'When we educate children about climate change we also e
few years have shown, is that it is our children who are teachin,
change seriously, because it affects their future and the future c
live. But they have also given us hope, something we all need as   ...ner.'

Minister Eamon Ryan, *T.D. Minister for Climate Action, Comm.   ...on Networks and Transport*

'Addressing climate change is a critical issue for the work of the Irish Aid programme at the Department of Foreign Affairs. I very much welcome this book which will support teachers to engage their pupils on the impacts and implications of climate change across the world and what we all can to do to be responsible climate aware global citizens.'

Minister Colin Brophy, *T.D. Minister for Overseas Development and Diaspora*

'At last! Here is a book that provides authoritative but accessible guidance on teaching about climate change in primary schools. Students and teachers everywhere will welcome this thoughtful and wide-ranging exploration of what is arguably the defining issue of our age.'

Stephen Scoffham, *Visiting Reader (Sustainability and Education), Canterbury Christ Church University, UK*

'A must read for every teacher, this is such a rich and timely resource. Not shying away from the starkness of the climate science but always seeking to cultivate children's natural wonder and hope, this is the perfect handbook for teachers who want to equip their students to be active citizens in a climate-disrupted world.'

Oisín Coghlan, *Director of Friends of the Earth, Ireland*

'Young students are already well aware of the many environmental and climate change challenges we face. They have already been to the forefront of the struggle for climate action and climate justice. Supporting and guiding them in their reflections on the issues is a privilege as well as an opportunity. Teachers also need support and this publication is an essential guide. This book offers much that is practical and immediate for classroom and whole school practice. Of particular value is the emphasis on placing climate change in the framework of citizenship education and the emphasis on hope and positive engagement, a key component of any education-based approach. To say this collection is a timely and relevant contribution is an understatement.'

Colm Regan, *Human Rights Activist and Teacher, University of Malta*

'Climate change and biodiversity loss are the greatest challenges confronting humanity in the 21st century. Education is key to addressing them, and this has to begin at primary school level. I warmly welcome this important new resource for students and teachers and believe it will play an invaluable role in helping the next generation better understand and confront these profound challenges.'

John Gibbons, *Environmental Writer and Commentator and Co-author of the* Routledge Handbook of Environmental Journalism

'Children and young people across the world have redefined political priorities in recent years and provided a refreshing insight that sees through the complexities and obstacles that have bedevilled a generation's efforts to tackle climate change. This text provides an excellent vehicle to harness and direct the energy and curiosity of young people by providing powerful insights into how and why the education system should respond to a growing demand by them to choose a different future and become advocates for a new sustainable global society.'

Emeritus Professor John Sweeney, *Irish Climate Analysis and Research UnitS (ICARUS), Maynooth University*

'In my outreach work on climate change, I am often asked by principals, teachers and parents how and when this topic should be taught in primary schools. This new book is very welcome indeed and fills an important gap in the curriculum. It offers fresh perspectives on how young children can engage with and learn about climate change across a range of subject areas. It also offers much needed guidance and practical ideas for teachers on how to broach this topical issue in sensitive ways that generate hope and action, rather than anxiety and fear. I sincerely hope it will be used widely and help to generate more widespread teaching of climate change in primary schools.'

Lorna Gold, *Author of* Climate Generation: Awakening to *Our Children's* Future

'*Teaching Climate Change in Primary Schools: An Interdisciplinary Approach* is a very welcome and essential new text. Primary children are well aware of the significance of climate change and of the actions being taken by young people to demand that it is tackled by us all. This book provides primary teachers with a wealth of knowledge for approaching the climate emergency in their classrooms. It could not be more timely nor more important, showing how this is a whole school and whole curriculum matter which primary schools must address with and for their children.'

Professor Emeritus Simon Catling, *Oxford Brookes University*

'Climate change education has to be part of our personal, local and global responses to the challenges facing a planet on the brink. With its enlightening focus on action, hope and empowerment, this book will help primary teachers to engage creatively and critically with climate change education.'

Koen Timmers, *Educator, Author and Co-founder of the global educational projects Climate-Action.info and ProjectKakuma.com*

'Climate Change is the biggest challenge in the world today. Our students want to take action and it is an area in which they can individually and collectively make a difference. As educators, it is our responsibility to empower our students to take that action. The pedagogical insights from this book are invaluable.'

Kate Murray, *Principal Teacher, St. Augustine's National School, Clontuskert, Ballinsaloe, Galway*

Teaching Climate Change in Primary Schools

This important and timely book provides an overview of climate change and highlights the importance of including climate change education in primary schools. It emphasises the importance of cross-curricular pedagogical approaches with a focus on climate justice, providing in-depth assistance for teaching children aged 3–13 years.

Informed by up to date research, the book helps teachers to remain faithful to climate change science whilst not overwhelming children. Accompanied by online resources, this book includes practical and easy to follow ideas and lesson plans that will help teachers to include climate change education in their classrooms in a holistic, cross-curricular manner. Specific chapters address the following topics:

- Inter-disciplinary approaches to climate change
- Early childhood education
- Pedagogies of hope
- The importance of reflective practice
- Ideas for including climate change education in curricular areas such as literacy, geography, science, history and the arts

Designed to promote climate change education in primary schools, this resource will help primary teachers, student teachers, geography specialists and all those interested in climate change education develop their own conceptual knowledge and that of the children in their class.

Anne M. Dolan is a lecturer in primary geography with the Department of Learning, Society and Religious Education in Mary Immaculate College, University of Limerick, Ireland.

Teaching Climate Change in Primary Schools

An Interdisciplinary Approach

Edited by Anne M. Dolan

Routledge
Taylor & Francis Group

LONDON AND NEW YORK

First published 2022
by Routledge
2 Park Square, Milton Park, Abingdon, Oxon OX14 4RN

and by Routledge
52 Vanderbilt Avenue, New York, NY 10017

Routledge is an imprint of the Taylor & Francis Group, an informa business

British Library Cataloguing-in-Publication Data
A catalogue record for this book is available from the British Library

Library of Congress Cataloging-in-Publication Data
Names: Dolan, Anne M., editor.
Title: Teaching climate change in primary schools: an interdisciplinary process / edited by Anne Dolan.
Description: Abingdon, Oxon; New York, NY: Routledge, 2021. | Includes bibliographical references and index. | Identifiers: LCCN 2021003678 | ISBN 9780367631673 (hardback) | ISBN 9780367631680 (paperback) | ISBN 9781003112389 (ebook)
Subjects: LCSH: Climatic changes--Study and teaching (Primary) | Environmental justice--Study and teaching (Primary) | Environmental education.
Classification: LCC QC903 .T4295 2021 | DDC 372.35/7--dc23
LC record available at https://lccn.loc.gov/2021003678

ISBN: 978-0-367-63167-3 (hbk)
ISBN: 978-0-367-63168-0 (pbk)
ISBN: 978-1-003-11238-9 (ebk)

Typeset in Bembo
by KnowledgeWorks Global Ltd.

In memory of Professor Emeritus Peadar Cremin:
Former President of Mary Immaculate College and
eternal development education pioneer.

Contents

List of figures   xi
List of tables   xiii
Case studies   xv
List of contributors   xvi
Foreword   xxi
Acknowledgements   xxiii

Introduction   1
Anne M. Dolan

SECTION 1
Theory and philosophical approaches   7

1 Teaching climate change: Setting the context   9
   Anne M. Dolan

2 A thematic approach to teaching climate change   29
   Fionnuala Tynan

3 The world's religious traditions and global climate disruption   46
   Patricia Kieran

4 A reflective approach to climate change education   60
   Kathleen Horgan

5 Early beginnings: Fostering positive dispositions towards climate education
   in early years classrooms   72
   Deirdre Breatnach, Mary Moloney and Jennifer Pope

SECTION 2
Climate change education: Literacy-based approaches   87

6 Climate change, picturebooks and primary school children   89
   Mary Roche

7 Listening, re-acting and acting: Stories from plants and animals to elicit empathy
   and dialogue about climate change, in the classroom and beyond   99
   Miriam Hamilton

8 Using climate change as the context for a Content and Language
   Integrated Learning (CLIL) approach in the primary classroom   110
   Siobhán Ní Mhurchú

SECTION 3
Climate change education: STEAM   119

9   Bringing climate change alive in the science classroom through
    science, communication and engineering STEM challenges   121
    Maeve Liston

10 Exploring climate change education outside the classroom   138
    Anne O'Dwyer

11 Do you see what I see? A visual lens for exploring climate change   152
    Anne Marie Morrin

12 The Grow Room: An artistic exploration of climate change   168
    Tanya de Paor

13 Is plastic really fantastic or is it something more drastic?   181
    Anne M. Dolan

SECTION 4
Climate change education: Pedagogies of hope and action   195

14 Geography, global learning and climate justice: Geographical aspects
    of teaching climate change   197
    Anne M. Dolan

15 Exploring climate change with an historical lens   214
    Anne M. Dolan and Eileen O'Sullivan

16 Climate change education through active citizenship   226
    Margaret Nohilly

17 Ecological awareness: A cornerstone to developing a healthy Christian spirituality   238
    Maurice Harmon

18 Creating teaching resources in response to the rapidly changing
    nature of climate change   247
    Brighid Golden

19 Negotiating environmental protection through drama   258
    Margaret O' Keeffe and Joanna Parkes

20 Moving towards change: The contribution of physically educated communities   272
    Richard Bowles

21 Pedagogy of hope: Futures teaching for climate change   284
    Anne M. Dolan

    Appendix 1: Climate Change Glossary   305
    Appendix 2: Sample lesson plans (as Gaeilge)   313
    Appendix 3: Sample lesson plans   317
    Appendix 4: Letter from the President of Ireland to the children in St. Augustine's
    *   NS, Clontuskert, Ballinasloe*   322
    Appendix 5: Timeline cards: History of climate change   323
    Index   328

Figures

1.1 The Keeling Curve: A graph showing the ongoing change in the concentration of carbon dioxide in the Earth's atmosphere 11

1.2 Presentation of the greenhouse experiment presented by children from St. Nessan's primary school at the Science Blast exhibition in Limerick 13

1.3 The Lost Words of Walney (title page of children's self-published work) 16

1.4 Elements of climate change 21

1.5 Four dimensions of learning needed to explore climate change effectively 23

2.1 When you think of climate change, what topics come to mind? 32

2.2 Examples of climate change topics 33

2.3 Blank flowchart for curriculum planning 37

3.1 Young Buddhist monks learning using a mobile phone 47

3.2 Aim of Belief Circles Game 49

3.3 Interbelief dialogue café 51

3.4 Sacred cow in Hinduism 53

3.5 Origami moments 54

3.6 Muslim girl enjoying nature 55

3.7 Extension activities 56

3.8 The land: general pointers for exploring this theme with students 57

4.1 The process of critical reflection 62

4.2 River of formative experiences 63

4.3 A time to change 65

4.4 Imagine the future 66

5.1 Positive dispositions that enable young children to engage with climate education 75

5.2 Image of a bug hotel taken in O'Briensbridge, Co. Clare, Ireland 82

6.1 Cover image You're Snug with Me 94

8.1 The benefits of Content and Language Integrated Learning (CLIL) 112

9.1 Prensky's Tomorrow's 'Better Their World' Paradigm 123

9.2 Engineering design process (EDP) for STEM lessons and activities 130

10.1 Central role of the child as Climate Change Champion at home, in school and in the community. 141

10.2 A rain gauge designed by a 10-year-old child 143

10.3 An anemometer designed by a 9-year-old child 143

10.4 A weather vane designed by an 11-year-old child 144

10.5 Suggested sequence to develop a school-community garden project – ready, steady grow 149

11.1	The five sequences of design thinking	154
11.2	Researching bee vision – extract from a journal (12 years)	158
11.3	Researching bee vision – extract from a journal (12 years)	159
11.4	Researching bee vision – extract from a journal (12 years)	159
11.5	Constructing insect-inspired pseudoscopes in the classroom (child 11 years)	161
11.6	Children investigating how light travels by using lenses and mirrors. Findings documented in their personal journals (child 12 years)	162
12.1	Daniel with sunflower, Limerick	173
12.2	Student's design work for bee bombs	175
13.1	The Mobius Loop	188
13.2	The Green Dot	188
13.3	Art installation inspired by the impact of plastic on ocean life (Patrician Academy, Mallow)	190
14.1	The Sustainable Development Goals infographics	201
14.2	*(a)* Climate change haiku	209
14.2	*(b)* Climate change haiku	209
14.2	*(c)* Climate change haiku	209
14.3	Climate Action Project: Six-week plan for schools	210
14.4	Children from St. Augustine's, NS, Clontuskert discussing climate change with a class teacher in Dubai	211
16.1	Sample Beliefs Circle on climate change	231
16.2	Sample 'Diamond 9'	236
17.1	Ecological Awareness Tree	244
18.1	Climate change around the world	249
18.2	Twisted game of climate change	250
20.1	The elements of Cooperative Learning	274
20.2	Five progressive levels for Teaching Personal and Social Responsibility (TPSR)	275
21.1	Sample cross-curricular plan for climate change education based on the book *The Promise* by Nicola Davies and illustrated by Laura Carlin	288
21.2	Examples of protest banners	290
21.3	Problem solving with LEGO	296
21.4	A selection of pages from *Nabi's Story:* The picturebook created by second class (8 years) and fifth class (11 years) children	299

Tables

2.1   Possible subject areas to be included in thematic plan on climate
       change (younger children (3-7 years) or children of an early
       developmental stage)   33
2.2   Possible subject areas to be included in thematic plan on climate
       change (older children (8-13 years) or children of an advanced
       developmental stage)   35
2.3   Blank KWL chart   38
2.4   Curriculum planning grid for climate change   39
3.1   Belief Circles Game: some suggested topics for educators   49
4.1   Retrospective review   64
4.2   Stepping into the uncertainty of climate change   67
4.3   A framework of questions for reviewing an experience of teaching
       climate change education adapted from Rolfe et al. (2001)   68
5.1   Overview of the IBL process in the infant (children 4-6 years)
       classroom   78
5.2   Sunflower investigation   80
5.3   Activity plan: making a bug hotel   83
9.1   What is *Science Capital*?   124
9.2   PMI (Plus, Minus, Interesting) activity to encourage higher
       order thinking about topics related to climate change   126
9.3   Global warming investigation   127
9.4   Characteristics of STEM education and STEM lessons   129
9.5   Stages in the engineering design process   131
9.6   Pedagogies incorporated into engineering for sustainable
       development activities   133
10.1   Scaffolding design & make skills   145
10.2   Suitable activities to scaffold scientific and geographical
       skill development at home   147
11.1   A suggested framework for STEAM workshops constructed
       around children's findings (using the Science Foundation
       Ireland [SFI] framework)   161
13.1   Rethinking our relationship with plastics   185
13.2   How long does it take to break down?   190
13.3   What the numbers mean: numbers used on plastics   191
14.1   *Find Someone Who* Statements for Climate Change Go Bingo
       (statements should be adapted in line with local social, economic
       and cultural factors)   199
14.2   Why is Zaria worried about the animals on her family farm
       in Uganda?   206
14.3   Why did Jack miss the bus to Cork?   207
14.4   Climate Action Project: A framework for enquiry   211

15.1	Activities for children based on the Ps of history framework (Buchanan, 2013:25–26)	220
16.1	Ideas for discussion	230
16.2	Timelines for implementation	230
16.3	Belief Circle discussion: Rules of the game	232
16.4	Aims, target groups and actions of the project	233
16.5	Energy audit questionnaire administered to classroom teachers	233
16.6	Sample of children's research	234
16.7	A child's account of a visit to a windfarm	235
16.8	Outcomes of the project	235
18.1	Beginning the process	248
18.2	Choosing resource type	249
18.3	Sample cards for taboo game	251
18.4	Role cards for carbon cycle simulation	253
21.1	Three sources of hope from children's investigative project work on plastic packaging and recycling symbols	286
21.2	Key sources of hope	287
21.3	Selection of slogans from protest banners	290
21.4	Key elements of climate change education	300
21.5	Actions for climate change	301

Case studies

1.1   Science Blast   12
14.1   Climate Action Project   210
21.1   Youth assembly on climate   291

Contributors

Deirdre Breatnach is a lecturer in the Department of Reflective Pedagogy and Early Childhood Studies at Mary Immaculate College, Limerick. A former primary school teacher and principal, she teaches modules on curriculum, research and pedagogy in early childhood education. Her research interests include: communication, language and literacy in the early years; the transition from early years settings to primary school; immersion education within early years and primary school settings; reflective practice and student learning during placement, and blended learning within the third level context.

Richard Bowles is a member of the Department of Arts Education and Physical Education in Mary Immaculate College. He is a teacher educator with responsibility for undergraduate and postgraduate physical education modules. As a former primary teacher, he has a deep interest in issues pertaining to teaching and learning within primary school physical education and sport. His current research activities centre on using self-study to explore teaching, coaching and teacher education practices.

Tanya de Paor is a lecturer in Visual Art Education, Mary Immaculate College, Limerick. She has been lecturing in visual arts education since 1998 at undergraduate and postgraduate levels. Her teaching, research and creative practice are informed by emergent developments in creative and critical pedagogies. Her research activities are informed by her multidisciplinary art practice, teaching preservice teachers, developments in STEAM education and through making art with children in formal and informal contexts. She sees art as a tool which can bring about societal transformation.

She is currently a PhD candidate at the Burren College of Art and the National University of Ireland, Galway. Her doctoral work is concerned with creative inquiry into the contested conceptual framework of the Anthropocene, defined as the Age of Man, in which the greatest impacts on the Earth System are influenced by humans. Her work is framed by the interconnectedness of art, ecology, pedagogy, relational and collaborative practices. Her research deploys art education methodologies, socially engaged practices, aesthetics and speculative fabulation to co create pathways from the Anthropocene to a Symbiocene.

Anne M. Dolan is a lecturer in primary geography with the Department of Learning, Society and Religious Education in Mary Immaculate College, University of Limerick, Ireland. She is the author of *Powerful Primary Geography: A Toolkit for 21st Century Learning* (published by Routledge in 2020) and *You, Me and Diversity: Picturebooks for Teaching Development and Intercultural Education* (published by Trentham Books/IOE Press in 2014). Anne is particularly interested in creative approaches to geography, inter-disciplinary collaboration and the use of the arts in geographical explorations.

Brighid Golden lectures in Global Education at Mary Immaculate College. She is a member of the national DICE (Development and Intercultural Education) Project and through this project delivers CPD on issues of global social justice to staff, students and community members at Mary Immaculate College. Brighid has a joint masters in International Approaches to Education and International Development from the University of Birmingham and is currently undertaking her PhD at the University of Glasgow exploring the area of critical thinking and its interconnections with teacher education and global education.

Kathleen Horgan is a former member of the Faculty of Education, Mary Immaculate College. During her early career, she worked as a primary teacher with a specialism in early years' education. She subsequently held the position of Education Officer with a non-governmental development agency where she devised curricula and provided professional development for teachers in Ireland and abroad in the areas of environmental sustainability, social justice education and development education. In recognition of her contributions to research and teaching, she has been awarded a Government of Ireland Senior Research Scholarship and a National Award for Excellence in Teaching in Higher Education.

Her primary research interests embrace reflective pedagogy, professional development and teacher learning. She has undertaken longitudinal research studies on the evolution of student teachers' personal theories of teaching through undergraduate and induction years. She has published and presented her work nationally and internationally and has collaborated with educational institutions, government agencies and philanthropic organisations at home and abroad.

Patricia Kieran is a British Foreign and Commonwealth Chevening Scholar who teaches Religious Education at Mary Immaculate College, University of Limerick. She was a team member of the Enquiring Classroom Project which sought to develop strategies to support teachers and students in engaging in difficult ethical conversations about identity, religions and beliefs, democratic values, diversity, belonging and violence (O'Donnell, A., Kieran, P., Cherouvis, S., Bergdahl, L., with Langmann, E. [2019] *The Enquiring Classroom: Values, Identity, Exploratiion*). She is a member of the Mid-West Interfaith Network and the Religions and Beliefs in Changing Times Research team as well as Director of the Irish Institute for Catholic Studies. She has co-written and edited books on a range of topics including Children and Catholicism, Catholic Theology, and Religious Education in an Intercultural Europe. Her most recent book *Connecting Lives: Inter-Belief Dialogue in Contemporary Ireland* (2019) focuses on dialogue among belief diverse communities. She has published numerous chapters and articles on the subject of inter-religious education, Catholic Education, Roman Catholic Modernism and gender.

Miriam Hamilton is a lecturer in education in Mary Immaculate College, Limerick, Ireland and a member of the Department of STEM Education. Having spent much of her career teaching at second level, she transitioned in recent years to teacher education, where she teaches science education to undergraduate and postgraduate pre-service teachers. Her research studies and publications span a variety of educational domains including; the social context of education, student experience, cultural pedagogy and reflective self-study inquiry. This writing of this chapter facilitates a new challenge with the exploration of storytelling as a pedagogy for teaching biological and climate change concepts.

Maurice Harmon is a Lecturer in Religious Education and a member of the Department of Learning, Society, and Religious Education at Mary Immaculate College, Limerick. He lectures across the Bachelor of Education (B.Ed.), Professional Master in Education (PME) and Certificate in Religious Education Programmes in the Faculty of Education. His research interests include Religious Education, Catholic Education, Spirituality, Student Voice and Initial Teacher Education at Primary Level.

Maeve Liston is a Senior Lecturer in Science Education at Mary Immaculate College. She has extensive experience in teaching science and science education at all levels in education (primary, second and third level). Dr. Liston is also the Director of Enterprise & Community Engagement. In her role she manages, designs and delivers a wide variety of different STEM (Science, Technology, Engineering and Maths) and STEAM (Science, Technology, Engineering, Art and Maths) Educational outreach initiatives promoting creativity, innovation and problem solving. She also runs a wide variety of programmes in the areas of Entrepreneurial Education, 21st Century Skills and careers, with a wide variety of key stakeholders in enterprise and industry.

Mary Moloney is a researcher, author and lecturer in Early Childhood Education and Care at Mary Immaculate College, Limerick. Mary believes in the critical importance of early childhood education and in supporting early childhood teachers to creating optimal learning environments for young children. Her work is influenced by visits to a broad range of countries including Slovenia, Norway, Denmark, Sweden, New Zealand, Reggio Emilia in Northern Italy and more recently by her work as a volunteer with refugee children and their families in Greece. Her latest book '*Intentional Leadership for Effective Inclusion in Early Childhood Education and Care*' (Routledge) which she co-authored with Eucharia McCarthy motivates educators to work towards the common goal of creating a truly inclusive culture in which all children, with or without disabilities, are supported and enabled to fully participate in every aspect of daily life and learning.

Anne Marie Morrin is a lecturer in Visual Art Education in the Department of Arts Education and Physical Education in Mary Immaculate College. As a researcher and teacher she is interested in interdisciplinary approaches to visual art education; educational environments as pedagogy; reflective journals as a tool in the classroom, a/r/t/ography and other forms of art based research. Her art practice directly influences her practice as a teacher – and vice versa. Within this binary role, Anne Marie places the role of practice and enquiry central to the acquisition of knowledge and explores new technologies to provide and adapt unique teaching and learning experiences for all involved.

Before taking up her current position in Visual Art Education at Mary Immaculate College, Anne Marie worked in a variety of educational and cultural settings including, theatre, fashion industry, galleries, school and community projects. The collection of experiences has afforded her the creative capacity and skills to approach her teaching and art practice in an inter-disciplinary manner. The most recent research projects Anne Marie instigated were highly engaging art installations that were conceptualised in collaboration with contemporary artists, pre-service students and primary school teachers and children. These projects include Art/Science participative urban intervention project entitled Particles or Waves? (City of Culture 2014), Visual notebooks for Hall of Mirrors (Farmleigh Gallery, Dublin and Limerick City Gallery of Art) and The Studio Classrooms (educational art and research project involving visual artists, primary school teachers and children who develop their art practice through online residencies).

Siobhán Ní Mhurchú is a lecturer in the Department of Language and Literacy Education in Mary Immaculate College, Limerick, Ireland since 2004, where she works with undergraduate and postgraduate students in the teaching of the Irish language as a first and a second language. She has a keen interest in Content and Language Integrated Learning (CLIL). Prior to her position in Mary Immaculate College, she worked as a Department of Education Inspector in the South East region, as a facilitator with the Primary Curriculum Support Programme (Gaeilge), as an education officer with Tiobraid Árann ag Labhairt in Nenagh and as an assistant principal in Scoil Gharbháin in Dungarvan, Co. Waterford.

Anne O'Dwyer is a member of the Department of STEM Education at Mary immaculate College. She lectures in Science Education. She teaches undergraduate pre-service elementary teachers and teaches on the MA in STEM Education programme. Anne's research interest is in Science Education and facilitating professional development to support learners. She is interested in self-study as a methodology to understand and improve teaching practices.

Margaret O'Keeffe is a lecturer in Drama Education in Mary Immaculate College and coordinator of the college's Teacher Education Access Programme (TEAP). Margaret holds a B.Ed. from Mary Immaculate College and a M.Ed. from Dublin City University (DCU) (formerly St. Patrick's College). She previously worked as drama lecturer in DCU, a primary school teacher and as an Education Director for TEAM Educational Theatre Company. During her time with TEAM theatre she devised theatre for young audiences and facilitated drama workshops in schools throughout Ireland for teachers and children. She supported the production of performances for young children in the Abbey and Project Theatre.

Margaret is co-author of *Discovering Drama: Theory and Practice for the Primary School* (Gill & MacMillan, 2006). She is an active member of ADEI (Association for Drama in Education in Ireland) since its foundation in 1999. Margaret has led numerous professional development courses for teachers and is actively involved in community projects. She has presented her research both nationally and internationally. Her research interests include: Drama Education; Applied Theatre; Teacher Education; Teacher Identity; Socially Justice; Embodied Pedagogies and Assessment in Higher Education.

Eileen O'Sullivan, is a lecturer in Primary History in the Department of Learning, Society and Religious Education in Mary Immaculate College, Limerick. Her research interests and publications include local history, children's temporal cognition and related implications for policy and curriculum development. Eileen has engaged in an in-depth study of the degree to which history textbooks reflect constructivist approaches to learning, as advocated in the Irish Primary Curriculum. In addition, she has worked as Director of School Placement in Mary Immaculate College and works as a Consultant Supervisor of student teachers while on placement. She has published a number of community-based curriculum development projects in history for primary schools, a comprehensive curriculum project entitled 'Viking Ireland' for Primary Schools, as well as curriculum projects in Social, Personal and Health Education.

Joanna Parkes has been working in the field of Creative Arts Education as a Drama Facilitator for many years, in very diverse contexts. Primary education has been the focus of much of her work: designing and implementing educational drama projects, delivering teacher training and producing teacher resources. She co-wrote two popular Drama Resource books for teachers, called *Step By Step Together* – Drama and Development Education in the Primary Classroom (NAYD, 2010) and *Step By Step Educational Drama-A* cross curricular use of Drama in the Primary classroom (NAYD, 2006). She has been a part-time lecturer in several third-level institutions including Mary Immaculate College, Marino Institute of Education and Trinity College. Joanna was one of six lead Artists chosen for a National research initiative in 2014: called Exploring Teacher/Artist Partnership. Since 2013, she has also been working in Early Years contexts, completing a Masters in Early Childhood Education from Marino Institute of Education in 2018. In 2019, she was awarded a year-long residency at the Ark (the John Coolahan Early Years Artist Residency) where she is exploring the value of using drama, story and play to support children's holistic creative and personal development.

Jennifer Pope is an early childhood expert and has been lecturing in the Department of Reflective Pedagogy and Early Childhood Studies in Mary Immaculate College since 2004. She graduated with a PhD in Paediatric Epidemiology in 2006 and has a particular interest in the role of early life experiences in promoting children's health and well-being now and for the future. Jennifer's recent research has focused on children's experiences of outdoor play.

Mary Roche is author of *Developing Children's Critical Thinking Through Picturebooks* (Routledge 2015). The book received a *United Kingdom Literacy Association (UKLA) Academic Book Award (2015)*. Mary lectured in teacher education, both primary and post-primary, and is now a tutor in the School of Education, University College Cork. An education consultant and school adviser, she is a co-convenor of Network Educational Action Research Ireland (NEARI) and co-author of several books on action research. Mary's *'Critical Thinking and Book Talk'* (CT&BT) approach, developed during her many years of research while a primary teacher, has been adopted by the National Council Curriculum Assessment Ireland (NCCA). You can follow Mary on Twitter @*marygtroche*.

Fionnuala Tynan is a lecturer in inclusive educational methodologies in the Faculty of Education in Mary Immaculate College. She is the coordinator of the Graduate Certificate in Autism Studies. Her research interests include inclusive and special education and wellbeing.

Margaret Nohilly is a Lecturer in SPHE and Wellbeing at Mary Immaculate College. She teaches at both undergraduate and postgraduate levels. She coordinates the Professional Master of Education programme. Her research interests include Child Protection, SPHE, Wellbeing and Policy in Education. She is the co-author of the recently published 'Wellbeing in School's Everyday: A whole-school approach to the practical implementation of Wellbeing.'

Foreword

Mary Robinson

Climate change is possibly the single most important issue facing humanity. Human behaviour is altering the planet's ability to regulate itself, dramatically impacting lives and livelihoods. The UN's COP 26 climate change summit due to take place in the Scottish city of Glasgow in November, 2020 has been postponed to November 2021 due to the coronavirus pandemic. While this may remove climate change from headline news, scientific evidence is irrefutable and we face a climate crisis.

There are many reasons why science has failed to convince citizens about the urgency of addressing climate change. These include a lack of leadership, the power of climate change deniers and the lack of a coherent education agenda. While environmental education has featured on the margins of the curriculum for many years, it remains under-resourced and low on the list of educational priorities. The need for climate change education with a clear focus on climate justice is now absolutely essential.

Teaching Climate Change in Primary Schools: An Interdisciplinary Approach was born out of a collaborative climate change education project by teacher educators in Mary Immaculate College (MIC) Limerick. In their mission to help student teachers teach about climate change, MIC academics have pooled their expertise in this publication. Informed by the most up to date scientific research and methodological approaches for primary teaching, the book moves from theory to practice in a way that is meaningful for primary teachers. Innovative approaches for teaching climate change are presented through early childhood education, literacy, science, history, geography, religious education, art, drama, physical education and cross-curricular themes.

This book makes a coherent argument for climate change education in primary schools. Framed by the Sustainable Development Goals, it provides an overview of climate change including its causes and impacts. It recognises the agency of children and it is written in a spirit of hope. Despite the staggering evidence of climate change in our local and global communities, it is important for us to retain this sense of hope and agency. My own publication *Climate Justice: Hope, Resilience and the Fight for a Sustainable Future* (Bloomsbury Publishing) *features* numerous accounts from innovative grassroots activists whose impressive results reveal how individuals can make a difference. Many groups and communities are responding with innovative approaches demonstrating resilience and the power of working together.

Climate justice is at the heart of this publication. A transformative concept, climate justice demands a shift from a discourse on greenhouse gases and melting icecaps into a civil rights movement, with the people and communities most vulnerable to climate change at its heart. Climate justice informed by science, responds to science and acknowledges the need for equitable stewardship of the world's resources. The warnings contained within Intergovernmental Panel on Climate Change (IPCC) reports couldn't be clearer – the scientists tell us that, by 2030, we need to have reduced global emissions by 45% and set ourselves on a path to a safer, fairer future. The struggle to secure climate justice is a global struggle – from communities in California ravaged by forest fires, to communities in rural Kenya affected by drought to increased flooding here in Ireland – climate change is already affecting all of our lives. Indeed, it was through my work on human rights in Africa that I came to understand that any advances in development were threatened by the impacts of climate change.

Climate change is an intergenerational issue. As Chair of The Elders, a global peace and human rights organisation founded by Nelson Mandela, I am constantly reminded of the global impact of climate change as an issue of accelerating concern. However, it is young people who have the most to lose. When I was in the UN General Assembly during the Climate Action Summit in 2019, I heard Greta Thunberg (aged 16 at the time) say, 'You have stolen my childhood.' This was a startling statement. Yet, it is young people who keep me hopeful. Greta has achieved more in her year of activism than many of us have achieved in a lifetime. Greta, and millions of children, call upon us all to be angry, to take action and to demand change. These young climate activists are articulate, effective and determined. They know what is at stake. Climate change education is having an effect. However, it needs to be established and indeed prioritised within curricula and education policies. We have the technological skills and knowledge required to solve this problem. A just transition to a zero carbon, zero poverty future is an enormous challenge, but we must succeed.

Dealing with a theme that is close to my heart, this book is essential reading for the Department of Education and Science, the National Council for Curriculum and Assessment, for every primary teacher, student teacher and teacher educator. I would like to congratulate Dr. Anne Dolan and the staff of Mary Immaculate College, Limerick, for this important publication which will make an extraordinary contribution to our children's education. I hope that my grandchildren will experience the wonderful ideas from this book.

Acknowledgements

Personally, it is an honour and privilege to write this note of appreciation to my colleagues and friends who participated in this important project. As teacher educators we are acutely aware of the importance of teaching about climate change. Yet, student teachers have expressed their worries and concerns about their own personal knowledge and ability to engage with this subject. Notwithstanding, their appreciation of the importance of climate change, sometimes it is easier to continue with a 'business as usual' approach to teaching. This book was written to help student teachers and primary teachers introduce climate change education into their classrooms. The contents are in line with the most recent research in curriculum, pedagogy and active enquiry-based learning.

I am grateful to all of the authors who have journeyed with me for the last three years. Colleagues in the Faculty of Education and the Department of Learning, Society and Religious Education, Mary Immaculate College enthusiastically volunteered to write a chapter. An active community of practice was established. Once a month we met for climate conversations where we ran workshops, invited guest speakers and discussed emerging trends. In groups, we wrote, re-wrote and peer reviewed chapters. Thanks to Lorna Gold for travelling to Limerick to share her expertise with us. A special word of thanks is also due to student teachers who piloted some of the activities and shared their ideas with us. The highlight of this project was a visit to the Cloughjordan Eco Village in County Tipperary. Thanks to Professor Emeritus Peadar Kirby for facilitating this visit.

A foreword from Mary Robinson sets the tone for this book. A passionate advocate for climate action, Mary Robinson the first female President of Ireland and former UN High Commissioner for Human Rights, continues to raise the issue of climate justice locally, nationally and internationally. It is an honour to have such an esteemed contribution to this publication.

I would like to thank my fellow geographers and friends from the Charney Primary Geography Group. My thinking and writing has been greatly enhanced as a result of feedback from this insightful community. Special thanks are due to Professor Emeritus Simon Catling and Dr. Stephen Scoffham for reading sections from the publication and providing me with feedback and encouragement.

This book has been inspired by the wonderful teachers and children who have shared their work and ideas with us. A special word of thanks is due to the children and teachers in my own former school St. Augustine's National School, Clontuskert, Ballinasloe. Their inspirational principal Kate Murray is a role model in exemplary climate change education. Kate introduced me to the wonderful Climate Action Project (https://www.climate-action.info). I would strongly encourage all teachers to become involved in this magnificent project under the stewardship of Koen Timmers.

This book showcases the development of creative and critical thinking in the context of climate change education. I would like to acknowledge the *National Forum for the Enhancement of Teaching and Learning in Higher Education* for funding received under the Strategic Alignment of Teaching and Learning Enhancement Funding in Higher Education 2019. A project entitled *Developing Studio Habits of Mind Across the Curriculum: Creative Teaching and Learning Approaches* has informed the philosophy of this book in general and Chapter 11 in particular. I would like to extend a word of thanks to my colleagues from this project Dr. Sandra Ryan and Anne Marie Morrin for their generosity, creativity and source of inspiration.

I am grateful to Routledge for agreeing to publish this book and in particular I would like to thank Bruce Roberts and Molly Selby for their professionalism, diligence and attention to detail. The magnificent artwork on the cover page of this publication was designed by my former student Saoirse Bradley and I will be eternally grateful to her for her dedication, art work and commitment to justice and global issues.

I was fortunate to obtain both sabbatical and professional leave of absence for the completion of this project. I would like to note my appreciation to the Research Office in Mary Immaculate College and Professor Michael Healy for facilitating my leave and for his ongoing support.

Finally, thanks to my inspirational family, my husband Professor Padraic Kenna for his generous support, love and patience, my mother Margaret Dolan for always being a source of encouragement and my two wonderful daughters, Laura and Emily.

Anne M. Dolan (Editor)

Introduction

Anne M. Dolan

The 50th anniversary of the Apollo 11 moon landing was celebrated in 2019. In the aftermath of World War II, the United States and the Soviet Union competed for nuclear dominance on Earth. With the launch of Sputnik, the contest expanded to space. During the Apollo 8 lunar mission on Christmas Eve, William Anders captured an image of the Earth appearing over the lunar horizon. The image of a fragile Earth hanging suspended in the void would later give rise to the metaphor 'Spaceship Earth'. In 1972, astronauts from the Apollo 17 spacecraft captured another iconic image of the Earth, a stunning blue-green beacon in a vast black cosmos. The Blue Marble image, as it came to be known, was adopted by the environmental movement as a symbol of global consciousness. It remains the most famous photo of Earth ever taken and is still the most requested photo from the NASA archives.

The descriptions of awe, connection and transcendence experienced by the astronauts have been well documented (Kluger, 2017). Interviews with astronauts have recorded the experience of a global consciousness, an intense dissatisfaction with the state of the world and a compulsion to do something about it. Psychologists call this cognitive shift of awareness during spaceflight the 'overview effect'. This state of mental clarity generates feelings of awe and wonder about the Earth and an inherent awareness of the fragility of the planet. It has also been linked with a sense of personal connection and an appreciation of the interconnected nature of life on Earth. These astronauts were blissfully unaware that half a century later, Planet Earth would be under threat from a human created catastrophe known as climate change.

Ten years after the Apollo 11 moon landing, another scientific event occurred. A group of climate scientists gathered for the first meeting of the 'Ad hoc group on carbon dioxide and climate'. This led to the publication of the Charney Report (National Research Council and Carbon Dioxide Assessment Committee, 1983), the first comprehensive assessment of global climate change due to levels of carbon dioxide in the atmosphere. While these predictions were controversial in the 1970s, the persistence of climate deniers continues today, despite irrefutable scientific evidence and devastating first hand experiences.

Fortunately, many are beginning to accept the validity of the scientific evidence. In her inaugural speech, *A European Union that strives for more* (2019), Ursula von der Leyen, the newly elected *President* of the *European* Commission, prioritised the issue of climate change as follows:

> Our most pressing challenge is keeping our planet healthy. This is the greatest responsibility and opportunity of our times. I want Europe to become the first climate-neutral continent in the world by 2050. To make this happen, we must take bold steps together.

Tens of thousands of school children and students in more than 100 countries have organised Friday protests, demonstrating their frustration at the lack of local and international political action. Inspired by a 16-year-old Swedish girl Greta Thunberg, young people have mobilised their voice in a spectacular and noteworthy manner. These protests have included a call for obligatory climate change education.

As teacher educators, we are acutely aware of our responsibility to teach climate change education. Our student teachers need to be able to respond to complex climate change questions raised in the classroom. Children are inherently curious – they want to understand the world around them, how it works, and how to interact with it. Their curiosity is evident through their questions. Enquiry-based learning (Roberts, 2013) encourages and supports a questioning approach. The research conducted for this publication was based on a constructionist, enquiry-based approach to teaching and learning. The first step in the research is an acknowledgement that we, as teacher educators, have many questions about climate change. Our initial questions are summarised as follows:

Questions about climate change

Questions about impact of climate change (personal context)

- How does climate change affect my life (or the life of a school child)?
- What can I do in my day-to-day life to reduce my carbon footprint?
- What are the likely local impacts of climate change?
- What can we realistically do to adapt to/stop climate change?

Questions about the science of climate change

Causes

- What are the causes of climate change?
- How does the phenomena associated with climate change differ from extreme weather phenomena of the past?
- How do we know about climate change?

Effects

- What are the physical effects of climate change?
- What impact has climate on weather patterns and seasonal changes?
- What impact has climate change on human life and lifestyles?

Responses

- What are the current individual, community-based, national and international responses to climate change?
- How should we respond to climate change? (personally, regionally, nationally and internationally)
- How is the natural world coping with climate change?
- Who studies it? What evidence is there? What does the research tell us?

Questions about children and climate change

- What relevance does climate change have for children?
- What can a child do about climate change?
- How complex is the concept for young children?
- How do children perceive climate change?
- How can we engage children in imaginative transformation towards a 'good Anthropocene'?

Questions about teachers and climate change

- How can teachers talk about climate change without making young children anxious?
- What is the best way to teach climate change?
- How do we model climate action in our classroom, school, home and community?

Questions about climate change and college community

- As a college community, what can we do to raise awareness of climate change and act to reduce it?
- What can we do to reduce our carbon footprint?
- What kind of climate change education resources should be available for staff and students?

Questions about climate change, teaching approaches and curricular areas

- How can stories and resources be used to illustrate different elements of climate change?
- What are the implications of the language of climate change for literacy education?
- How can the curricular areas of PE, citizenship, history, geography and science support climate change education?
- How can climate change education be enhanced through spirituality and religious education?
- How can art practice and drama education empower citizens to think about adapting to climate change for a more sustainable future?
- In what ways can visual art practice facilitate co-creation of knowledge and understanding of climate change among artists, teachers and children?

This book has been written as a reflective response to our climate change education questions. Indeed, the process of research and reflection has generated further questions. As you begin reading this book, we strongly encourage you to list your own questions about climate change education. While this publication will not answer all of your questions, it will provide a foundation for beginning to address climate change education in the primary classroom.

The book is divided into four sections. Each section includes theoretical and practical dimensions.

- Section 1: Climate change education: Theory and philosophical approaches
- Section 2: Climate change education: Literacy-based approaches
- Section 3: Climate change education: STEAM – An educational approach to learning that uses Science, Technology, Engineering, the Arts and Mathematics
- Section 4: Climate change education: Pedagogies of hope and action

Section 1: Introduction to theories and practices of climate change education

In Chapter 1, I set out the rationale for including climate change education as part of the core primary curriculum. The chapter explores the nature of climate change and climate change education. Climate change caused by global warming is already beginning to transform life on Earth. It is the defining challenge of our time, perhaps the most significant challenge facing all citizens today. This chapter sets the context for the book. It provides a definition and rationale for climate change education in primary schools. Fionnuala Tyson explains thematic teaching, provides a rationale for its use and presents appropriate models for the teaching of climate change thematically. Patricia Kieran's chapter illustrates how the world's spiritual and religious traditions can help us to address the ethical dilemma of climate change.

Kathleen Horgan's chapter examines how reflective practice can be promoted and developed explicitly as a means of interrogating beliefs, culture, pedagogy and practice within the field of climate change education. A review of selected theoretical perspectives on reflection is provided, as well as an overview of strategies and approaches which facilitate reflection. Reflective practice is viewed as a transformative approach to professional learning. It creates opportunities for exploration, discussion and debate about the nature of professional learning and its relationship to personal and social change. In essence, reflective practice is about the processes through which we produce a shift in the way we see and make meaning of our personal and professional worlds and the nature of those changes. The chapter presents reflective practice as a lens through which teachers and students can consider critically the dominant assumptions, values and beliefs which underpin modern society and how these are implicated in the current ecological crisis. It highlights the importance of creating spaces where teachers and students can reflect critically on these dominant assumptions, their personal worldviews and relationships with the natural world.

The final chapter in this section, discusses the importance of including climate change education in early years' settings. The authors Jennifer Pope, Deirdre Breathnach and Mary Moloney outline the importance of fostering positive dispositions in young children and provides practical examples for early childhood education.

Section 2: Climate change education: Literacy-based approaches

In her chapter, Mary Roche outlines how discussing picture books about conservation and climate change can help raise awareness and create in children a sense of agency around 'being part of the solution'. Miriam Hamilton uses narrative to introduce us to the colourful coral, the powerful polar bear, the busy bee, the ancient sea turtle and the alpine flora. Using dialogical methodologies motivated by the stories of these plants and animals from the air, land and sea, the text provides thought-provoking scenarios of danger, balanced with activities focused on exploring actions of hope to save these species. Siobhán Ní Mhurchu's chapter provides some ideas, pedagogies and methodologies on how to approach a *Content and Language Integrated Learning* (CLIL) lesson using climate change as a context while teaching through the medium of a second or foreign language.

Section 3: Climate change education: STEAM (Stem + art)

This section focuses on addressing climate change education through STEM and STEAM. STEM stands for science, technology, engineering and math and the additional

'A' in STEAM stands for arts. The main difference between STEM and STEAM is that STEM symbolizes a modern approach to science and related subjects focusing on solving problems with critical thinking and analytical skills. STEAM education explores the same subjects, but incorporates creative thinking and applied arts into teaching about real life situations.

Art is about discovering and creating ingenious ways of problem-solving, integrating principles and presenting information. By adding the elements of art to STEM-based thinking, educators believe that students can use both sides of their brain – analytical and creative – to develop the best thinkers for today and tomorrow. Maeve Liston discusses the nature of STEM education and the potential of engineering projects for generating climate change solutions. Anne O'Dwyer encourages us to explore climate change outside the classroom. Anne Marie Morrin introduces us to an innovative arts project: *The School of Looking*. This project aims to develop an understanding and awareness around human and animal vision, exploring the biology and physics of insects (bees, flies and spiders) and the impact climate change and habitat loss have on a declining population. A second arts project is presented by Tanya de Paor: *The Grow Room Project*. This project is based around a greenhouse structure within an educational institutional setting. In the project, undergraduate and postgraduate pre-service teachers have the opportunity to develop creative and critical pedagogies to explore new pathways to visually think about climate change. Chapter thirteen focuses on the connections between plastic and climate change and includes some children's artistic responses to the plastic crisis.

Section 4: Climate change education: Pedagogies of hope and action

Climate change is considered by some teachers as a controversial topic especially as it challenges the neo-liberal consumerism promoted by so many sectors of society. Yet, if children are going to learn to think critically, teachers should be prepared to contest the prevailing dominant economic, political and social orthodoxies. Children need to have an opportunity to consider a different future and to imagine the world differently.

In this section, I discuss the central role of geography in addressing climate change issues. This is followed by a chapter co-written with Eileen O'Sullivan which deals with the importance of including an historical lens. Margaret Nohilly provides a range of practical ideas to support climate change education through the lens of 'Citizenship Education' as a component of Social, Personal and Health Education. Maurice Harmon argues that in addition to learning about climate change, hearts must be moved to feel passionately about it. Through practical activities, children can become active in saving their planet. Through the development of a spiritual identity within the education system, a keen sense of climate justice can be awakened. Brighid Golden provides guidelines on creating educational resources for exploring climate change. In his chapter, Richard Bowles explores how climate change issues can be addressed within physical education curricula. By promoting a culture of movement, informed by a desire to be socially responsible, his chapter provides guidance for raising climate change awareness and action through physical education. Finally, my chapter on a pedagogy of hope, focuses attention on futures education and possibilities of forging pathways to a sustainable future.

A climate change glossary is included (Appendix 1) and further resources are available on the padlet which accompanies this book: https://padlet.com/annedolan/uir0u3bwz3octwz0.

References

Kluger, J. (2017) *Apollo 8: The thrilling story of the first mission to the moon.* New York: Henry Holt and Company.

National Research Council and Carbon Dioxide Assessment Committee, (1983) *Changing Climate: Report of the Carbon Dioxide Assessment Committee.* National Academies.

Roberts, M. (2013) *Geography through enquiry.* Sheffield: Geographical Association.

von der Leyen, U (2019) A European Union that strives for more. http://europa.eu/rapid/press-release_SPEECH-19-4230_en.htm Strasbourg, 16 July 2019.

Section 1

Theory and philosophical approaches

1 Teaching climate change

Setting the context

Anne M. Dolan

Introduction

Climate change caused by global warming is already transforming life on Earth. It is the defining challenge of our time, the most significant issue facing all citizens today. Evidence of climate change is compelling. There is widespread consensus amongst the international scientific community that human-induced climate change is happening. According to the *United Nations Framework Convention on Climate Change* (2015), greenhouse gas emissions from human activities driving climate change are now at their highest levels in history. Without action, the world's average surface temperature is projected to rise over the 21st century and is likely to surpass 3° C this century – with some areas of the world expected to warm even more.

Over 30 years ago, climate change was first declared a human-generated phenomenon by NASA climatologist James Hansen. In the meantime, a steady drum beat of scientific reports have sounded warnings about climate change predictions (Dolan, 2018). While the situation is beyond serious, there is cause for hope. In response to the science of climate change, the issue is now being recognised as a serious threat by mainstream media, educators and some politicians. At the Paris Climate Conference (the 21st meeting of the Conference of the Parties, otherwise known as COP21) in December 2015, 195 countries adopted the first-ever universal, global climate deal. An agreement to maintain global warming below 2° C was the official outcome. This commitment marks an unprecedented international consensus on the need to transition from fossil fuels within the next few decades. In 2015, 193 countries adopted the 2030 Agenda for Sustainable Development and its 17 Sustainable Development Goals, one of which addresses climate change (United Nations, 2017). To maintain hope and a sense of agency, climate change education has to be part of the solution to the challenges posed by a warmer Earth.

Climate change is considered a controversial topic by some teachers. Causes of climate change are embedded in neo-liberal approaches to development which embrace capitalism, excessive consumerism and unnecessary waste. Yet if children are going to learn to think critically, teachers should be prepared to contest the prevailing dominant economic, political and social orthodoxies. Children are currently affected by climate change albeit in differing ways depending on geographical, social and economic factors. As interested citizens, they have a right to a comprehensive and robust climate change education, to ensure they become responsible decision makers now and in the future. Children need to have an opportunity to consider a different future and to imagine the world differently (Andreotti, 2016; Hicks, 2014).

This chapter aims to:

- Explore the science of climate change.
- Examine the causes and implications of climate change.
- Discuss the importance of teaching and learning about climate change.

The science of climate change

Climate change education requires in-depth teacher knowledge of climate change science. In 1859, Irish scientist John Tyndall discovered that gases including carbon dioxide (CO_2) and water vapour absorb heat. Subsequently, he realised that any change in the amount of water vapour or CO_2 could potentially change the climate. Referred to as the greenhouse effect, this natural process warms the Earth's surface. A simple explanation is as follows: A greenhouse constructed of glass allows sunlight to warm the air and plants inside. The heat not absorbed by the plants is trapped by the glass and cannot escape. Throughout the day, sunlight continues to warm the air, the air is trapped, so this heat remains even after the sun sets. Greenhouse gases build up in the atmosphere and act in a similar manner to the glass in a greenhouse, attracting and maintaining the heat from the sun. Some of the sun's energy is reflected directly back to space, the rest is absorbed by land, ocean and the atmosphere. CO_2, methane (CH_4) and other 'greenhouse gases' trap heat that would otherwise escape from the Earth's atmosphere. The accumulation of greenhouse gases is a natural process and in the correct proportion, these gases ensure that the earth is sufficiently warm to support life. The problem arises when greenhouse gas levels increase exponentially due to human activity. Hence, the natural systems regulating our climate become disrupted. Children's exploration of the greenhouse gas concept is discussed later in this chapter (Case Study 1.1 and Figure 1.2).

Since the industrial revolution, hundreds of millions of years' worth of stored carbon have been released into the atmosphere. Fossil fuels such as coal, oil and gas are stores of carbon buried deep below the earth's surface. Once burnt, these fuels release carbon atoms which combine with oxygen atoms in the air to produce CO_2. The molecular structure of CO_2 traps heat that would otherwise have been radiated back to space. The current use of the term 'climate change' refers to an increase in the planet's temperature due to human-generated emissions of greenhouse gasses. These include CO_2, CH_4, nitrous oxide (N_2O), halogenated fluorocarbons (HCFCs), ozone (O_3), perfluorinated carbons (PFCs), hydrofluorocarbons (HFCs) and water vapour. Even small changes in the global average temperature can cause major and dangerous shifts in climate and weather. The difference between 0 and 1° Celsius (or 32° and 33° Fahrenheit) for instance, is the difference between ice and water. The planet has warmed by 1° degree Celsius since we began to burn coal. If we continue with a 'business as usual approach' temperatures will rise by four times this amount by the end of the century. The last time there was this level of CO_2 in the atmosphere, humans did not exist (Klein, 2019).

Globally, we have emitted more industrial carbon since 1988 than in all of prior human history. The Keeling Curve is a graph of the accumulation of CO_2 in the Earth's atmosphere based on continuous measurements taken at the Mauna Loa Observatory on the island of Hawaii from 1958 to the present day (Figure 1.1). Dr. Charles David Keeling began studying atmospheric CO_2 in 1956 by taking air samples and measuring the amount of CO_2 they contained. Over time he noticed a pattern of consistent

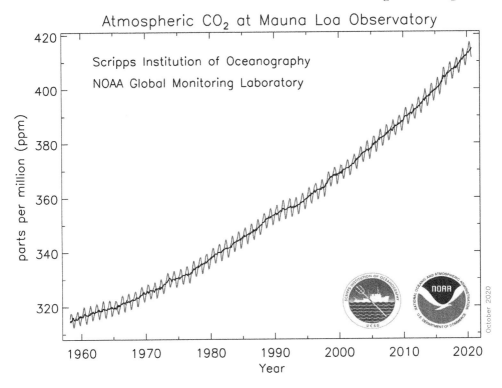

Figure 1.1 The Keeling Curve: A graph showing the ongoing change in the concentration of carbon dioxide in the Earth's atmosphere

Source: https://www.esrl.noaa.gov/gmd/ccgg/trends/

rising levels of CO_2 in the atmosphere. In addition, he also noticed interesting seasonal patterns. In the Northern Hemisphere, during the Spring and Summer months, plants absorb a substantial amount of CO_2 through photosynthesis, thus removing it from the atmosphere. During the Autumn and Winter months, trees and plants begin to lose their leaves and decay, increasing the release of CO_2 in the atmosphere. Hence, concentrations of CO_2 in the atmosphere increase throughout the Winter, reaching a peak by early Spring.

Since its creation, the Keeling Curve has served as a visual representation of Keeling's data, which scientists have continued to collect since his death in 2005. By analysing the CO_2 in his samples, Keeling was able to link rising levels of CO_2 to an extensive use of fossil fuels. The results, which are now largely undisputed, are catastrophic. Hence, the time for climate action is now. To enable teachers and children to engage with the science of climate change, a glossary of key climate change terms is included in Appendix 1.

To illustrate the process of releasing CO_2, Gold (2018) uses a wonderful metaphor of blowing up a balloon (beyond its capacity). Initially, the balloon inflates slowly and when it is full, one usually stops blowing and ties a knot. There is only a certain amount of air we can put into a balloon which Gold equates to the notion of a carbon budget. If one keeps blowing air into the balloon, it will eventually burst. As greenhouse gases including

CO_2 are continuously being pumped into the atmosphere, we are now facing the prospect of the balloon bursting or in the case of the Earth, extreme climate change. A second powerful metaphor is that of driving a car. If one drives a car and skids towards a vehicle, one immediately tries to stop the car by engaging the break. Engaging the accelerator is akin to our continued release of greenhouse gases into the atmosphere. We have to stop driving this metaphorical car.

The Intergovernmental Panel on Climate Change (IPCC) is the authoritative voice of climate science. Established in 1988, by the United Nations Environment Programme and the World Meteorological Organisation, the IPCC is a partnership between climate scientists and governments. It aims to supply an objective perspective of the current state of knowledge regarding climate change and its likely impacts. In 2018, the (IPCC; October 8, 2018) reported that the world has 12 years left for global warming to be kept to a maximum of 1.5°, that's 9 years from the publication date of this book. Any increase beyond this will significantly increase the risks of drought, floods, extreme heat and poverty for hundreds of millions of people. This IPCC report describes a world of extreme weather events, worsening food shortages and wildfires combined with a significant reduction of coral reefs.

The perceived complexity of climate change may discourage teachers from raising this issue in classrooms. Nevertheless, it is our duty as educators to assist children in understanding this important local and global issue. While climate statistics and data maybe a little removed from our daily concerns, a personal timeline can help us to make links with the science of climate change. In a doodle on the back of an envelope, Lorna Gold places herself on the historical timeline of carbon emissions (Colour Plate, section 1). A parent of two children, Lorna plotted out different scenarios for her world in line with different levels of carbon in the atmosphere. This doodle is a powerful image for helping teachers to make their own personal connections with climate change data.

Case study 1.1 Science Blast

In 2019, the inaugural primary science education festival, Electricity Supply Board (ESB) Science Blast took place in Ireland. The festival is designed to equip up to 13,000 primary school children with the fundamental skills of STEM (science, technology, engineering and maths) at a crucially early point in their academic lives. Science Blast involves an entire class investigating the science behind a straight-forward question and conducting simple experiments with items commonly found in schools or homes, before displaying their findings at an exhibition in one of the three national venues: Dublin, Limerick and Belfast. Children from 35 Limerick schools participated in Science Blast at Mary Immaculate College. Typical questions for investigations include: 'How can we make the best slime?' 'Why does cake go hard but biscuits go soft?' 'Can cows' eyes be blue?' and 'Can I charge my mobile device with a fruit?' The children from St. Nessan's Primary School, Mungret, Limerick investigated the following question: What is the Greenhouse effect and how do human activities affect it? (Figure 1.2). Using cling film (plastic covering) to trap heat, they illustrated the greenhouse effect with the following experiment:

Equipment

- Two transparent jars
- Water
- A teaspoon

Figure 1.2 Presentation of the greenhouse experiment presented by children from St. Nessan's primary school at the Science Blast exhibition in Limerick

- Two thermometers
- Clingfilm
- Rubber band
- Sticky tape
- Soil

Procedure

1 Fill each jar with some soil so that the bottom is covered. Add 2–3 drops of water.
2 Place the thermometers in the jars so that they do not touch the soil. Use the sticky tape to attach the thermometers to the jars.
3 Cover the top of one jar with the clingfilm. Use the rubber band to hold the cling film in place.
4 Leave the second jar open
5 Record the initial temperature of each thermometer.
6 Put both jars in the sun (or below a strong, warm light).

Results

1 *Did one of the thermometers in your experiment show a higher temperature?* Yes, the thermometer in the jar with clingfilm was hotter because heat was trapped inside.
2 *Which jars represents Earth with an atmosphere and Earth without an atmosphere?* The jar without a cover represents Earth without an atmosphere.

Climate change and biodiversity

Biodiversity refers to the variety of life that can be found on Earth including plants, animals, fungi and micro-organisms, the communities they form and the habitats in which they live. As climate change threatens the habitats of numerous species, biodiversity is in decline. The *World Wildlife Fund's Living Planet Report* (2020) reported that approximately 68% of mammals, birds, fish and reptiles have been wiped out since 1970. This is largely due to human's overconsumption of land, food and natural resources. Moreover, this report proves that human activity is destroying eco-systems at an unacceptable rate, ultimately threatening the well-being of current and future populations. The situation with insects is even more alarming. Insects are essential for the functioning of all ecosystems, as pollinators, food for other creatures and recyclers of nutrients. According to a longitudinal international study, the world's insects are moving towards extinction, threatening a 'catastrophic collapse of nature's ecosystems' (Sánchez-Bayo et al., 2019:17). There has been a 40% decline of insect species and a third of the remaining insect population is endangered. Indeed, the rate of extinction is eight times faster than that of mammals, birds and reptiles. The total mass of insects is falling by a staggering 2.5% a year, suggesting they could vanish within a century (Sánchez-Bayo et al., 2019). The main cause of this decline is agricultural intensification and the way we produce our food. Furthermore, intensive farming is linked to climate change, the destruction of wildlife and the pollution of rivers and oceans. Our unsustainable food production and specifically our consumption of beef has been raised by scientists as part of the *EAT – Lancet Commission on Food, Planet and Health Research Project* (Willett et al., 2019). According to this research, beef consumption in western countries needs to drop by 90%, replaced by five times more beans and pulses.

The importance of healthy ecosystems is a central concern of these scientific reports. Healthy ecosystems require a substantial variety of plant and animal life from soil microbes to predators such as tigers and wolves. If one or more species is removed from this environment, the ecosystem will be damaged in some way. Changing precipitation patterns can lead to desertification of once teeming ecosystems. Rising water temperatures and acidification are already fundamentally changing our oceans; while land degradation including deforestation and destruction of wetlands directly contribute to climate change and they are also responsible for the destruction of ecosystems. Biodiversity is important for our health, in terms of high quality food and access to pharmaceutical raw materials. Healthy functioning ecosystems are also important for a healthy economy. Biodiversity supports diverse industries including agriculture, cosmetics, pharmaceuticals, horticulture, construction and waste treatment. Consequently, the loss of biodiversity threatens our food supplies, opportunities for recreation and tourism, and sources of food, medicines and energy.

Trees are often referred to as the 'lungs of the earth' due to their ability to absorb and store CO_2 from the atmosphere. The Amazon rainforest plays a significant role in mitigating climate change. While forest fires are a natural occurrence during the dry season, the devastating 2019 fires led to international concern about the fate of the Amazon forest, the world's largest terrestrial CO_2 sink. Similarly, bushfires are a regular part of the Australian summer. Nevertheless, the scale and intensity of fires during the summer of 2019–2020 shocked and devastated local communities. Fewer trees reduces the Earth's capacity to store and sequester atmospheric carbon.

Furthermore, the process of deforestation generated by fire, a demand for fuel or a requirement for agricultural land, leads to more greenhouse gases in the atmosphere and a further disruption of the climate system. Indeed, woodlands are particularly vulnerable to the effects of climate change. Storms and droughts weaken and break up habitats including woodlands. Seasonal patterns are knocked out of sync and climate change also increases the likelihood of tree pests and diseases. Notwithstanding their vulnerability, trees are part of the climate change solution. In addition to storing carbon, they help mitigate flooding, offer shade to reduce temperatures and provide renewable alternatives to fossil fuels. Planting trees, an enjoyable and accessible climate action for all children is discussed in greater detail in Chapter 10.

Not only are we witnessing a loss of species, we are also experiencing a loss of words. In 2015, the Oxford children's dictionary dropped 50 words relating to nature (including *fern, willow, starling, bluebell, conker, heron, acorn and kingfisher*) in favour of words/phrases such as *broadband, cut and paste* and *analogue*. Robert Macfarlane and Jackie Morris protested with the production of a masterpiece 'The Lost Words' (Macfarlane and Morris, 2018). Robert Macfarlane, a prize-winning poet and writer, created 'a book of spells', the intention being to spell the lost words back into our memories and usage. Each spell is introduced by a double-page spread where letters blow and tumble among grasses or fern or trees – as if the lost words were being broken and scattered.

The poems are powerful acrostics, as the word in danger of being lost is spelled, not only in the title, but also in the reading and writing of the spell. The book is beautifully illustrated with Jackie Morris' celebrated paintings of acorns, brambles, owls, bluebells and magpies. According to Macfarlane, the book is for everyone aged between 3 and 100, so it is an excellent starting point for beginning to consider the impact of climate on our locality. Many schools including South Walney Junior School in England are using 'The Lost Words' as a lens for exploring their own locality. The Isle of Walney is an island off the west coast of England, at the western end of Morecambe Bay in the Irish Sea. In a self-published book, the staff and children at South Walney Junior School produced their own version of 'The Lost Words' to celebrate their locality in poetry and art (Figure 1.3, Colour Plate, section 2).

A magnificent sequel 'The Lost Spells' (Macfarlane and Morris, 2020) conjures up the magic of British wildlife in a time of ecological crisis. This pocket-sized book celebrates barn owls, swifts, gorse and foxes through poems and art-work. Both of these books by Macfarlane and Morris are designed to re-awaken awe and wonder about our bewildering, complex and interconnected world. Ultimately, they are about learning and relearning to love nature.

The interrelationships in the natural world are numerous and affect us in many ways. Relationships within ecology and between humans and nature have direct impacts on the food chain, water supplies, air composition and on the quality of life itself. The impact of climate change on biodiversity can be challenging to teach. The threats to biodiversity and species is unnerving. It is somewhat alarming to realise that climate change is no longer just about polar bears and penguins; it's not only about coral reefs and sea turtles; it is about our survival on planet earth (Dolan, 2020). It is important for children and teachers to realise that we live within a system and our actions have a direct impact on other parts of the system. Indeed, the impact of humans is now so significant, a new epoch has been proposed – The Anthropocene. This epoch defines Earth's most recent geologic time period as being influenced by humans or anthropogenic, based on overwhelming global evidence that atmospheric, geologic, hydrologic, biospheric and other earth systems are now altered by humans. Geologic time is discussed in greater detail in Chapter 15.

Figure 1.3 The Lost Words of Walney (title page of children's self-published work)

Covid-19 and climate change

In Chapter 6, Mary Roche discusses her childhood memories of the potential threat of nuclear war, an apocalyptic scenario guaranteed to threaten the security and well-being of all. The Greek word *apocalupsis* means to *reveal* or *disclose*. In the final book of the Christain Bible, the Book of Revelation (or the Apocalypse of John) is an apocalyptic letter which relies on visions, symbols and Old Testament references to reveal the ultimate fulfillment of God's promise given to Abraham in Genesis. The book provides a vision of suffering enduring by people before the potential of eternal salvation. Many people refer to the end of the world as the Apocalypse or the time of the Apocalypse. As this book was being compiled, the global scourge of Covid-19 emerged. Transforming the way we live our lives, the pandemic provided the world with a crash course in apocalypse management. Similar to nuclear war, Covid-19 is deadly and similar to climate disruption, it is global.

Covid-19 illuminated global interconnections through the spread of the virus and the resulting health, social and economic chaos which ensued. The greatest disaster since World War II, Covid-19 was an unanticipated event of epic proportions that exposed human fragility in an interconnected and interdependent world (Dolan and Usher, 2020). A global calamity, Covid-19 left thousands dead, millions vulnerable, supply lines collapsed, economies derailed, factories closed and cities under lockdown. A coronavirus is a type of common virus that causes an infection in the nose, sinuses or upper throat. Most coronaviruses are not dangerous and spread in the same fashion as the common cold. The coronavirus has the appearance of a crown (Latin for corona) images of which have been well documented in the media. Like other coronaviruses, it has transferred to humans from animals. Following the World Health Organization's (WHO) declaration of a pandemic, mass quarantines and nationwide lockdowns were implemented by several countries across the globe. The year 2020 will forever be known as the year when time stopped. Not only did the virus infect hundreds of thousands of people across the planet, but it brought the global economy to a virtual standstill, crushing millions of businesses, large and small, while driving tens of millions of people out of work. Ironically, the virus was good for nature. The level of carbon emissions and air pollution were reduced while swans and fish returned to the canals of Venice. While the COP26 UN climate change conference, set to take place in Glasgow in November 2020 was postponed, the virus generated an important discussion about nature, sustainability, resilience and community-based approaches to energy, security and co-operation.

Although the virus originated in Asia, the global pandemic was a product of a multitude of factors including air links connecting every corner of the planet and the failure of governments to act quickly to stop its spread. Connections between the virus and climate change became apparent. Covid-19 was designated as a zoonotic disease, an emerging infectious disease transmitted between domestic or wild animals and humans. The human destruction of natural ecosystems increases the numbers of rats, bats and other animals capable of harbouring deadly diseases. Collectively, deforestation, haphazard urbanisation, climate change and our complete disregard for the important role of nature contributed to the emergence of the Covid-19.

The effects of Covid-19 pandemic will be felt for some time to come. The fragile nature of the earth and its inhabitants have been highlighted. An awareness of our interdependent relationship with nature has been re-established. We have learnt so much about the management and distribution of risk. Many politicians ignored scientific advice and downplayed the warnings from health experts. Former President of the United States of America, Donald Trump called it a 'hoax'. Similar instances of denial about climate change are evident, where political leaders have dismissed the warnings of scientists for years.

Post Covid-19, a renewed appreciation of our environmental interdependence must be maintained. During the pandemic, there was much discussion about 'a new normal' or 'building back better'. In the case of climate change, it is incumbent upon all of us to transition from a carbon fuelled way of living. We do not have to face a choice between economic collapse and climate breakdown. An investment of trillions of dollars in decarbonisation will be required. Potentially, this offers a golden opportunity for economic development to be re-imagined in more sustainable terms. It is important to conceptualise new ways of living or 'a new normal' as we simply cannot return to a 'business as usual' approach.

A climate justice response

Climate justice involves sharing the burdens and benefits of climate change and its resolution equitably and fairly. The injustice of climate change continues to be raised by several environmental campaigners and non-governmental organisations (NGOs) including Oxfam, Christian Aid, Friends of the Earth and Trócaire. By calling for a climate justice response, there is a recognition that people who have contributed least are most affected (Waldron et al., 2016). Geographical and economic analysis demonstrates that the richest 10% of the world's population pollute the atmosphere dramatically more than the rest (Dorling, 2018).

While everyone is vulnerable, the impact is far greater on those in low-income countries. Those who have contributed least to the problem, people in the Global South, face the worst consequences of climate change, and are struggling to cope with drought, storms and floods. The compounded nature of the impact of climate change on the most vulnerable has been noted by several commentators. Khazem (2018:128) states, 'climate change can worsen the living conditions and human rights of people who may already suffer from human rights violations and so further contribute to social injustice and inequality and engender social ills and conflicts'. For instance, severe drought helped destabilise Syria, sparking the conflict which sent a million people to Europe in search of refuge (McKibben, 2019). Commentators such as Dorling (2018) argue that equitable income distribution has to be part of the response to climate change. Dorling claims that in countries with more equitable income distribution, people including the rich consume and pollute far less.

The world's poorest and most vulnerable are seriously at risk with many having to migrate due to sea level rise, crop failure and pollution. Although there are few instances of climate change as the sole factor in migration, climate change is widely recognised as a contributing and exacerbating factor in both migration and conflict. A 2018 World Bank study predicted that further climate change will displace as many as 143 million people from Africa, South Asia and Latin America by 2050 (Rigaud et al., 2018). Indeed, the term 'climigration' is now used to describe large scale population displacement due to climate change. For example, in the South Pacific, 3,000 Carteret Islanders have to migrate to Papua-New Guinea as a consequence of rising sea-levels. The residents of Tuvalu, where the highest point is just 4.6 metres above sea level, are facing a similar threat. In Kenya, prolonged drought has forced many of the nomadic Turkana people into towns and relief camps. However, the legal protections afforded to refugees does not extend to climate refugees as they are not covered by the 1951 Refugee Convention. The latter extends only to people who have a well-founded fear of being persecuted on grounds related to race, religion, nationality or membership of a particular social group or political opinion, and are unable or unwilling to seek protection from their home countries.

Climate change has a direct impact on the realisation of internationally recognised human rights, including those protected by the International Covenant on Economic, Social, and Cultural Rights (UN General Assembly, 1966a) and the International Covenant on Civil and Political Rights (UN, General Assembly, 1966b). Climate justice links human rights and development to achieve a human-centred approach, whereby the rights of the most vulnerable are safeguarded and the burdens and benefits of climate change are shared by all. Climate justice begins at home, it begins with each decision we make in relation to energy, transport and lifestyle. Poverty and food security cannot be tackled without addressing the issue of climate change and helping people to adapt to it impacts.

The moral dimension of climate change

Climate change has been described as a 'perfect moral storm' as it brings together three major challenges to ethical action in a mutually reinforcing way (Gardiner, 2011). The first challenge is the global nature of climate change. Once emitted, greenhouse gas emissions can have climate effects anywhere on the planet, regardless of their source. Many of the most vulnerable countries and people are those who have emitted the least historically, and whose levels of greenhouse gas emissions continue to be relatively low. The second challenge is the intergenerational aspect. Emissions of the most prominent greenhouse gas,

CO_2, typically persist in the atmosphere for a long time, contributing to negative climate impacts for centuries, or even millennia. This places an unfair and unethical burden on future generations, especially if the impacts are severe and cumulative.

The third challenge to ethical action is that our theoretical tools are underdeveloped in many of the relevant areas, such as international justice, intergenerational ethics, scientific uncertainty and the appropriate relationship between humans and the rest of nature. For instance, climate change raises issues about our moral obligations to care for nature and our environment. By contributing significantly to climate change, this current generation is passing most of the burden on to their children, grandchildren and people in other parts of the world. This illustrates the global and intergenerational dimensions of the perfect moral storm of climate change. The ongoing political inertia in developing robust climate action is an example of shoving one's proverbial head in the sand hoping that somehow this crisis will go away.

Pope Francis (2015), well known for his interest in environmental issues, dedicated his encyclical Laudato Si' to the issue of climate change. The encyclical, discussed in greater detail in Chapter 17, draws from the deep well of Catholic teaching on creation. Pope Francis has criticised world leaders for their weak response to this global catastrophe. However, some commentators also raise questions about the Catholic Church's response to climate change. While Woodworth (2020) credits the encyclical as a 'remarkable document', he notes the use of aspirational rather than pragmatic language, the focus on economic accounting rather than natural capital accounting and most importantly, the absence of a clear call for specific actions. Woodworth acknowledges the confined space of conservative Catholicism within which Pope Francis operates. Nevertheless, it behoves Pope Francis and other world leaders to make a clarion call to action in line with current scientific evidence.

The Paris Agreement, which committed nations to limiting climate change to 2°, will necessitate extensive and substantial economic, political and lifestyle changes. We need a radical shift towards comprehensive solutions for the environmental and social aspects of our collective crisis. In religious terms, an 'ecological conversion' is required. The exploitative/extractive mindset that underpins global capitalism contrasts with the more holistic vision of a unified web of life that is central to a sustainability mindset and which forms part of indigenous wisdom. To date, many humans have subjugated and neglected the environment. The price of this abusive relationship is now obvious to all. We have a moral and ethical duty to reconsider our relationship with nature.

Responding to climate change

The threat of climate change increasingly recognised by young people. During 2019, hundreds of thousands of students in more than 2,000 cities from Australia and Uganda to Germany and Italy left their classrooms, to take to the streets in peaceful marches protesting about governments' climate inaction. Young generations in 125 countries demanded attention from politicians, international institutions and their elders. They have issued a call to save the planet under the banners 'Youth Strike 4 Climate' and 'Fridays for Future'. This spontaneous global activism by young students, worried about the future, was inspired by the commitment and messages of (the then 16-year-old) Swedish schoolgirl, Greta Thunberg. This young climate activist who made headlines for her action against climate change was nominated for the Nobel Peace Prize. Subsequently, she sailed from Europe to New York in a zero emissions sailboat. Upon arrival, she addressed international leaders at the UN Climate

Action Summit in New York. In December 2019, she was named TIME magazine's Person of the Year. Her speeches have been published in several languages and her story has been retold in multiple publications for different age groups.

In addition to the student strikes, many more have mobilised under the collective banner of *Extinction Rebellion*, a global environmental movement with the stated aim, of using non-violent civil disobedience to compel government action. In response to the global mobilisation of young people, some governments are beginning to take climate change seriously.

Global climate change is a complex issue. A complete reconceptualisation of how we view climate is required. The British newspaper *The Guardian* announced a style guide change for journalists writing about climate change. From now on, journalists are required to use terms such as *climate crisis* or *breakdown*, and *global heating* over the more common *climate change* and *global warming*. Furthermore in 2019, Oxford Dictionaries declared 'climate emergency' the word of the year, following a hundred-fold increase in its usage. Hundreds of cities, towns and even countries have also declared "climate emergencies" during 2019 – including Ireland, the UK, Canada and France. It remains to be seen how these declarations will influence industrial, economic and social policies.

The Guardian columnist George Monbiot argues that the language we use to describe our world, our environment and our assault on life and beauty has become sanitised, neutral and somewhat disinfected. Even the term *climate change* he argues, confuses natural changes with the more serious catastrophic disruption caused by humans. While teachers have to be careful to minimise use of alarmist terminology, they must use environmental and climate terminology honestly. Language frames the way we perceive the natural world. For instance, terms such as *living planet* and *natural world* are far more evocative than *environment*. The term 'place of natural wonder' communicates a sense of awe and wonder enjoyed by simply being in a place. Children can be invited to find better ways of describing nature and their relationships with it.

Teaching climate change education is conceptually challenging (Shepardson et al., 2012). It requires teachers who are knowledgeable about climate change, its causes and consequences. Children should be able to understand the processes that contribute to climate change and discuss its impact on living things, people and the environment. Responses to climate change include denial, adaptation and mitigation. Figure 1.4 illustrates a framework for exploring different elements of climate change.

Impacts

Due to an increase in temperature, the world's weather patterns are changing. Earth-orbiting satellites and other technological advances have enabled scientists to monitor these changes, collecting many different datasets about our planet and its climate on a global scale. This body of data, collected over many years, reveals the signals of a changing climate. The planet's average surface temperature has risen about 1.33° F (0.74° C) since the late 19th century, a change driven largely by increased CO_2 and other human-made emissions into the atmosphere. The ten hottest years on record have occurred since 1998. Rising sea levels, declining arctic sea ice, changes in precipitation patterns resulting in extreme flooding, droughts and more extreme weather events such as heat

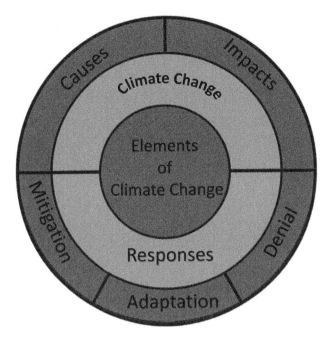

Figure 1.4 Elements of climate change

Source: Adapted from Sheppard (2012) and Hicks (2019)

waves, cyclones and tropical storms are just some of the effects of changes to the global climate. Other impacts include increased acidification and warming of the oceans, decreased snow cover, glacial retreats and shrinking ice sheets. Each of these changes are resulting in serious knock on effects such as increased poverty, species extinction, conflict and migration (Dolan, 2020).

Causes

It is now widely recognised that climate change is caused by human-instigated global warming, the result of burning fossil fuels (oil, coal and gas) and the use of their by-products in every area of modern life. Levels of CO_2 in the atmosphere have increased dramatically since the Industrial Revolution and will continue to do so for centuries to come (Hicks, 2014). According to the *United in Science Report* (WMO and Science Advisory Group of the UN Climate Action Summit, 2019), carbon dioxide concentrations in the atmosphere increased at a higher rate between 2015 and 2019 than in the previous five years. With levels of carbon dioxide and other greenhouse gases rising more quickly than heretofore, further warming is already locked in, according to the World Meteorological Association (WMO). The science is unequivocal. For more than 25 years, WMO has issued an annual *Statement on the State of the Global Climate*. It is based on data provided by international meteorological organizations. These reports have been published in the six official languages of the United Nations (Arabic, Chinese, English, French, Russian and Spanish) to inform governments, international agencies, other WMO partners and the general public about the global climate and significant climatic trends at global and regional levels.

Denial

In spite of devastating climatic events including flooding, forest fires and drought, climate change deniers continue to ignore scientific evidence. Certain political ideologies along with the fossil fuel industry have collectively invested money in climate denial. In the United States, fossil fuel interests and ideological conservatives sponsor fierce disinformation campaigns to discredit climate-science warnings and resist proposed solutions. One of the most sinister examples has been the use of mass media to discredit climate change research. For example, in the United States, major business interests associated with the energy sector, fund reports by scientists willing to contest the universal research evidence linking human activities, the oil industry and climate change. These reports are then presented by segments of the US media including the Fox network (owned by Rupert Murdoch), certain radio stations and newspapers. Manufactured studies are presented as the ultimate research evidence, denying the culpability of humans for climate change (Dunlap and McCright, 2010). Sustained attacks have been conducted against those endorsing the evidence of global warming including authors of scientific peer reviewed journal articles and institutions such as the National Academy of Sciences.

Adaptation

Adaptation seeks to lower the risks posed by the consequences of climate change. It involves learning to live with changing temperatures and seasons, extraordinary weather conditions, higher sea levels, extensive flooding and drought. Humans have always taken action in response to local climatic conditions including introduction of new crop types, revised building practices and flood relief schemes. However, climate shifts including temperature, storm frequency and flooding may place unbearable pressure on communities. Those least responsible for climate change have few options available to them for adaptation. Adaptation measures include large-scale infrastructure changes and flood relief schemes as well as behavioural shifts such as water conservation and building of passive houses.

However, not all adaptation is positive or well-intentioned. Klein (2019) uses the term 'climate barbarism' as a form of climate adaptation. This represents a marrying of white supremacist violence with vicious anti-immigrant racism. A rise of far right politics globally and stricter border controls, corresponds with higher levels of prejudice toward immigrants.

Mitigation

Climate change mitigation consists of actions to limit the magnitude or rate of global warming and its related effects. Mitigation involves reducing the flow of heat-trapping greenhouse gases into the atmosphere, either by reducing sources of these gases (for example, the burning of fossil fuels for electricity, heat or transport) or enhancing the sinks that accumulate and store these gases (such as oceans, forests and soil). Mitigation strategies in climate change education include education about renewable energy, the design of eco-technologies and energy conservation.

Both climate change mitigation and adaptation strategies are required now. Even if emissions of greenhouse gases dramatically decrease in the next decade, adaptation will still be needed to deal with the global changes that have already been set in motion (Selby and Kagawa, 2013).

Climate change education: Dimensions of learning

There are increasing calls for the inclusion of climate change education in formal and non-formal education from religious, spiritual, environmental and civic groups (Francis and McDonagh, 2016; United Nations Framework Convention on Climate Change, 2015). Mainstreaming climate change education as part of formal education systems has to be one of the most important and effective means of developing capacities for addressing climate change (Mochizuki and Bryan, 2015). Article 12 of the Paris Agreement focuses on education as follows:

> Parties shall cooperate in taking measures, as appropriate, to enhance climate change education, training, public awareness, public participation and public access to information, recognising the importance of these steps with respect to enhancing actions under this agreement.
> (United Nations Framework Convention on Climate Change, 2015:28)

Shepardson et al. (2009:550) argue that understanding global warming and climate change 'is essential if future citizens are to assume responsibility for the management and policy-making decisions facing our planet'. Our generation and future generations will have to learn how to live with the challenges posed by climate change. However, complex issues such as climate change will not be resolved by education programs which focus on knowledge alone (Hicks, 2019). Figure 1.5 outlines four important dimensions of effective climate change education namely: Knowing; feeling; choosing and acting. These dimensions represent a holistic, human, ecological and social understanding of

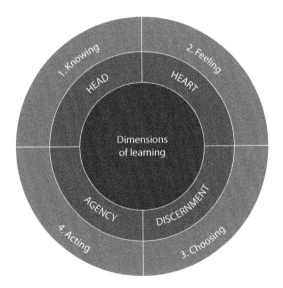

Figure 1.5 Four dimensions of learning needed to explore climate change effectively

Source: Hicks (2019:23)

climate change. While climate change knowledge is important, it is not sufficient without attitudinal change; an ability to choose wisely and a sense of agency.

The following reflections from student teachers illustrate some of the challenges raised by their experiences of climate change education:

Student teacher reflections

What I've learnt is that climate change is a huge problem which the young generation need to be educated about. As a teacher, I was surprised at how much I did not know. Now I know there are so many resources for teachers and children. Because it is affecting all of us, everywhere we live rural or urban areas, the ability to make it local can have a huge impact on pupil's learning. They will be more engaged especially in the aftermath of an extreme weather event.

As a teacher you need strong knowledge of climate change so that you can teach it effectively. It is a topic which you can easily integrate with other subject areas and one which is of interest to children.

I do not have much prior knowledge about climate change. However, I did teach a climate change lesson during school placement. I realized that the children know more than me. They are aware of the effects and causes of climate change and they know about the role everyone has in order to solve the issue.

There is definitely a major change occurring in our climate that needs to be addressed at every level of society. I don't believe that our dependence on oil and gas will change due to the huge amount of revenue and wealth associated with fossil fuels. Educating children is our last hope before it's gone too far.

Sadly, I feel climate change is out of control. It's no longer about switching off an appliance when it's not in use or having a shower instead of a bath. The world needs something big or someone big to make a change. I am still horrified about the level of corruption in our society today and the level of collusion between fossil fuel industries and politicians. However, children are naturally full of hope. I will strive to educate future generations and hopefully educate that 'someone big' to make the changes we desperately need.

Personally, climate change is a huge topic for me. I really see it as a global issue and as a teacher it is something I have always incorporated into my teaching particularly during school placement. I have found that children respond really well to the topic and have a significant interest and creative initiatives that are not being brought to light or being challenged during their everyday school life. I find it's an important topic for school children and it is completely diverse and can be used and integrated into every curricular subject. I love learning and exploring the topic of climate change however, the deeper I delve into it and the more information I gain the more it frustrates me to see government officials and even educators not doing enough to shed light on the topic.

My views on climate change have remained the same. I am invested in the topic and wish to make a change. As a teacher I see that teaching climate change and what we can do about it as one of the most important things we will ever teach. It is all very well having literacy and numeracy schemes but what good is it if we have no planet to live on. I am optimistic that a positive change will come soon.

Climate change has become the biggest threat and disregarded subject of our generation. It is unfortunate to see the economy overruling sustainability as people in power invest in fossil fuels instead of renewable sources. Power and money have skewed politicians and businesses into believing global warming and climate change are mythical in nature. We know the effects of things like war. We do not fully appreciate the impacts of climate change on our lives. Money is being pumped into cures instead of prevention e.g. flooding in Miami. More significant governmental and stricter UN policies must be demanded. Penalise with fines because money seems to be the only language that people understand.

The reflections from student teachers demonstrate an awareness of the importance of the issue, high levels of children's interest and anxiety about levels of personal climate change knowledge. However, some of the reflections illustrate a disconnect between awareness and action. In some cases, student teachers are not aware of the importance of their own personal agency in terms of lifestyle choices but focus instead on the importance of teaching others about climate change. Some student teachers are optimistic about the future whereas others are more pessimistic.

Teaching about climate change involves scientific knowledge, familiarity with appropriate pedagogy and resources and confidence to explore the complexities of the subject, including moral and ethical aspects (Hestness et al., 2011). Critical thinking and an appreciation of personal/collective agency is also essential. However, many teachers and student teachers are unsure about their own personal climate change conceptual knowledge. Some teachers are nervous about their ability to engage children in appropriate actions, while others have concerns about the perceived controversial nature of the issue.

Conclusion

The transition to a low-carbon, climate-resilient economy has to be part of the solution as it makes economic, social and environmental sense (Hicks, 2014). Political will and leadership are needed for this to happen. Politicians will not gamble their political careers on climate actions unless the public call for them to do so. Without a comprehensive education programme, short-term political pay backs will remain more popular than long-term environmental actions. Often framed as a green or left wing agenda, climate action and holistic environmental protection are challenges for people of all political persuasions, ethnicities and religious beliefs. Humanity has the fundamental scientific, technical and industrial knowledge to solve the carbon and climate problem within the next 50 years (Pacala and Socolow, 2004). However, considerable buy-in will be required by citizens, corporations, businesses communities and agricultural sectors. The uneven responses from state, corporate and civil actors across the world clearly signify the challenges and opportunities that lie ahead. Even though the scientific evidence is clear, the power of fossil fuel interests continues to influence policy and practice. Alternately, the reality of climate change is encouraging people to consider alternative sustainable ways of living.

As humans, we are all living on this one interdependent planet with its incredible biodiversity and natural wonders. Challenges faced by the planet will have direct consequences for us. Collectively, we need to appreciate the implications of our actions or inaction, hence the need to act co-operatively has never been greater. If we continue as we are adopting a 'business as usual' approach, experts predict that we face a global temperature rise of 5%. In other words, if levels of global consumption equalled levels of consumption in the United States of America, we would need four planets. Hence, the need for a comprehensive, robust climate change education programme in schools.

As a resource for all primary teachers and student teachers, this book is written to address the challenges of teaching about climate change. Specifically, the book aims to alleviate teachers' fear and anxieties about their own perceived knowledge gaps and confidence levels. Climate change education needs to feature prominently across the curriculum, in links with the local community and through pre-service and in-service teacher education. As educators, we have a duty to prepare young people for a climate changed world. We need to imagine our world in 2050, 2060 and 2070 with an anticipated population of ten billion people, and make the correct decisions now to ensure that our children and grandchildren inherit a liveable world (Tutu and Robinson, 2011).

Useful websites

- Climate change education, UNESCO: https://en.unesco.org/themes/education-sustainable-development/cce.
- Creating Futures, Climate Change Education for Senior Primary: https://www.dcu.ie/chrce/news/2016/sep/creating-futures-climate-change-education-for-senior-primary.shtml.
- Education for Global Citizenship: A Guide for Schools: https://www.oxfam.org.uk/education/resources/education-for-global-citizenship-a-guide-for-schools.
- IPCC: Intergovernmental Panel on Climate Change: http://www.ipcc.ch.
- Trócaire Climate Change Education resources: https://www.trocaire.org/getinvolved/education.
- Animation of Keeling Curve History: https://www.youtube.com/watch?v=1ZQG59_z83I&feature=emb_rel_end.

References

Andreotti, V. (2016) The educational challenges of imagining the world differently. *Canadian Journal of Development Studies/Revue canadienne d'études du développement, 37*(1), pp. 101–112.

Dolan, A.M. (2018) Climate Change and Geography. *Irish Times,* December 27th https://www.irishtimes.com/opinion/letters/climate-change-and-geography-1.3741007.

Dolan, A.M. (2020) *Powerful primary geography: A toolkit for 21st-century learning.* London: Routledge.

Dolan, A.M and Usher, J. (2020) The geography of Covid-19 *In Touch,* INTO Teacher's magazine November/December 2020, pp. 52–53.

Dorling, D. (2018) Geography and climate breakdown. *The Oxford Magazine,* (402) pp. 11–12, November 30th.

Dunlap, R.E. and McCright, A.M. (2010) Organized climate change denial. Lever-Tracy, C. (ed.), *Routledge handbook of climate change and society.* London: Routledge.

Francis, P. (2015) *Laudato Si'.* Dublin: Veritas.

Francis, P. and McDonagh, S. (2016) *On care for our common home, Laudato Si': The encyclical of Pope Francis on the environment.* New York: Orbis Books.

Gardiner, S.M. (2011) *A perfect moral storm: The ethical challenge of climate change.* Oxford, UK: Oxford University Press.

Gold, L. (2018) *Climate generation: Awakening to our children's future.* Dublin: Veritas.

Hestness, E., Randy McGinnis, J., Riedinger, K. and Marbach-Ad, G. (2011) A study of teacher candidates' experiences investigating global climate change within an elementary science methods course. *Journal of Science Teacher Education, 22*(4), 351–369.

Heuser, S. and Midgley, A. (2018) *Groundswell: Preparing for internal climate migration.* Washington, DC: World Bank.

Hicks, D. (2014) *Educating for hope in troubled times: Climate change and the transition to a post-carbon future.* London: Trentham Books/Institute of Education Press.

Hicks, D. (2019) Climate change: Bringing the pieces together. *Teaching Geography*, Spring, 20–23.

Khazem, D. (2018) Critical realist approaches to global learning: A focus on education for sustainability. *International Journal of Development Education and Global Learning*, 10(2), pp. 125–134.

Klein, N. (2019) *On fire: The (burning) case for a Green New Deal*. New York: Simon & Schuster.

Macfarlane, R. and Morris, J. (2018) *The lost words*. London: Hamish Hamilton.

Macfarlane, R. and Morris, J. (2020) *The lost spells*. London: Hamish Hamilton.

McKibben, B. (2019) *Falter: Has the human game begun to play itself out?* Melbourne: Black Inc.

Mochizuki, Y. and Bryan, A. (2015) Climate change education in the context of education for sustainable development: Rationale and principles. *Journal of Education for Sustainable Development*, 9(1), pp. 4–26.

Pacala, S. and Socolow, R. (2004) Stabilization wedges: Solving the climate problem for the next 50 years with current technologies. *Science*, 305(5686), pp. 968–972.

Rigaud, K.K., Jones, B., Bergmann, J., Clement, V., Ober, K., Schewe, J., Adamo, S., McCusker, B., Heuser, S. and Midgley, A. (2018) *Groundswell: Preparing for internal climate migration*. Washington, DC: World Bank.

Sánchez-Bayo, F. and Wyckhuys, K.A. (2019) Worldwide decline of the entomofauna: A review of its drivers. *Biological Conservation*, 232, pp. 8–27.

Selby, D. and Kagawa, F. (2013) *Climate change in the classroom: UNESCO course for secondary teachers on climate change education for sustainable development*. Paris, France: United Nations Educational, Scientific and Cultural Organization. http://unesdoc.unesco.org/images/0021/002197/219752e.pdf.

Sheppard, S. (2012) *Visualising climate change: A guide to visual communication of climate change and developing local solutions*. London: Routledge.

Shepardson, D.P., Niyogi, D., Choi, S. and Charusombat, U. (2009) Seventh grade students' conceptions of global warming and climate change. *Environmental Education Research*, 15(5), pp. 549–570.

Shepardson, D.P., Niyogi, D., Roychoudhury, A. and Hirsch, A., (2012) Conceptualising climate change in the context of a climate system: Implications for climate and environmental education. *Environmental Education Research*, 18(3), 323–352.

Tutu, D. and Robinson, M. (2011) Climate change is a matter of justice. *The Guardian*, December 5. http://www.guardian.co.uk/environment/2011/dec/05/climate-change-justice?intcmp=122.

UN General Assembly (1966a) International covenant on economic, social and cultural rights. *United Nations, Treaty Series*, 993(3).

UN General Assembly (1966b) International covenant on civil and political rights. *United Nations, Treaty Series*, 999(171).

United Nations Framework Convention on Climate Change (2015) *Adoption of the Paris Agreement*. Retrieved from: https://unfccc.int/resource/docs/2015/cop21/eng/l09r01.pdf.

United Nations (2017) *Goal 13: Take urgent action to combat climate change and its impacts*. Retrieved from: https://unstats.un.org/sdgs/report/2017/goal-13/.

Waldron, F., Ruane, B., Oberman, R. and Morris, S. (2016) Geographical process or global injustice? Contrasting educational perspectives on climate change. Environmental Education Research, 25(6), pp. 895–911.

Willett, W., Rockström, J., Loken, B., Springmann, M., Lang, T., Vermeulen, S., Garnett, T., Tilman, D., DeClerck, F., Wood, A. and Jonell, M. (2019) Food in the Anthropocene: The EAT–Lancet Commission on healthy diets from sustainable food systems. *The Lancet*, 393(10170), pp. 447–492.

WMO and Science Advisory Group of the UN Climate Action Summit (2019) *United in Science Report*. Retrieved from: *https://ane4bf-datap1.s3-eu-west-1.amazonaws.com/wmocms/s3fs-public/ckeditor/files/United_in_Science_ReportFINAL_0.pdf?XqiG0yszsU_sx2vOehOWpCOkm9RdC_gN*.

Woodworth, P. (2020) "We were nowhere. We've got somewhere". Does Laudato Si' go far enough, and is the Church on board for the climate journey? In McKim, R. (ed.), *Laudato Si' and the environment: Pope Francis' green encyclical*. London: Routledge.

World Meteorological Organization (2019) WMO statement on the state of the Global Climate in 2016. *World Meteorological Organization (WMO)*. Retrieved from: https://public.wmo.int/en/our-mandate/climate/wmo-statement-state-of-global-climate.

World Wildlife Fund (2020) *Living Planet Report*. Retrieved from: https://www.worldwildlife.org/publications/living-planet-report-2020.

2 A thematic approach to teaching climate change

Fionnuala Tynan

Introduction

One of the criticisms of the climate change discussion is that it has been academic and political, typically presented through a single lens. Arguably, teaching through a traditional curriculum model with distinct, fragmented subject areas fails to recognise the integrated nature of knowledge and of lived experiences. The concept of an integrated curriculum is not new. In 1933, Dewey promoted this idea through a pragmatist view of education. This approach to teaching and learning was advocated in the Plowden Report (Central Advisory Council for Education, 1967) in the UK and in the Primary School Curriculum (Department of Education, 1971) in the Republic of Ireland. Despite the existence of some critics of curriculum integration (see George, 1996), curriculum integration gives children a broader experience of education and helps them to connect seemingly fragmented disciplines through a central theme (Reid, 2005). It also contributes to stronger classroom relationships, greater emphasis on pedagogy and enhanced efficiency in teaching (DeLuca et al., 2015). Not without its critics (Reid, 2005), curriculum integration enhances learning outcomes in knowledge, skills, values and attitudes (Chumdari et al., 2018). Traditionally, climate change has been explored through specific disciplines such as science or geography, yet now there is a trend to promote the teaching of this topic through a cross-curricular approach (Flynn, nd). Considering the multi-disciplinary causes of implication of climate change, a cross-curricular approach makes sense. This chapter outlines the pedagogical nature of thematic teaching. It provides an academic rationale for its use and considers different applied models for the thematic teaching of climate change. It also provides reflective activities or prompts for teachers to help in future planning.

What is thematic teaching?

If we want our children to be effective citizens, we must inspire them to engage with lifelong learning (Golden, 2016). There is an increased call to move away from examining climate change through one discipline (such as science or geography) and presenting it to children in a cross-curricular way, integrating many subject areas. Climate change isn't a mere topic; it concerns 'personal values and requires collective action, systemic reform and innovation' (Flynn, nd:4). Yet, it also concerns exploring the emotive aspect of the topic and acknowledging pupils' fears and emotions, while also allowing them to understand the effects of different actions (Ibid.). In addition to knowledge, skills, attitudes and values, thematic teaching also encompasses feelings, emotions and actions. It is particularly important when teaching about climate change that children do not feel unduly anxious about the future of the planet or feel there is no point in taking action. Ultimately, teaching about climate change should promote critical thinking and possible action.

Teachers tend to use the terms *thematic teaching, cross-curricular approach* and *curriculum integration* synonymously. Thematic teaching can be seen as a way of integrating curriculum areas (Loughman, 2005) and is likened to 'a pedagogy of connection' (Dillon, 2006:69). It aims to transform fragmented knowledge and acquisition of isolated facts into personally useful tools for learning new information (Lipson et al., 1993:252). But the *intentional teaching* of a theme matters, not just the use of the approach in its own right. Alleman and Brophy (1991:7) warn that if activities are worthwhile, it is because 'they fulfil important curricular purposes, not just because they cut across subject matter lines.' They found that some of the 'integrated' activities suggested in pupils' textbooks 'lack educational value in any subject and are just pointless busy work' (Ibid.:4). For instance, drawing a picture of a polar bear at the end of a geography lesson does not comprise a focus on art. This 'busy work' does not enhance geographical or art conceptual development. It is not thematic teaching. Alleman and Brophy also warn of the risk of contaminating other subjects by 'integrating' literacy or numeracy with them and while attaining outcomes in literacy or numeracy, failing to teach curriculum content or subject-specific skills in the target subject. Interestingly, Esprívalo Harrell (2010:146) reminds us that an integrated curriculum does not necessarily facilitate integrated comprehension within an individual as this is an internal process. This means quality teaching matters.

Teaching children about climate change thematically is linked to social constructivism and the works of Piaget, Bruner and Vygotsky. Advances in neuroscience have also informed the study of thematic teaching, including the contextual and constructivist nature of knowledge. Through studies in neuroscience, we know that learning is both social and emotional (Immordino-Yang, 2015). Self-efficacy and self-determination are enhanced through thematic teaching, and these concepts are particularly important in the context of climate change. Self-efficacy is the belief we have in our own abilities, to be able to complete tasks, make decisions, effect control over certain things and meet the challenges we face in life. Self-determination, by contrast, is the development of intrinsic motivation through meeting three basic human needs: competence, autonomy and relatedness (Deci and Ryan, 1985). The teaching of climate change can, at times, feel depressing at best. Children need to feel that they can make informed decisions that will impact positively on their world. Thematic teaching supports this as the topic of climate change can be explored in a myriad of ways through a wide range of activities, linked to children's interests.

According to Lipson et al. (1993:253), the assumption exists that thematic teaching is a self-evident way to achieve integration in curriculum, but it is very much dependent on teacher content knowledge (Esprívalo Harrell, 2010). Chapter 1 addresses the interconnected nature of climate change. It is imperative that teachers have a thorough conceptual understanding of climate change before they teach it to a class. But thematic teaching is much more than knowledge transfer. It has, at its core, an understanding that children are:

- Central to the process
- Actively constructing their own knowledge
- Supported by their classroom environment
- Have positive interactions with their teacher and peers (Loughman, 2005)

Fogarty (1992) presents ten different models of curriculum integration ranging on a continuum from integration within single subjects, to integration across several subjects/disciplines to integration with the pupils themselves and then across a network of learners. This chapter presents the webbed model, whereby one topic is selected and linked in a web to other subjects. However, it is also acknowledged that a 'nested model' allows for natural integration of one topic with another and may typically be used in a classroom. Ultimately, we are working towards the immersed model where all learning, and indeed life itself, is viewed through the theme and everything revolves around it! The immersed learner is constantly making connections to their subjects and sees links in everyday experiences.

What is the value of thematic teaching for climate change?

A host of literature outlines the value of thematic teaching which is relevant in the context of climate change:

1 It provides a longer timeframe to work on a topic/theme. This means there can be higher levels of dialogue and negotiation which contribute to children's civic education (Gaughan, 2003).
2 It makes learning more meaningful (Nurlaela et al., 2018).
3 It enables teachers to address issues in a holistic manner which achieves better understanding (Ignatz, 2005).
4 It can provide a framework for children to make connections in learning (Roser and Hoffman, 1992).
5 It promotes child involvement (Chumdari et al., 2018).
6 It facilitates a balance between content and process (Ignatz, 2005).
7 It promotes the generalisation of skills and knowledge enabling pupils to transfer their learning (Lipson et al., 1993).
8 It emphasises conceptualisation rather than memorisation, thus promoting higher-order thinking skills (Chumdari et al., 2018).
9 It enhances children's social skills through co-operative tasks (Nurlaela et al., 2018).
10 Children can be independent in their learning and experience higher levels of intrinsic motivation (John, 2015).

What are the disadvantages of thematic teaching?

1 Sometimes the integrated curriculum is described in terms of activities rather than in terms of curriculum (Lipson et al., 1993). Over time this can lead to an impoverished curriculum with some subject areas inadequately covered in terms of knowledge, skills and attitudes.
2 There is a significant workload associated with the approach and a need for professional development for its successful implementation (Leung, 2006).
3 It can be difficult to assess children's learning across a wide range of disciplines. Thorough and continuous assessment of various techniques can be difficult to implement (Wolfinger and Stockard, 1997).
4 Many 'thematic' activities in textbooks lack educational value in any discipline and do not promote progress towards specific outcomes in the target subject area. Teachers have to be able to ensure the integrity of the curriculum (Alleman and Brophy, 1991).

What are the considerations in using thematic teaching?

• Each theme should be carefully chosen and be of interest to both children and teacher. If 'climate change' is selected, ensure that the children are involved in identifying the aspects of climate change to be explored.

- The theme should allow for broad exploration of different disciplines.
- Curriculum objectives/outcomes for different subject areas should be outlined in the thematic plan so that the integration is not 'trite' but meaningful.
- No subject area should be 'forced' into the thematic plan. Links should be natural and sensible.
- The theme should allow for the development of knowledge, skills and attitudes. It should not be for the development of cognitive capacities alone.
- Specific teaching and learning activities should be identified and appropriately sequenced, with assessment *of* and *for* learning planned in advance to support the learner.
- Authentic materials should be sourced where possible. This may include internet clips and photographs. Materials need to be fully vetted by the teacher in advance to ensure they suit the cognitive and developmental stages of the children.
- The teacher needs to be knowledgeable in the different aspects of the theme showing a high level of content knowledge and to have identified appropriate sources of reference for the children.
- Managing co-operative learning activities requires a skilful approach and careful preparation to ensure children are consistently focused on the theme.

Teaching climate change thematically … step by step

In working through the development of teaching climate change thematically, Loughman's elements for successful thematic projects (2005) are applied as follows:

1   Consider the theme (climate change): where might/can the theme lead? You need to be clear on what the possibilities are and how you can manage the different fronts that emerge. Before you initiate the theme with your pupils, think about your own knowledge of climate change (Figures 2.1 and 2.2).
2   Consider the possible subject area that could be linked to the theme of climate change. This means that if the children are limited in their suggestions, you can prompt them and encourage a broader range of sub-themes. There are two examples given below, one for younger classes or children of a younger developmental stage (Table 2.1) and another for older classes or children at a later developmental stage (Table 2.2).

Figure 2.1 When you think of climate change, what topics come to mind?

Figure 2.2 Examples of climate change topics

Table 2.1 Possible subject areas to be included in thematic plan on climate change (younger children (3–7 years) or children of an early developmental stage)

Subject area	Climate change sub-theme	Ideas
Language	Weather (or any sub-theme!)	• Vocabulary development • Presentation (weather forecast) with a focus on tenses (past, present, future).
Literacy	Weather	• Matching words to pictures • Reading/writing local weather reports • Reading/writing local weather reports for different times of the year • Reading/writing weather reports for other parts of the world • Developing comprehension skills: impact of weather on activities, such as clothes and food.
Mathematics	Weather	• Reading a pictogram • Creating a pictogram • Counting 'days of sun' or 'days of rain' • Sorting/classifying clothes • Develop a sense of chronology as weather changes across the seasons • Capacity: measuring rainfall (more or less than yesterday) • Creating patterns (algebra) using weather symbols

(Continued)

Table 2.1 (Continued)

Subject area	Climate change sub-theme	Ideas
Science	Animal life	• Pets, suitable pets • Care for pets • Visit to a pet shop • The work of a vet • Animals on a farm • The story of milk • Mammals • The value of animals to humans • The impact of human activities on animals (e.g. urban areas versus rural areas)
History	Story/chronology	• Folk tales about the earth
Geography	Local environment	• Walk of school grounds • Distinguish between built and natural environments • Finding places of beauty • Types of homes in the school community • Features in homes that accommodate the weather, e.g. sloping roof
Social, Personal and Health Education	Food	• The food pyramid • Natural versus processed foods • Where food comes from • Food hygiene and impact of lack of food hygiene • Making healthy choices • Sharing with people who don't have food, e.g. at lunch time • Food and waste • Food and packaging (composting and recycling)
Visual arts	Recycling	• Creations from recycled materials • Appreciation of 'junk art' by professionals • Upcycling containers for different uses
Music	Animals	• Taking a sound walk to listen for animal/bird sounds • Recreating animal/bird sounds using the body, household objects and instruments. • Adding sound effects to a poem about animals • Listen to pieces of music that represent animals, e.g. Carnival of the Animals (Saint-Saens).
Drama	Environmental protection	• Exploring the roles of different people in our community who protect the environment (e.g. waste management, architect, gardener, town planner, bee-keeper and farmer)
Physical Education	My locality	• Walking the school grounds • Walking in a place of natural beauty (field trip) • Orienteering to get to know and notice the school environment
Other		

Table 2.2 Possible subject areas to be included in thematic plan on climate change (older children (8-13 years) or children of an advanced developmental stage)

Subject area	Climate change sub-theme	Ideas
Language	Weather (or any sub-theme!)	• Vocabulary development • Presentation (weather forecast) • Listening to stories related to weather • Retelling stories related to weather • Reciting poems related to weather
Literacy	Land use (or any sub-theme!)	• Reading of newspaper or magazine or website information • Developing criticality • 'Fake news' • Comprehension skills • Report writing • Persuasive writing • Debates
Mathematics	Deforestation	• Link to area and perimeter • Reading large numbers • Reading graphs • Creating graphs
Science	Animal life	• Animals in the Arctic/Antarctic • Animals on safari • Animals that hibernate • Endangered species • Food chains
History	The Stone Age people	• Waste management • Land use • Food • Clothes • Beliefs
Geography	Climate	• Climate in different parts of the world • Evidence for climate change • Causes of climate change • Impact of climate change • Interventions to reduce climate change effects
Social, Personal and Health Education	Vegetarianism/veganism	• Media education: how it's portrayed • The food pyramid • Making informed choices
Visual arts	Natural products	• Creating colour from natural sources, e.g. berries/grasses (possible links to cave painting!)

(Continued)

Table 2.2 (Continued)

Subject area	Climate change sub-theme	Ideas
Music	Listening and responding	• Taking a sound walk in a place of natural beauty vs the school corridor • Recreating natural sounds using household objects • Adding sound effects to a poem about the earth • Listen to pieces of music that represent places of natural beauty, e.g. The Moldau (Smetana), The Hebrides Overture (Mendelssohn), Sunrise (Grieg)
Drama	Activism	• Interviews with women heroes from history. Hearing 'herstory' • Character representation of environmental activists
Physical Education	My locality	• Cross-country running • Orienteering • Walk/cycle in a forested area
Other		

This blank flowchart (Figure 2.3) allows teachers to consider the possibilities across the curriculum for teaching about climate change.

> This means you are now mentally prepared to present the theme of climate change to children and can guide them in a discussion about the theme. This does not mean you have to know EVERYTHING, but you can begin to prepare sources of information.

3 Present the children with a stimulus to introduce the theme of climate change and to increase their motivation. This can be done in many different ways:

- children's literature
- a poem
- a news item
- a field trip
- a film
- an interview
- a song

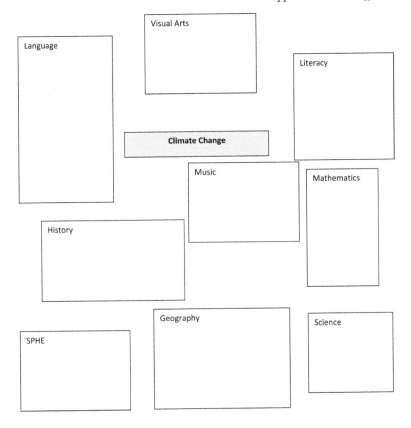

Figure 2.3 Blank flowchart for curriculum planning

Possible stimuli

Video clips	https://www.climaterealityproject.org/video (older children)
	https://cafod.org.uk/Education/Primary-teaching-resources/Climate-and-environment (older children, 8–13 years)
	https://climatekids.nasa.gov/ocean/ (older children, 8–13 years)
	Clips from any of the following animations … you'll need to watch them to select appropriate sections. It is not appropriate to watch the full film with children as they are likely to become passive:
	• Bee Movie • Happy Feet • The Nut Job 2 • Dolphin Tale • Legend of the Guardians
Websites	https://climatekids.nasa.gov/menu/teach/
	https://cafod.org.uk/Education/Primary-teaching-resources/Climate-and-environment

	https://www.ecowatch.com/5-ways-to-teach-children-about-climate-change-1882006127.html
Poetry	*The Barefoot Book of Earth Poems* (compiled by Judith Nichols)
	All the Wild Wonders, Poems of Our Earth edited by Wendy Cooling
Books	*The Barefoot Book of Earth Tales* by Dawn Casey and Anne Wilson
	The Lorax by Dr. Seuss
	The Tragic Tale of the Great Auk by Jan Thornhill
	The Magic School Bus and the Climate Change by Joanna Cole and Bruce Degan
	It's Your World by Chelsea Clinton
	One World by Michael Foreman
	The Last Wolf by Mini Grey
	First Light by Rebecca Stead
	The Last Wild by Piers Torday
	How to Bee by Bren MacDibble

4 After presenting the stimulus, bring the discussion around to the theme of climate change which may arise organically from the children or it may need to be scaffolded. With younger children (3-7 years), you could approach this by presenting the theme of looking after Planet Earth or caring for our environment, expanding on what the children know. One approach is to do a KWL (What do I **k**now? What do I **W**ant to find out? What have I **L**earned?) (see Table 2.3) to identify children's interests, knowledge and experiences related to the topic. This works best when written on a flipchart which can be displayed in the classroom for the length of time the topic is being explored. Such a chart can also serve as an assessment at the end of the process.

5 Plan appropriate teaching and learning activities based on what the children want to find out. The teacher's role will vary from being a catalyst inspiring learning – a teacher providing instruction and modelling, to a facilitator of learning. S/he will need to consistently observe and guide, check responses and gauge levels of enthusiasm. This needs to be planned so that curriculum objectives are actually attained and to ensure that children's knowledge, skills and attitudes are developed. Table 2.4 provides an outline of curricular areas. Climate change learning objectives can be generated for each area. This is an important planning document that highlights specific conceptual content to be taught thematically. It may seem repetitious, but remember, in the stages above (Tables 2.1–2.3 and Figure 2.3) teachers and children are pre-empting initial ideas. Once these stages have been completed, a comprehensive thematic work plan can be created. Rigorous planning facilitates effective thematic teaching and efficient allocation of time on a daily/weekly basis.

Table 2.3 Blank KWL chart

What do I KNOW? K	What do I WANT to find out? W	What have I LEARNED? L

Table 2.4 Curriculum planning grid for climate change

Subject area and sub-theme	Ideas	Curriculum objectives/outcomes Skill development
Language: weather	• Vocabulary development • Presentation (weather forecast) with a focus on tenses (past, present, future).	Oral Understanding: • Sentence structure and grammar • Vocabulary Oral Exploring and using: • Description, prediction and reflection
Literacy: weather	• Matching words to pictures • Reading/writing local weather reports • Reading/writing local weather reports for different times of the year • Reading/writing weather reports for other parts of the world • Developing comprehension skills: impact of weather on activities, clothes, food and food	Reading/Writing • Communicating: engagement • Understanding: conventions of print • Vocabulary • Phonics • Word recognition • Genre • Comprehension
Mathematics: weather	• Reading a pictogram • Creating a pictogram • Counting 'days of sun' 'days of rain' etc. • Sorting/classifying clothes • Develop a sense of chronology as weather changes across the seasons • Capacity: measuring rainfall (more or less than yesterday) • Creating patterns (algebra) using weather symbols	Data: • Represent, read and interpret simple tables and charts (pictograms) • Sort and classify objects Time: • Use the vocabulary of time to sequence events Capacity: • Develop an understanding of the concept of capacity through exploration and the use of appropriate vocabulary Algebra: • Identify, copy and extend patterns
Science: animal life	• Pets, suitable pets • Care for pets • Visit to a pet shop • The work of a vet • Animals on a farm • The story of milk	Plants and animals: • Observe, discuss and identify a variety of plants and animals in different habitats in the immediate environment • Recognise and identify the external parts of living things

(Continued)

Table 2.4 (Continued)

Subject area and sub-theme	Ideas	Curriculum objectives/outcomes Skill development
	• Mammals • The value of animals to humans • The impact of human activities on animals (e.g. urban areas versus rural areas)	**Caring for my locality:** • Appreciate that people share the environment with plant and animal life • Identify, discuss and implement simple strategies for improving and caring for the environment
History story/ chronology:	• Folk tales about the earth	**Stories:** • Listen to local people telling stories about their past • Discuss the chronology of events (beginning, middle, end) in a story • Express or record stories through art work, drama, music, mime and movement and using information and communication technologies
Geography: Weather and homes	• Types of weather • The seasons • Impact of weather on clothes and activities • Types of homes in the community • Homes in other countries • Features in homes that accommodate the weather, e.g. sloping roof	**Weather:** • Observe and discuss a variety of weather conditions using simple vocabulary • Record weather observations using a weather chart or diary • Become aware of some of the effects of different weather conditions on human, animal and plant life in the local environment • Discuss the suitability of different kinds of clothes for different weather conditions • Recognise that some weather patterns are associated with seasonal change and distinguish between summer and winter **Living in the local community:** • Acquire some awareness of different types of homes in the locality • Begin to appreciate the need for shelter for a family **People and places in other areas:** • Develop some awareness of people living in other areas • Acquire some awareness of different types of homes in places outside the locality

Table 2.4 (*Continued*)

Subject area and sub-theme	Ideas	Curriculum objectives/outcomes Skill development
Social, personal and health education: food	• The food pyramid • Natural versus processed foods • Where food comes from • Food hygiene and impact of lack of food hygiene • Making healthy choices • Food and waste • Food and packaging (composting and recycling)	Taking care of my body: • Appreciate the need, and understand how to care for his/her own body in order to keep it healthy and well • Recognise and practise basic hygiene skills • Become aware of the importance of food for growth and development • Explore food preferences and their role in a balanced diet • Discuss and explore some qualities and categories of food • Realise the importance of good hygiene when preparing food to eat Developing citizenship: • Appreciate the environment and realise that each individual has a community and individual responsibility for protecting and caring for the environment
Visual arts: recycling	• Creations from recycled materials • Appreciation of 'junk art' by professionals • Upcycling containers for different uses	Construction: • Explore and experiment with the properties and characteristics of materials in making structures • Look at and talk about his/her work and the work of others
Music: animals	• Taking a sound walk to listen for animal/bird sounds • Recreating animal/bird sounds using the body, household objects and instruments. • Adding sound effects to a poem about animals • Listen to pieces of music that represent animals, e.g. Carnival of the Animals (Saint-Saens).	Exploring sounds: • Listen to, identify and imitate familiar sounds in the immediate environment from varying sources • Use sound words and word phrases to describe and imitate selected sounds • Discover ways of making sounds using body percussion • Explore ways of making sounds using manufactured and home-made instruments Listening and responding to music: • Listen to a range of short pieces of music or excerpts

(*Continued*)

Table 2.4 (Continued)

Subject area and sub-theme	Ideas	Curriculum objectives/outcomes Skill development
Drama: environmental protection	• Exploring the roles of different people in our community who protect the environment (e.g. waste management, architect, gardener, town planner, bee-keeper and farmer)	Exploring and making drama: • Develop the ability to play in role as an integral part of the action Reflecting on drama: • Experience the relationship between story, theme and life experience
Physical education: My locality	• Walking the school grounds • Walking in a place of natural beauty (field trip) • Orienteering to get to know and notice the school environment	Walking: • Undertake short walks within or adjacent to the school grounds • Find an object in a confined area of the school site, given simple clues Orienteering: • Identify areas of the hall, playing-field or school site
Other		

6 Respectful group exploration and reflection is essential for children to make sense of material covered in class. Several methodologies allow children to communicate their thoughts and feelings about climate change, express their interests and show their new learning. This phase can enhance a child's sense of values and promotes a sense of community. Children need to be reminded that they bring different life experiences to their understanding of climate change. Bringing in parents or communicating with them can enhance a community-based exploration of climate change. Children should be encouraged to make connections between climate actions at home, in school, nationally and internationally.

Ideally, children can make decisions about the aspects of climate change they would like to explore. Children should document what they want to know about their chosen climate change sub-theme, where they will access the information, the roles of everyone in the group and how they will share the information. This is subject to change, but it facilitates the development of important cognitive, social and affective skills. By carefully managing groups, teachers ensure that the children stay on task, core learning objectives are achieved and maximum learning is taking place.

Methodologies that support discipline specific aspects of climate change are explored in more detail throughout the book. They include some of the following:

• Enquiring classroom methodologies (Chapter 3)
• Reflective discussions and activities (Chapter 4)
• Local investigations (Chapters 5 and 10)
• Use of story (Chapters 6, 7 and 13)

- Discussion activities based on the language of climate change (Chapters 8 and 9)
- Art based explorations (Chapters 11 and 12)
- Environmental trails and outdoor education (Chapters 10 and 20)
- Walking debate (Chapter 14)
- Poetry (Chapter 14)
- Timelines (Chapter 15)
- Ranking (Chapter 16)
- Games (Chapter 18)
- Role play and hot seating (Chapter 19)
- Cooperative learning (Chapter 20)

Over the course of the teaching of the theme (which could be a week, a fortnight, a month, a term), the teacher allocates some aspects of climate change education for whole class teaching while others will be explored through children's investigations.

7 Building and maintaining spirit and enthusiasm: successful thematic teaching 'can become a contagious agent that expands each student's imagination and eagerness to learn' (Loughman, 2005:117). It's important for children to feel that their work is valued and of interest to others, that their efforts at finding out information are successful and that they are contributing to the learning of all. Opportunities for children to express what they have learned will help to maintain their enthusiasm for climate change. They should be encouraged to present what they have learned in multiple ways, rather than simply writing a report or doing a class presentation. Suggestions include:

- Podcast
- Concept map
- Cartoon
- Song
- Poem
- Drama
- Freeze frame
- Photograph
- PowerPoint
- Poster
- Debate
- Infographic

8 The final stage of thematic teaching is pulling the theme together. The children will have amassed a lot of new knowledge over the course of the week/fortnight/month/term and should have the opportunity to share it with a wider audience. If not already done, this is a good time to make links between all the sub-themes of climate change that have been explored. Ideally, children can decide on how the material is presented and to whom the material will be presented (e.g. other classes, the principal and/or parents).

While not part of Loughman's approach, the inclusion of critical reflection at the end of climate change exploration is necessary. Children should identify 'take home messages,' they should consider their role as informed citizens and make a decision for personal action. If a child feels very strongly about climate change, s/he could be supported to share their views with a wider audience, such as writing a letter to a politician or submitting a podcast to a local radio station.

Conclusion

Climate change is a multi-dimensional issue that affects every person and living thing on planet Earth. It cannot be explored exclusively through one subject area if children are to understand the complexity of the topic or to learn how to act responsibly. Thematic teaching allows for the exploration of climate change in a multi-disciplinary fashion that builds on, and harnesses, the interests, motivations, knowledge and skills of children.

This chapter presents a pedagogical basis for thematic planning to enable practitioners to justify this approach in the classroom. It highlights the advantages, disadvantages and considerations for taking such an approach to teaching about climate change. The chapter sets out a structured, step-by-step approach to thematic teaching for climate change to support student teachers and beginning teachers who have little or no experience of such a teaching approach. Teachers need to be well informed about the nature of thematic teaching and the potential benefits of its adoption in the case of climate change education.

References

Alleman, J. and Brophy, J. (1991) *Is curriculum integration a boon or a threat to social studies? Research Series No. 24*, East Lansing: The Institute for Research on Teaching, Michigan State University.

Casey, D. and Wilson, A. (2013) *The barefoot book of earth tales*. Cambridge (MA): Barefoot Books.

Central Advisory Council for Education (1967) *The Plowden Report, children and their primary schools*. London: HMSO.

Chumdari, Anitah, Budiono, S. and Suryani, N. (2018) Implementation of thematic instructional model in elementary school, *International Journal of Educational Research Review*, 3(4), pp. 23–31.

Clinton, C. (2017) *It's your world*. New York: Puffin.

Cole, J. and Degan, B. (2010) *The magic school bus and the climate change*. New York: Scholastic Press.

Cooling, W. (Ed.) (2010) *All the wild wonder, poems of our earth*. London: Francis Lincoln Ltd.

Deci, E.L. and Ryan, R.M. (1985) *Intrinsic motivation and self-determination in human behavior*. New York: Plenum.

DeLuca, C, Ogden, H and Pero, E (2015) 'Reconceptualizing elementary pre-service teacher education: Examining an integrated-curriculum approach', *The New Educator*, 11(3), pp. 227–250.

Department of Education (1971) *Primary school curriculum*. Dublin: The Stationery Office.

Dillon, P. (2006) Creativity, integrativism and a pedagogy of connection, *International Journal of Thinking Skills and Creativity*, 1(2), pp. 69–83.

Dr. Seuss (1971) *The Lorax*. New York: Random House.

Esprívalo Harrell, P. (2010) Teaching an integrated science curriculum: linking teacher knowledge and teaching assignments, *Issues in Teacher Education*, 19(1), pp. 145–165.

Flynn, F. (nd) *Teaching about climate change in Irish primary schools*. Dublin: Trócaire. https://www.trocaire.org/sites/default/files/resources/edu/teaching_about_climate_change.pdf.

Fogarty, R. (1992) Ten ways to integrate curriculum, *The Educational Digest*, 57(6), pp. 53–57.

Foreman, M. (2011) *One world*. London: Anderson Press.

Gaughan, J. (2003) A dose of thematic teaching, *English Journal*, 92(5), pp. 18–21.

George, P.S. (1996) The integrated curriculum: A reality check, *Middle School Journal*, 28, pp. 12–19.

Golden, B. (2016) Exploring global citizenship education through integrated curricula, *Policy and Practice: A development education review*, 23, from https://www.developmenteducationreview.com/issue/issue-23/exploring-global-citizenship-education-through-integrated-curricula [last accessed 12 December 2019].

Grey, M. (2018) *The last wolf*. London: Jonathan Cape.

Ignatz, M. (2005) Curriculum integration: Preparing prospective teachers, *Journal of College Science Teaching*, 34(5), pp. 38–41.

Immordino-Yang, M.H. (2015) *Emotions, learning, and the brain: Exploring the educational implications of affective neuroscience (the Norton series on the social neuroscience of education)*. New York: WW Norton & Company.

John, Y.J. (2015) A "new" thematic, integrated curriculum for primary schools of Trinidad and Tobago: A paradigm shift, *International Journal of Higher Education*, 4(3), pp. 172–187. DOI: 10.5430/ijhe.v4n3p172.

Leung, W.L.A. (2006) Teaching integrated curriculum: Teachers' challenges, *Pacific Asian Education*, 18(1), pp. 88–102.

Lipson, M.Y., Valencia, S.W., Wixson, K.K. and Peters, C.W. (1993) Integration and thematic teaching: Integration to improve teaching and learning, *Language Arts*, 70, pp. 252–263.

Loughman, S.B. (2005) Thematic teaching in action, *Kappa Delta Pi Record*, 41(3), pp. 112–117.

MacDibble, B. (2018) *How to bee*. Fittleworth: Old Barn Books.

Nichols, J. (Ed.) (2016) *The barefoot book of earth poems*. Cambridge (MA): Barefoot Books.

Nurlaela, L., Samani, M., Asto, I.G.P. and Wibawa, S.C. (2018) The effect of thematic learning model, learning style, and reading ability on the students' learning outcomes, *IOP Conference Series: Materials Science and Engineering*, 296, pp. 1–8.

Reid, V. (2005) Interdisciplinary curriculum: Advantages and disadvantages of implementation, *Canadian Music Educator*, 46(3), pp. 36–40.

Roser, N.L. and Hoffman, J.V. (1992) Language charts: A record of story time talk, *Language Arts*, 69(1), pp. 44–52.

Stead, R. (2008) *First light*. New York: Random House.

Thornhill, J. (2016) *The tragic tale of the great auk*. Toronto: Groundwood Books.

Torday, P. (2015) *The last wild*. London: Quercus Editions.

Wolfinger, D.M. and Stockard, J.W. (1997) *Elementary methods: An integrated curriculum*. New York: Longman.

3 The world's religious traditions and global climate disruption

Patricia Kieran

Introduction

With the current disruption of climate and urgent need for action (Robinson, 2018), it is timely to explore what the teachings and traditions of some of the great religions of the world might offer to educators. This chapter suggests that, as we face the greatest challenge of this age, we have much to learn from the spiritual teachings and ethical wisdom of the religions of the world that may guide, support and sustain our response to climate change. In this Anthropocene age, we realise that human actions are the dominant cause of climate change (Gold, 2018). Since our beliefs impact our actions, they have enormous potential to foster hope and to motivate us to act decisively to address climate disruption. This chapter proposes that selected sacred teachings from some of the world's religions have enormous potential to reorient educators in innovative ways as we navigate current environmental challenges. The chapter aims to:

- Overview three classroom methodologies suitable for exploring climate change with students (ages 8–18)
- Summarise key sacred teachings relevant to climate change from selected religious traditions
- Explore ways of seeing, thinking and acting in response to climate change inspired by world religions

Religious traditions as powerful resources to guide human responses to global climate disruption

Many great religions were founded hundreds and thousands of years before the current awareness of global warming, yet their sense of sacred reverence for life in the universe is striking. In Western Europe, we are facing this global challenge at a time when there is much disillusionment with traditional 'organised' religions and their teachings. For some, religion might seem outdated, irrelevant or unhelpful (Dawkins, 2019; Hitchens, 2007) with little to offer educators in the face of global climate change. However, for thousands of years, many of the world's great living religious traditions have reminded us that humans are not the measure of all (Weeks, 2017) and that planet Earth is not to be exploited simply to gratify immediate human needs. Many religions give humans a sense of place in the universe, often connecting the natural world with a supernatural or divine origin and destiny, inviting people to live ethically and justly, expressing a deep sense of mystery, awe, wonder and delight in animate and inanimate life as illustrated in

Figure 3.1 Young Buddhist monks learning using a mobile phone
https://pixabay.com/photos/children-learning-video-game-boys-1346149/

Figure 3.1. While each tradition is complex and vastly different, many sacred songs and stories celebrate the heavens and the stars, caution humans to act lovingly and responsibly, to take care of the earth and to live in harmony with animal and plant life. Indeed, the current environmental crisis represents a spiritual crisis as humans lose that sense of sacred connection with the universe.

Religions

Some estimate that there are more than 4,000 religious traditions in the world and that over 85% of the world's population belong to some form of religious tradition (Hackett and McClendon, 2017). Interestingly, while religion may be declining in Europe and North America, other areas in the world are becoming more and not less religious (Sherwood, 2018). Organisations such as the Alliance of Religions and Conservation (ARC), GreenFaith and Yale Forum on Religion and Ecology provide resources on religious traditions that cultivate a deep sense of devotion and reverence for the cosmos. Many texts and resources on spirituality and ecology (Mc-Donagh, 1986, 1999; Palmer and Finlay, 2003) bring together a range of teachings and materials that can be useful for exploring this topic with students (Sponsel, 2012). As previously stated there is a vast diversity within and among religions, yet many of their vibrant teachings and sacred rituals provide a sense of the interconnectedness of all life (Bahá'í Spiritual Assembly, 2010; McFague, 2008). It is worthwhile to combine scholarly accounts of religions with the testimonies of practitioners and believers within a tradition. It is also important to remember that religion and beliefs are complex and contested categories. There can be an incredible diversity of teachings and practices within each tradition. People from similar backgrounds may live their identities in vastly different ways (e.g. conservative, liberal, radical, cultural, lapsed etc.), and a person's religious or belief identity can change during the course of their life. It is noteworthy that within families, individual members might have very different religious or belief identities. It is always best to avoid generalisations, or any type of (positive as well as negative) stereotyping, exoticising (romanticised presentations of traditions as 'exotic' or 'foreign') or homogenising (we all believe the same thing) of religions and beliefs. It is important to stress that the religions of the world and their spiritual practices and ethical teachings should not be viewed simply as objective banks of information or educational resources. To their practitioners, these religions are sacred, life-transforming traditions, containing ultimate meaning and they provide foundation and orientation in life. While this chapter explores the teachings of some of the world's religions on the environment, it is also important to note that many ancient and modern teachings about the environment come from non-religious traditions like Humanism, Atheism and new-age spiritualties.

Classroom methodologies

The Enquiring Classroom (TEC) was a two-year (2017–2019) international Erasmus + project, with partners in Ireland, Sweden and Greece, that sought to develop an innovative model of enquiry-based learning to enable teachers to support students (ages 8–18) as they engaged in difficult discussions around a range of topics including religions and beliefs and ethics. The project worked closely with educators, sharing ideas, knowledge and practices in peer groups, in order to develop skill-sets that could help to foster educational environments that allow for the careful and sensitive exploration of ideas, questions and values that matter to teachers and students. TEC suggests that students need to be given opportunities to discuss and critically examine complex issues, e.g. global warming, in safe educational contexts with trusted facilitators to foster critical thinking skills, refine moral perception and imagination and develop the ability to engage with conflict and disagreement.

A *TEC Handbook* for teachers is available online (O'Donnell et al., 2019). This contains a range of the project's innovative pedagogies and resources (on religions and beliefs, philosophy for children and living values) designed to support educators and students in enquiring and learning together. The Handbook is divided into key areas (the ethical, the political, the aesthetic, the historical and the sacred) and presents a broad range of arts-based, practical, interdisciplinary and experimental methodologies. Educators are invited to adapt these non-prescriptive methodologies to suit learners' specific needs and contexts. The following three TEC methodologies are inspired by its '*Rough Guide to the Sacred*' section of the handbook. (See resources section for more information about the handbook and the project).

Enquiring classroom methodology 1: Belief Circles Game

Human beliefs are complex and contested. Belief is generally the acceptance that something exists, is true, good or reasonable (Schwitzgebel, 2010). Religious beliefs usually concern ultimate reality and often (but not always) relate to the supernatural existence of a deity (or deities) or teachings of a spiritual leader and tradition. When teaching about global warming and climate change, it is important to invite students to think and talk about their own beliefs while also learning from and about beliefs that are sacred to world religions. Beliefs can have an enormous impact on how humans view the world and act as 'every action that we take is grounded in an elaborate web of beliefs and goals' (Tullett et al., 2013).

Beliefs are most important when it comes to responding to climate change. The Belief Circles game draws on students' lived experience of religious or secular world views and their sacred texts and traditions so that their diverse religious or philosophical beliefs are spontaneously woven into their responses. Environmental topics for discussion can be generated collaboratively with students. The aims of Belief Circles Game are set out in Figure 3.2 while sample topics are indicated in Table 3.1.

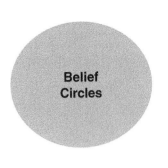

- Provide a safe structured space for students to think & talk about personal beliefs

- Facilitate student's respectful engagement with a variety of belief perspectives

- Negotiate points of difference and commonality

- Invite students to listen attentively to others without comment

- Facilitate student's engagement with the teachings of selected world religions.

Figure 3.2 Aim of Belief Circles Game

This methodology gives a space and a place for students (in small groups of four–six) to talk about their personal beliefs relating to environmental issues while listening to other belief perspectives. Students can make their own Belief Circle with paper (reusable and recyclable) plates segmented into eight sections, each containing a handwritten topic for discussion. Alternatively, teachers can adapt an online randomiser wheel (https://wheelde-cide.com/) by filling in topics for discussion used in conjunction with an online stop watch.

Table 3.1 Belief Circles Game: some suggested topics for educators

Potential Belief Circle topics		
Trees	Global warming	Holy places
Sunshine	Rain	Bio fuels
Water	Earth	The sea
Veganism	The stars	Fears
How the earth was made	Cars	Environmental action
Prayers	Buying things	Creation
Climate change denial	Happiness	Vegetarianism
Religion	Bees	Upcycling
Love	Conservation	God/gods
Animals	Travel	Species extinction
Sacred stories	Eco warriors	Children
Pollution	Recycling	Climate justice
Adults	Carbon footprint	Hopes
Biodiversity	Fossil fuels	Nature
Beliefs	Money	Meat

Rules of the Belief Circles Game

- Everybody is invited to speak but nobody is forced to speak
- Silence is a valuable form of participation and communication
- Students speak about their own views … 'I think' or 'I believe' or 'I feel' or 'For me …'
- Students talk (clockwise rotation) for an equal amount of time (e.g. initially 30 seconds, extending to 1–2 minutes in subsequent rounds, using a timer or speaking object if desired)
- Everybody agrees to *listen actively* and not to interrupt
- Criticising or belittling another person's beliefs (e.g. 'you're wrong' … 'that's ridiculous'…) is not acceptable
- Attempts to convert fellow group members to different religious persuasions are inappropriate
- Confidentiality must be respected at all times
- Everybody has a first go at speaking for 30 seconds
- Go around the circle a second time so students can hear each other (extending time with each spin of the wheel) on the existing topic
- Alternatively spin the wheel so the dial lands on a new topic. Teacher does not join any group and ensures students actively listen to each other

Method

1 Group(s) sit in a circle
2 Agree the rules of the game
3 Start the discussion by spinning the dial on the belief wheel until it randomly lands on a topic for discussion

In their groups, before the game ends, students identify:

- Something they liked about somebody else's belief
- Something they heard that made them think differently about their own belief
- Some action they might take to limit global warming

Additional questions

- What really matters to you and does this matter to everyone else?
- Did any beliefs surprise you?
- What does it feel like to agree/disagree with somebody else?

Enquiring classroom methodology 2: Interbelief environmental dialogue café

This methodology gives students an opportunity to think about their own beliefs and ideas on environmental topics while engaging in dialogue with members of diverse religious traditions as illustrated in Figure 3.3. It should take place in a large space (e.g. hall) with four tables, each designated to a different religion and covered in paper tablecloths. The number of chairs around each table (ideally five or six) varies depending on the number of student participants. Coloured markers are left on each table so students can draw, doodle and write questions or comments on the paper tablecloths. Four members of different religious traditions, ideally from the local community, familiar with environmental

Aim

- Excite curiosity and interest in how religious believers understand & respond to climate change

- Listen, ask questions, and engage in interbelief dialogue

- Understand what different religious traditions teach about the environment.

Figure 3.3 Interbelief dialogue café

issues and interbelief dialogue and briefed by the teacher, are invited to 'host' the students at the table designated to explore their faith's teaching on the environment. (This activity can be adapted to include additional tables hosted by members of diverse philosophical convictions and beliefs, e.g. atheism, agnosticism and humanism.) Faith members put sacred artefacts from their tradition on the table for students to explore. Students spend an identical amount of time in dialogue with the faith member at each table and after 10 or 15 minutes, they rotate in a clockwise direction while the hosts remain in situ. Students are encouraged to ask questions about each faith's teachings on the environment (e.g. earth, life forms, humans and global warming). A bank of laminated cards containing identical questions is provided at each table as a stimulus for discussion (downloadable). In the course of an hour, students get to visit all four tables and dialogue with four members of different faiths.

Resources: Four tables with paper tablecloths, markers, artefacts, prompt questions and talking object (if desired).

Method

Divide students in groups of five–six and seat them around the tables. Agree ground rules (e.g. nobody forced to talk, respectful engagement/one person speaks at a time/we can disagree without being disagreeable, etc.). Explain signal, notifying all students of the need to move tables in clockwise direction after 10–15 minutes.

1 Members of the different faith traditions stand together in front of the students (who are seated at tables), welcome them and explain how the interbelief environmental dialogue café works
2 Optional choral reading of interbelief text by faith members to show solidarity between their different traditions (downloadable on padlet)
3 Invite students to ask questions – no such thing as a silly question
4 Faith members return to the table they are hosting and welcome everyone
5 Looking at the objects on the table, students guess what tradition the faith member is from
6 Invite spontaneous questions relating to the faith tradition and the environment – give students thinking time and invite them to write down any questions
7 Optional use of talking object. Faith members respond to participants' questions but also expand them to include broader questions 'Does anybody else here believe anything similar? Different?'

8   When time is up, educator concludes the event by asking the students: 'Could you tell us one thing you learned?'; 'One interesting question?'; 'One thing that surprised you?'; 'One way you might act differently?'; 'One thing you'd like to know more about?', etc.

Belief Circles and interbelief dialogue activities can be enriched by students' simultaneous exploration of key teachings and traditions from selected world religions. At the outset it may be helpful to present a very brief survey of key teachings from selected traditions, so that students' exploration of potential responses to climate change might be informed and guided through dialogue with them (Kieran, 2019).

Snapshot of teachings from three selected world religions

Hinduism

The Hindu religion is sometimes described as the oldest living religion in the world, and it stretches back more than 4,000 years. Brahman (Supreme Reality), is not separate from the elements of the cosmos and the earth. The Upanishads (ancient sacred text) teach about the five elements of space, air, fire, water and earth: *'From Brahman arises space, from space arises air, from air arises fire, from fire arises water, and from water arises earth'* (Gandhi, 2018). Everything comes from Brahman, and humans should not exploit the earth. All life forms including insects, plants, animals and geographical features mediate the spiritual presence of Brahman. Among the many Hindu avatars or manifestations of divinity on earth, we find sacred animals closely connected to the gods as illustrated in Figure 3.4 (e.g. cows, tigers and cobras). Hindu gods are represented in human and animal form (e.g. Ganesh, the elephant god and Hanuman, the monkey god). Gandhi is perhaps the best-known modern advocate of the Hindu principle of Ahimsa (non-violence) or not harming any living thing (common to Hinduism, Buddhism and Jainism). Since the spirit of god is present in all life forms, to destroy or exploit even the smallest insect is to disrespect the divine. For this reason, vegetarianism is common among many (but not all) devout Hindus who would literally not want to harm a fly!

Jainism

The ancient Jain religion is almost 3,000 years old, and has such environmental consciousness and reverence for life that devout followers often deliberately try to limit their needs and movements as much as possible so as not to disrupt nature. Jainism teaches us that personal care and care for nature are indivisible. Its principles have been summarised as: 'no waste, no overuse, no abuse, no polluting. Jainism calls on us to stop destroying our environment, to preserve its resources and to ensure that fruits of the earth are shared equally. If there are more resources available for all, then the poor will also get a fair share thereof' (Chandaria, 2008). Some practicing Jains wear white mouth guards called *Mahapatti* so that they do not ingest and injure micro-organisms.

Buddhism

The Buddhist tradition is based on the teachings of Siddharta Gautama, the Buddha who lived around 500 BCE. The Buddha's four noble truths taught that a life lived through craving for material things (what we might call rampant consumerism and individualism

Figure 3.4 Sacred cow in Hinduism

https://pixabay.com/photos/cow-holy-sacred-india-hinduism-2610663/

today) based on envy, greed and desire, inevitably leads to suffering (dukkha). Humans tend to always desire more. Buddha taught non-attachment to material things. His teaching involved living simply as well as the spiritual practice of meditation. The Buddha taught the eightfold path as the way to be free from suffering. Buddha taught 'Right Livelihood' or respect for all life and 'Right Action' or working for the good of others as well as compassion for all living things. Activities like snail meditation (https://www.youtube.com/watch?v=L0D6Le3Bf3Q) might foster a sense that humans are not the measure of all things.

Enquiring classroom methodology 3: Origami moment

This informal methodology encourages teachers to pause momentarily in the middle of an exercise and invite students to play an origami game in paired or small group settings, to foster imaginative and critical thinking as illustrated in Figure 3.5. A downloadable blank version of the origami template is provided by TEC. This methodology can be adapted to cover a range of interdisciplinary topics.

Origami moments scaffold higher order thinking and paired dialogue. Students can contribute their own questions related to climate issues. They may enjoy creating and making the origami pieces and asking each other questions that can range from the silly to the philosophical, to the religious and historical. Not all participants will be familiar with how to make the origami piece or play the origami game. Teachers may need to give additional time for this.

Origami
Moment

- Create opportunities for students to engage in playful, paired dialogue on environmental topics
- Respond to the spontaneous opportunities for imaginative thinking about their potential to act positively to combat climate change.

Figure 3.5 Origami moments

Method

At the beginning of a unit of learning provide each pair of participants with the origami template and invite them to make the origami piece (TEC Origami). As students engage in learning, the teacher decides when it would be appropriate to punctuate the learning with paired/small group dialogue scaffolded by the origami pieces. The students are invited at intervals to open their origami figures and play the game and read the question or quotation. Suggested questions are given below:

- What do you think of the statement that 'Every leaf is precious?'
- What is your favourite sacred story or teaching about the earth?
- Why might some people think 'cute' animals like pets should be protected and not care what happens to other species?
- If you could be an insect, what insect might you chose and why?
- Look around you. Can you see any upcycled or recyclable materials?
- Some people say 'I've no control over my carbon footprint.' Are you OK with this?
- 'Young people are the protectors of the earth.' Agree/Disagree?
- Do you think humans are superior to other species?
- What would you say to someone who said 'I have a right to use earth's resources as I wish?'
- The more you buy the more you want to buy. True/False?

Snapshot of teachings from selected monotheistic religions

Judaism

In the Jewish tradition's ancient account of creation in the Torah (sacred scriptures), 'eretz' or earth brings forth life. Earth is not a passive object to be used and abused by humans. God created humans by taking the dust of the earth and breathing life or spirit into it. Without God's breath (Hebrew ruaḥ חור) there is no human life. The created world is made in the image of the Creator. The ancient scriptures teach that every seven years (Hebrew shəvi'it תיעיבש) should be a Sabbatical year (Leviticus 25:1–7; Deuteronomy 15:1–11), a period of rest for the land and release of debts, where farmers do not plough or work it (British Library). The Jewish philosopher Maimonides (1135–1204) said the Sabbatical year was there to make the earth stronger and more fertile by letting it lie fallow so there was no planting, pruning or harvesting. Further, whatever grew during the sabbatical year must be shared with everyone as the earth's produce belongs to everyone. Humans do not own the land and must respect its rhythms and its need to rest and recuperate.

Christianity

The same creation accounts connect the three monotheistic prophetic faiths (Judaism, Christianity and Islam), and recount that after God created the earth and the heavens, the seas and the land, the animals and the insects, God saw that they were good (Gn. 1:31). Humans are asked by God to be stewards of creation, to take care of it. The gospel stories show Jesus' deep connection with nature. He teaches through stories of plants, seeds, harvest, trees, animals (Mt. 13:31), and birds and 'not one of them is forgotten before God' (Lk. 12:6). Pope Francis reminds us that human life is grounded in three intertwined relationships, 'with God, with our neighbour and with the earth' (Pope Francis, 2015, p. 39). In medieval times Saint Francis of Assisi (1181–1226) introduced animals into the crib, telling the story of the birth of Jesus as an acknowledgement that Jesus came not just for humans but for the salvation of all creation (Hobgood-Oster, 2008). *The Amazon Synod* (2019) called for socially just sustainable development, and recognised the gravity of sins against the environment and sins against future generations as sins against God (*Vatican News*).

Islam

Allah created the world and the cosmos, and everything in the universe points in the direction of God. Humans should not destroy the universe because to do so is to destroy the signs of Allah's presence across all species and life forms. Allah's process of creation is ongoing and continues with the birth of each new child, the planting of each new tree, the life of each species on earth as illustrated in Figure 3.6. The Holy Koran (57:4) tells us, 'He it is Who created the heavens and the earth in six days, then established Himself on

Figure 3.6 Muslim girl enjoying nature
https://pixabay.com/photos/hijaber-gorgeous-doll-girl-1907180/

the Throne. He knows what enters within the heart of the earth, and what comes forth out of it, what comes down from heaven, and what mounts up to it. And He is with you wherever you may be. And Allah sees well all that you do.' Islam forbids cruelty to animals and humans should show love and respect for other species because all are made by Allah and all belong to Allah. 'There is not an animal that lives on the earth, nor a being that flies on its wings, but they form communities like you. Nothing have we omitted from the Book, and they all shall be gathered to their Lord in the end' (Koran 6:38).

Extension activities

Many of the world's religions teach that humans are given a sacred ethical task of caring for, protecting and guarding the earth with its myriad life forms and species. For billions of believers in their distinctive traditions, religious understanding, sensibility and practice, connects them with the divine so that they perceive the beauty and presence of the sacred in nature and the world around them (Kennedy, 2010). Through the eyes of faith ordinary everyday realities such as trees, cobwebs and insects can be seen with a new reverence and openness as illustrated in Figure 3.7.

Leaf activities

Explore countless things such as leaves (or insects) with a new reverence and openness. Teachers invite students to explore a leaf through the senses. Pay attention to it. Spend time simply observing. Make simple drawings. Imaginatively see the world from the leaf's perspective. Write the autobiography of the leaf including its hopes, dreams and fears. Many websites (see bibliography) provide additional nature imagery and sounds to support this kind of exploration. Educators might introduce quotes from a variety of sources for discussion e.g. No leaf is like another (Nietzsche). 'To the caterpillar the leaf is the universe' (Feuerbach).

Natural World

Explore sacred stories about Trees. For instance the Tree of Knowledge of Good and Evil in Judaism & Christianity; the Lote Tree (Sidratul Muntaha) in Islam; the Baobab Tree in Madagascan and South African spiritual tradition (Sponsel) or the Bodhi tree in Buddhism & others. After reading a short sacred text, go on a nature walk and invite students to look intensively and attentively at the natural world (e.g. clouds), to appreciate the way the writers of the sacred scriptures fall in love with the universe when they poetically talk of the sky, the stars, the sea, land and the universe (Psalm 8).

Figure 3.7 Extension activities

The Chelsea gold winner Mary Reynolds talks of the needs and wishes of the lands as well as 'listening to the land' (Reynolds 2016). Students might listen to sacred stories and poems about the land. Teachers might invite children to gaze at nature's shapes and colours, notice its sounds, breathe in its smells, sense its touch. This can be done on a nature walk, in the school garden, stretched out or barefoot on grass, lying down looking at the clouds breeze by, or just listening to the rain. The weeds and insects in the school grounds, as they yearn for life, can become a source of wisdom and deep understanding for students. Reynolds speaks of the need to let the land recover and go wild to heal itself.

Figure 3.8 The land: general pointers for exploring this theme with students

Students might explore the natural world (Reynolds, 2016) and its role in religious rituals that express the need for ethical action and reverence for the preciousness of life as illustrated in Figure 3.8. Meditation in the Jain, Buddhist, Christian and many other traditions with different postures (e.g. sitting down, standing and walking) through remaining still, breathing gently and clearing the mind, is part of many spiritual rituals. While mindfulness as a practice is found in many non-religious disciplines (e.g. psychology, education and business), it is important to remember that, in origin, mindfulness and meditation are ancient religious practices (Irish Bishops' Conference, 2019). Some skilled educators, have used them (indoors and outdoors), to connect students with movement, breathing, inspired by and in nature. In the classroom, students might be invited to engage in some of the imaginative spiritual practices like being observant of and attentive to nature.

Conclusion

The world's religions have the potential to support educators as we address the urgent challenge of global climate change. Religious wisdom often reminds us that we are called upon to take care of the earth, to be reverent before its incredible biodiversity, and not to exploit and disrespect our planet. In the face of this environmental crisis, religious traditions have the potential to recalibrate how we see ourselves and the world as well as mobilise us to see, think, judge and act differently. Religions pose deep questions and ask us 'have your attitudes, beliefs and actions helped or harmed this planet? What are you going to do to make the world a better place for all species?' As educators we need to provide students with a space where they can see and think differently about themselves and the world, and move beyond a functionalist, consumerist culture. Educators can invite students to slow down, stop and notice the beauty and preciousness of life. Many religious traditions involve going beyond self (self-transcendence) into the area of mystery, awe, wonder, silence, stillness, beauty and a sense of oneness with all creatures and the universe. They are also rooted in the search for meaning and address complex, ethical, ultimate questions about how we view the divine, humans, other species and the universe. Many religions involve an urgent call to climate justice and ethical action to heal the earth in the face of climate change. Our learning contexts, whether urban or rural, provide unique opportunities to make a place and space for students to engage with inspiring religious traditions which invite us to live justly and compassionately, pay attention to nature and to cherish the preciousness of our universe.

Resources

The Enquiring Classroom project seeks to develop strategies to support teachers and students in engaging in difficult ethical conversations about identity, religions and beliefs, democratic values, diversity, belonging and violence, in order to establish a firm foundation for inclusive and tolerant schools and classrooms.

The Enquiring Classroom project seeks to develop an innovative model of enquiry-based learning to enable teachers to use the tools of philosophical enquiry to engage in difficult ethical discussions and to support students' capabilities in this regard. The project also seeks to promote peer knowledge transfer and exchange of pedagogical content, strategies and practice to support students' lived encounters with philosophical and religious thought; to develop a skill-set for teachers that supports careful and sensitive facilitation of complex issues such as migration, climate change and an unequal distribution of resources. The Enquiring Classroom project can be accessed using the following link: http://nebula. wsimg.com/b34a2e21e05d30983c68342cf6de3918?AccessKeyId=C0264DFDC5E0FB-B4FF37&disposition=0&alloworigin=1.

Websites

- Amazon Synod:http://www.synod.va/content/sinodoamazonico/en/documents/final-document-of-the-amazon-synod.html.
- Birdsong meditation: https://www.youtube.com/watch?v=qJldwNFpar0.
- British library discovering sacred texts: https://www.bl.uk/sacred-texts.
- Bugs with Therevada Buddhist chanting: https://www.youtube.com/watch?v=K1UnpVVGqS4.
- Chandaria, Chairman of the Institute of Jainology: https://www.jainology.org/address-by-nemu-chandaria/.
- Chester Beatty Resource Ways of Seeing Part 11: https://chesterbeatty.ie/assets/uploads/2018/11/Ways-of-Seeing-II.pdf.
- Children's books: https://kiddingaroundyoga.com/blog/teaching-ahimsa/.
- Green Faith: https://greenfaith.org/index.html.
- Forum on Religion and Ecology at Yale: http://fore.yale.edu/climate-change/statements-from-world-religions/.
- Meadow with flowers and rabbits: https://www.youtube.com/watch?v=razjcetumEM.
- Meditation on snails: https://www.youtube.com/watch?v=L0D6Le3Bf3Q.
- Native American 10 commandments: https://www.nativevillage.org/Inspiration-/ten_native_american_commandments.html.
- Pew Research Centre: https://www.pewresearch.org/fact-tank/2017/04/05/christians-remain-worlds-largest-religious-group-but-they-are-declining-in-europe/.
- Rain meditation: https://www.youtube.com/watch?v=yoTa0lhYO9Q.
- Rain, thunder and lightening sounds: https://www.youtube.com/watch?v=Fm0sToWtatw.
- Sea and moon: https://www.youtube.com/watch?v=q6UB8sKMZrA.
- TEC origami: http://www.enquiring-project.eu/origami-moment-templates.html.
- Vatican News: https://www.vaticannews.va/en/vatican-city/news/2019-10/amazon-synod-day-2-the-church-confesses-ecological-sins.html.
- Waterfall and river sounds and image: https://www.youtube.com/watch?v=lE6RYpe9IT0.

References

Bahá'í Spiritual Assembly (2010) *Spirit of Faith: The Oneness of God*. Illinois: B ahá'í Publishing.

Dawkins, R. (2019) *Outgrowing God: A Beginner's Guide*. New York: Random House.

Gandhi, S. (2018) *Hinduism and Brotherhood*. Chennai: Notion Press.

Gold, L. (2018) *Climate Generation: Awakening to Our Children's Future*. Dublin: Veritas.

Hackett, C. and McClendon, D. (2017) *Christians Remain World's Largest Religious Group but They are Declining in Europe*. Washington: Pew Research Centre.

Hitchens, C. (2007) *God is Not Great: How Religion Poisons Everything*. London: Atlantic Books.

Hobgood-Oster, L. (2008) *Holy Dogs and Asses: Animals in the Christian Tradition*. Illinois: University of Illinois.

Irish Bishops' Conference (2019) *A Reflection on Mindfulness: Rediscovering the Christian Tradition of Meditation and Contemplation*. Dublin: Veritas.

Kennedy, S. (2010) *I Can Feel My Toes Breathe: Bringing Meditation and Stillness to Young People*. Dublin: Veritas.

Kieran, P. ed., (2019) *Interbelief Dialogue in Contemporary Ireland*. Dublin: Veritas.

Mc-Donagh, S. (1986) *To Care for the Earth*. London: Chapman.

Mc-Donagh, S. (1999) *Greening the Christian Millennium*. Dublin: Dominican Publications.

McFague, S. (2008) *A New Climate for Theology: God, the World and Global Warming*. Fortress Press.

O'Donnell, A., Kieran, P., Cherouvis, S., Bergdahl, L. and Langmann, E. (2019) *The Enquiring Classroom: Values, Identity, Exploratiion*. Erasmus + http://nebula.wsimg.com/b34a2e21e05d30983c68342cf6de3918?AccessKeyId=C0264DFDC5E0FBB4FF37&disposition=0&alloworigin=1.

Palmer, M. and Finlay, V. (2003) *Faith in Conservation*. Washington: World Bank.

Pope Francis. (2015) *Laudato Si: On Care for Our Common Home*. Dublin: Veritas.

Reynolds, M. (2016) *The Garden Awakening: Designs To Nurture Our Land and Ourselves*. Cambridge: Green Books.

Robinson, M. (2018) *Climate Justice*. London: Bloomsbury.

Schwitzgebel E. (2010) 'Belief.' In Zalta E.N. ed., *The Stanford Encyclopedia of Philosophy*. Stanford: Stanford University.

Sherwood, H. (2018) 'Religion: Why faith is becoming more and more popular.' The Guardian. August 27, 2018.

Sponsel, L.E. (2012) *Spiritual Ecology: A Quiet Revolution*. Santa Barbara, CA: Praeger.

Tullett A.M., Prentice M.S., Teper R., Nash K.A., Inzlicht M. and Mcgregor I. (2013) 'Neural and motivational mechanics of meaning and threat.' In Markman K.D., Proulx T. and Lindberg M.J. eds., *The Psychology of Meaning*. Washington, DC: American Psychological Association, 401–419.

Weeks, M. (2017) *Religion in Minutes: The World's Great Faiths Explained in an Instant*. New York: Quercus.

4 A reflective approach to climate change education

Kathleen Horgan

Introduction

Teaching is a complex, sometimes puzzling and often dilemma-ridden endeavour. This is especially true when engaging as a teacher with the interrelated, multifaceted dimensions of climate change education. Developing the disposition and skills of critical reflective practice can assist teachers of climate change education to unpack teaching experiences, to explore different perspectives and to develop greater insight into their practice. This chapter will demonstrate how the skills of reflective inquiry can be adopted by teachers as a pedagogy, to assist children to engage critically with climate change issues.

Reflective teaching

Reflecting involves interrogating formative teaching 'moments' through the lens of personal experience, informed by educational theory. A reflective approach to teaching helps teachers to become flexible, self-analytical and responsive to the complex dynamics of classroom interaction, especially in the context of engaging with contested and controversial issues such as climate change education. Becoming a reflective teacher involves a commitment to growth and professional development, and to being aware of a range of possible choices and responses to every classroom situation (Bonfield and Horgan, 2016). Reflection can help teachers of climate change education to become aware of any limiting assumptions that they may hold about themselves, learners, learning and teaching, thereby enabling them to act in a more intentional manner while taking responsibility for pedagogical actions and their effects.

An explicit goal of reflective practice is to create deeper understanding and insight, forming the basis for not only considering alternatives, but also for taking action to continually improve practice throughout one's teaching career (Horgan and Gardiner-Hyland, 2019). Building the habit of reflective practice allows teachers to remain fluid in the dynamic environment of the classroom. Over the past three decades in particular, it has become clear that promoting and encouraging a reflective approach to teaching and learning is an important starting point for pedagogical development particularly when exploring complex and contested issues (Brookfield, 2017). Hence, the ongoing reflective process of understanding behaviours, clarifying values and interrogating actions is a critically important dimension of the practice of climate change education:

> Understanding values is an essential part of understanding an individual's own worldview and that of other peoples. Understanding your own values, the values of the society you live in, and the values of others around the world is a central part of

educating for a sustainable future. Each nation, cultural group, and individual must learn the skills of recognizing their own values and assessing these values in the context of sustainability.

(UNESCO, 2005:3)

Critical reflection and climate change education

Critical reflection locates our analysis of professional thought and action within the wider historical, social, environmental and cultural contexts (Bonfield and Horgan, 2016). Using a critically reflective approach, we strive to uncover the spectrum of intended and unintended influences on and consequences of our actions. This necessarily raises questions about the ethical and moral aspects of our work. By taking this broader context into consideration, we come to see ourselves as agents of change, capable of understanding what is, but also of working to create what should be. Given the myriad complexities, ambiguities and dilemmas that characterise our relationship with the natural world, teachers of climate change education in particular can benefit from critical inquiry and thoughtful reflection, both hallmarks of critical reflective practice. Larrivee and Cooper (2006) state that the characteristics of critical reflection include:

> Questioning of underlying assumptions, biases, and values one brings to bear on their teaching.
> Conscious consideration of the ethical implications and consequences of practices on learners and their learning.
> Examination of how instructional and other classroom practices contribute to social equity and to the establishment of a just society.
> Extended awareness beyond immediate instructional circumstances to include caring about democratic foundations and encouraging socially responsible actions.

(Larrivee and Cooper, 2006:12)

Figure 4.1 outlines the stages involved in critical reflective practice. These stages involve:

- Interrogating personal biography, beliefs, values & assumptions
- Examining current practice to determine whether particular actions, reactions or interactions are achieving what is desired
- Struggling to let go of familiar patterns and ways of viewing the world
- Transformation, the final stage of the cycle, which involves embracing new ways of thinking, new perspectives and pedagogical practices

The paragraphs which follow will explore key aspects of this model as they relate to teachers of climate change education. The pedagogical opportunities presented by the model will also be explored to assist teachers in their practice of engaging in climate change education. Adopting such reflective strategies may help teachers of climate change education to avoid stagnating in what Schon (1987) referred to as the 'swampy lowlands' of 'unexamined judgements, interpretations, assumptions and expectations' (Larrivee, 2000:294).

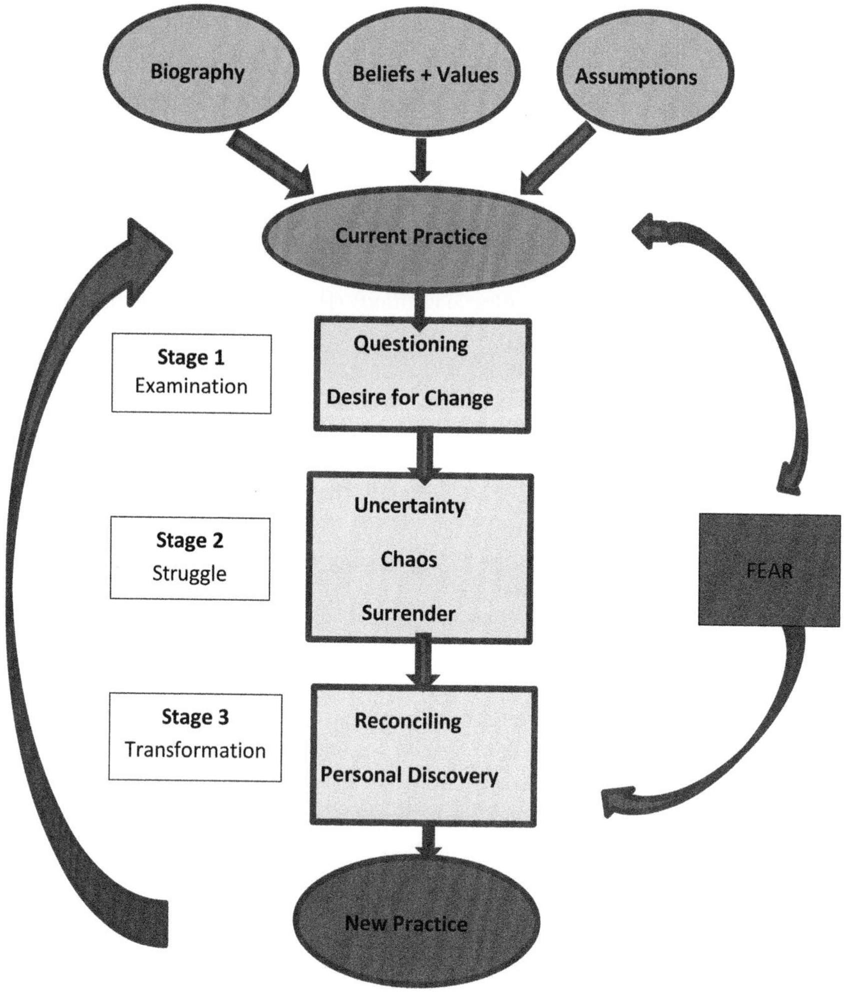

Figure 4.1 The process of critical reflection

Source: Horgan (2019) adapted from Larrivee (2000)

Interrogating personal biography, beliefs, values & assumptions

The process of engaging in reflective practice inevitably raises the issue of identity – who is the 'I' who teaches? (Palmer, 1998). How do my beliefs, values, assumptions and biographical experiences influence how I teach? This approach to identity can therefore raise provocative, uncomfortable and challenging questions about taken-for-granted dispositions that we may hold and point to the possible fallibility of some traditions and precedents that have been assimilated in terms of how we view and relate to the natural world. It suggests a more critical interrogation of comfortable routines, and supports a view of the self as 'a continuous reflexive project' (Hargreaves, 1994:71), involving struggle, reassessment and openness to change. As Bamford (1999:171) states, teachers 'need to escape their own enculturation' if they are to genuinely address environmental concerns.

Personal biography

Brookfield (1998:198) considers this lens as 'one of the most important sources of insight into practice'. Our biographies as learners have significant implications for how we teach because our experiences are remembered and felt at a visceral level, which is much deeper than at the level of thought. We might think that we have developed our teaching style and orientation towards learners as a result of our study of education only to find that 'the foundations of how we work have been laid down in our autobiographies as learners' (Brookfield, 1998:198). Analysing our autobiographies as learners often helps us to understand why we are so deeply committed to certain ideals and values.

Beliefs, values & assumptions

Research has shown that reflection and enquiry are necessary in order to expand and modify our beliefs. Reflection helps to challenge our well-worn, taken-for-granted assumptions through a process of systematic inquiry, thereby promoting professional growth and development.

Interrogating personal biography, beliefs, values & assumptions: Reflection activities

Teacher reflection activity 1: What has sparked my interest in climate change education?

You are reading this book because you have an interest in climate change education.

Take a moment to think about your life experiences and relationship with the natural world up to this point in time and to identify certain key or formative moments that have sparked your interest in climate change education. How do these experiences inform who you are and what you value?

You may represent this experiential trajectory as a timeline as shown below in Figure 4.2.

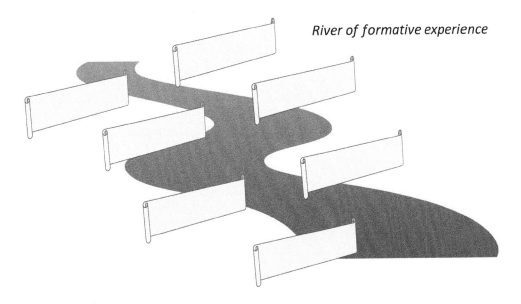

Figure 4.2 River of formative experiences

Teacher reflection activity 2: Personal beliefs about climate change education

Write a paragraph beginning with each of the following:

- Given my current understanding of climate change education, I would like to be a teacher who …
- My current understanding of learning means that, as a teacher of climate change education, I will endeavour to …

Reflective activity for children (8–13 years): Recalling experiences in nature

Using soft background music, settle the class into a relaxed reflective state and invite them to recall moments in their lives where they have enjoyed being outdoors in nature. It may be a time when they were playing in the park, walking in the woods, growing plants, playing on the beach ….

Invite the learners to draw the images that come to mind and, under each image, to write the feelings they associate with it.

For younger learners, you may wish to prepare them for this activity by exploring the language of feelings and using written words or emojis to express their feelings.

Stage 1: Examination

In the first stage, the *examination stage*, we begin to question whether particular actions reactions, or interactions are achieving what is desired. For example, we might question if our current practice is:

- Promoting deep and meaningful connections with the natural world
- Fostering age-appropriate understandings of the inter-relationships between people and nature
- Cultivating questioning dispositions and critical thinking skills
- Affirming of the different perspectives and contributions of all members of the learning community
- Solution-focused and empowering

Through reflecting on questions such as those outlined above, we pause the momentum of our habitual behaviour and begin to observe certain patterns of thinking and behaving and, ultimately, assess the benefits and limitations of our current practice. We realise the aspects of our behaviour that are sustaining a state that we want to change and this realisation creates a desire for change. Table 4.1 presents a format which can be used to reflect on or take stock of current practice in respect of climate change education.

Reflective activity for teacher: Examining current practice

Take a blank sheet of paper and create four quadrants on the page as outlined in Table 4.1 below. Under the title 'Last Term', reflect on how you felt about your teaching and your

Table 4.1 Retrospective review

Last Term	This Term
Next Term	What I Notice

children's learning last term. Draw the images that come to mind or write the words which best describe your reflections. Engage in a similar process when reflecting on your feelings about your current work as teachers and the children's experiences as learners under the heading 'This term'. Next, take a moment to consider your aspirations for next term. Having completed these three quadrants, list your observations under the heading 'What I Notice'.

Reflective activity for children: A Time to Change (8-13 years)

The aim of this activity is to provide children an opportunity to reflect on the ways in which they can help to care for the planet and all its systems and life forms. Distribute copies of *A time to change (Figure 4.3)*. Invite children to think and talk about how they could make the world a better place, encouraging them to focus on potential personal actions for change. Based on the individual commitments and priorities identified by the children, a class 'Charter for the Planet' could be generated. Displayed in a prominent position in the classroom, such a charter should be reviewed regularly to assess progress.

Reflective activity for children: Imagine the future (children 8–13 years)

The aim of this activity is to encourage children to reflect on the power of individuals, groups, governments and international agencies to work together to protect the planet for current and future generations.

Using an *Imagine the Future* activity (Figure 4.4), ask the children to imagine that they are looking at the monitor of a time machine which allows them to see the world in the year 2050. Invite them to depict the images that they see using words, symbols and drawings.

In pairs or small groups, encourage children to share and discuss their images, focussing on how individuals, groups, governments and international agencies can help to protect the planet, including its systems and life forms. A review of the childrens' images, will provide valuable information for the teacher regarding the levels of optimism or worry that individual children have about their future.

Think about yourself, your school, your locality, your county, your country, and your planet. What needs to be changed in each of these in order to make the world a better place?

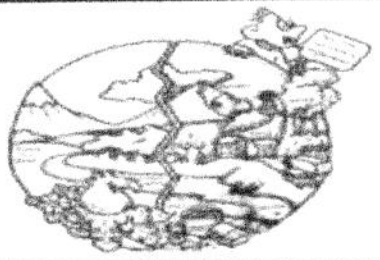

A CHANGE WHICH I FEEL SHOULD BE MADE

Myself: ______

School: ______

Locality: ______

County: ______

Country: ______

The Planet: ______

Look at the list of changes that you have suggested. In your copy, write how you can help to bring about these changes.

Figure 4.3 A time to change

Source: Horgan & Murphy (1993:48)

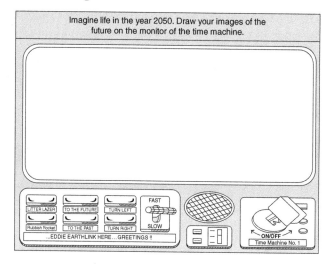

Figure 4.4 Imagine the future

Source: Horgan & Murphy (1993:49)

Stage 2: Struggle

Schultz et al. (2013:14) state that '… uncertainty, surprise, and change' are critical in dealing with global change. When we attempt to let go of familiar patterns and ways of viewing the world, Larrivee (2000) states that this leads to a struggle and we find ourselves in conflict. This signals a critical stage in the reflective process:

> If this state of inner turmoil brings about too much fear and doubt, the choice may be to close down the process and either stay with the old practice or seek a quick fix. We look for a ready-made solution, a 'prescription' for change. However, when we do this, we circumvent an essential stage in the critical reflection process.

If instead we are able to face the conflict, surrendering what is familiar, we allow ourselves to experience the uncertainty. This not knowing throws us into chaos. In this phase, if we 'move into the eye of the storm', we 'weather' the turmoil and a deeper understanding emerges.

Embracing climate change education can present challenges for teachers in a myriad of different ways as it involves stepping into the unknown, where we do not have the certainty that we may feel when engaging with other aspects of the curriculum. We cannot, for example, anticipate the impact of climate change on our lives in the short term and its long-term effects are beyond the predictive scope of even the most eminent climatologists.

Therefore, climate change education may challenge latent beliefs that teachers as 'experts' in the classroom should have all the answers. However, climate change education defies clear solutions or precise explanations, leaving teachers vulnerable to feelings of inadequacy and helplessness. It requires teachers to focus on the processes of learning; to resist the simplistic, mechanical world view which predominates and to draw on diverse perspectives and cultural contexts. This often requires that teachers 'move into realms that are counter to existing dominant values' (Bamford, 1999:170). Table 4.2 below invites teachers to consider their levels of comfort with different aspects of the pedagogy and content of climate change education.

Table 4.2 Stepping into the uncertainty of climate change

Teacher reflection: Stepping into the uncertainty of climate change education

Reflect on the statements below and their implications for your engagement with change education. What opportunities and challenges does each present for you, your teaching beliefs and your current pedagogical approaches?

Pedagogy	*Opportunities*
The pedagogy of climate change education is open and exploratory where learners and teachers are co-learners and co-investigators.	*Challenges:*
Subject content knowledge	*Opportunities*
The content knowledge of climate change education is life itself. It is multidisciplinary and complex. The teacher's role is to mediate the content so that it is complex enough to allow deep engagement, yet not too complex to prevent an active response.	*Challenges:*
Exploratory talk	*Opportunities*
The type of talk that allows this complexity to emerge is described by Mercer (2000) as exploratory talk. Exploratory talk allows children to explore meaning and try out new ways of understanding and to modify existing ideas. It involves experimentation with new ideas, enabling children to talk their way into meaning.	*Challenges:*
Class management	*Opportunities*
Active, inquiry-oriented learning involves 'productive noise' where learners move around, talk to each other and act independently on focused tasks. It is the antithesis of the traditional classroom.	*Challenges:*
Curriculum design	*Opportunities*
Climate change education is a cross-curricular area which spans all subjects in the curriculum. Planning for climate change education involves an integrated, thematic approach.	*Challenges:*
Different learner responses to climate change	*Opportunities*
With the increased focus on climate change in the media and elsewhere, some learners experience 'climate fatigue' others feel 'climate overwhelm' while many feel 'climate fears' and are concerned about their futures and the futures of those they care about.	*Challenges:*
Learner agency	*Opportunities*
While acknowledging the challenges associated with climate change, this form of education is committed to learner agency and cultivates a pedagogy of hope where learners are empowered to make changes.	*Challenges:*

Table 4.3 A framework of questions for reviewing an experience of teaching climate change education adapted from Rolfe et al. (2001)

Teacher reflection: Reviewing an experience of teaching climate change education

What?

- What aspect of the teaching/ learning encounter am I focussing on?
- What was I trying to achieve?
- What did I do?
- What was the learner response?
- What were the outcomes?
- What feelings did it evoke in the learners? Myself? Others (if relevant)?
- What were the positive and negative aspects of the experience?

So what?

- What can I learn from this experience?
- What was my thought process prior to and during the learning experience?
- What new knowledge can I bring to the situation now?
- What could I have done to make it better?
- What wider issues arise from this experience?

Now what?

- What do I need to do now?
- How can I learn from this experience?
- What theoretical insights can inform my learning?

Rolfe et al. (2001) developed a framework for reflection based on three simple questions: What? So what? Now what? To assist teachers in reflecting on their experience of teaching climate change education, the author has generated a list of questions based on this framework (Table 4.3).

Stage 3: Transformation

Engaging with the turmoil, the conflict, the uncertainty and the chaos allows personal discovery to emerge. By completing the cycle and moving through the struggle stage, we undergo a transformation. 'When learning surfaces from within, tapping our own resources, we experience an "ahah" and no longer need to take on other's solutions. This shift restructures our way of thinking and changes our overall perspective. We are now capable of critically reflective practice' (Larrivee, 2000:306).

Activity for children (4–7 years): A new beginning

The aim of this activity is to help young children to appreciate the many connections we have with the forest and its creatures.

Read and discuss the story: A new beginning

Explore the events which ensued when the trees ran away.

- Why did the people not wake at dawn?
- Why were the people frightened when they looked out of their windows?
- Why was the mayor angry when she heard what really happened?

- How did the people find the forest?
- What did Aodh and Aisling do when they found Oisín Oak?
- What did the people say?
- Why did the forest trees decide to come back?
- How did they return to Baile Glas?

Retell the story and encourage the children to dramatise what happened.

Story: A new beginning

Once upon a time, in the middle of a forest there was a little town called Baile Glas. The forest was home for hundreds of creatures who lived on the trees. But the people became greedy and began to cut down the trees. The trees and the forest creatures were sad and angry. They asked their magic friend Labhraidh Leprechaun to help them. One night, he used his magic to give them feet to run away. The trees took all the forest creatures with them and went to another valley.

The following morning, the people of Baile Glas were not awakened at dawn by the sweet singing of the forest birds but slept on until the afternoon. Finally, the people yawned, stretched, looked at their clocks and jumped up with a start. It was 1 pm, lunch time! Whatever could have happened? Why hadn't they been awakened by the birds? They jumped into their clothes, pulled back the curtains, looked out and rubbed their eyes in shock. Everything was so different. Baile Glas looked just like the surface of the moon with monstrous brown holes where the green forest once stood. The people were frightened and ran to the mayor's house.

The mayor was at her bedroom window. All the people stood on the steps below. 'Does anybody know what is going on?' asked the mayor. Some people said that the sky was falling down. Others said that aliens from outer space had stolen the trees. 'Now stop all the guessing', said the Mayor. 'Does anybody here have any idea what really happened?' The people looked at each other, scratched their heads, but said nothing. Then a tiny voice was heard from the middle of the crowd. It was a little girl called Aisling. 'Excuse me Mrs Mayor', she said, 'but I think I know what really happened. My brother and I were in the forest when the trees decided to leave'. Aisling spoke out as loudly as she could, telling the people about everything that she and her brother, Aodh, had seen and heard in the forest. As she spoke the people grew quieter and some faces became redder and redder and more ashamed.

The people were sad and worried. They had to think of a plan to make things better. Aodh spoke next. 'I think I have an idea', he said. The people listened attentively. 'In order to move, the trees had to grow feet, and, as you know, heavy feet leave big footprints. So let's follow the footprints and we're sure to find the forest'. 'What are we waiting for? Let's go!' they all said.

It wasn't difficult to find the enormous footprints left by the forest trees. They were so big that mothers and fathers had to hold their children's hands tightly because if they fell in they were sure to be lost forever. They followed the footprints up hill and down dale, until eventually the footprints stopped. The people looked up and there in front of them was a forest just like the forest of Baile Glas. Aodh and Aisling ran into the forest looking for their friend Oisín Oak. When they eventually found him, they hugged him tightly and told him how much they missed him. The children explained that the people were sorry for harming the forest and had come to invite the trees back to Baile Glas. When the people saw Oisín Oak, they ran towards him, threw their arms around him and said 'Sorry'. Then they stood in a circle around the forest, joined hands and recited this poem which they had made up on their way.

Oisín, please come back to stay
We're so lonely since you away.
No trees, no flowers, no birds to cheep,
Baile Glas has gone to sleep!
If we get another chance,
Through the forest we will dance,
We'll feed the birds,
We'll mind the flowers,
We'll water you when there are no showers,
We'll even plant new baby trees,
We'll make a hive for the bumble bees,
We'll keep your forest bright and green,
If you come back to us, Oisín

Oisín Oak and all the forest trees and creatures were very happy to go back to Baile Glas. They missed the town where they had lived for hundreds of years. The animals and birds looked forward to having their young at home in the forest in Baile Glas, so they forgave the people and promised to go home. They called on Labhraidh Leapreachaun to work his magic again. Labhraidh appeared instantly. He was very happy that his plan had worked to make the people take more care of the forest. Once more he got some rainbow dust and mixed it up with the forest dew and this time he said these words:

You were sad and ran away,
Now you want to return to stay,
So I'll give you back your sturdy feet,
And wish you well till next we meet.

All of a sudden, there was a great rocking and rumbling in the ground beneath the forest and once again the tree roots turned into legs and feet. 'Climb aboard said Oisín Oak, 'We'll give you all a lift back to Baile Glas', The people climbed up onto the sturdiest branches they could find and held on tightly as the trees ran back to Baile Glas. From that day on, the people of Baile Glas took care of their precious forest, and the people, the creatures and the trees lived happily ever after.

Adapted from *Team Planet: Nurturing* (Horgan, 1994:26).

Conclusion

In asking the above questions and exploring the above processes, we are exercising our innate sense of criticality and stimulating critical thinking amongst our learners in their engagement with climate change education. Central to this chapter is the view that critical thinking empowers us. Based on discernment, critical thinking is inherently democratic and it helps to ensure a strong link between theory and practice. Ultimately, it requires a willingness to detach ourselves from our established views and maintain the belief in the fallibility of our inquiry. Re-examining some of our previously held views may be difficult or troubling, and yet may yield a sense of freedom and deep insight. bell hooks, while writing in terms of the classroom, posits the view that such a sense of criticality is deeply inherent to our own development and the development of societal well-being:

> The classroom with all its limitations remains a location of possibility. In that field of possibility we have the opportunity to labour for freedom, to demand of ourselves and our comrades an openness of mind and heart that allows us to face reality even as we collectively imagine ways to move beyond boundaries, to transgress. This is education as the practice of freedom.
>
> (hooks, 1994:207)

References

Bamford, B. (1999) From environmental education to ecopolitics. Affirming changing agendas for teachers. *Educational Philosophy and Theory, 31*, 157–173.

Bonfield, T. and Horgan, K. (2016) *Learning to Teach: Teaching to Learn.* Dublin: Gill Education.

Brookfield, S. (1998) Critically reflective practice. *Journal of Continuing Education in the Health Professions, 18*(4), 197–205.

Brookfield, S.D. (2017) *Becoming a Critically Reflective Teacher.* San Francisco, CA: Jossey-Bass, A Wiley Brand.

Hargreaves, A. (1994) *Changing Times, Changing Teachers.* London: Cassell.

hooks, b. (1994) *Teaching to Transgress: Education as the Practice of Freedom.* London: Routledge.

Horgan, K. and Gardiner-Hyland, F. (2019) Irish student teachers' beliefs about self, learning and teaching: A longitudinal study. *European Journal of Teacher Education, 42*(2), 151–174.

Horgan, K. (1994) *Team Planet: Nurturing.* Limerick: The Primary School Development Education Project. https://www.developmenteducation.ie/teachers-and-educators/primary-education/team-planet/introduction.html.

Horgan, K. and Murphy, H. (1993) *Team Planet: Webs of Dependence.* Limerick: The Primary School Development Education Project. https://www.developmenteducation.ie/teachers-and-educators/primary-education/team-planet/introduction.html.

Larrivee, B. and Cooper. J.M. (2006) *An Educator's Guide to Teacher Reflection.* Boston: Houghton Mifflin Company.

Larrivee, B. (2000) Transforming teaching practice: Becoming the critically reflective teacher. *Reflective Practice, 1*(3), 293–307.

Mercer, N. (2000) *The Guided Construction of Knowledge: Talk Amongst Teachers and Learners.* Clevedon: Multilingual Matters Ltd.

Palmer, P.J. (1998) *The Courage to Teach.* San Francisco: Jossey-Bass.

Rolfe, G., Freshwater, D. and Jasper, M. (2001) *Critical Reflection in Nursing and the Helping Professions: A User's Guide.* Basingstoke: Palgrave Macmillan.

Schon, D.A. (1987) *Educating the Reflective Practitioner.* San Francisco; London: Jossey-Bass.

Schultz, M., Rockström, J., Öhman, M.C., Cornell, S., Persson, Å. and Norström, A. (2013) Human prosperity requires global sustainability—A contribution to the post-2015 agenda and the development of Sustainable Development Goals. *A Stockholm Resilience Centre Report to the Swedish Government Office.* Stockholm: Stockholm Resilience Centre.

UNESCO (2005) Draft consolidated international implementation scheme. Available online at: http://unesdoc.unesco.org/images/0014/001403/140372e.pdf.

5 Early beginnings

Fostering positive dispositions towards climate education in early years classrooms

Deirdre Breatnach, Mary Moloney and Jennifer Pope

Introduction

Children are primed for learning from birth, and they learn at a rapid pace between birth and six years old. The early childhood period provides a critical foundation for lifelong learning. The types of learning experiences and opportunities that young children encounter within classrooms at this point in their educational journey affects them as they progress through primary school and beyond. This chapter focuses on early childhood climate education approaches, and how they can be introduced effectively in early childhood classrooms. Firstly, the chapter provides a rationale for why it is important to consider climate education in the early years of a child's life. Drawing upon international early childhood curriculum frameworks (Ireland, New Zealand, Australia, Norway and England), the chapter then outlines both the importance of fostering positive dispositions in young children as well as, how this can be undertaken in the early childhood years. This chapter illustrates how inquiry-based learning (IBL), using various playful, relevant and meaningful learning experiences, nurtures positive dispositions towards learning about the environment in the early years.

Early childhood education (ECE) – The formative years

Across the world, and depending on the school starting age in individual countries, ECE is concerned with the early years of a child's life from birth to approximately six to eight years of age. This period is critical in building the foundations of lifelong health, well-being and education. Ensuring these foundations are solid is vital for a society to promote a prosperous and sustainable future (Centre on the Developing Child, Harvard University, 2010). Neuroscientific and brain research shows that early childhood is the most intensive period of brain development during the human lifespan, when the rate and depth of children's learning is greater than at later stages (Ibid., 2008). The early childhood period, therefore, is highly significant as 'children's early years are the foundation of their lives as students, adults and citizens' (OECD, 2019:4).

Some people may argue that introducing young children to climate change too soon may frighten or scare them and suggest waiting until they are older. However, children are curious about and, receptive to the world around them. While the concept of climate is vast and certain elements may be too abstract for young children to grasp, teachers of young children in early childhood settings and school classrooms can introduce core concepts in accessible and developmentally appropriate ways through early childhood climate education. Without access to early years climate education, children may draw their own conclusions based on snippets of information from adults and media footage.

Consequently, children may develop pessimistic or defeatist concepts of climate change which may ultimately underline their own sense of powerlessness.

It is possible for teachers to weave or infuse climate education through all aspects of the child's day in school or the early childhood setting, maximising on any potential teachable moments. Through their interactions and modelling, teachers can nurture a culture that promotes respect and care of self, others and the environment. This encapsulates all interactions with children and their relations with each other and, the environment – indoors and outdoors. It, therefore, extends beyond traditional subject-based lessons. Consider, for example, how the outdoor space around a school can be cultivated to promote engagement with nature during lunch or recess times. Many outdoor areas in schools are bare, asphalt-dominated spaces. These sterile schoolyards do not allow opportunities to support children's natural curiosity about the environment and, their propensity for observation and questioning in the early years. Yet, there may be scope to introduce raised beds for planting, sensory gardens to encourage wildlife, birdfeeders to attract birds or opportunities to utilise recycled material to promote open-ended play and exploration. These spaces could then foster an appreciation of the natural surroundings, develop climate awareness and provide a platform for ongoing environmental education (Department of Education, Employment and Workplace Relations (DEEWR), 2009:16).

Young children's learning occurs informally for the most part during the early childhood period, through their everyday routines inside and outside their homes. Many countries, therefore, have developed ECE programmes and curricula to support this vital phase of a child's learning and development. In Ireland, for example, the Early Childhood Curriculum Framework: *Aistear* (the Irish word for journey) encompasses the period from birth to six years and, focuses upon the care and education of young children from birth through to the early years of primary school (National Council for Curriculum and Assessment (NCCA), 2009). Congruent with early childhood curricula in other countries such as *Te Whāriki* (Ministry of Education, New Zealand, 2017); *Belonging Being and Becoming* (DEEWR, Australia, 2009); Framework plan for Kindergartens (Norwegian Directorate for Education and Training, 2017) and the *Early Years Foundation Stage* (Department for Education (DfE), England, 2017), *Aistear* posits that 'all children can grow and develop as competent and confident learners within loving relationships with others' (NCCA, 2009:6). Early childhood curricula generally recognise that young children are experiential learners, who learn by doing and who are active participants rather than passive recipients of knowledge. Similarly, core principles of early childhood underpin these various curricula. Drawing upon *Aistear*, in the Irish context, three core principles shape children's learning in the early years:

1 Children and their lives in early childhood
2 Children's connections with others
3 Children's learning and development

Children and their lives in early childhood

Aligning with the United Nations Convention on the Rights of the Child (UNCRC, 1989), a key principle when working with children is to recognise that they are citizens with rights, roles and responsibilities within society, including the responsibility to respect and care for others and the environment (NCCA, 2009). In an early childhood classroom, a central element of children's experiences should involve opportunities to exercise these citizenship rights and social responsibilities in an age-appropriate way. As discussed later, teachers can support young children to develop a sense of social responsibility, justice and ethics and, engage as citizens by providing opportunities for them to develop positive dispositions towards all aspects of learning including climate change.

In Chapter 1 of this book, Dolan stresses that climate knowledge although important is not sufficient. It needs to be accompanied by attitudinal change, wise decision-making and a sense of agency. The capacity to make informed decisions and develop this sense of agency should therefore be nurtured from the earliest years. In terms of children's sense of identity and belonging, teachers can play an important role in fostering strong self-identities in young children. There are many ways to support children in considering their own lives in the early years' classroom through participation and documentation. Young children can use their drawings, stories or photographs to document their lives (Martin, 2019). These processes of documenting who we are, where we live, how we live, what we eat, where our food comes from and how we travel provide an initial stepping stone towards supporting children to consider the experiences of others. Practical strategies such as learning journals or portfolios based on children's lives and interests and developed in conjunction with children themselves can be very valuable tools.

While climate education in the early years involves informing children about various issues, the potential to have a long-term impact depends on the development of 'attitudes and values like respect for themselves and others, care for the environment, and positive attitudes to learning and to life' (NCCA, 2015:1). Thus, it is essential for fostering positive dispositions towards climate education in the early years and beyond. Katz (1993) defines dispositions as enduring habits of mind and action, the 'tendency to respond to situations in characteristic ways' (NCCA, 2009:54). Thus, learning dispositions, which develop 'in conjunction with children's acquisition of knowledge, skills, attitudes and understanding' (NCCA, 2015:2) are a key component of a child's educational journey. Figure 5.1 provides an overview of the types of positive dispositions outlined in *Aistear, Te Whāriki, NZ, Belonging Being and Becoming, Australia, the Framework Plan for Kindergarten Teachers, Norway* and the *Early Years Foundation Stage* in England.

Katz (1993) defines dispositions as enduring habits of mind and action, the 'tendency to respond to situations in characteristic ways' (NCCA, 2009:54). Thus, learning dispositions, which develop 'in conjunction with children's acquisition of knowledge, skills, attitudes and understanding' (NCCA, 2015:2) are a key component of a child's educational journey. While climate education in the early years involves informing children about environmental issues, the potential to have a long-term impact depends on the development of 'attitudes and values like respect for themselves and others, care for the environment, and positive attitudes to learning and to life' (NCCA, 2015:1). Thus, it is essential for fostering positive dispositions towards climate education in the early years and beyond. Figure 5.1 provides an overview of the types of positive dispositions outlined in *Aistear, Te Whāriki, NZ, Belonging Being and Becoming, Australia, the Framework Plan for Kindergarten Teachers, Norway* and the *Early Years Foundation Stage* in England.

Children's connections with others

Although certain dispositions are innate, because young children's dispositions are influenced by the significant adults in their lives (parents and grandparents), they are robust in most children upon entry to school (Katz and Chard, 2000). The Centre on the Developing Child, Harvard University (2010) states that one of the foundations of lifelong health and well-being is safe and supportive physical, chemical and built environments, which should provide 'physical and emotional spaces that are free from toxins and fear, allow

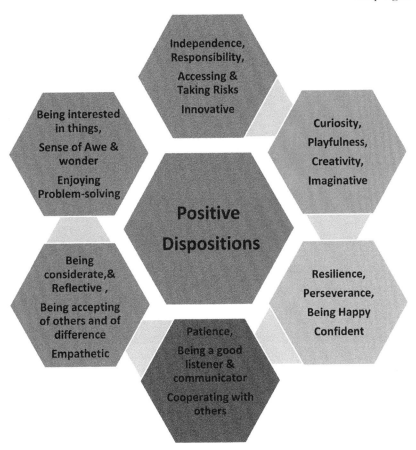

Figure 5.1 Positive dispositions that enable young children to engage with climate education

active exploration without significant risk of harm, and offer supports for families raising young children'. Bronfenbrenner's (2005) bio-ecological framework also suggests that wider factors influence children's development operating at different system levels. Bronfenbrenner's model seeks to 'understand how the characteristics of the developing person, including their dispositions, knowledge, experiences and skills, interact with aspects of the environment to invite or inhibit engagement' (MoE, NZ, 2017:61). Beyond the micro-system factors (home and school) as highlighted earlier, wider factors within local communities and macro policy decisions, the local environment, litter and traffic pollution all affect children's development.

How do young children get to and from school? Is there an opportunity to encourage them to 'park and ride' using their scooters, bicycles, walk or even skip a small part of the way? Young children's shorter stature means they are closer than adults to exhaust fumes from traffic. To promote wise decisions in terms of transport and air pollution, some schools have introduced initiatives to avoid parking close to the school gate at drop-off and collection times. While these initiatives can generate discussions about traffic restrictions near the school and, can have a direct impact on very young children, they require building relationships with parents, staff and local communities. This may be challenging. Nonetheless, such initiatives are a concrete way of showing young children that personal and collective choices can make a difference for them and others. Children can experience first-hand how the lack of cars means fresher air, greater health and safety and, more space for them to play and explore.

Furthermore, many schools urge children to reduce, re-use and recycle. Children's lunchtime presents an ideal opportunity to seize on a teachable moment. For example, a teacher can engage children in considering what it would be like if everyone just threw their rubbish on the floor. Teachers can support the extension of this simple discussion to a larger scale discussion and project about recycling from a citizen's viewpoint, encouraging children, to undertake a 'rubbish hunt' around the school once a week. When given responsibility, children will take ownership of activities, thus fostering their sense of personal and collective agency, as well as their emerging social responsibility. Often, very young children are the most adept at reminding peers, older children and adults about their responsibilities with regard to keeping a school clean and tidy. Over time, this can be extended to the wider community and local initiatives such as Tidy Towns. The national Tidy Towns initiative has been in operation in Ireland since 1958. The ethos is to encourage people of all ages within the community to work together outdoors to enhance the environment where they live and work.

Most children are naturally curious about their surroundings and have a particular interest in exploring and investigating how things work and why things happen. They also have an innate sense of wonder and awe and, a natural desire for inquiry. Their sense of curiosity and wonder is characterised by 'how', 'why', 'where', 'when' and 'what' questions, leading to scientific learning, which helps them develop the capacity to predict, observe and experiment from early childhood (De la Blanca et al., 2013). All of this has implications for how children learn and, how teachers teach in the early childhood classroom. As mentioned, it is important to foster a sense of personal agency in young children while nurturing a sense of collective agency and, social responsibility. Children need opportunities to work and play together to develop these dispositions. They can work collaboratively to take care of their collective environment, the early childhood classroom, their outdoor play spaces, homes and local communities. According to Wall et al. (2015), how children learn and develop in early childhood is not subject solely to what teachers intend to teach, but also upon how it is facilitated. Thus, inferring a proactive role for the teacher who must utilise a repertoire of pedagogical strategies to motivate and engage children, satisfy their natural curiosity and nurture positive dispositions.

Children's learning and development

The early childhood classroom provides the optimal environment to capitalise on children's natural curiosity. Children learn best when dealing with topics they can explore in depth. As mentioned, abstract concepts such as climate education can be difficult for young children to conceptualise as they may struggle to see any situation from a point of view other than their own (Piaget and Cook, 1952). By focusing on the natural world in the children's immediate locality, or on events and objects that arouse children's existing interests, teachers may raise awareness of climate education in relevant and authentic ways.

Early childhood pedagogy: IBL

Inspired by Dewey, IBL is a constructivist approach where the overall goal is for children to make meaning with the teacher acting as a guide and role model for children (Byrne et al., 2016), allowing them considerable freedom to interact (MacDonald, 2016). Oğuz-Ünver and Arabacioğlu (2011:304) describe IBL as the 'art of questioning or the art of raising questions'. It emphasises the child's role in the learning process and involves hands-on activities, which relate to real-life situations and events as children learn by doing (NCCA, 2009). During IBL, the teacher becomes a co-learner working together with children to investigate a topic, guiding them through their inquiry with the use of appropriate scaffolding. This not only encourages children to construct their own knowledge actively and bring personal ideas and concepts to the learning experience, but also encourages them to make changes in their attitudes and behaviours (Kuhlthau et al., 2007) enhancing the development of positive dispositions such as curiosity, perseverance and responsibility.

The Ministry of Education, New Zealand (2017) notes that throughout early childhood, children are critical thinkers, problem-solvers and explorers who are able to connect with and care for their own and wider worlds. Therefore, young children are perfect candidates for IBL because it embraces active explorations that awaken their interest for learning involving: observing; touching; listening; smelling; comparing; sorting; classifying and ordering (MacDonald, 2016).

Through an IBL process, both teachers and children collaborate and share genuine curiosity, wonderment and questioning about the area of interest. In addition, children are involved actively in constructing understandings through hands-on experiences, research, processing and communicating their understandings in various ways (e.g., photographs, drawings, discussions). In Chapter 1, Dolan refers to a deficit in children's vocabulary in relation to the natural world (words such as willow, bluebell and conker). It is essential, therefore, that teachers avail of teachable moments throughout the day to make concerted efforts to introduce new language and expose children to experiences which contextualise such words. Ideally, this should involve hands-on experiences, such as having a willow den within an outdoor play space. However, picture books, accompanying story sacks and puppetry, rhymes and songs also appeal to young children, bringing learning to life in a playful and engaging way.

Within the early childhood classroom, children need multiple opportunities to express ideas, opinions and to 'broaden their understanding of the world by making sense of experiences through language' (NCCA, 2009:35). This ensures that the child's voice is central and that teachers listen to and act upon children's questions. For example, in everyday conversations such as in news-sharing and informal discussions, children often converse about topics and areas of interest such as the weather. Teachers can use these teachable moments to introduce children to conversations related to climate change. When engaging in these types of exchanges with young children, the ideas explored must always connect with what is already familiar to the children to ascertain and build upon prior knowledge. When discussing the weather outside, teachers can make connections with climatic conditions in other parts of the world. A wet day can lead to discussions or stories about monsoon conditions and the importance of rain. Indeed, weather discussions can lead to more in-depth investigations and tracking of weather patterns over the course of a number of weeks (see sample lesson plan below). Due to their innate curiosity, young children can be quite enthralled by tasks such as observing the amount of rainfall in containers on a daily basis and can be guided to speculate as to why this might occur. This type of learning takes place in a social context where children learn from each other, together with others and from those outside the classroom context. Table 5.1 provides an overview of the IBL process in the infant classroom.

The following lesson plan, **Our Changing Environment**, builds upon everyday discussions which arise during news-time, outdoor play, nature walks and reading books. The lesson is designed to deepen children's awareness and knowledge of climate education.

Table 5.1 Overview of the IBL process in the infant (children 4-6 years) classroom

Aspects of the child's inquiry process	Context for climate education examples	When engaged in the inquiry process, children	When modelling or supporting the inquiry process, teachers
Initial engagement: noticing, wondering, playing	Examining the natural world looking for insects under rocks/container pots etc. Noticing changing seasons Wondering about wind, rain and sunshine (see sample lesson plan 1: 'Our changing environment')	raise questions about objects and events around them	observe and listen
Exploration: exploring, observing, questioning	Observing and exploring types of insects in different habitats (see sample activity plan 2: 'Making a bug hotel') Exploring what we grow and what we could grow (Book Oliver's vegetables could prompt discussion) Observing what happens to grass, soil and plants during rainfall or warm weather (see sample lesson plan below) Observing and asking why bees visit flowers	explore objects and events around them and observe the results of their explorations make observations, using all of their senses and generate questions	act as facilitators to guide children with thoughtful, open-ended questions encourage children to observe and talk among themselves and to the teacher
Investigation: planning, using observations, reflecting	Planning, building and examining a bug hotel Planting and growing herbs/fruit/vegetables Measuring rainfall, checking temperature (see sample lesson plan)	gather, compare, sort, classify, order, interpret, describe observable characteristics and properties notice patterns, and draw conclusions, using a variety of simple tools and materials	provide a rich variety of materials and resources and strategically question and observe children to clarify, expand or discover the children's thinking model how to plan, observe and reflect
Communication: sharing findings, discussing ideas	Evaluation of position of bug hotel, consider moving, review construction, the lives of the insects... Protecting insects Or considering what grows well...	work individually and with others, share and discuss ideas and listen to ideas	listen to the children to help them make connections between prior knowledge and new discoveries

Adapted from: Ministry of Education, Ontario, 2010

Based upon active learning, it utilises four strategies when applying IBL in ECE: scientific activities that are authentic and meaningful for the children, age-appropriate questions that challenge children, opportunities for children to interact and encourage them to search for evidence and collect data (Dejonckheere et al., 2016).

Lesson plan 1: Our changing environment

The environment is all around us and is a natural part of our daily lives. This lesson encourages children to explore the concept of change in the environment by tracking weather patterns and conducting a 'Sunflower investigation' (Table 5.2).

Lesson objectives

Children will:

- Chart, graph, identify and analyse local weather patterns Investigate plant growth conditions through a 'Sunflower investigation'
- Use a process of predict, observe and explain (P.O.E.) for their investigations
- Become familiar with and utilise key vocabulary (e.g., Climate, compost, drought, earth, environment, pollution, seasons, weather)

Key questions

- What is the environment?
- What are habitats?
- Are there different types of habitats?
- What are the basic needs of all living things? (e.g., air, water, food, shelter and sunlight)

What do you think would happen if these five basic needs are not met?

Necessary materials and equipment

- Computer and internet for videos and National Geographic-Climate and weather: www.watchknowlearn.org/video.aspx?videoID=3929&CategoryID=2671
- 'This Land is Your Land'. www.youtube.com/watch?v=3C4iRf9gOdY
- Camera
- Chart paper
- Markers
- Map and/or globe
- Clear, clean 2-litre plastic bottles (clear so children can see root growth), cut in half (three per group of three children)
- Scissors
- Potting compost
- Sunflower seeds

Duration

Two weeks (10 days, 30–40 minutes/day).

Table 5.2 Sunflower investigation

Tell children they are going to investigate sunflower growth under different conditions. Review the five conditions necessary for life and, ask children to predict what will happen if one of these is missing. This investigation explores healthy growing conditions, drought conditions in which sunlight is interrupted from particulate matter in the air, simulating air pollution.

Predict: as you prepare for the Sunflower investigations, ask children to respond to each of the following questions for the various conditions simulated in the investigation:

- What does your seed need to sprout into a seedling? (Light and water)
- How long will it take your seed to sprout into a seedling?
- How much will your seed grow each week?

Help children to complete a Predict Observe Explain (POE) record

Predict	Observe	Explain

Each group of three children should have all the materials needed to begin their sunflower investigation at their table/area. Each group should create three sunflower planters to simulate the conditions in the three investigations:

Investigation 1: the seed will be properly watered daily, and placed in the window sill where they will receive direct sunlight

Investigation 2: the seed will be properly watered daily but placed in a dark area of the classroom to restrict sunlight

Investigation 3: the seed will not be watered but placed on the window sill where they receive appropriate daily sunlight

Ask children to:

- Clear, clean 2-litre bottles (clear so children can see root growth)
- Cut the bottle in half
- Poke holes in the bottom of the bottle to allow drainage
- Fill the bottle bottom with potting compost
- Plant sunflower seeds into the compost
- Have children label each planter with their team names and 1, 2 or 3 to correspond with the conditions outlined for investigations 1, 2 and 3.

Observe
For each investigation, have children observe how long it took for the seed to sprout into a seedling and, how much the seedling grew each week.

Explain
Support and encourage children to:

- Revisit predictions from before the Sunflower investigation
- Explain why they think what happened actually happened
- Discuss whether their predictions were accurate, close or not accurate and why
- Share their ideas with the whole class

Adapted from: Morrison et al., 2015

Lesson preparation

Assemble all materials for each day. As children will only be working on this theme/project for ten days, you should prepare sample sunflower planters one–two weeks in advance, simulating the various conditions described in the activity, so they can see a longer-term example of the various environmental conditions. You may also wish to create a daily weather chart for children to use to chart weather conditions.

Lesson plan components: Introduction

Introduce the lesson by telling the children they are going to act as investigators and reporters during the lesson. Just like professionals investigating and reporting news stories, children are going to investigate the local environment and factors that affect it. Introduce the concept of environment and habitats by holding a class discussion, asking questions such as:

- What is the environment?
- What are habitats?
  - Are there different types of habitats?
  - What are the basic needs of all living things?
  - What happens when these five basic needs are not met?
  - Why is it important for all living things to have these basic needs met at all times?
  - Why do some living things become extinct?
  - Why are their basic needs not met?
  - What can we do to make sure the basic needs of all living things are always met?

Show the video 'This Land is Your Land' www.youtube.com/watch?v=3C4iRf9gOdY asking children to watch for various habitats on the video. Ask children to share what habitats they saw during the video. Document their responses on chart paper and post on classroom wall.

Have children draw two different habitats they have seen (e.g., forest, prairie, desert, wetland, tundra, ocean and mountain). Help children to label the habitats.

Activity/investigation: Weather chart

Use every day for the duration of the theme. Children will chart and graph their local weather to begin to identify and analyse patterns in weather and make connections among climate (the weather conditions over an extended period) and changes in the environment.

At the start of every class:

Have children describe the weather (e.g. sunny, cloudy or rainy) and document their responses?

At the end of the week or month:

Have children identify the numbers of sunny, windy and rainy days in a week/month and document their responses. This introduces children to the concept of pattern analysis in an informal age-appropriate manner?

IBL results in multiple learning outcomes. It provokes intelligence and creativity (Lawson, 2010), enables the acquisition of scientific literacy, vocabulary knowledge, conceptual understanding and attitudes toward science (Minner et al., 2009). It enhances critical thinking, science processing skills, cognitive development (Panasan and Nuangchalerm, 2010), content learning (Minner et al., 2009) as well as discipline-specific reasoning skills and practices (Hmelo-Silver et al., 2007). As such, it is an appropriate strategy for raising awareness of climate education with young children in early childhood classrooms.

Throughout this chapter, we have emphasised children's sense of curiosity, awe and wonder of the world. Children love to explore, particularly in the outdoor environment where they overturn stones and soil to see what lies beneath. Bugs, insects and their habitats fascinate children. Again, these explorations provoke immense discussion, debate and excitement among young children. Introducing items such as birdfeeders, raised planting beds and bug hotels can bring more wildlife into a schoolyard, promote biodiversity and offer opportunities for children to consider how ecosystems work. While a purchased bug hotel can look very pleasing aesthetically, insects may find that homemade hotels provide a more five-star experience as illustrated in Figure 5.2. As shown in the sample activity plan, homemade bug hotels are inexpensive and easy for children to make, exposing children to a wealth of relevant and meaningful learning experiences. Children can design their own hotel, or work in small groups, collect materials and make decisions about their hotels and enjoy looking for guests as the stay in their hotels! Throughout discussions about the children's bug hotel, the importance of biodiversity and our insect population can be highlighted (as illustrated in Figure 5.2 and Table 5.3).

As noted previously, these lesson plans may be implemented as formal aspects of a primary school or early childhood curriculum. However, it is essential not to overlook the incidental learning that occurs throughout the day. There are many teachable moments that teachers can use to their advantage to cultivate awareness of climate education. Indeed, many of these teachable moments, emerging from children's interests often provide the

Figure 5.2 Image of a bug hotel taken in O'Briensbridge, Co. Clare, Ireland

Table 5.3 Activity plan: making a bug hotel

Making a bug hotel

Necessary materials and equipment

- Wooden box or pallets for a larger hotel;
- Bits of old Bamboo sticks;
- Bits of Bark and dead wood;
- Broken old tiles (use for the roof of the hotel);
- Old small bricks with holes;
- Old plant stems;
- Twigs, small logs, dry leaves;
- Straw

Duration: ongoing through different seasons

Directions

1 Children can bring in materials from home and teacher can provide material also.
2 Together access the suitability of the materials and decide on suitable location/s for the bug hotels.
3 Plan together for construction design, children can be creative.
4 Children can construct the bug hotels with assistance from adult, if necessary.
5 Use magnifying glasses to inspect the guests in the hotel.
6 The book *Bug Hotel* by Robin Clover can help introduce the children to different insects.

Discussion

Predict: where is the best place to put the bug hotels and exploring why location may matter (Bees might like sunshine, other insects may like more cool damp conditions)?

What insects might you find in this ecosystem?

Observation

What insects do we observe?

Are there particular areas that are more populated in general?

Do particular species prefer particular areas in the hotel?

Explain

Has wildlife increased in the school yard?

Why do particular species like the hotel or particular areas of the hotel?

---

starting point for follow-on class-based inquiries about weather and climate. Furthermore, this work supports education about biodiversity highlighted in Chapters 7, 10, 11 and 12.

Conclusion

This chapter has provided a rationale for the key role of climate education within the early childhood classroom. It outlines the importance of fostering positive dispositions in young children and provides practical examples of how to support this in the ECE classroom. When fostering young children's positive dispositions, teachers play a vital role in challenging, extending or stretching children's learning throughout the school day. Although climate change information should be introduced in an age-appropriate and developmentally suitable manner in early childhood, knowledge alone is not sufficient, particularly if it is out of context or too abstract. Early childhood teachers are well-placed to nurture and capitalise upon children's innate sense of curiosity about the world and can appreciate how young children learn constantly through all types of experiences. Thus, teachers can use this as a framework to introduce climate education and promote children's sense of personal and collective agency. This chapter illustrates how IBL, using various playful, relevant and mean-ingful learning experiences, can nurture positive dispositions towards learning in the earliest years. When climate education is introduced in an age-appropriate manner, and when it builds upon children's own interests, this approach lays the foundations for an appreciation of the child's immediate environment, leading to more in-depth discussion and exploration over time. It is essential that this learning journey commence in early childhood in order to develop enduring habits of mind that remain with children throughout their lifespan.

Resources

The Windy Day (2012), Anna Milbourne and Elena Temporin, Usborne Publishing Ltd.
Feel the Wind (2001), Arthur Dorros, William Morrow.
Rosie's Hat (2015), Julia Donaldson and Anna Currey (illus). Pan Macmillan Publishers Ltd.
Like a Windy Day (2008), Frank Asch and Devin Asch (illus), Houghton Mifflin.
The Sunny Day (2012), Anna Milbourne and Elena Temporin, Usborne Publishing.
The Magic School Bus and the Climate Challenge (2014), Joanna Cole and Bruce Degen (illus), Scholastic Press.
The Problem of the Hot World (2015), Pam Bonsper and Dick Rink (illus), CreateSpace Independent Publishing Platform
Hello World Weather (2016), Jill McDonald, RH Children's Books.
Giddy Godspeed and the Felicity Flower (2017), Maria-Pilar Landver, Independently published.
May I Come in (2018), Marsha Arnold, Sleeping Bear Press.
The Lonely Polar Bear (2018), Khoa Le, Happy Fox Books.
Only a Tree Knows How to be a Tree (2020), Mary Murphy, Candlewick Press.

Additional websites

- Book Trust: https://www.booktrust.org.uk/booklists/e/environment-childrens/.
- Gardening for biodiversity: https://www.naturenerd.ie/gardening-for-biodiversity.
- Weather symbols for young children: http://www.clipartbest.com/weather-forecast-symbols-for-children.
- Weather songs: https://www.prekinders.com/weather-seasons-songs-kids/.

References

Bronfenbrenner, U. (2005). *Making Human Beings Human: Bioecological Perspectives on Human Development*. London: Sage.
Byrne, J., Rietdijk, W. and Cheek, S. (2016). Inquiry-based science in the infant classroom: "letting go". *International Journal of Early Years Education, 24* (2), 206–223.
Center on the Developing Child, Harvard University (2008). *The Science of Early Brain Development*. Harvard, Author. Available at: https://46y5eh11fhgw3ve3ytpwxt9r-wpengine.netdna-ssl.com/wp-content/uploads/2007/03/InBrief-The-Science-of-Early-Childhood-Development2.pdf.
Center on the Developing Child, Harvard University (2010). *The Foundations of Lifelong Health Are Built in Early Childhood,* Harvard: Author. Available at: https://developingchild.harvard.edu/wp-content/uploads/2010/05/Foundations-of-Lifelong-Health.pdf.

De la Blanca, S., Hidalgo, J. and Burgos, C. (2013). Children's School and Science: The scientific inquiry to understand the surrounding reality. IX International Congress on Research in Didactics of Science (979–983). Retrieved from http://studylib.es/doc/4720850/escuela-infantil-y-ciencia--la-indagación.

Dejonckheere, P., Van de Keere, K., De Wit, N. and Vervaet, S. (2016). Exploring the classroom: Teaching science in early childhood. *International Electronic Journal of Elementary Education, 8* (4), 537–558. Available at: http://xurl.es/t9bx9t of Education and Science (DES) (1999). *Primary School Curriculum*. Dublin: The Stationery Office.

Department for Education (DfE), England (2017). *Statutory Framework for the Early Years Foundation Stage Setting the Standards for Learning, Development and Care for Children from Birth to Five.* Available at: https://assets.publishing.service.gov.uk/government/uploads/system/uploads/attachment_data/file/596629/EYFS_STATUTORY_FRAMEWORK_2017.pdf.

Department of Education, Employment and Workplace Relations (DEEWR) (2009). *Belonging, Being and Becoming. The Early Years Learning Framework for Australia.* Available at: https://education.nt.gov.au/__data/assets/pdf_file/0009/258084/BelongingBeing-Becoming.pdf.

Hmelo-Silver, C.E., Duncan, R.G. and Chinn, C.A. (2007). Scaffolding and achievement in problem based and inquiry learning: A response to Kirschner, Sweller, and Clark (2006). *Education Psychologist, 42* (2), 99–107.

Katz, L. (1993). Dispositions: *Definitions and Implications for Early Childhood Practices.* Perspectives from ERIC/EECE: A Monograph Series, No. 4.

Katz, L. and Chard, S. (2000). *Engaging Children's Minds: The Project Approach* (2nd ed.). Stamford, CT: Ablex.

Kuhlthau, C. C., Maniotes, L. K. and Caspari, A. K. (2007). *Guided Inquiry: Learning in the 21st Century.* Wesport, CT and London: Libraries Unlimited.

Lawson, A.E. (2010). *Teaching Inquiry Science in Middle and Secondary Schools.* Los Angles: Sage.

MacDonald, K. (2016). *Back to the Garten: Inquiry-Based Learning in an Outdoor Kindergarten Classroom.* St. Catherines, Ontario: Brock University. Available at: https://www.dr.library.brocku.ca/bitstream/handle/10464/9325/Brock_MacDonal d_Kate_2016.pdf?

Martin S. (2019). *Circle-time, Selfies, Friends and Food: Researching Children's Voices in Early Years Settings in the Young Knocknaheeny ABC Programme.* Cork: Young Knocknaheeney.

Ministry of Education, New Zealand (2017). *Te Whāriki: Early Childhood Curriculum.* Available at: https://education.govt.nz/assets/Documents/Early-Childhood/ELS-Te-Whariki-Early-Childhood-Curriculum-ENG-Web.pdf.

Ministry of Education, Ontario (2010). *The Full-Day Early Learning – Kindergarten Program* (Draft). Available at: http://www.edu.gov.on.ca/eng/curriculum/elementary/kindergarten_english_june3.pdf.

Minner, D., Levy, A. and Century, J. (2009). Inquiry-based science instruction. What is it and does it matter? Results from a research synthesis years 1984 to 2002. *Journal of Research in Science Teaching, 47* (4), 474–496. Available at: http://xurl.es/gxpbs.

Morrison, V.B., Milner, A.B., Walton, C.C., Johnson, C.C. and Peters-Burton, E.E. (2015). *Optimising the Human Experience, Our Changing Environment.* Indiana: Purdue University. Available at: https://www.doe.in.gov/sites/default/files/elme/kindergarten-lessons-our-changing-environment.pdf.

NCCA (2009). *Aistear: The Early Childhood Curriculum Framework.* Dublin: Author.

NCCA (2015). *Aistear Síolta Practice Guide: Helping Young Children to Develop Positive Learning Dispositions.* Available at https://ncca.ie/media/3193/dispositions-3-6.pdf.

Norwegian Directorate for Education and Training (2017). *Framework Plan for Kindergartens.* Available at: https://www.udir.no/globalassets/filer/barnehage/rammeplan/framework-plan-for-kindergartens2-2017.pdf.

OECD (2019). *Providing Quality Early Childhood Education and Care: Results from the Starting Strong Survey 2018.* Paris: TALIS, OECD Publishing. Available at: https://doi.org/10.1787/301005d1-en.

Oğuz-Ünver, A. and Arabacioğlu, S. (2011). Overviews on inquiry based and problem based learning methods. *Western Anatolia Journal of Educational Sciences (WAJES)*. Special issue: Selected papers presented at WCNTSE. ISSN 1308 – 8971, pp. 303–310.

Panasan, M. and Nuangchalerm, P. (2010). Learning outcomes of project-based and inquiry-based learning activities. *Journal of Social Sciences, 6* (2), 252–255.

Piaget, J., and Cook, M.T. (1952). *The Origins of Intelligence in Children*. New York, NY: International University Press.

UNCRC (1989). United Nations Convention on the Rights of the Child. Geneva: Office of High Commissioner for Human Rights (OHCHR). https://www.ohchr.org/en/professionalinterest/pages/crc.aspx.

Wall, S., Litjens, I. and Taguma, M. (2015). *Pedagogy in Early Childhood Education and Care (ECEC): An International Comparative Study of Approaches and Policies*. Available at: https://assets.publishing.service.gov.uk/government/uploads/system/uploads/attachment_data/file/445817/RB400_-_Early_years_pedagogy_and_policy_an_international_study.pdf.

Section 2

Climate change education: Literacy-based approaches

6 Climate change, picturebooks and primary school children

Mary Roche

Introduction

When I was a child, there was a moment in history when the world's future hung in the balance. It is difficult to believe now, but in 1962, there was an imminent threat of an all-out nuclear war. We prayed in our convent school every day that the world would not end. At home, my father, a member of Civil Defence Casualty Corps, had a box filled with very real-looking artificial wounds and radiation burns, and, as I stuck them on myself and studied the grisly effect, we discussed radioactive fallout and sickness. But I didn't worry too much because I had a job helping my Dad to deliver the booklets that, I was sure, would help people survive if atomic war broke out. In the end, we were spared that horror:

> World relief as Cuban missile crisis ends: The world has breathed a collective sigh of relief after the superpowers reached an agreement ending the immediate threat of nuclear war.
>
> (http://news.bbc.co.uk/onthisday/)

Some people are reluctant to introduce the topic of climate change, or impending ecological collapse, in the primary school, because they worry that it will make children feel helpless and frightened. My reason for relating the anecdote above is to suggest that children might not be overly anxious if they have appropriate information and can take some action. They must first become aware of the beauty of the natural world; second, learn about our interdependency as inhabitants of the world; third, be given information about problems like climate change; fourth, be provided with opportunities to critically discuss and problematise issues to do with climate justice and fifth, feel a sense of agency around taking action to be part of the solution. For teachers, this does not mean a tokenistic approach where children perhaps, fill in a worksheet, draw pictures, create posters or write essays *about* climate change. It means a willingness to tackle critical literacy.

This chapter will:

- Look at the concept of critical literacy
- Explore choosing suitable literature
- Examine discussing Picturebooks: Critical Thinking and Book Talk (CT&BT)
- Provide an exemplar for classroom practice
- Conclusion: Being part of the solution

Critical literacy

Comber (2001) argues that being critically literate is essential in everyday daily life in our western, developed, media-driven, world:

> Critical literacies involve people using language to exercise power, to enhance everyday life in schools and communities, and to question practices of privilege and injustice. … Critical literacy means practicing the use of language in powerful ways to get things done in the world.
>
> (Comber 2001:2)

Critical literacy has no clear definition. It draws on the work of Freire (1972) and from educationalists like those who took up Freire's challenge of literacy for 'reading the world and the word.' Luke and Freebody (1999) changed how many people viewed the literacy learner when they introduced the 'Four Resources' model of literacy. These were: breaking the code; participating in understanding the texts; using texts and analysing texts.

Literacy is seen now as more than reading, writing, listening and speaking. It positions the literacy learner as an active participant in the meaning-making process rather than a passive receiver of information (Freebody and Luke, 2003). In the 'text critic' role or the 'analysing text' practice, there is an understanding that texts are never neutral but represent particular points of view. Critical readers must: acknowledge that texts (and images are included in this understanding of 'text') can manipulate and influence how people think; realise that texts can empower or silence; notice where there are gaps or dominant readings in a text; understand that texts are shaped according to the values of the author; and finally, accept the text's point-of-view or offer an alternative position. As you can see, a superficial reading of a text will not suffice. Children need to be given ample opportunities to read between the lines, and co-construct knowledge through discussion. Teachers need to be text critics too and judiciously choose texts that allow such exploration.

Choosing suitable literature

Drawing on Vygotskian theory, Boggs et al. (2016) suggested that children's literature should stimulate their higher-order pro-social processes. Sometimes adults present sugar-coated versions of 'reality,' forgetting, or not realising, that even young children are quite capable of high levels of understanding if the issues to be thought about or discussed are presented in a way that makes sense to them. We need to select 'quality literature that stimulates children's contextualized understanding of Earth's changing climate' (665).

I am not arguing that books themselves will change attitudes or habits or even raise awareness. What has influenced children are the discussions that we have had where the children were listened to seriously by their peers and by their teacher, as they formed, refined and articulated their thinking. Boggs et al. (2016) argue that children's books on climate change invite students to expand their understanding of difficult scientific concepts that affect their day-to-day lives. They suggest that as students engage with these texts, they can learn how they can make a difference in the world.

> For teachers, the task of choosing classroom texts is a multidimensional process that must combine the characteristics of high- quality children's literature with a focus on the quality of the climate change message (666–667).

Books for raising awareness of the beauty of the natural world

Before we can present climate change as an issue to be discussed, however, we need to expose children to literature that will encourage them to appreciate the wonders of the earth, to explore how children live in other areas of the earth and to empathise with those who are disadvantaged by the socio-political contexts in which they live. The latter is important for bringing about an awareness of climate justice. We need children to see that the changes they make and the actions they take must go beyond the immediate local environment.

In Roche (2015), I explained how the book *'Think of an Eel'* (Wallace and Bostock, 2008) raised gasps from my class of 8- and 9-year-olds. This book has rich lyrical language, beautiful illustrations and an abundance of information about the life-cycle of the eel. If I were using this book again, I would extend the discussion around the current problems of plastic waste in the ocean and explore with the children how we might raise awareness about recycling plastic in the school. We could approach our local shops and supermarkets to discourage the overuse of plastic packaging. We could approach the local deli to promote awareness of the dangers of single-use plastic straws, cups and cutlery. We could also look at the food chain of which the eel is a part and ask: 'how and why would it matter if eels became extinct?'

There are hundreds of beautiful fiction and non-fiction books, that could be used to build up an awareness and love of nature: for example Baker-Smith's (2018) *The Rhythm of the Rain*; Davies and Chapman's (2015) *One Tiny Turtle*; Davies and Fox-Davies' (2015) *Bat Loves the Night*; King-Smith and Jeram's (2008) *All Pigs are Beautiful*; MacFarlane and Morris' (2017) *The Lost Words*; Soundar and Mistry's (2018) *You're Safe with Me*; Teckentrup's (2018a) *Birds and Their Feathers*; Thomas and Egnéus' (2018) *Moth* and Waters and Preston-Gannon's (2018) *I Am the Seed that Grew the Tree*.

Our interdependency as inhabitants of the world

Children need to be shown how we all inhabit this one planet called Earth. Books that can be used to illustrate our interdependency include: Heinz and Marstall's (2000) *Butternut Hollow Pond*; Schimmel's (1994) *Dear Children of the Earth*; Teckentrups' (2018b) *We are Together*, (2017) *Under the Same Sky* and Godkin's (2007) *Wolf Island*.

Information about global warming and climate change

Before we can discuss solutions, we need to understand the problem. The following picturebooks are useful resources: Bonsper and Rink's (2015) *The Problem of the Hot World*; Donnelly and MacAree's (2019) *The Great Irish Weather Book*; Foreman's (2017) *Hello Mr World*; Herman and Hinderliter's (2018) *What is Climate Change?* and Kurlansky and Stockton's (2014) *A World Without Fish*.

Discussing picturebooks

It is important that teachers are very careful in their choices of picturebooks for discussing topic as sensitive and serious as climate change and ecological conservation. If we accept that readers are positioned by the writer's points of view, then we adults need to ensure that the point of view is one agreed by naturalists and climate experts – and not one taken by climate change deniers, or those with vested interests:

> …texts have designs on us as readers, listeners or viewers. They entice us into their way of seeing and understanding the world into their version of reality.
>
> (Janks, 2010:61)

Of course, older children could compare and contrast the positions taken in different texts and media reports regarding climate change, but that is not our brief here. We are discussing the use of picturebooks specifically.

Literacy researchers have argued that although critical literacy skills are complex, even young children can learn and use them in their everyday literacy work (Comber and Simpson, 2001; Leland and Harste, 2000; Vasquez, 2003). Young children can be helped to see that even a simple story such as 'You're Snug with Me' (Soundar and Mistry, 2018) can have layers of meaning. The story opens 'in the far north' where Mama Polar Bear has given birth to two cubs. Like most toddlers, they are bursting with questions about their world. As Mama patiently answers them, they learn that their frozen home might be threatened. She tells them, however, that they will never go hungry – as long as the ice stays frozen. She teaches them about the importance of safeguarding the delicate balance of nature – the ice will only melt if we don't take care of it. And, as she teaches them (and us), Mama also reassures them with the refrain 'you're snug with me.' As the little cubs' knowledge grows, young readers' knowledge grows too. On the surface, it is a reassuring baby-animal-and-mother-animal tale. But there is a gentle, yet strong, factual environ-mental message too. We learn that even the coldest places on our earth are endangered by climate change, and that we share responsibility. I'm sure that any teacher could see the potential here for using such a book to stimulate discussion and possibly, action.

Before we examine how we can use such picturebooks for classroom discussion about climate change, we need to explore the CT&BT (Roche, 2010, 2015) pedagogical approach, as recommended in the new Primary Language Curriculum (Ireland, 2008, 2013).

Critical Thinking and Book Talk (CT&BT)

For many years I have been encouraging children to discuss picturebooks through an approach I call CT&BT. Initially, my aim was to help children develop their oral language or oracy skills. Gradually, I realised that there was far more going on as they argued and debated the meaning. I began to see that they were thinking critically, and that the process was a dialogical approach to critical literacy.

The CT&BT approach seems like a simple enough approach. You will need a 'good' picture book, a child or a group of children who can see the pictures and hear the story and who will discuss the book, using previously negotiated rules of respectful behaviour. The children sit in a circle, with the teacher sitting with them. The book is displayed slowly via the visualiser or using scans of each page. Children must have time to study the illustrations as the story is read aloud. They then discuss the book, prompted by questions the book has raised for the children or by a question from the teacher/adult, who is a *par-ticipant* in the discussion. The children take turns democratically in sharing ideas, agreeing or disagreeing with each other and with the teacher (Ireland, 2008, 2013). Research shows that learning grows, and knowledge is produced in classrooms that are dialogic commu-nities (Alexander, 2018; Mercer, 2000; Roche, 2007, 2015).

Exemplar: Using 'You're Snug with Me' in a classroom

The children are seated initially in a semi-circle facing the whiteboard where, initially the cover of the book is being displayed. The teacher introduces the process by reminding the children that: *'Each time we discuss a book together, we create knowledge – and think thoughts that no one might ever have thought before. If the talk goes to the right (clockwise) around the circle, then we will think different thoughts than if it goes to the left (or anti-clockwise). This is because we get ideas when we listen to what other people are saying. So, let's remind ourselves of the golden rules: looking carefully, listening carefully, thinking hard, replying respectfully when it is our turn, and no interrupting. The author and the illustrator had a reason for making this book. We will try to discover any hidden messages in the pictures or the words.'* [NOTE: DO NOT TELL THEM WHAT YOU THINK THE BOOK IS ABOUT.]

The teacher reads the story, pausing and allowing the children ample time to view the images which are beamed up for all to see. They can initially discuss the cover image and try to infer what the book might be about.

When the story is finished, the teacher invites the children to close their eyes and individually think of how they felt as the story was read, what they thought, if anything puzzled them. Then invite them to share one idea quietly with the person next to them. Then the circle is closed so that the discussion can begin.

The teacher then says: *'Now we will begin the discussion: who would like to start?'* If there is a volunteer, then she reminds them that when they are finished, they must 'pass the tip on' (gently tap the shoulder) of the person either to their right or left. Then each person speaks, or passes on the tip, with the teacher waiting her turn for the tip to come to her. [This will become quite automatic after a few experiences of the process. In the first few sessions also, the teacher, when it is her turn, can model and or teach the language of *'I agree with X … because … and I disagree with X because … or I kind of agree/disagree because ….'* The 'because' is very important: children must supply reasons for their statements).

If no-one volunteers to start, then the teacher can begin by asking an open-ended question, such as *'I wonder does the Mama Bear feel as safe as the baby bears?'* and she 'tips' the person to her right or left.

The discussion goes around the circle until it is back to the first speaker. If there were children who were not ready to speak and who passed in the first circuit, the teacher invites a 'hands-up' if they wish to speak now. If the class is eager to keep talking, let another circuit begin. As a wrap-up, the teacher could invite the children to tell the person beside them something new that they learned or some new thought they had.

Teachers should resist the temptation to immediately follow the discussion with what children call 'work' – we are not looking for a product here, merely better thinking and understanding. It can demotivate those children who do not shine with pencil or crayon, if they feel that every discussion will be followed by a task. However, canny teachers will choose books that lend themselves to cross curricular links – in this case, the next Geography lesson could focus on shrinking Polar Ice and children could use the knowledge they have generated through their discussion, to suggest some actions they could take.

Note: See Ireland (2008, 2013) and Roche (2015) for further examples of how to do the 'CT&BT' process.

Figure 6.1 Cover image *You're Snug with Me*

Copyright: Lantana Publishing Limited

Critical thinking

Critical thinking is thinking for oneself. In the exemplar above, we notice that at no time are the children being told what to think. This is important. To be able to think for oneself is necessary for making sense and meaning of our lives and our world. Without it, we risk being mere receivers and consumers of others' knowledge. Critical *thinking* is essential for critical *literacy*. Critical thinking about literacy enables us to see it as a 'highly complex socio-cultural practice' (Hall et al., 2016:286). Many educators (Comber, 2001; Leland et al., 2013) see critical thinking and critical literacy as requirements for challenging the taken-for-granted assumptions, values and norms of the world. Other critical pedagogues think that we should not only challenge such norms but transform them.

In a chapter entitled 'The future of critical literacy,' Janks (2010:203–234) provides a serious overview of the 'on-going socio-historical imperative for critical literacy' (203). She speaks about how information becomes altered through 'spin' and how necessary critical literacy is: 'in a world of spin critical literacy helps us to understand whose interests are served by the stories we are told and the stories we tell' (204). However, she concludes on a hopeful note when she says: 'Critical literacy work in classrooms can be simultaneously serious and playful. We should teach it with a subversive attitude, self-irony and a sense of humour' (234).

This last point is really important: if we are dealing with young children, then we must choose our texts with care and pose our questions sensitively. We must never destroy their innocence or make them anxious about the world or the future. This is tricky with a subject as scary as global warming and climate change. Children need to feel a sense of empowerment and agency (Roche, 2015).

Opportunities to discuss and problematise issues to do with climate justice – An example from practice

In 2002, I read '*Oi! Get Off Our Train*' (Burningham, 1991) and discussed it with a class of 5- and 6-year-old Senior Infants. The children displayed remarkable understanding about why the animals might want to get on the train. They talked about the shrinking polar icecaps, the draining of marshes and how people need 'roads, houses food and stuff and so trees get cut down.' Then the discussion took a turn:

S: 'some tigers are evil because they try to kill people.'
    I asked him if the people who kill tigers were evil in that case.
S: No. they're actually not sort of evil – they're sort of greedy. Cos all they're doing that for is the money. They're killing animals for money, which is actually destroying the world.
    The discussion went on to the issue of whether there were good animals and bad animals. The children began to classify 'biters and stingers' as bad, and 'cuddly' animals as good.
EN: I'm thinking about good and bad animals – well cats do a little bit of good: they eat the mice and rats and things, but what about snakes – they just bite you.
A: I think I can answer the question about why animals bite you – they don't know that you're afraid of them, but they do know that they're afraid of you.
                                            (Research notes 2001–2006 in Roche, 2007)

Eventually, there was some consensus around deciding that animals were neither bad nor good, but that, perhaps, we humans ascribe human characteristics to them. The children were unwilling to let the topic go and they returned to it again and again over the next few days. I used to have regular meetings with parents to view videoclips and read transcripts (as part of my PhD research). Some parents told me that the children had begun to show an interest in nature programmes on the TV, that they requested nature books from the library and that 'they were remarkably well informed' about endangered species and the consequences for us. The thing is – I didn't 'inform them' – we just read and discussed books. The children themselves had amazing levels of prior knowledge.

The following year I was teaching 3rd class. We discussed '*Dear Greenpeace*' (James, 2006). Again, the conversation ranged widely, and the children amazed me with their understanding of the threats to ocean life and to animals 'even as big as whales.' Then, as always, the discussion took a philosophical turn as to whether animals could think, and what they might think about. And, if they could think and feel emotions, was it right to farm them and eat them? And was it right that so much land was given to pasture when, as M said, 'it could be used for growing food crops for humans?' Their awareness of animals as sentient creatures may well inform future life choices. During that year, several discussions were initiated in the course of Geography lessons about climate change and deforestation and slash-and-burn practices. One lesson on the Amazon was completely hijacked into a discussion about food industries like McDonalds. C immediately suggested that we should 'be videoing the discussion, for our research' and proceeded to get the tri-pod, camera and microphone out of the cupboard. The discussion raised huge questions about globalisation. One boy, JO'M, stated that he suspected that 'McDonalds and Disney were friends' because the toys in the Happy Meal boxes were usually marketing products for children's films (Roche, 2007).

I recently met some of those now adult students. We spoke about their classroom discussions and the first one they all recalled was 'the McDonald discussion.' We watched some clips from the video from 2006.

> K said that, following that discussion, she understood how parents were exposed to 'pester power' in fast-food restaurants, the psychology of the colours used, the use of standardised 'American food' all over the world. She said she became an activist, talking her family and friends out of eating fast-food.
>
> P felt that being able to do some research, being empowered to take some action helped allay fear and anxiety.
>
> This was agreed by the group – they all said that when you feel that you can do something, you feel less frightened. I reminded them of the day of the Lord Mayor's visit, when the Principal was amazed at how they had spoken up about littering, the need for recycling centres, and the absence of safe playgrounds in their area, and how he later congratulated them.
>
> JB also now in her 20s said: 'it was about more than that though – discussing the picturebooks, agreeing and disagreeing with each other; learning that some solutions are complex because some issues are a contest of two or more rights – all of this helped us to find our voice, use our voice and make us accept each other as people. It made us better human beings.'
>
> JB added that during that year, because of all the discussions we had had, she became highly concerned about water and energy conservation and recycling and 'drove her family mad.' She then said: 'it has influenced my whole life: because our awareness was raised about all these issues to do with conservation, climate change, women's rights, I decided to do Development Studies and specialise in micro-funding women in poorer countries.'
>
> (Research notes, Dec 2016)

The videos of that interview with JB, and of the meeting with the now-adult former students show that as teachers, we can never underestimate the ripple effect of the lessons we teach, the messages we convey and most of all how dialogue and discussion lead to sustainable attitudinal change.

Conclusion: Being part of the solution

We need to create in children a sense of agency around 'being part of the solution.' Echterling (2016) argues that much of the eco-citizen education of young people focuses too heavily on making small lifestyle changes in the private sphere and explains how that is not enough to make any dent in the serious global issues facing us as a human race. For very young children, small local changes may be all they can do, though. Striking a balance between raising awareness without causing anxiety is tricky. One practical activity that we did that year was the 'Green Wave' Project where we did some research on when certain trees budded. This was added to a national project and the greening of Ireland was visible on an animated map when all the data was collated. Several students remember this as something that made them aware of their native trees, and of hedgerow cutting and nesting.

> P, now in his 20s said: I suppose the biggest environmental themed thing I remember was the green wave project we took part in as a class, where we investigated signs of Spring approaching. Like, we measured rainfall and had a calendar sheet to track when leaves started to bud on trees locally. It was certainly something that made an impact.
>
> He added: I remember a kind of personal protest where I stopped eating KitKats because I knew they used palm oil that was harvested from shrinking orangutan habitats.
>
> C, now 22 said: It did raise awareness. We said what we thought and felt. It showed us how we impact others and the planet, a rather advanced topic for 'children.' These books and talks showed how we as children knew more than we acknowledged, and when given the chance to speak in a comfortable and 'safe' environment, we were able to state what we knew, understood and interpreted about the world and how things were going. It definitely changed how I viewed ecological issues.
>
> (Research notes)

Discussing picturebooks with children is only a start, but what it can do is help create articulate critical thinkers who demand evidence and who think for themselves as responsible and active citizens of the world.

Children's books

Baker-Smith, G. (2018) *The Rhythm of the Rain*. London: Templar Publishing.

Bonsper, P. and Rink, D. (illus.) (2015) *The Problem of the Hot World*. California: CreateSpace Independent Publishing Platform.

Burningham, J. (1991) *Oi! Get Off Our Train*. New York: Red Fox.

Davies, N. and Chapman, J. (illus.) (2015) *One Tiny Turtle*. New York: Penguin Random House.

Davies, N. and Fox-Davies, S. (illus.) (2015) *Bat Loves the Night*. London: Walker Books.

Donnelly, J. and MacAree, F. (2019) *The Great Irish Weather Book*. Dublin: Gill Books.

Foreman, M. (2017) *Hello Mr World*. London: Walker Books.

Godkin, C. (2007) *Wolf Island*. Toronto: Fitzhenry & Whiteside.

Heinz, B.J. and Marstall, B. (illus.) (2000) *Butternut Hollow Pond*. MN: Millbrook Press.

Herman, G. and Hinderliter, J. (illus.) (2018) *What is Climate Change?* New York: Penguin

James, S. (2016) *Dear Greenpeace*. London: Walker Books.

King-Smith, D. and Jeram, A. (illus.) (2008) *All Pigs are Beautiful*. New York: Penguin Random House.

Kurlansky, M. and Stockton, F. (illus.) (2014) *A World Without Fish*. New York: Workman Publishing.

MacFarlane, R. and Morris, J. (illus.) (2017) *The Lost Words*. New York: Hamish Hamilton.

Schimmel, S. (1998) *Dear Children of the Earth*. US: Northword Press.

Soundar, C. and Mistry, P. (illus.) (2018) *You're Snug with Me*. Oxford: Lantana Publishing Limited.

Teckentrup, B. (2017) *Under the Same Sky*. Munich: Prestel.

Teckentrup, B. (2018a) *Birds and Their Feathers*. Munich: Prestel.

Teckentrup, B. (2018b) *We are Together*. Munich: Prestel.

Thomas, I. and Daniel Egnéus (illus.) (2018) *Moth*. London: Bloomsbury Children's Books.

Wallace, K. and Bostock, M. (illus.) (2008) *Think of an Eel.* London: Walker Books.

Waters, F. and Preston-Gannon (illus.) (2018) *I Am the Seed That Grew the Tree: A Nature Poem for Every Day of the Year.* London: Nosy Crow.

References

Alexander, R.J. (2018) Developing dialogic teaching: genesis, process, trial. *Research Papers in Education,* 33(5): 561–598.

BBC: On this Day. Available: <http://news.bbc.co.uk/onthisday/hi/dates/stories/october/28/newsid_2621000/2621915.stm≥ accessed 20-02-19.

Boggs, G.L., Wilson, N.S., Ackland, R.T., Danna, S. and Grant, K.B. (2016) *The Reading Teacher,* 69(6): 665–675.

Comber, B. (2001) Critical literacies and local action: Teacher knowledge and a new research agenda. In Comber, B. and Simpson, A. (Eds.), *Negotiating Critical Literacies in Classrooms* (271–282). Mahwah, NJ: Erlbaum.

Comber, B. & Simpson, A. (Eds.) (2001) *Negotiating Critical Literacies in Classrooms.* Mahwah, NJ: Erlbaum.

Echterling, C. (2016) How to save the world and other lessons from children's environmental literature. *Children's Literature in Education,* 47:283–299.

Freebody, P. and Luke, A. (2003) Literacy as engaging with new forms of life: The 'four roles' model. In G. Bull and M. Anstey (Eds), *The Literacy Lexicon* (2nd edn) (51–66). Frenchs Forest, NSW: Pearson Education Australia.

Freire, P. (1972) *Pedagogy of the Oppressed.* London: Sheed and Ward.

Hall, K., Cremin, T., Comber, B. and Moll, L. (2016) *International Handbook of Research on Children's Literacy, Learning and Culture.* Chichester, Sussex: Wiley-Blackwell.

Ireland: National Council for Curriculum Assessment, NCCA (2008) *Assessment in the Primary School Curriculum – Guidelines for Schools,* Available: <https://curriculumonline.ie/getmedia/b124cf04-457c-4360-80ab-e1371b1ad1f9/SM_Critical-Thinking-Book-Talk2.pdf?ext=.pdf> Accessed 01-03-19.

Ireland: National Council for Curriculum Assessment, NCCA (2013) *Aistear Toolkit* Available: <http://action.ncca.ie/resource/Childrens-thinking-and-talking/65> Accessed 01-03-19.

Ireland: National Council for Curriculum Assessment, NCCA (2017) *Primary Language Curriculum Ireland: NCCA.* Support Materials: Available: <https://www.curriculumonline.ie/getmedia/e08e89b8-bc55-4fca-a6cb-2a8ccc3e24f3/List_SM_Onsite.pdf> Accessed 01-03-19.

Janks, H. (2010) *Literacy and Power.* New York and Abingdon, Oxon: Routledge.

Leland, C., Lewison, M. and Harste, J. (2013) *Teaching Children's Literature: It's Critical!* New York and London: Routledge.

Leland, C.H. and Harste, J.C. (2000) Critical literacy: Enlarging the space of the possible. *Primary Voices K–6,* 9(2): 3–7.

Luke, A. and Freebody, P. (1999) A map of possible practices: Further notes on the four resources model. *Practically Primary,* 4: 5–8.

Mercer, N. (2000) *Words and Minds.* London and New York: Routledge.

Roche, M. (2007) *Towards a Living Theory of Caring Pedagogy: Interrogating My Practice to Nurture a Critical, Emancipatory and Just Community of Enquiry,* unpublished PhD thesis, University of Limerick. Available: < http://www.eari.ie >Accessed 01-03-19.

Roche, M. (2010) 'Critical Thinking and Book Talk: Using Picturebooks to Promote Discussion and Critical Thinking in the Classroom'. *Reading News.* Autumn 2010. Literacy Association of Ireland (np).

Roche, M. (2015) *Developing Children's Critical Thinking Through Picturebooks: A Guide for Primary and Early Years Students and Teachers.* Abingdon: Routledge.

Vasquez, V. (2003) *Getting Beyond "I like the book": Creating Space for Critical Literacy in K–6 Classrooms.* Newark, DE: International Reading Association.

7 Listening, re-acting and acting

Stories from plants and animals to elicit empathy and dialogue about climate change, in the classroom and beyond

Miriam Hamilton

Introduction

Biodiversity and healthy ecosystems are crucial to human wellbeing and the survival of all life on planet Earth. Nonetheless, vast numbers of plant and animal species are under significant threat from climate change. Toxic outputs, habitat destruction and intensive agricultural and industrial practices are having a significant impact on other living things sharing this planet with us. This chapter enables teachers and teacher educators to appreciate how storytelling provides a powerful framework for teaching and learning about climate change with children. The chapter illustrates ways in which learners can explore and evaluate the effects of climate change, through stories that highlight the perspectives of a particular group of unique living things. The stories are written in the voice of the organisms with some suggested activities for teachers to explore the plights of these five diverse living things under significant threat from climate change. Teacher, teacher educators and children are invited to enter the intimate worlds of living things from across the continents.

Read on to experience how the narrative stimulates in-depth interactions with the *colourful coral*, the *powerful polar bear*, the *busy bee*, the *ancient sea turtle* and the *alpine flora*. Using dialogical methodologies motivated by the stories of these plants and animals from the air, land and sea, the chapter provides thought-provoking scenarios of danger, balanced with activities focused on exploring actions of hope to save these species. There are key scientific, biological and moral moments embedded in the stories to be explored by the teacher and their class. Importantly, the stories aim to engender empathy through the structuring of group-based reflective dialogue among the children, their teachers and parents.

Each of the five stories that follow are conceptualised to be versatile; for use in a scheme of work to examine climate change and its effects, or as integrated learning moments used to create connections between diverse concepts in the primary classroom. Teachers may use the stories to arouse children's initial interest and curiosity in climate change, and in this way, they can operate as powerful stimuli to engage a class, before further discussion and dialogue. They can also form the basis of investigative group-based tasks in a lesson or series of lessons. The integrated learning can be further exploited if used in conjunction with suggested questions, thinking pauses and calls to action, suggested for the teacher following the story texts. It is important to note that the suggested methodologies are not intended to be prescriptive, but offer a broad template of ideas for the teacher to adapt to their context, class or teaching approach. A digital illustration follows each story to bring the stories to life in a visual way for children.

This chapter dovetails in a useful way with Chapter 6 where Mary Roche presents an argument for the use of appropriate literature to develop critical literacy skills among children. Mary provides many suggestions for suitable reading material to foster awareness of the beauty of the natural world among children and provides a theoretical rationale for text, literature and story to be central resources to awaken curiosity, imagination and criticality among children. This chapter supports many of the central facets of Mary's argument in the stories and resources focused on living things, for use, adaptation and modification with children in the primary classroom.

The ancient sea turtle

Psst … Come over here … no closer. You hardly expect me to come over there to all of you, when I am carrying this heavy bony load on my back, not to mention trying to walk on these big awkward limbs. Look at me, is it any wonder I spend most of my time at sea? How would you like to carry your house around, and unlike those annoying tortoises that people are always confusing me with, I cannot even bring my head and limbs inside. Now that is much better, you can see me and I can see you, well hello! My name is *Dermochelys Coriacea,* but you can call me *Dermo.* Well, you are probably wondering why a leatherback sea turtle like me is talking to you. You see I have a problem I am hoping you might help me with … but first let me tell you a little more about me, so we can become friends.

Well, I am a relative of the first true sea turtles from the cretaceous period, who lived on Earth 110 million years ago. My ancestors shared the Earth with the dinosaurs for a long time and we outlived the dinosaurs, but are in a bit of trouble today. *I will explain why a little later.* There are 6 other species of sea turtle and myself, the leatherback, but I am the oldest and the biggest, measuring up to 2 metres long and weighing around 700 kg. There are many pictures of me online, have a look!

I can dive deep down into the sea and if I have to, I can hold my breath for a whole hour. Do not try that mere humans, us sea turtles are born with these special skills. How do you think my body helps me survive living in the Atlantic, Pacific and Indian oceans to find those juicy jellyfish to feast on? Remember, I am the one who protects you from jellyfish stings because one of my jobs is to keep their numbers under control and what fun I have preying on those glistening tasty treats. I love the sea, swimming fast and diving. I expect some of you enjoy that too, but sometimes we have to come to land to lay eggs so our babies can hatch. This is where our problems start. Let me tell you why.

Unfortunately, we cannot see very well out of the water and did you know they don't make glasses for sea turtles … so finding a quiet beach is becoming hard because there seem to be humans everywhere. The seas have also become so busy and I hear you have a similar problem with all those cars on your roads. But these are not my only problems. There is a much more recent problem and a very deadly one. You see, your plastic rubbish, especially the clear or white type, looks just like a tasty jellyfish to me and my sea turtle friends. We cannot tell the difference. In the last few years, our human scientist friends who are trying to help us found that many sea turtles died because they ate waste plastic rubbish from the sea.

My sea turtle friends and I are now endangered, and there are not that many of us left. I know you may not realise this but you could really help us. Would you help us? Great, so what I need you to do is not too hard. Could you reduce how much plastic you use, especially with the grocery shopping and recycle as much as you can so the plastic does not find its way into the sea? Maybe you could discuss what else you might do this at school with your teacher or at home. It has been fun talking to you and I feel confident that after hearing from me and hearing about my story, you and your friends will help me. If you do, I promise I will help you back, by continuing to control the jellyfish. We can help each other … isn't that what we living things should do?

The alpine flora

Hello to all you boys and girls out there! Do you know that not only animals but plants too are suffering because of climate change? Even worse, some groups of plants are at risk of disappearing forever. Could you imagine how sad that would be?

My name is Flora and I am an alpine plant living high in the beautiful mountains of the world. This means I am especially good at growing in very high places where most plants would never survive. I can seek out little spaces between rocks on mountains, where I can firmly attach myself to grow strong. I stay low to the ground and this protects me from the wind, rain and snow. My narrow stem is designed not to freeze, so I am happy in cold places; well, happier than most other plants would be. It can be rather chilly at times. I am able to survive with very little water because I have small leaves that keep the water in, and I can produce flowers quickly once the warmth of summer comes. This allows me to make new seeds faster than other plants. Really, us alpine flora are amazing, and very unique plants.

The problem we have is that the constant warming of the Earth is making us move further and further up the mountain, where really there is a limit as to how high living things can survive. I like the high mountains but not the barren sections at the top. There is no easy way to attach and grow there; it is too harsh a place to live. Some of my plant neighbours from further down the mountain have been causing trouble for us lately. As it is getting warmer and warmer each year, some of the plants from lower down are moving up and trying to take the spaces of the alpine plants. We have to fight to keep our community together as some of the invading plants are faster than we are at growing, so we are being forced upwards to a place we cannot survive. It is very worrying and if only the plants from below would stay where they belong.

The solution to my families' problem is very clear. The invading plants will stop pushing us up if their area cools down. That is what they say anyway. They are moving up because they like a certain cool temperature like us. We need to cool things down, literally!

You humans could really help us by using less energy and releasing fewer gases from your cars, homes and industries. Simple steps you could take to save energy include: walking to school, riding your bike, saving water by turning off the tap while brushing your teeth and saving electricity by turning off the lights when you leave a room. If you like walking in the mountains or on other rocky trails, please do not walk on me or collect me. Feel free to take many photos though. I know I look nice when in flower, but I need to stay where I am to ensure there are seeds for the new population of alpine flora. I hope that while we are fixing the planet's temperatures, that you might look after those of us who are hanging on in there. I believe you will help the plants as well as the cute animals, remember we all need each other and we all have a very important job to do.

The busy bee

So much to do … busy, busy, dash, rush, fly here and there, flowers to visit, pollen to collect …

Well, hello and how are you children this fine day? Let me stop and take a breath to chat to you today. Apologies, how rude of me, I haven't introduced myself. My name is Bertie and I am a very busy bee. You may be wondering why I am so busy. Let me explain. Are you comfortable and ready to listen?

Okay, here goes. Just after I was born in my hive, a child of our queen bee, I began work immediately as a hive cleaner. Did you know that bees are very clean and the queen refuses to lay her eggs without a spotless hive? I have 70,000 in my family now, so a very busy household, as you can imagine. How many people are in your family? My second job was much more fun than cleaning the hive because I nursed the newborn baby bees, as well as helping build the honeycomb for our hive by collecting pollen and nectar from lots of flowers. This keeps me very busy indeed. Those little balls of busy bee fluff are just so cute and need lots of care and attention from us older bees. Now that I am fully mature, my job is to be a forager for the rest of my life. A very tiring and busy job, but I do love it. Every day I forage for nectar and pollen to make honey, to feed our large bee population.

You might not know how much I help you humans as I fly from flower to flower. Sometimes, I accidently drop some of my pollen and this helps with *pollination*. I am not going to talk much about pollination today but your teacher might chat with you about that later. Pollination helps plants to make new baby plants. What is very important is that honeybees like me are needed for the growth of new plants, because we are *pollinators*. This means we help with transporting the pollen needed for new baby plants to form. We are good at pollinating cocoa, vanilla, strawberries and many other fruits and crops. If you enjoy chocolate treats and vanilla flavoured foods, I am your friend.

Sadly, our honeybee populations have been declining for a number of years now, which is quite worrying. We love to have a wide choice of different flowers to hop on and hop off. This keeps us very healthy, just like humans needing a balanced diet with lots of different type of food from the different food groups. When humans grow one type of plant over huge areas for human or animal food, we really struggle. Last week, in order to get a balanced diet, I had to search for miles for something different to eat. I was exhausted getting home to the hive. Also, the nectar has tasted a little strange lately. We hear that humans are spraying their crops with lots of chemicals, and these are not nice or safe for us bees to eat. Wouldn't you get bored of eating the same food every day, and think '*Yuck*' if you knew bad tasting chemicals were sprayed onto it? Sometimes we get so tired and sick, we do not survive and the honeybee populations, my species, my family, are getting smaller every year.

The good news is each one of you can help me by doing just two small things. Would you like to know what they are? Okay, so listen carefully. If you have a garden, please do not cut the grass so often. Let me enjoy the daisies, buttercups and dandelions because these are some of my favourite flowers. Also, if you could find a few old containers and plant some wildflower seeds, ones with wide open flowers are just great for collecting pollen and nectar, so these would be amazing. Perhaps this is something you might consider doing at school if you cannot at home. It would be my food dream come true, just like you arriving at a party and seeing the things you most like to eat … except maybe my flowers are a little healthier than your favourites!

Thank you for helping me out with this. I am very grateful and in return will make plenty of honey for you to enjoy with your pancakes for many years to come.

The colourful coral

Hey everybody, my name is Cora. What is the weather like where you are? I can't see much down here in the coral reef today. The water is murky, not too clean. I wish I could see the blue skies through the clear water as it used to be …

Forgive me; I must explain a little more about who I am in case some of you have not heard of me. I live in the Great Barrier Reef in Australia, the largest reef in the world, and it is visible from space, so I hear. Did you know that corals have existed on Earth for over 400 million years, and we are related to jellyfish? We live happily together in groups called colonies in shallow tropical waters. We provide shelter and homes for thousands of species of fish and we are often referred to as 'The rainforest of the seas'. I have heard that some people think we are not alive, because we do not move about much. Let me assure you that we are very much alive, but we are also fragile and sensitive animals. I don't mean sensitive in the feelings way, what I mean is small changes to the water like a change to the temperature can hurt us or even kill us.

Coral reefs where lots of us live are essential to you humans. We give you food, medicines and tourism, as coral reefs have some of the most beautiful colours you have ever seen. I love living here but things are not too good here now. This is because a huge number of the world's reefs have been lost and many more like mine are in big trouble. Remember I mentioned I couldn't see the sky lately. This is not just sad for me but also very dangerous. You see what is happening is that when trees are cut down, you know, to build houses and factories for humans, the waste and bits left over wash into the seas and block out the light, oxygen for breathing and the algae that give us our great colour cannot make food. The same happens when rubbish, dirt, oil and chemicals wash into the seas.

The other thing that has been happening is that it has also been getting far too warm lately. Don't get me wrong, I love the warm water like you do at the beach, but if it gets too warm, the algae I share my home with leave and no longer make the food I need to survive. I also lose my wonderful colours and turn pure white. I like being a colourful coral, so this is not good.

So, I have three favours to ask you so that I can see the sun again. These favours will help me especially if your whole class or even school could do them. Are you ready?

Favour number 1: if you could waste less water by turning off the tap when you brush teeth, and stop taking showers that would be great! Okay, I am joking about the showers, you do need those, but 5 minutes is plenty! Saving water means less wastewater returns to the seas.

Favour number 2: try not to forget your rubbish when you go to the beach, take it with you and if you can recycle it, even better. This prevents solid waste getting into the seas, which is much safer for coral.

Favour number 3: the water needs to cool down a little, so we need to burn less fuels that make the gases that warm the planet up. I know you do not light the fire or drive the car, but you could cycle or walk more. Carpool or take the bus instead of all of you each taking your car on every journey. Hey, you would get some more exercise too and be heathier, if you used the car less.

Ohh my goodness, look at the time! I must go now because groups of tourists are coming to snorkel by and see how good I look today. I hope that when we chat again, you can tell me what you have been doing and maybe the sun will come out again for all of us. Here's to hoping!

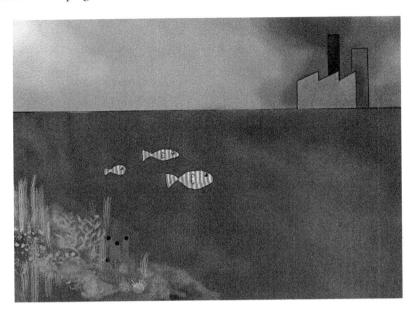

The powerful polar bear

Dear Children,

I am writing to you with a very heavy heart. My name is Pete and I am a powerful polar bear from the Arctic Ocean. Have a look at a map or globe, and you will see my home of sea ice. I am the largest land carnivore in the world and so I only eat meat, no vegetables or fruit for me. Of course, you do need to have your lots of fruit, because humans are omnivores and eat a more varied diet than me. I weigh as much as 10 men and am a brilliant swimmer with big paws for pulling myself through the water. I hunt alone and only like eating seals. It isn't good to be a fussy eater as seals are fast and very hard to find.

I need the sea ice so that I can search for seals to eat and when I was younger, there was plenty of ice and plenty of seals for me to hunt and eat. The seals live at the edges of the ice and for many years now the sea ice area has started becoming smaller and smaller, because it is melting year by year. The atmosphere is getting warmer and melting the ice, a little like an ice-lolly on a hot day. It drips and turns to back to liquid. With less ice to hunt on and more and more of the ice melting earlier every year, I now have a very short time to hunt and have to survive long spells without food. I do not like being hungry and I imagine you don't either, it feels bad.

When I am very hungry, this sometimes means I have to steal food from humans and they do not like me coming around bothering them. We try to stay away from each other and do our own thing. I do not want to visit humans' bins for food because I would rather eat seals, but sometimes, I have no choice. The dens we build for our young have also become dangerous because the warmer winters have caused the dens to collapse and melt, leaving my cubs exposed to the harsh conditions with little shelter. Life has become very hard and I am feeling like I need some help from you children. I need to have hope for the future and I know you can help me.

I need you and your friends to take action. You could help to stop the sea ice melting and my home disappearing, so how about you do some things in your home to help me protect mine. If you could reduce the amount of energy you use, this would help me so much. We get most of our energy from burning fuels that release many gases. These gases are warming up the Earth and melting my home. If I share my *five top tips challenge* for you to take on to help me save my home. Will you accept my challenge and help me out? Can you guess what any of my tips are to save energy? Go on … have a try!

Pete's top tips for protecting the sea ice melting by saving energy

- Use energy-efficient light bulbs in every room.
- Insulate your home to use less energy and keep the heat in.
- Turn the heating down and wear another layer if you are cold.
- Turn off and power down all electrical devices when you are not using them.
- Use the car less and shop local.
- Reduce, reuse and recycle as much as you can.

I want to thank you from the bottom of my furry feet for all your help with this. I hope you take on my challenge. I believe in you and know you can make a difference,

Yours,

Pete, *the powerful polar bear.*

Suggested activities

Colour images for the story characters featured in this chapter are available to download on the padlet accompanying this book. The following short group of activities are developed with due consideration of the broad and central methodologies underpinning primary curricula in many jurisdictions. All suggested activities promote talk and discussion, active learning, collaboration, knowledge & skill development and creativity. In addition, all activities include many opportunities for linkage and integration within and across curricular areas in primary education. In addition, the activities facilitate varied differentiation and assessment strategies to be incorporated by the teacher, for the diverse and inclusive classroom. It may be helpful to discuss the prior knowledge of each creature with the children, prior to engaging with the stories. It may also be useful to display the accompanying picture of each creature on the interactive whiteboard in the introduction to the lesson or as you tell the story.

Exploiting the learning moments structured within the stories

Using the story *as* active learning by incorporating some activity, after a complete read-through. This would serve to facilitate a discrete lesson with knowledge (e.g., habitats, adaptation & the role of different living things), skills (measurement, observation and questioning) and attitudes (helping others/solidarity/empathy) into the story. Much used cooperative learning strategies such as the *'Jigsaw', 'Read and Explain Pairs' and 'Triads'* are all ideal to break up the text for peer learning, enhanced comprehension and to generate active learning.

Pupils as researchers

Consider exploiting extension opportunities for group research on related aspects of the stories. For example, structure age-appropriate research, presentation, discussion and feedback on a relevant and age-appropriate topic:

*   Organism structure, anatomy, habitat, niche, feeding, factors affecting, lifespan.
*   Pollination and the role of pollinators.
*   Plastics and sea creatures.
*   Warming seas and global warming.
*   Human activity and living things.

Living thing on the hot seat

There are ample possibilities where the teacher could integrate drama to develop pupil knowledge skills and interaction with the characters in the stories. For example, the teacher could use symbol or dress to personify any of the stories' characters and the children can prepare questions in advance to ask each character, in order to learn more about the organism and the climate change issue. Alternatively, the children can be the character either as a whole class activity or in small groups to maximise participation. This could work very well after a research phase or a jigsaw activity, where expert group members could take the hot seat. Other pupils can ask questions with the child in character sharing the new knowledge their group has acquired through their research. In this way, the children learn new knowledge, skills and attitudes together as well as developing confidence and elements of performance in a creative and enjoyable context.

Art and creativity

Consider linking with visual arts by asking the children to think of an image or scene they have in imagined from listening to one of the stories. They could create aspects of this image as a group or independent activity using a variety of materials (recyclable ideally), in keeping with the central theme. Allow time for class discussion where some children can share what their art represents and why they decided to create this image/scene, in the way it is presented. Teachers could provide opportunities for use of digital art resources, if available, to incorporate technology as appropriate for the class and context.

Problem-solving

With an older class, consider concept mapping to generate short-term, medium-term and long-term solutions to each or any of the organisms' problems. Groups could engage in action planning small initiatives, in school, at home and in their communities to highlight and take a small step in addressing some of the key issues presented in the stories.

Generating hope

Following any of the suggested activities above, it would be important to give children a sense of hope for the future and for them to understand that they are part of the solution and agents of change. There is considerable scope for a range of classroom activities in order to engender hope. For example, consider a '*Finish my story activity* …' where independently or in groups the children create and share a positive outcome for the story characters, generating hope and a sense of action and citizenship. Alternatively, children could be introduced to or be challenged to seek out hero stories where positive outcomes have ensued because of direct action to address climate change-related issues. Finally, perhaps organise a visit to a seed saver bank, eco farm, wildlife sanctuary, wetlands, nature reserve, recycling plant or sustainable woodland, to demonstrate how positive actions generate hope.

Conclusion

I hope you will use this chapter in the spirit it is written. That you as educators and citizens can connect with the moral and ethical tragedy that climate change is fast becoming. That you realise the great power you possess to centralise climate change in what you do with children every day. Notwithstanding all the knowledge and skills inherent in formal curricula, there is no greater gift to give to our youngest children, but the knowledge that it is in our hands to take collective responsibility to halt the demise of our planet. Schools have a significant role to play in both educating for change and activating change among the pupils and indeed the staff. I believe our genetic links to other living things knitted into our DNA from millions of years of evolution connects us to the animals and plants we share the planet with. We all have an inherent empathy for the care of living things, for sustaining life. This chapter re-awakens this empathy with the hope that it will translate in many small ways to positive actions to begin to reverse the damage we are doing to planet Earth.

Useful websites providing biology-related resources for climate change

- Ask About Ireland. 2019. Learning-zone/primary-students. [ONLINE] Available at: http://www.askaboutireland.ie.
- Marine Institute: Home. 2019. Education-outreach/teachers-resources. [ONLINE] Available at: https://www.marine.ie.

- Heritage in Schools. 2019. Teachers-resources. [ONLINE] Available at: http://www.heritageinschools.ie.
- Royal Society of Biology. 2019. Teaching resources. [ONLINE] Available at: https://www.rsb.org.uk/education/teaching-resources.
- Association for Science Education. 2019. Teaching resources. [ONLINE] Available at: https://www.ase.org.uk.
- *Sincere thanks to Paul Hamilton (age 16) for the digital art pictures.*

8 Using climate change as the context for a Content and Language Integrated Learning (CLIL) approach in the primary classroom

Siobhán Ní Mhurchú

Introduction

Content and Language Integrated Learning (CLIL) involves teaching another curriculum subject or certain aspects of another subject through the medium of a foreign language or through a second language. According to Coyle et al. (2010:1), 'Content and Language Integrated Learning is a dual-focused educational approach in which an additional (foreign or second language) is used for the learning and teaching of both content and language.' In this chapter, *Gaeilge* or the Irish language has been chosen as an exemplar but any foreign/second language can be utilised.

The objective of this chapter is:

* To explain the concept of CLIL
* To explain the Irish context
* To emphasise important aspects that need to be taken into consideration prior to introducing CLIL in the classroom
* To provide exemplar CLIL lesson plans based on climate change through the medium of *Gaeilge* (the Irish language) for middle grades (*Rang 3/4*; 9/10-year-old children) in the primary school

Teaching and learning a second or foreign language – The Irish context

Language is a means by which we think, dream, express our thoughts and opinions, communicate and connect with others. Learning a second language or a foreign language can be challenging and requires time, persistence, dedication, competence and confidence. There are four language skills which merit attention – Listening, Speaking, Reading, Writing and different languages may have a specific sound system, a specific alphabet and may have a specific written format.

Irish, or *Gaeilge*, is an autochthonous language spoken in Ireland and is a core subject in government-funded Irish and English-medium primary schools. Primary education in Ireland is an eight-year cycle from junior infants at the age of four/five to sixth class at the age of twelve/thirteen. The curriculum for primary education covers the following key areas: Irish (*Gaeilge*); English; mathematics; social, environmental and scientific education (SESE) incorporating history, geography and science; arts education including visual arts, music and drama; physical education; and social, personal and health education and the same teacher is responsible for teaching all subjects.

The majority of primary schools are English-medium schools where Irish or *Gaeilge* is taught through the medium of Irish for approximately 40 minutes per day and all other subjects are taught through the medium of English. The majority of Irish speakers who use the Irish language communicatively and as their first language are located in regions known as *Gaeltacht* areas and Irish-medium primary schools are available to the children in these areas. Also, there are Irish speakers outside those regions who have made Irish their first language of choice or who have a keen interest in the language. Irish-medium primary schools or *Gaelscoileanna* have become increasingly popular in towns and cities outside the Gaeltacht area. The Irish language is taught as an L1 (First Language) in Gaeltacht areas and in Irish-medium schools and the Irish language is the medium of instruction during the school day in these schools while English is taught as an L2 (Second Language).

It is a general view that both the quantity and quality of Irish teaching in English-medium primary schools varies greatly (Department of Education and Science, 2007; Department of Education and Skills, 2013; Harris et al., 2006). Implementing a convincing pedagogy to teach a second language effectively within a time frame of 40 minutes per day is only one of the challenges experienced by Irish teachers. For both learners and teachers, the absence of a functional context impacts negatively on Irish language learning, on attitudes towards the language and on the motivation to learn the language as noted by Harris (2007). The lack of linguistic proficiency among some teachers is also well documented (Department of Education and Skills, 2005, 2007; Harris et al., 2006; National Council for Curriculum and Assessment, 2008). Therefore, the introduction of CLIL in Irish primary schools is being encouraged by the Department of Education and Skills to give a greater function to second and foreign language learning and the teaching of PE through the medium of Irish is being piloted in 22 schools in September 2019.

Introducing a content and language integrated lesson in the classroom

Consistent with communicative, task-based and content-based language teaching, CLIL stresses the idea that any fluency in the use of a target language can be achieved best by its use as a functional medium of communication and information, and not by making it the object of analysis in class (de Graaff et al., 2007). The benefits of CLIL are well documented (Figure 8.1).

Prior to implementing a content and language integrated lesson, the CLIL teacher may need support in all or some of the following aspects:

- Understanding the CLIL approach
- Language proficiency in the target language
- Language teaching methodologies
- Curriculum content (specific language and subject knowledge)
- Planning in advance for CLIL

Understanding the CLIL approach

According to de Graaff et al. (2007:606), in their comparison between L1 and L2 teaching, 'CLIL involves additional language learning objectives and specific opportunities for communication and language use.' Keeping a balance between language and content learning is very important in CLIL as there can be a tendency to prioritise language

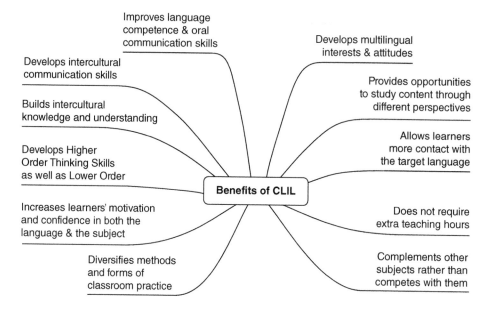

Figure 8.1 The benefits of Content and Language Integrated Learning (CLIL)

Source: Adapted from Attard Montalto et al. (2014:10)

over content or content over language as was evident in the research by Ó Ceallaigh et al. (2016). To complement a communicative approach to language teaching, the CLIL teacher needs to focus on fulfilling communicative needs and empowering the learners to do so also. Language functions such as giving and asking for information, asking and answering questions, expressing an opinion, describing something will be necessary for communication. To ensure engagement, understanding and learning for our learners, we must encourage and accommodate meaningful interaction (interaction between learners and teachers, interaction between learners and other learners). The CLIL teacher must constantly encourage, motivate and praise efforts as learners articulate and discuss their learning and thoughts in a language in which they are most likely unable to express themselves confidently. Being a very effective communicator, ensuring the comprehension of all learners at all times, recognising moments of poor concentration due to poor understanding and having the skills to resolve these issues on the spot are crucial.

Language proficiency in the target language

As a CLIL teacher, one is expected to model accurate use of the target language at all times. To allow for effective language planning by the teacher and to enable successful language acquisition for the learner, we need to differentiate between: (i) the language of learning; (ii) the language for learning and (iii) the language through which the learning happens. This is based on the *Language Triptych* developed by Coyle et al. (2010).

i   Language of learning refers to the language needed to access basic concepts relating to the content including subject-specific vocabulary, fixed expressions and subject typical grammar ii Language for learning is the enabling language of the classroom including teacher language necessary to conduct classroom activities and language for the learner to communicate and work with learning skills, i.e., co-operative work and questioning

iii Finally, language through learning is the language that allows for learning, thinking, questioning, re-telling and acquisition of new knowledge as well as progression of language learning

Language teaching methodologies

Coherent, relevant, effective methodologies which maximise language learning and yet maintain high levels of academic achievement at the same time are paramount. Initially teacher talk will exceed learner talk in quantity, and therefore, planning for the exact or close levels of language being utilised by the teacher is crucial where relevant key words are revised often in many different ways and brought to the attention of the learners through visual prompts (labels or flashcards), appearing on images, using a variety of questions. Teachers may need to vary voice intonation to emphasise language and would be expected to adjust their language output to ensure clarity at all times.

The following methods are common language teaching methodologies in the formal Irish language lessons and can also be used during CLIL lessons to teach, revise and consolidate new language, e.g., direct method, audio-lingual method, total physical response, audio-visual, series method and a structural approach method.

Willis (1996) speaks of three essential conditions of language:

i Good quality exposure to the target language through the different skills of listening and reading (input)

ii Opportunities to communicate, use and interact allowing the learner to express what they feel or think through the skills of speaking and writing (output)

iii Motivation to learn new knowledge and skills and to share that learning

She adds an additional desirable condition:

iv Form-focused instruction (FFI) to consolidate accuracy

Only texts with an appropriate language level should be utilised. Each text can be adapted by changing key words, re-arranging the layout, adding images to support comprehension and highlighting vocabulary.

The following techniques to enhance comprehensibility in immersion are also helpful in the CLIL classroom (Cloud et al., 2000:125):

- *Use of cognates, controlled vocabulary and shorter phrases*
- *Limit idiomatic speech during instruction for students at beginning stages*
- *Use natural redundancy in phrasing*
- *Repeat key vocabulary*
- *Reinforce key ideas*
- *Pace instruction appropriately*
- *Provide natural pauses between phrases to give students time to process language*
- *Give students the 'wait time' they need to interpret questions and formulate a response*
- *Check frequently on student understanding*

Body language, gestures and facial expressions also facilitate comprehension as well as visual aids, realia, images, graphic aids, film, media, multimedia presentations, information and technological supports and manipulatives.

Preparing numerous fun-filled opportunities to revise and consolidate the learning, repeat key words and sentence structures using a variety of strategies, e.g., chants, a series of dance moves, crosswords, quizzes, group activities and games are also very beneficial to create a positive experience and attitude and to motivate all participants.

Curriculum content (specific language and subject knowledge)

Gaeilge, the target language in this case, can be challenging for the learner as root words can be changed when mutations (*séimhiú/urú*) alter the spelling and the sounds of initial consonants (*bord – ar an mbord, ó bhord go bord, faoin mbord*) and when genitive and plural forms alter the root nouns (*lár an bhoird/na boird*). It can be helpful to refer to or underline the root word in these situations to support the language learner's understanding, e.g., *ar an mbord*, and later in this chapter, I refer to Form-focused instruction (FFI) which supports the learner with language analysis. Syntax or sentence structure are also challenging but as a CLIL teacher you need to persist!

Formal language lessons (*Gaeilge*) are timetabled daily and it is hugely beneficial if relevant and appropriate language functions and forms are integrated in these lessons to support the learner. It is very helpful to teach some prerequisite language formally in the 'Gaeilge' language lessons, i.e., language that supports the learners in their learning in the CLIL lessons (topics like weather/vacations/clothes; verbs in different forms; comparative and superlative adjectives; etc.).

While the learners may be aware of language structures and forms, the vocabulary pertaining to the content or the discipline-specific language may be new for the learners and will need to be revised regularly in many different ways and consolidated at every opportunity. Revising previous lessons using cloze procedures, true or false, putting sentences in order, fill the blanks, drills, quizzes helps to strengthen that foundation on which we build the new learning.

As previously mentioned, teacher talk will exceed learner talk initially and the methodologies in use will reflect that, but as time progresses and the students become more familiar with the CLIL approach, more co-operative methods and more active learning methodologies can be utilised like station-teaching, the jigsaw technique, group work and collaborative work that involves group discussion and feedback. Catering for different learning styles to motivate and engage language learners is challenging initially.

Therefore, a good understanding of the target language and accuracy in the language as well as effective language methodologies for the different learners are crucial for the CLIL teacher. In Chapter 1, Anne Dolan speaks of the importance of '*teachers who are knowledgeable about climate change, its causes and consequences,*' and for CLIL teachers, this content knowledge and discipline-specific language must be imparted through the medium of a second/foreign language.

Planning in advance for CLIL

Proactive pre-planning is vital to ensure high levels of teaching and learning. To begin with, an appropriate topic (age-appropriate, interesting and relevant to their lives, on which they have some prior knowledge) will be necessary to provide a context. In the context of climate change, the much-discussed topic of weather provides an excellent entry point for CLIL teachers.

At the early stages, two short lessons per week are more productive instead of one long lesson as levels of misunderstanding and confusion may be high and also the second lesson provides an opportunity to revise both language, content and learning within a shorter period of time to support consolidation.

Gibbons (2002:38) suggests that 'productive talk does not just happen' but needs to be 'deliberately and systematically planned.' Specific, achievable language objectives and content objectives are required to keep focus. Both language and content objectives should carry an equal weight. Identifying the language of learning (subject-specific language), the language for learning (communicative language both for the teacher and for the learners) and the language through learning (which allows for processing the learning) in advance will be helpful and language functions should be identified to ensure learners can communicate their learning. Preparing relevant and useful resources must be planned for. Careful planning including the use of relevant and useful resources is required to teach and to consolidate learning.

A variety of language and content methodologies are required to cater for a wide range of learners and these also need to be planned for and executed effectively. Strategic integration planning with the formal Irish language lessons is also necessary with a view to focusing on forms are required in both classes, e.g., verbs in the present/past/future tense.

Pre-planning may also include Form-focused instruction. FFI aims to engage the learners in some degree of language analysis such as identifying grammatical rules and uses elements from cognitive theory, specifically noticing, awareness and practice activities. Noticing activities are predominantly receptive and bring learner's attention to linguistic aspects through input enhancement (Sharwood Smith, 1993; cited in Lyster, 2007:66). Controlled practice activities ask learners to use the correct form of the language while discussing subject matter content.

As lessons require a wide variety of methodologies and a constant awareness of the learners' progress and success, CLIL teachers need to be flexible in their approach. It may be necessary to change style, methodology, focus and emphasis. Teachers may be required to simplify the content midway through lessons to ensure the language and subject objectives planned for at the beginning are being achieved by the language learners. Hence, the need to plan for assessment of learning, for learning and through learning.

To consolidate the learning, all opportunities to revise should be maximised and the recommendation by Met (2008) to document all the new language in a specific notebook during or at the end of lessons is very supportive.

Conclusion

The CLIL approach requires patience and perseverance and its benefits will not be realised overnight. There can be an assumption among teachers that they may continue their normal classroom approach, methodologies and routines, and merely exchange the medium of instruction from English to *Gaeilge* (a second/foreign language). However, the reality is quite different, particularly if one would like the CLIL experience to be beneficial and enjoyable for the learners.

Cammarata and Haley (2018) talk about the power of doing and thinking together. Certainly, working collaboratively with another colleague with a similar CLIL vision can be worthwhile. The sharing of ideas, reflections, challenges and experiences to achieve a common goal will be hugely beneficial to all involved. *Ní neart go cur le chéile!*

The notion of teaching 'climate change' through a second or foreign language might seem daunting. Be realistic in your language and content learning objectives and in what you hope to achieve. The learner's levels of understanding, of language learning and of content learning will increase with each lesson. However, it is important that the content is at an age-appropriate level and that the medium of instruction is at the correct level to ensure comprehension and new learning. It is advisable to use the target language at all times during the lessons and not to revert to the first language, particularly when the challenging times arrive, e.g., lack of understanding, trying to explain complex concepts.

I suggest you try the CLIL approach in your classroom for at least one term, and if possible, try it for one year to reap many of the benefits mentioned above. It will be a challenge for you and for your learners at first but if you persevere, you will be pleasantly surprised with the achievements of your learners. *De réir a chéile a tógtar na caisleáin!*

To support your work in this area, I have designed some lesson plans to support you on your journey while using climate change as the context and *Gaeilge* as the second or foreign language for a CCLIL approach in the primary classroom. These lesson plans are available on the padlet accompanying this book. A sample lesson plan is available as Gaeilge (Appendix 2) and for language learners learning English as a second/foreign language, a translated version is included in Appendix 3.

References

Attard Montalto, S., Walter, L., Theodorou, M. and Chrysanthou, K. (2014) The CLIL Guidebook. https://www.languages.dk/archive/clil4u/book/CLIL%20Book%20En.pdf.

Cammarata, L. and Haley, C. (2018) Integrated content, language, and literacy instruction in a Canadian French immersion context: A professional development journey. *International Journal of Bilingual Education and Bilingualism, 21*(3), 332–348. DOI:10.1080/13670050.2017.1386617.

Cloud, N., Genesse, F. and Hamayan E. (2000) *Dual-language instruction: A handbook for enriched education.* Boston: Heinle and Heinle.

Coyle, D., Hood, P. and Marsh, D. (2010) *CLIL – Content and Language Integrated Learning.* London, England: Cambridge University Press.

de Graaff, R., Jan Koopman, G.J, Anikina, Y. and Westhoff, G.J. (2007) An observation tool for effective L2 pedagogy in Content and Language Integrated Learning (CLIL). *International Journal of Bilingual Education and Bilingualism, 10*(5), 603–624.

Department of Education and Skills (2005) *Beginning to teach: Newly qualified teachers in primary schools.* Dublin: Government Publications.

Department of Education and Science (2007) *Irish in the primary school: Inspectorate evaluation studies.* Dublin: Department of Education and Science.

Department of Education and Skills (2013) *Chief Inspector's Report 2010-2012.* Dublin: Department of Education and Skills.

Gibbons, P. (2002) *Scaffolding language scaffolding learning: Teaching second language learners in the mainstream classroom.* New Hampshire: Heinemann.

Harris, J. (2007) National trends in achievement in Irish listening at primary level: A challenge for language revitalisation and language policy. In Conrick, M. and Howard, M., eds., *From applied linguistics to linguistics applied: Issues, practices, trends* (Vol. 22, pp. 25–42). London: British Association of Applied Linguistics.

Harris, J., Forde, P., Archer, P., Nic Fhearaile, S. and O' Gorman, M. (2006) *Irish in primary schools – Long term national trends in achievement.* Dublin: Government Publications.

Lyster, R. (2007) *Learning and teaching languages through content: A counterbalanced approach.* Amsterdam: John Benjamins Publishing Company.

Met, M. (2008) Paying attention to language: Literacy, language and academic achievement. In Fortune, T.W. and Tedick, D.J., eds., *Pathways to multilingualism: Evolving perspectives on immersion education* (pp. 49–71). Clevedon: Multilingual Matters.

National Council for Curriculum and Assessment (2008) *National curriculum review, Phase 2 – Research Report No. 7.* Accessed at http://www.ncca.ie/en/Publications/Reports/Primary_Curriculum_Review,_Phase_2_Final_report_with_recommendations.pdf.

Ó Ceallaigh, T.J., Ní Mhurchú, S. and Ní Chróinín, D. (2016) Balancing content and language in CLIL: The experiences of teachers and learners. *Journal of Immersion and Content-Based Language Education, 5*(1), 58–86. DOI:10.1075/jicb.5.1.03oce.

Smith, M.S. (1993) *Input enhancement in instructed SLA: Theoretical bases. Studies in second language acquisition* (Vol. 15, pp. 165–179). London: Cambridge University Press.

Willis, J. (1996) *A Framework for task-based learning.* Edinburgh: Addison Wesley Longman Ltd.

Section 3

Climate change education: STEAM

9 Bringing climate change alive in the science classroom through science, communication and engineering STEM challenges

Maeve Liston

Introduction

Primary science is a way of thinking and doing. Science in primary school is concerned with asking questions and finding ways of answering them through exploration, investigation and innovation. The main reason for teaching primary science is to extend the children's innate curiosity and natural urge to explore their immediate environment. The emphasis is on developing a way of exploring and thinking in order to investigate ourselves and the environment. It allows children to see an experimental world where everything they encounter can be subject to scientific exploration. STEM activities and the practice of scientific process skills can play a key role in exploring and providing possible solutions to the causes and impacts of climate change through questioning, observing, predicting, investigating, analysing information and communicating (Liston, 2013c).

Prensky (2016) argues that a guaranteed approach to world improvement involves producing a population of adult citizens empowered by their education, to create solutions to real-world problems. Those adults will inevitably create real, world-improving solutions for the rest of their lives, becoming 'Solutionaries' (Weil, 2016). In the words of Prensky (2016:1):

> Our kids now need an education that is far more connected and real than in the past – an education system that gives them not only knowledge, but also provides them with empowerment and agency. They need an education whose ends are not just to improve themselves, but rather to improve the world they live in.

In recent times, there has been an increasing emphasis on climate change in the media and increasing awareness among our younger generations, in particular as a result of the inspiring young activist Greta Thunberg (Thunberg, 2019). Her actions have sparked a global movement for action against the climate crisis, inspiring millions of school children to go on strike for our planet. Such actions have intrigued and sparked further curiosity among teachers, children and entire school communities, with a hunger to learn more about sustainability, energy conservation and climate change (Liston et al., 2019; Waldron et al., 2011). A recent research study, reviewing an educational outreach programme on sustainable energy and climate change in Irish schools, found that teachers acknowledged that the strong focus now being placed in the media around climate change, energy usage, fossil fuels and plastics is encouraging entire school communities to get even more involved with such initiatives. This is also acknowledged by the NCCA (2010), stating that 'schooling finds itself at the centre of a set of global concerns about the future of the planet, about food and water security, and about the movement of peoples in the face of climate disasters….and increasingly, schools are being asked not simply to teach students about these issues but to shape the next generation of creative problem solvers who can quite literally "save the world"' (NCCA, 2010:6). Therefore, it can be argued that education has a very important role to play in achieving our global sustainability goals into the future (Dolan, 2012, 2015, 2020; Liddy, 2012).

Integrating Education for Sustainability (EfS) and climate change across the curriculum at all age levels in both formal and informal education systems is one of the most important and effective means of developing capacities for addressing climate change (Mochizuki and Bryan, 2015; DES, 2014). There are particularly strong links between STEM (Science, Technology, Engineering & Mathematics) education and EfS that need to be made more explicit and further utilised in the classroom. This chapter explores the importance of primary science and STEM in the context of EfS. It suggests a range of strategies for developing *Science Capital* and STEM literacies with a view to facilitating the development of Prensky's (2016) 'Solutionaries' and 'Globally Empowered Child(ren)'.

Importance of STEM

Globally, the demand for STEM graduates is increasing at an unprecedented rate (Vandeweyer, 2016; Wilson, 2009). Currently enterprise, industry and governments across the world are continuously publicising the need for highly skilled STEM workforces (Douglass and Edelstein, 2009; Orpwood et al., 2012). Reports, strategies and action plans highlight the importance and need for STEM populations with creativity, problem-solving, critical thinking and communication skills to ensure economic prosperity (Augustine et al., 2010). However, there is not enough emphasis being placed on the importance of STEM literacies and competences in order to make informed decisions about everyday life (Howarth and Scott, 2014). STEM not only contributes to the economy but also to social and cultural prosperity, making the world a better place to live in (Roberts, 2002, 2012; Vasquez et al., 2017). We need our future population to be able to apply knowledge, skills & abilities associated with STEM within and across disciplines and in real-life situations in order to begin tackling the problem of climate change in a logical and systematic way (Carnevale et al., 2011; DES, 2017).

STEM education, social responsibility and active citizenship

STEM education is now recognised as a powerful means of refocusing education, concentrating on critical thinking and a willingness to explore and engage with the real world. STEM lessons and educational experiences can significantly contribute in developing a sense of ethics and social conscience among students (Jolly, 2017). This can be achieved by exposing young people to real social and environmental challenges and ideas locally, regionally, nationally or internationally (Howarth and Scott, 2014; Jolly, 2017; Tytler et al., 2008; Wilson and Mant, 2011). Positioning the problems in context and increasing relevance of a topic in STEM lessons acts as a hook to engage curiosity, encouraging children to find solutions to such problems and developing their capacity to make informed decisions about political and civic issues and about their own lives (Beatty, 2011). Incorporating climate change into STEM education allows children to identify problems that need to be solved, carry out research and brainstorm ideas.

The Organisation for Economic Co-operation and Development (OECD) has also recommended that science curricula should be redesigned to better reflect the reality of modern science and place an emphasis on the contribution of science in society, concentrating on the understanding and the application of scientific concepts rather than on

Figure 9.1 Prensky's Tomorrow's 'Better Their World' Paradigm

Source: Adapted from Prensky (2016)

the retention of information (OECD, 2006). The Royal Academy of Engineering (2011) urges that 'now is the time to stop our children being channelled by a constraining curriculum into making weather vanes and CD Racks, and to begin taking on projects that stimulate creativity, focusing on those borne out of product need, problem solving and sustainability' (Royal Academy of Engineering, 2011).

It is suggested that implementing teaching strategies, such as problem-based learning through a STEM curriculum, may reinvigorate students' desires to understand the world around them and engage them in classroom instruction (Havice, 2009). STEM activities allow students to learn and apply content, practices and skills of the STEM disciplines to situations they encounter in their lives (Bybee, 2013). True authentic STEM education incorporates Prensky's 'Better Their World' Paradigm (Figure 9.1), that is, STEM-educated students are problem-solvers, innovators, inventors, self-reliant, logical thinkers and technologically literate (Huling and Speake Dwyer, 2018; Kennedy and Odell, 2014). We need these individuals in order to raise awareness about the immediate effects and impacts of climate change before it is too late.

The question is, where do we begin in the classroom? The first step is to develop *Science Capital* and STEM literacies of our children and teachers.

STEM literacy

A STEM literate society will allow people to practice STEM skills, making informed decisions about their everyday lives. STEM literacy involves an awareness of how STEM disciplines shape our material, intellectual and cultural environments and willingness to engage in STEM-related issues and with the ideas of science, technology, engineering and mathematics as a constructive, concerned and reflective citizen (Bybee, 2013). STEM literacy is 'the knowledge and understanding of scientific and mathematical concepts and processes required of personal decision making, participation in civic and cultural affairs and economic productivity' (National Research Council, 2011:5).

In today's increasingly technological world, we are bombarded with information and news feeds. We now require citizens that can discern real facts, recognise bias and make decisions on a variety of issues. Such issues include: Causes and impacts of climate change; advantages and disadvantages to a wide variety of alternative energy production; and anticipated impacts of industrial development.

Science Capital

Science Capital is the measure of people's knowledge, attitudes, skills and experiences with science. People with *Science Capital* engage with science as part of their normal, everyday life. It looks at what and how they know, what and how they think and who they know (Table 9.1).

Table 9.1 What is *Science Capital?*

Science Capital involves:

- Scientific literacy, i.e., knowledge and understanding about science and how science works.
- Confidence/ ability to use and apply science knowledge, principles, language and scientific processes into everyday life.
- Seeing the relevance and value of science in everyday life.
- Awareness of where and how science skills, knowledge and understanding are useful for all careers and walks of life.
- The exposure to science through unstructured science activities (e.g., watching science related TV programmes, reading science books, playing science games).
- Taking part in informal science activities both inside and outside of school.
- Family science skills, knowledge and qualifications.
- Recognising the science skills and knowledge that are used in the everyday activities and in the work of people you know in a meaningful way and.
- Talking to others about science in everyday life.

STEM literacy and *Science Capital* are affected by a variety of factors and experiences. These include exposure and engagement with science at school, at home, during informal learning experiences through educational outreach both in and out of school and everyday life experiences (Archer et al., 2015). Education is key, beginning at the grassroots level with the individual (children and young people and teachers), spreading outwards towards family, the community and society. Therefore, STEM education involving curricula, pedagogies and educational outreach needs to focus on building STEM literacy and *Science Capital* around climate change in the primary classroom. An integrated approach to STEM education and climate change within and across subject areas and topics provides opportunities to link what is happening in the classroom to society, thus developing responsible citizenship (Stohlmann et al., 2012).

Building STEM literacy and Science Capital around climate change in the primary classroom

We need to consider how can we *Engage* learners at a deeper level with the topic of climate change? What will we use as a *Trigger* to stimulate discussions, debates and ideas? How can we get them *Wondering and Exploring?*

STEM activities that promote exploratory talk and speech involving questioning, eliciting ideas, probing understanding, reflection, assimilation and accommodation of new knowledge and communication on the topic of climate change will significantly contribute to developing STEM literacy and *Science Capital* of children (Harlen and Qualter, 2004). Science communication can empower children in our classrooms to develop a greater interest, understanding of and interaction with climate change. Consequently, this develops their confidence to conduct conversations and debates about this very important topic (Burns et al., 2003; Davison et al., 2008; Mihelich et al., 2016; Varner, 2014). Effective sustainability communication in the classroom can introduce an understanding of the human-environment relationship, thereby promoting awareness of responsible human interactions with the natural and social environment (Godemann and Michelsen, 2011).

Science communication activities and engagement strategies for the primary STEM classroom

This section provides examples of science activities that promote engagement with the topic of climate change through *Triggering, Wondering, Exploring* and *Communicating.* The aim of these strategies is to develop *Science Capital* and STEM literacies of our children and teachers.

1 **Climate change displays:** In the classroom, make a display or a climate change learning wall including the following:

   - *Climate change/STEM on the news display board:* Include news reports on current environmental issues (regionally, nationally and internationally).
   - *Imagery and 'picture in time' activities:* Use infographics and images on the causes and impacts of climate change to stimulate discussion. Include the following questions: What is happening/has just happened? What will happen next/in an hour/day/week/month? What happened/would it have been an hour/a day/a week/a month/a year before the picture was taken?
   - *Word webs/concept maps:* Children develop a word web including concepts and scientific terminology they discover around the topic of climate change (Liston, 2013a,b).

2 **Consultation and Mentoring:** Invite scientists, engineers and industry representatives into the classroom or go on fieldtrips to relevant industries (e.g., renewable energy industries). Facilitate discussions regarding how industry, scientists and engineers are working on tackling the problem of climate change and making a social difference. Follow-up activities could include researching the following websites and organisations to highlight the importance of STEM and environmental engineering for the 21st century:

   - *Engineering a better world* is a unique programme focused on achieving sustainable development, through innovative, collaborative, challenge-led engineering.
   - *Engineering for change* is a knowledge organisation dedicated to preparing the global workforce to deliver solutions that improve the quality of life of underserved communities.
   - *Engineers without borders* involves initiatives explicitly focused on creating global citizen engineers through international humanitarian engineering projects.

3 **Media:** Incorporate relevant documentaries and TED Talks on climate change into your teaching.

4 **STEM Clubs:** Set up a STEM sustainable energy club in your school: Monitoring energy consumption, managing energy consumption and recycling projects.

5 **Debates/Ridiculous Arguments:** Organise groups of children to debate against each other on the following questions: Is climate change real? Can we do anything about climate change? Scientists and engineers have caused climate change? Is STEM the answer in tackling the problem of climate change? Ensure the children are provided with enough time to research the topics as debates allow for the opportunities for argumentation, decision making, discerning real facts and recognising bias.

6 **Research Projects:** Research projects allow groups of children to explore a topic, gather data and evidence, make informed decisions and present their findings to their

peers. Research promotes higher-order thinking, analysis of information and arriving at conclusions. Possible titles for research projects could include:

- Why is the Earth's climate changing? How do we know the climate is changing?
- How do humans/science change the planet?
- How are energy and climate change connected?
- What is global warming and how can we stop it?
- What are scientists and engineers doing to tackle climate change?
- Why is energy essential in achieving the new Sustainable Development Goals (SDGs)?
- What prevention methods and equipment and solutions have been developed to tackle climate change?

7 **Thinking activities**

Thinking Cap: Ask children to put on their thinking caps, asking them the following:

- Have you noticed any problems around your local area/nationally/across the globe? What could you do to change or fix this? How could you go about doing this?
- Can we use STEM to develop solutions to climate change?
- Who decides what happens about climate change?
- How could STEM industries save energy?

The Science Talk Ball: Stick questions regarding climate change onto an inflatable ball or dice. Children throw it around the classroom from one person to another. The child who catches reads a question out and the class must answer. A blank talk ball could also be designed, where children stick their own questions onto the ball.

'What If', Plus Minus Interesting Activities: Ask children to complete a Plus, Minus, Interesting (or Positive, Negative, Interesting) rubric (Table 9.2) for the following 'What If' statements:

- What if we ran out of fossil fuels?
- What if all the ice caps melt?
- What is there were no scientists and engineers in the world?

Demonstrations and Modelling: Demonstrations and modelling activities allow children the opportunities to explore abstract and concrete phenomena. Children discuss this and try to provide explanations to what is happening and how it is happening. The global warming experiment outlined in Table 9.3 is an example of one such activity.

Table 9.2 PMI (Plus, Minus, Interesting) activity to encourage higher order thinking about topics related to climate change

What If ....

Plus	Minus
Interesting	

Table 9.3 Global warming investigation

Materials

One large clear glass jar (large enough to hold a plastic or paper cup); two paper cups; soil (potting or topsoil); outdoor thermometer (small enough for the base to fit in the cup) and spray bottle with water.

Part 1

Procedure

1 Place the soil in each of the cups so the cups are almost full. Label one cup 'A' and the other cup 'B'.
2 Place the thermometer in cup 'B' so that the base (the bulb of the thermometer) is slightly buried by the soil.
3 Place both cups in direct sunlight (such as on a table outside). Wait about 10 minutes and record the temperature in cup 'B'.
4 Move the thermometer to cup 'A' and repeat the temperature measurement. Both cups of soil should be at the same temperature, if not, wait a few more minutes before taking the temperature.
5 Place the large glass jar (upside down) over cup 'A' keeping the thermometer in the soil.
6 Wait several minutes and remove the jar and record the temperature.
7 Move thermometer to cup 'B' that was not covered, wait several minutes, and record the temperature again.

Results

The cup of soil covered by the inverted glass jar will be warmer than the uncovered cup. The glass jar acts like a greenhouse trapping reflected heat energy.

Teacher: What did the temperature do when the soil was covered by the glass jar?

Temperature observations

Cup A:

At the beginning: _____

After covered by glass jar: _____

Cup B:

At the beginning: _____

At the end: _____

Teacher: Why do you think the temperature changed when the earth (soil) was enclosed by the glass jar?

What is the source of the heat?

Why did it not affect cup 'B' that wasn't covered?

Part 2

Teacher background information: Sunlight is the source of the earth's heat. There is a natural balance of sunlight that enters the atmosphere and energy that is reflected and not converted to heat. Anything in the atmosphere that 'traps' sunlight energy will add heat to the atmosphere and can result in an increase in temperature.

Repeat the entire experiment with one addition. After you have recorded the temperature in the soil covered by the jar, spray water mist into the jar before turning it over and covering the cup. Wait and record the temperature again.

What happens?

Is the temperature higher or lower when the water mist is sprayed in the 'atmosphere' of the earth (the cup)?

Why do you think the water mist makes a difference?

Once children have been introduced to and begin to develop an understanding and knowledge around climate change (*Science Capital* and STEM literacy), more experimental inquiry-based climate change STEM investigations, projects and challenges can be introduced. The activities detailed above can be used as the first steps in STEM lessons to engage children with the topic of climate change. The following sections will include ideas on how to allow children to investigate the topic further through more hands-on activities. These activities will focus on STEM climate change challenges incorporating the engineering design process (EDP). Firstly, the concept of STEM education, characteristics of STEM education and STEM lessons and the EDP will be explored.

Solving real-world problems with STEM

STEM education is an interdisciplinary approach to learning, removing the traditional barriers that separate the four disciplines of science, technology, engineering and mathematics, integrating them together into real-world, rigorous and relevant learning experiences for students (Vasquez et al., 2013). STEM education isn't just one thing—it's a range of strategies that help students to build understanding and apply concepts and skills from different disciplines in contexts that make connections between school, community and work, in order to solve meaningful problems (Gerlach, 2012). STEM education is not fundamentally different from other teaching and learning, except that the children are asked to make additional connections, not only between the STEM subjects but also with other subject areas, concepts and ideas (Vasquez et al., 2013).

STEM projects and activities can encourage exploration of new ideas, resourceful problem-solving and risk-taking through providing engaging lessons linked to relevant environmental, societal and industrial issues (Ramirez, 2013). Real-world STEM projects based on solving real-world problems promotes creativity, problem-solving, sustainability and increases students interest in STEM by developing both their conceptual understanding of key scientific concepts and skills including collaborative, inquiry-based skills (Royal Academy of Engineering, 2011; Straw et al., 2011). Characteristics of STEM projects, activities and lessons are summarised in Table 9.4.

The engineering design process (EDP)

Engineering must take centre stage during STEM activities (Jolly, 2017). STEM activities and lessons use the EDP as a systematic, orderly, open-ended way of approaching problems and designing solutions for those problems (Figure 9.2).

Engineering is the glue that integrates science, mathematics and technology and forces them towards workable solutions (Liston, 2018). The EDP provides a model that guides students from identifying a problem—or a design challenge—to creating and developing a solution.

Children:

- Develop multiple ideas for solutions
- Develop and create a prototype
- Test the prototype
- Evaluate
- Redesign

Table 9.4 Characteristics of STEM education and STEM lessons

Characteristics of STEM projects and activities

- Removing traditional barriers of separating the four disciplines of science, technology, engineering and mathematics (Vasquez et al., 2013).
- Integrating and applying a deeper level knowledge and understanding of mathematics & science to create technologies and solutions for real-world problems using engineering design approach (Jolly, 2017).
- Integrating real-world, rigorous and relevant learning experiences for students (Vasquez et al., 2013).
- Inspiring creativity, problem-solving, inquisitive thinking and teamwork (Roberts, 2012).
- Supporting spontaneous questioning as well as planned investigations (Huling and Speake Dwyer, 2018).
- Incorporating habits of mind for students to use technology; integrates engineering design requiring collaboration and communication and troubleshooting (Morrison, 2006).
- Allowing for innovation and critical thinking (Jolly, 2017).

Components of a STEM lesson (Jolly, 2017)

1 Does the lesson present a real problem (an engineering challenge)?
2 Will students relate to the problem?
3 Does the lesson allow students multiple acceptable and creative approaches and solutions for successfully solving the problem?
4 Does the lesson integrate and apply important science and math grade-level content?
5 Does the lesson clearly use the engineering design process as the approach to solving problems?
6 Does the lesson use a student-centred, hands-on teaching and learning approach?
7 Does the lesson lead to the design and development of a model or prototype?
8 Is the role of technology in the lesson clear to the students?
9 Does the lesson successfully engage students in purposeful teamwork?
10 Does the lesson include testing the solution, evaluating the results and redesigning to improve the outcome?
11 Does the lesson involve students in communicating about their design and results?

The EDP includes the following stages: Ask; imagine; plan and design; create; test and evaluate; redesign/improve and communicate (Table 9.5).

Cross-curricular STEM challenges and projects

STEM activities can be categorised as follows:

- Developing solutions in dealing with the impacts of climate change.
- Developing innovations and prototypes in preventing climate change.

Developing solutions in dealing with the impacts of climate change

Some examples of possible STEM projects for children using the EDP include:

Solar Energy

- Design, build and cook using a solar oven.
- Design and make your own solar panels to charge a mobile phone.
- Design and make solar boats.

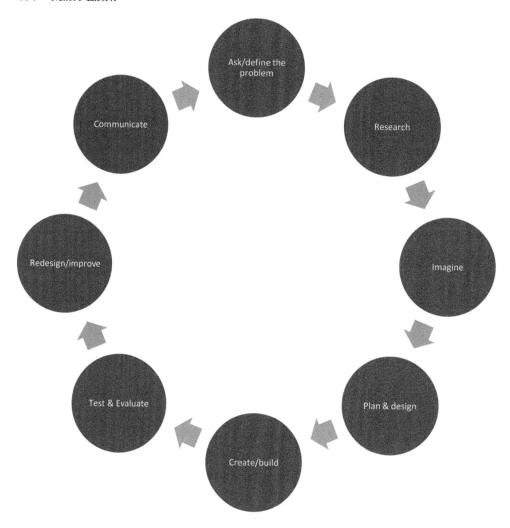

Figure 9.2 Engineering design process (EDP) for STEM lessons and activities

Wind energy

- Design and create a wind turbine for a power supply company using only recycled materials.

Hydropower

- How can we use water more to develop a more sustainable world?

Waste management

- Design and trial a waste/chemical free lunch programme in your school.
- Develop an environmentally friendly water and plumbing system at home/in school.

Table 9.5 Stages in the engineering design process

Stages of engineering design process	Activity
Ask/define the problem: Introducing criteria and constraints	The specific challenge the children are to address. Q: *What is the problem you want to solve?* *What needs to be designed and who is it for?* *Were there any specific requests or requirements?*
Conducting research	Children carry out research (documentaries, news reports, etc.).
Imagine	Team members explore ideas through brainstorming informed ideas on how to solve the problem and come up with possible solutions. Q: *What is the end product?* *What are the overall goals?* *What are the project requirements and limitations?*
Plan and design	The team choose an idea and decide on how to design their prototype by sketching their design. Q: *What will you need?* *What steps will you take?* *Why did you design it this way?*
Create/build	Team members create the design and prototype they selected.
Test and evaluate	The teams test their design to check if it works as they expected and as per the criteria. They evaluate the design based on how well the design met the criteria and solve the problem. Q: *How will you test your design?* *Did it work as you expected?*
Redesign/ improve	The team decide if they needed to change/alter/redesign the prototype in any way. Q: *Do you need to change or alter or improve your design in any way? Why?* *How will you do this?*
Communicate	The children present their prototypes to the class mentioning the problem, their design solutions and their results.

Coping with extreme weather conditions due to climate change

- Design and create a model floating garden that could survive a flood.
- Design and create a model house that can withstand rising flood waters/hurricane/ extreme temperatures (high and low).
- Design and create a drought-tolerant garden.
- Creating a ground water run off system to treat floodwaters.
- Design and build a roof structure to reduce the amount of storm damage during high-wind events.
- Invent an emergency shelter that can fit a person, and is sturdy and quick to build.

Developing innovations and prototypes in preventing climate change

Open-ended STEM projects

To ensure that global learning, sustainability and citizenship education are incorporated effectively into STEM education, refer children to the 17 Global Goals for Sustainable Development (discussed in greater detail in Chapter 14) and ask them to incorporate as many of the goals into the following STEM-focused projects on climate change.

How can we engineer a better, more sustainable world?

- Make the world a better place through STEM inventions.
- Use the ESD to develop a solution to climate change.
- Design to improve community resilience under six development themes: Self-supply water and sanitation, on and off grid energy systems, climate resilient infrastructure, and applying big data in the community.
- Develop prevention equipment/structures/technologies to tackle climate change.
- Design and test an energy-efficient model school.
- Design and test a sustainable home of the future.
- Design a local and sustainable amenity (e.g., a playground).
- Design and develop a more energy efficient hand dryer for toilet facilities.
- Create sensor technologies in detecting changes to our environment.

Research

After children have been asked to find a problem to a solution or a challenge has been posed, the next step in the EDP involves the children researching the topic and content.

There are many children's books and videos that may help the children with this process in developing their understanding of engineering and the work of engineers in developing a more sustainable world, for example:

1 Start Engineering (2013). *Dream, Invent, Create.* USA: Start Engineering.
    This book provides an introduction to the inspiring possibilities of engineering, helping them make a connection between the everyday world and engineering and that engineers can make the world a better place. Available at: http://start-engineering.com/kids-book.
2 Kamkwamba, W. (2009). *The Boy Who Harnessed the Wind.*
    When 14-year-old William Kamkwamba's Malawi village was hit by a drought, everyone's crops began to fail. Without enough money for food, let alone school, William spent his days in the library … and figured out how to bring electricity to his village. Persevering against the odds, William built a functioning windmill out of junkyard scraps, and thus became the local hero who harnessed the wind.
3 Bailey, J. (2010). *What's the Point of Being Green?*
    Written especially for young adult readers, this book covers the basics on all major environmental issues, presenting them in brief, illustrated copy blocks that are easy to read.
4 *Dream Big: Engineering Our World.*
    Dream Big video celebrates the human ingenuity behind engineering marvels big and small, and reveals the heart that drives engineers to create better lives for people around the world. Available at: https://dreambigfilm.com/.

Table 9.6 Pedagogies incorporated into engineering for sustainable development activities

Pedagogies incorporated into engineering for sustainable development activities
Cross-curricular: Interdisciplinary including approaches to analyse, reason and communicate as children pose, solve and interpret problems in a variety of novel situations (Jolly, 2017).
Empathy: The design and prototyping process in developing solutions to climate change are conducted through an empathetic lens (plant, animal and human life) (Plattner, 2010; Sun, 2017).
Minds-on, hands-on: Ideating, discussions, drawing diagrams, 'thinkering', prototyping, testing, re-testing, re-designing and 'iterating' after failures (Cox et al., 2017).
Discursive design practices: Valuing others' ideas and value communication (Gubrium and Holstein, 2000).
Mixing ideas concept: Each project team member is involved in the process of brainstorming ideas on how they could solve the problem or design responses to the STEM challenge (Guha et al., 2004).
The greening STEM model: An interdisciplinary and collaborative approach to teaching STEM subjects that uses the natural environment and real-world challenges to engage learners and deliver high-quality STEM education.
Community-based learning: Providing context and relevance of the STEM projects and challenges by exploring the local environment.
Innovators DNA:
• *Questioning:* Asking questions to understand how things work and really are today, why they are that way and how they might be changed or disrupted. Questions provoke new insights, connections, possibilities and directions.
• *Observing:* Observe the world around them to gain insights into and ideas for new ways of doing things.
• *Experimenting:* Trying out new experiences and piloting new ideas (Dyer et al., 2011).

The many strategies in how to engage children with the topic of climate change that were outlined previously in this chapter can also be used during the research step of the EDP.

Engineering for sustainable development

All the above-mentioned activities that are flexible, self-directed, social, productive and responsible incorporate not only the EDP within STEM education but also a variety of important skills and approaches outlined in Table 9.6.

Conclusion

Our future generations need to be ready to tackle an array of global challenges. EfS, and in particular, education about sustainable energy and climate change should and can feature prominently as part of STEM education. EfS is future-focused, change-orientated, learner-centred, community-connected and interdisciplinary, involving critical inquiry, empowerment and participation. STEM projects involving challenges based on local, national and global issues incorporate all such characteristics of EfS and play an important role in promoting EfS across the school community (Davis, 2010).

Interdisciplinary STEM engineering projects allow for a more flexible, emergent curriculum, that is relevant, integrated and embedding sustainability at its core (Pratt, 2010). Such projects allow children time for critical reflection and to question the world around them, how things work, how they might be changed or disrupted, thus encouraging more active and responsible citizens.

The cross-curricular STEM challenges and projects outlined in the chapter all incorporated the EDP and thus develop 'Engineering Habits of Mind' (EHoM) among children. The activities allow children to think and act like an engineer. Not only are the activities developing children's STEM skills and competencies but also the activities are designed to develop the children's STEM literacies and *Science Capital* to develop a generation of informed, proactive 'solutionaries' that can problem-find, problem-solve, visualise and improve. The Royal Academy of Engineering (2011) argues that a more extensive promotion of EHoM as a mechanism for improving *Science Capital* and engineering for sustainable development among young people is needed.

STEM challenges and projects based on developing solutions in dealing with the impacts of climate change and developing innovations and prototypes in preventing climate change, involve questioning … questioning everything, that is, how things work? Why were they designed it that way? How they might be changed? Questioning can provoke new insights, connections, possibilities and directions. Children should not be afraid to think outside the box and to ask the question 'why?' We need to provide the opportunity for children to start questioning why? We also need to allow children to step out of certainty into uncertainty, by exploring an ever-changing world, imagining the past and looking to the future (Liston, 2015). Therefore, these projects can also promote high levels of empathy, compassion and understanding.

The imagining, designing and creating elements of the EDP unleash children's creativity through ideating, thinkering, prototyping and piloting new ideas. Innovative STEM education can thus help in developing a population of future 'disruptors' that will not allow our world to be destroyed by climate change but that will design and engineer a better world for all. As Steve Jobs once said, 'Why join the navy if you can be a pirate?'

Resources

Examples of organisations that have developed STEM (Engineering) resources and ideas for STEM projects for the teaching of climate change:

- Teach Engineering: https://www.teachengineering.org.
- Engineering is Elementary: http://www.eie.org.
- Practical Action: www.practicalaction.org.
- STEM Learning: https://www.stem.org.uk/engineering-resources/primary.
- Royal Academy of Engineering: https://www.raeng.org.uk/publications/other/engineering-material-for-a-greener-planet-final.

References

Archer, L., Dawson, E., DeWitt, J., Seakins, A. and Wong, B. (2015) "Science capital": A conceptual, methodological, and empirical argument for extending Bourdieusian notions of capital beyond the arts. *Journal of Research in Science Teaching, 52*(7), 922–948.

Augustine, N.R., Barrett, C., Cassell, G., Grasmick, N., Holliday, C. and Jackson, S. (2010) *Rising above the gathering storm, revisited: Rapidly approaching category 5.* Washington, DC: National Academy of Sciences, National Academy of Engineering, Institute of Medicine.

Beatty, A. (2011) *Successful STEM education a workshop summary.* Washington, DC: National Academies Press.

Burns, T., O'Connor, D. and Stocklmayer, S. (2003) Science communication: a contemporary definition. *Public Understanding of Science, 12,* 183–202.

Bybee, R.W. (2013) *The case for STEM education. Challenges and opportunities.* Arlington VA: NSTA Press.

Carnevale, A.P. Smith, N.S. and Melton, M. (2011) *STEM.* Georgetown University: Center on Education and the Workforce.

Cox, C., Apedoe, X., Silk, E. and Schunn, C. (2017) Analysing materials in order to find design opportunities for the classroom. In Goldman, S. and Kabayadondo, Z eds., *Taking design thinking to school. How technology of design can transform teachers, learners and classrooms.* New York: Routledge, 205–220.

Davis, J.M. (2010) *Young children and the environment. Early education for sustainability.* Cambridge: Cambridge University Press.

Davison, K., McCauley,V., Domegan, C. and McClune, W. (2008) *A review of science outreach strategies north and south with some recommendations for improvement: A report for the Standing Conference on Teacher Education North and South.* Armagh: Centre for Cross Border Studies. Available at: file:///C:/Users/user/Desktop/Second%20Class/College/STEM%20Communications%20readings/science_booklet%20(1).pdf.

DES (Department of Education and Skills) (2014) *'Education for Sustainability': The national strategy on education for sustainable development in Ireland, 2014-2020.* Available at: http://www.education.ie/en/Publications/Education-Reports/National-Strategy-on-Education-for-Sustainable-Development-in-Ireland-2014-2020.pdf#sthash.XfgyNiGv.dpuf.

DES (Department of Education and Skills) (2017) *STEM education policy statement 2017-2026.* Dublin: Government of Ireland.

Dolan, A.M. (2012) Education for sustainability in light of Rio +20: Implications for reforms of the B.Ed. degree programme in Ireland. *Policy and Practice: A Development Education Review, 15,* 28–48.

Dolan, A.M. (2015) Education for sustainability: An inclusive, holistic framework for teacher education. In O'Donnell, A. ed., *The inclusion delusion? Reflections on democracy, ethos and education.* Oxford: Peter Lang, pp. 133–149.

Dolan, A.M. (2020) *Powerful primary geography: A toolkit for 21st century learning.* London: Routledge.

Douglass, J.A. and Edelstein, R. (2009) The global competition for talent: The rapidly changing market for international students and the need for a strategic approach in the US.

Dyer, J. Gregersen, H. and Christensen, C.M. (2011) *The innovator's DNA: Mastering the five skills of disruptive innovators.* Boston, MA: Harvard Business Review Press.

Gerlach, J. (2012) *STEM: Defying a simple definition.* NSTA Reports. Accessible at: http://www.nsta.org/publications/news/story.aspx?id=59305.

Godemann, J. and Michelsen, G. (2011) *Sustainability communication: Interdisciplinary perspectives and theoretical foundation.* New York: Springer.

Gubrium, J. and Holstein, J. (2000) Analysing interpretive practice. In Denzin, N. and Lincoln, Y. eds., *Handbook of qualitative research.* 2nd Edition. Thousand Oaks, CA: Sage, 487–508.

Guha, M.L., Druin, A., Chipman, G., Fails, J.A., Simms, S. and Farber, A. (2004) *Mixing ideas: A new technique for working with young children as design partners.* Proceedings of IDC 2004. College Park, Maryland: ACM Press.

Harlen, W. and Qualter, A. (2004) *The Teaching of science in primary schools.* 4th Edition. Great Britain: Fulton Publishers.

Havice, W. (2009) The power and promise of a STEM education: Thriving in a complex technological world. In ITEEA ed., *The overlooked STEM imperatives: Technology and engineering.* Reston, VA: ITEEA, 10–17.

Howarth, S. and Scott, L. (2014) *Success with STEM. Ideas for the classroom, STEM clubs and beyond.* London: Routledge.

Huling, M. and Speake Dwyer, J. (2018) *Designing meaningful STEM lessons.* Arlington VA: NSTA Press.

Jolly, A. (2017) *STEM by design: Strategies and activities for grades 4–8.* New York: Routledge.

Kennedy, T. and Odell, M. (2014) Engaging students in STEM education. *Science Education International*, *25*(3), 246–258.

Liddy, M. (2012). From marginality to the mainstream: Learning from action research for sustainable development. *Irish Educational Studies*, *31*(2), 139–155.

Liston, M. (2013a) Primary science–linking concepts and ideas. *Intouch*, *131*, 54–55 (March 2013). INTO (Irish National Teachers Association).

Liston, M. (2013b) Concept mapping. Linking scientific concepts together in the primary science classroom. *Intouch*, *137*, 58–59 (September 2013).

Liston, M. (2013c) Children acting like scientists. *Science*, *49*(1), 19–20, November 2013.

Liston, M. (2015) Science is just for 'nerds'? In *The inclusion delusion: Reflections on democracy, ethos and education*, Chapter 11. Oxford: Peter Lang Publishing, 181–196.

Liston, M. (2018) Designing meaningful STEM lessons, *Science*, *53*(4), 34–37.

Liston, M., Dolan, A.M., Brennan, A. and Taylor, M. (2019) Review and research on the impact of the sustainable energy authority of Ireland (SEAI) Schools Programme. Report compiled by Mary Immaculate College on behalf of the SEAI.

Mihelich, J., Sarathchandra, D., Hormel, L., Storrs, D. and Wiest, M. (2016) Public understanding of science and K-12 STEM education outcomes: Effects of Idaho parents' orientation toward science on students' attitudes toward science. *Bulletin of Science, Technology and Society*, *36*(3), 164–178. Available at: http://journals.sagepub.com.libraryproxy.mic.ul.ie/doi/pdf/10.1177/0270467616687217.

Mochizuki, Y. and Bryan, A. (2015) Climate change education in the context of education for sustainable development: Rationale and principles. *Journal of Education for Sustainable Development*, *9*(1), 4–26.

Morrison, J. (2006) *TIES STEM Education monograph series: Attributes of STEM education—the student, the academy, the classroom.* TIES: Teaching Institute of Essential Science.

National Research Council (2011) Successful STEM education: A workshop summary.

NCCA (2010) Curriculum overload in primary schools: Experiences and reflections from the learning site. http://www.ncca.ie/en/Curriculum_and_Assessment/Early_Childhood_and_Primary_Education/Primary_School_Curriculum/PSN_Curriculum_Overload/Curriculum_overload_voices_from_learning_site.pdf.

OECD (2006) *Evolution of student interest in science and technology studies—Policy report.* Paris: Global Science Forum.

Orpwood, G.W., Schmidt, B.A. and Hu, J. (2012) Competing in the 21st century skills race, 15.

Plattner, H. (2010) *Boot camp bootleg.* Palo Alto: Design School Stanford. Accessed at: https://dschool.stanford.edu/resources/the-bootcamp-bootleg.

Pratt, R. (2010) Practical possibilities and pedagogical approaches for early childhood education for sustainability. In Davis, J.M. ed., *Young children and the environment. Early education for sustainability.* Cambridge: Cambridge University Press.

Prensky, M. (2016) Education to better their world. *Unleashing the power of 21st-century kids.* New York: Teachers College Press (Columbia University).

Ramirez, R. (2013) *Save our science: How to inspire a new generation of scientists.* https://1lib.eu/book/2225688/4c6605?dsource=recommend&regionChanged=&redirect=236521497.

Roberts, G. (2002) SET for Success, review. Available at: http://www.nationalstemcentre.org.uk/stem-programme/stem-background.

Roberts, A. (2012) A justification for STEM education. *Technology and Engineering Teacher*, (May/June) 1–5.

Royal Academy of Engineering (2011) Notes for STEM clubs and STEM ambassadors resources, Engineering engagement project. Available at: http://www.raeng.org.uk/education/eenp/engineering_resources/pdf/Hazard_Sheet.pdf.

Stohlmann, M., Moore, T. and Roehrig, G. (2012) Considerations for teaching integrated STEM education. *Journal of Pre-College Engineering Education Research*, 2(1), 28–34. doi: 10.5703/1288284314653.

Straw, S., Hart, R. and Harland, J. (2011) *An evaluation of the impact of STEMNET's services on pupils and teacher*. Slough: NFER.

Sun, K.L. (2017) Empathy in STEM education. In Goldman, S. and Kabayadondo, Z. eds., *Taking design thinking to school. How technology of design can transform teachers, learners and classrooms*. New York: Routledge, 147–160.

Thunberg, G. (2019) *No one is too small to make a difference*. UK: Allen Lane.

Tytler, R., Osborne, J., Williams, G., Tytler, K. and Clark, J.C. (2008) Opening up pathways: Engagement in STEM across the primary-secondary school transition. Retrieved July 4, 2008: http://www.dest.gov.au/sectors/career_development/publications_resources/profiles/Opening_Up_Pathways.html.

Vandeweyer, M. (2016) *The growing need for developing (the right) STEM skills* [online]. Available at: https://oecdskillsandwork.wordpress.com/2016/05/06/the-growing-need-for-developing-the-right-stem skills/.

Varner, J. (2014) Scientific outreach: Toward effective public engagement with biological science. *BioScience*, 64(4), 333–340. Available at: https://doi.org/10.1093/biosci/biu021.

Vasquez, J.A. Comer, M. and Sneider, C. (2013) *STEM lesson essentials, grades 3–8. Integrating science, technology, engineering, and mathematics*. New York: Heinemann.

Vasquez, J.A. Comer, M. and Villegas, J. (2017) *STEM lesson guideposts. Creating STEM lessons for your curriculum*. New York: Heinemann.

Waldron, F., Oberman, R., Ruane, B., Kavanagh, R. and Murphy, C. (2011) *An Evaluation of SEAI's Education Programmes*. (A report by the Centre for Human Rights and Citizenship Education, St Patrick's College, Drumcondra).

Weil, Z. (2016) *The world becomes what we teach: Educating a generation of solutionaries*. Cheltenham, UK: Lantern Books.

Wilson, R.A. (2009) *The demand for STEM graduates: Some benchmark projections*. London: Council for Industry and Higher Education.

Wilson, H. and Mant, J. (2011) What makes an exemplary teacher of science? The pupils' perspective. *School Science Review*, 93(342), 121–125.

10 Exploring climate change education outside the classroom

Anne O'Dwyer

Introduction

Learning outdoors incurs several physical, cognitive and psychological benefits. Immersing the learner in his/her own local habitat when learning about the environment and climate change makes the abstract concrete and makes the global context applicable in a local place. For many children in today's society, much free time and playtime is spent indoors involving technology. This compares to previous generations of children who may have climbed trees, built tree houses and observed armies of ants in their playtime. This change has an impact on children's connection with their outdoor environment, both locally and globally. When children spend less time outdoors, they do not have the same physical, emotional and social connection with their local place. Local knowledge including knowing the names of trees, wildlife and birds is not validated in a technology-based society. Sir David Attenborough (2010) has stated, 'no one will protect what they don't care about; and no one will care about what they have never experienced'. Learning outdoors places children in a natural environment and thus provides opportunities for children to value and care for this space.

Research shows that although young children are aware of environmental problems such as climate change, knowledge of the causes and the solutions for these environmental problems appear to be more difficult for them to comprehend (Evans et al., 2007). In school science curricula internationally, there has been a shift towards a focus on skills-based teaching and learning, particularly at primary level, e.g., science programmes of study in the United Kingdom (Department of Education, 2015) and Next Generation Science Standards in the United States (National Research Council, 2012). This development of skills has been strongly associated with outdoor learning (Kerr, 2019). The focus of this chapter is learning about climate change outside the classroom.

This chapter aims to:

- Provide a rationale for teaching and learning about climate change in outdoor settings.
- Outline practical considerations for education about climate change through outdoor learning.
- Discuss the importance of cultivating school, home and community links.
- Facilitate the development of scientific and geographical skills through climate change education.
- Support sustainable and longitudinal approaches to climate change education.

Rationale for learning science and geography outdoors

Outdoor learning has long been regarded as a valuable schooling experience in Scandinavian countries, given its recognition in contributing to physical, emotional and intellectual development (Humberstone and Stan, 2011). Increasing the availability and accessibility of outdoor learning experiences may also provide for greater creativity and encourage life-long learning (Waite et al., 2006). Learning science outdoors provides opportunities to readily investigate topics affecting our climate in contexts and communities (Monroe et al., 2017). This helps to make learning more relevant and meaningful.

Climate change education involves a number of scientific and geographical skills: observing and recording environmental changes; collecting, analysing, seeking patterns and interpreting our own data as well as data from secondary sources; communicating with others; investigating and experimenting with materials. However, as well as skills and understanding, learners need to appreciate the importance of their environment for meaningful learning and to develop an inquisitive and proactive attitude towards climate change. People's feelings about the environment are paramount; thus, affective learning needs to be explored alongside the role of cognition (Omdahl, 2014). The affective learning domain is potentially a key entry point for environmental education (Staus and Falk, 2013), and thus positive climate action.

As well as developing an understanding of skills and content knowledge, the suggested pedagogies in this chapter strive to connect learners' curiosity about scientific concepts with their local places. A reliance on knowledge and skills alone may hinder environmental education (Pooley and O'Connor, 2000). Children's experiential learning produces affective-based attitudes; hence, the use of local contextual learning opportunities is important for the further development of positive environmental attitudes (Pooley and O'Connor, 2000). It is essential that children are informed and empowered to make critical decisions about how to contribute to a better environment on a local, national and international level. Consequently, learning science and geography outdoors, provides opportunities for learners to value and appreciate their outdoor space. This extends learning beyond the school and classroom to the home and community.

Practical considerations for outdoor learning

In a review of literature, Dillon et al. (2006) identified a number of challenges for teachers and schools when learning outdoors. These include prior knowledge and experience, fears and phobias, health and safety issues, learning styles and preferences (Dillon et al., 2006). These factors affect teachers' confidence and preparedness to situate learning outdoors. However, outdoor learning has potential to maximise children's learning. The following guidelines (Department of Education and Science, 1999) facilitate planning for outdoor learning:

- **The school setting:** Be aware of the habitats local to the school. These may include one or more mini-habitats such as hedgerow, footpath, lawn, tree, flower garden, wild flower area, meadow, pond and sand dune. The teacher should be knowledgeable about all potential learning sites before bringing learners outside.
- **Seasonal factors:** Where possible, the teacher should be flexible when planning an outdoor lesson, as plans are often subject to favourable weather conditions. It is important to consider outdoor learning across the different seasons to support observation of different habitats at different times of the year.

- **Extend area with age:** The site and setting identified for outdoor learning should be suitable for the age of the learners. It is recommended that younger children should be more restricted, while the extent and opportunities for outdoor learning will increase with older classes, e.g., teachers may begin with a focus on an individual tree with younger classes and extend to a forest walk with older classes.
- **Have a purpose:** Teachers should have a clear purpose outlined and shared with the children before going outdoors. Consider integration with other subject areas to prepare the children for the outdoor learning. Plan possible questions to initiate the outdoor investigation as well as preparing for possible questions the children may ask.
- **Stay safe:** It is essential that teachers have planned adequate supervision when bringing a class outdoors and/or off the school site. Ensure there are a number of adults to accompany the class. All adults should be cognizant of possible risks or hazards.
- **Be prepared:** Plan and consider the safe use of appropriate equipment when outdoors, e.g., laminated worksheets to mark with whiteboard pens are useful. When using equipment as part of their experiential learning, children need to be familiar with the safe-use of the equipment beforehand, e.g., they may need practice reading a thermometer.
- **Be organised:** Organise how the class group will work before you leave the classroom, e.g., paired tasks or group work. Consider the value and/or feasibility of some children completing different tasks to enable peer teaching. Plan and anticipate the timing of each activity. Ensure timing is realistic within the allocated time slot.
- **Have respect:** Encourage children to care for and respect plant and animal life. Act responsibly during outdoor learning.
- **Plan what's next:** Always plan follow-up work with the children when they return to the classroom. It is essential to maximise the potential of each opportunity to learn outdoors.

School, home and community links

The home and community are valuable settings in which to extend meaningful learning from the school classroom. Developing home and community links empowers children to become mini-ambassadors for climate change education beyond the school setting. There has been much research (Epstein et al., 2009) highlighting the important role of parents and communities as part of children's learning. Figure 10.1 represents the potential value of the child as the core participant in a three-way relationship between home, school and the community. To develop and maintain a partnership with home and community, schools and teachers need to work to develop and implement appropriate practices of partnership. As the common denominator, the child has the potential to become a *Climate Change Champion* by pollenating ideas within, across and between the three contexts.

Teachers may feel that they lack the necessary skills and knowledge to adequately teach about climate change (Plutzer et al., 2016). Furthermore, they may be hesitant about establishing home/school links for climate change education due to concerns about parents' responses (Wise, 2010). In some settings, teachers are concerned that addressing climate change in their community could affect their status and credibility, given public scepticism about climate change in some communities (Wojcik et al., 2014).

Moll et al. (1992) outline the mutual and collaborative benefits of involving parents, home, family, play and culture as part of classroom learning. They have used the term

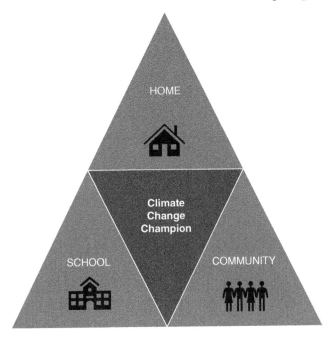

Figure 10.1 Central role of the child as *Climate Change Champion* at home, in school and in the community

'funds of knowledge' to refer to knowledge that has been developed historically and culturally and skills that are essential for household functioning and well-being. Environmental-friendly practices may form an example of such household funds of knowledge. Parents and community representatives could share their experiences with children, e.g., recycling, upcycling, composting and other everyday practices that support a better climate. Examples from the local community create a social context for informing, assisting, and supporting teachers' work. As people at every age are sensitive to social norms, community-based expectations can support efforts to change behaviours or take action against climate change (Flora et al., 2014).

Pedagogical approaches to develop scientific & geographical skills in outdoor learning

Experiential, inquiry-based and constructivist approaches are effective for science and environmental education (Bybee et al., 2006). The challenge of climate change education points to the potential need to combine experiential learning and social constructivist perspectives in a new way (Monroe et al., 2017). Experiential learning encompasses the process of active engagement and discovery with reflection and mental engagement (Kolb, 1984). Focusing on personally relevant and meaningful information and using active and engaging teaching methods are two necessary components of climate change education (Monroe et al., 2017). In acknowledging the impact of climate change may be more obvious in certain places in the world, it is important for primary school children that the distant, global threat of climate change is illustrated in a meaningful manner, relevant to their own local context.

A constructivist approach provides learners with the intellectual space needed for them to critically examine complex issues (Bruner, 1966). Bardsley and Bardsley (2007) have advocated the use of a constructivist approach to teaching and learning about climate change. Furthermore, social-constructivist perspectives emphasise that knowledge is constructed through social interaction (Dillon, 2003), and learning occurs through small group discussions and deliberations.

Child-centred strategies commonly used within the primary classroom are suitable for use in the outdoor classroom also. These could include walking debates, small group discussions and field trips. The following strategies help move learners beyond the basics of climate science (Monroe et al., 2017):

1 *Deliberative discussion* to help learners better understand their own and others' viewpoints and knowledge about climate change.
2 Opportunities to *interact with scientists and to experience the scientific process* for themselves.
3 *Uncover and address misconceptions* about climate change.
4 Involving learners in the *design and implementation of school or community projects* to address some aspect of climate change.

The ideas in the next section of this chapter include elements of these strategies. They illustrate pedagogical approaches and teaching ideas for each of the three domains outlined in Figure 10.1, home, school and community. The teaching ideas are outlined as units of work, thus encouraging a sustained and integrated approach to climate change education, as opposed to discrete stand-alone lesson ideas. Useful websites with further information to support development of individual lessons are included at the end of this chapter.

Teaching ideas to support outdoor learning

Each of the teaching ideas presented here explicitly focus on the development of skills through the context of learning outdoors at school, at home and in the community.

A longitudinal approach at school

Working with weather is an important part of climate change education (Dolan, 2020). To understand 'climate change', learners need to appreciate and understand the meaning of 'climate'. Climate refers to weather patterns over a very long time, e.g., 30 years. Weather conditions change seasonally and daily. While a school year is too short to gather data about local climate, local weather data can be collated. School weather data can be collated with information from secondary sources to make inferences about local weather and climate changes. Exploring our weather to understand climate change is suitable for children (8–13 years). In this longitudinal weather-recording project, the learners:

• Recognise that local weather represents short-term conditions of our environment.
• Observe and record weather changes day-to-day, week-to-week and season-to-season.
• Develop an understanding that climate refers to weather patterns over a long time.

Lessons can begin in the classroom by analysing weather forecasts, reports, charts and statistics from local, national and global sources. Learners should develop an awareness of

Figure 10.2 A rain gauge designed by a 10-year-old child

different climates across the globe. Encourage learners to interview a parent/grand-parent about their experiences of climate growing up, changes over time or perhaps experiences of living in different countries and climates, linking both the science and geography curricula. Middle classes could use recyclable plastic bottles to make a rain gauge (Figure 10.2). Older and senior classes could use plastic cups and other available materials to make an anemometer (Figure 10.3). Recycled materials can also be used to

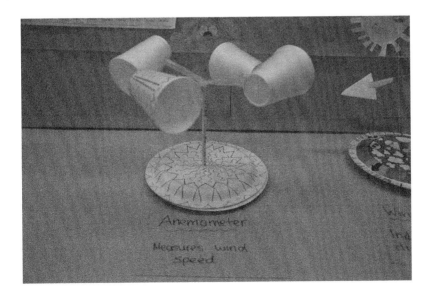

Figure 10.3 An anemometer designed by a 9-year-old child

Source: Dolan (2020:117)

make a weather vane (Figure 10.4). Instructions for designing and making equipment to measure different aspects of weather are available on the education sections of Met Éireann and Met Office websites.

The learners need to plan their weather recording database, i.e., design a table(s) to collate daily recordings for each weather type. Discuss where to set up the weather station(s), when to record (same time of day) and what to record (number of measurements and units of measurements). Depending on age and ability, different groups could take responsibility for collecting different types of data daily, e.g., temperature (ground & air), rainfall, wind (speed & direction) and cloud cover.

The following skills are developed over time, as the weather data is collected throughout the school year:

- *Predicting:* Weather forecasting, data collection.
- *Observing:* Weather conditions over a period.
- *Estimating & measuring:* Weather conditions daily.
- *Recording & communicating:* Daily data and representing graphically for communication.

Figure 10.4 A weather vane designed by an 11-year-old child

- *Analysing:* Interpreting data gathered by the class, as well as secondary data sources, e.g., sea level changes and global temperatures, to make inferences about climate change locally and globally.

Table 10.1 provides guidelines to scaffold learner development through the design and make stages (Department of Education and Science, 1999:21–22) for weather data collection instruments.

Table 10.1 Scaffolding design & make skills

Design & make skill development		Rain gauge (suggestions)	Anemometer (suggestions)
Explore	Free exploration of materials and available resources is essential.	Possible resources include plastic bottle (varying sizes), rulers, permanent markers, scissors and tape.	Possible resources include plastic cups, straws, pipes, lollypop sticks, plasticine, rulers and tape.
	Explore the available recyclable materials – manipulate to hypothesise possible design features and uses of materials.		
	Consider the technical and aesthetic uses of different materials.		
	Encourage adaptations to possible design ideas.		
Plan	This involves the imagining, planning and designing the weather instrument.	A possible plan may be to cut a plastic bottle in half. Invert the top half to sit into the bottom half. The top half forms a funnel to gather the water, the bottom half collects the water.	Straws / lollypop sticks may be attached to four cups. This will need to be supported in the centre.
	Encourage group work, share and communicate ideas.		One cup should be marked to facilitate counting of spins (wind speed) for data collection.
	Make simple annotated drawings, smaller scale (or partial) models.		
	Create a range of design proposals and compare and consider the merits of different designs. Through discussion, assess the feasibility of undertaking different design proposals.		
	Review and adapt designs.		

(Continued)

Table 10.1 (Continued)

Design & make skill development		Rain gauge (suggestions)	Anemometer (suggestions)
Make	Make and produce the instrument that was designed and planned. The development of craft-handling skills, such as cutting, joining, fastening, weaving and linking, will be essential for the construction of the weather data collection instruments.	Consider how to support the designed weather recording instrument.	
	Select and use appropriate tools.	Will it stand alone?	
	This requires careful supervision, and safety is an important skill and attitude for learners to develop at each phase of the designing and making process.	Will it be dug into the ground?	
		This discussion may continue from the planning stage.	
Evaluate	Evaluating the product that has been designed and produced by the children can help them to suggest improvements to their designs and to consider ways of modifying their way of working and planning.	After one week of use, review and evaluate the effectiveness of the designed instrument.	
	Children should be provided with opportunities to review what other groups have produced and to see how well the resulting products match their design proposals.	Is it fit for purpose?	
	Children should suggest modifications to designs and, in an atmosphere of positive criticism, be encouraged to try other design proposals in an effort to provide more appropriate solutions to the problems that were identified.	Is it reliable?	
		Is it in a suitable location?	
		Will it endure weather conditions for longitudinal data collection?	
		After one week, learners should make recommended changes to their designs.	

Supporting learning at home

This teaching idea is for children (4–8 years) in primary education. Through these activities, the learners:

- Observe, discuss and identify a variety of plants and animals in different habitats in the immediate environment.
- Recognise and identify the external parts of living things.
- Observe growth and change over time.

Table 10.2 provides a list of possible fun activities that learners can complete at home that support development of scientific and geographical skills. Further information to support these suggested activities is available in the useful websites (see *Professional Development Support for Teachers*) listed at the end of this chapter. Going on regular walks outside at home will help younger learners notice change over time. Each of the suggested

Table 10.2 Suitable activities to scaffold scientific and geographical skill development at home

Scientific & geographical skills	Suggested activities at home
Observation	*Sensory walk:* Engage all of the senses; sound, touch, smell, colour & shapes of living things.
	Bird watching: Observe and describe birds and their body parts. Listen to their song.
	Colour hunt: Find plants and leaves of different colours. This is particularly ideal for Autumn.
	Hula-hoop focus: Use a hula-hoop to mark a closed area to scaffold closer observation of living things. A magnifying glass may be used.
	Scavenger hunts: Select a number of objects for learners to spot in their home garden space, e.g., animal footprint, feather, different shape leaf, a flower, seeds and berries.
Identification	*'I Spy' game:* Provide parents with identification cards / keys describing the characteristics of living things, e.g., shape and size of leaves, legs / wings / size of mini-beasts etc. Parents can use the description of characteristics to support learners' identification of living things.
Recording	*Drawings:* Of observations, noting presence / absence of living things in different locations.
	Annotated drawings: Of the variety of plants and animals observed and/or identified in various habitats- wall / path/ under tree / lawn / hedge.
Sorting and grouping	Sort autumn leaves, fruits and/or seeds into big/small, rough/smooth, dull/shiny and red / brown. Discuss the similarities and differences.

activities in Table 10.2 could be repeated throughout the year to observe and recognise the changing seasons, and consequent effects on nature and biodiversity. It is recommended that learners and parents explore these activities in their home garden, local park, relative's garden or any available space near home that may provide a suitable and safe environment for the learners' skill development.

There is limited information about the types of living things in local habitats and limited collated evidence of the impact of creating 'micro habitats' to support their survival. These home-based activities are an important avenue to extending parents' and families' awareness of living things in their environment. It is hoped that these activities will encourage families and parents to support learners to understand the impact of our changing climate. Possible ideas could include birdhouses (made from plastic bottles), birdfeeders (made from coffee jars), insect hotels or mini-beast mansion (made from pallets, timber and carpet) and insect pots (made from yogurt cartons). Such activities have potential to contribute to global citizen initiatives, e.g., *Action for Pollinators* (see listed websites at the end of this chapter).

Stepping stones to learning in the community

Meaningful climate change education involves learners developing a relationship with their local place. This takes time, and is supported and sustained through long-term projects (Beames et al., 2012; Dolan, 2016). Place pedagogy is a dynamic and open approach used in Geography education. According to Dolan (2016:53), 'Learning contexts should be set in the real world of children; that is in their own localities'. This facilitates interaction between people and their local places (Somerville, 2010). Elements of place pedagogy include relationship to place, perspectives of place and lived experiences in place. Climate change education is particularly powerful where it is situated in the local place. Recent research (Perkins et al., 2018) has highlighted the need for climate change education to be simultaneously local and global. Situating learning in the local community helps learners to know and care about their local place. Authentic participation in child-centred pedagogies can be transformative and conducive to mitigating the effects of climate change (Perkins et al., 2018). Important elements such as insurance, child safety and protection should be discussed with school management in line with school policies before initiating community links. The suggested steps to support a classroom teacher in initiating and developing a school-community link are outlined in Figure 10.5. Through the *Ready Steady Grow* sequence of learning, the learners:

* Identify the variable factors that affect plant growth.
* Communicate findings of fair test investigation to community partner(s).
* Work with community partner(s) to develop a shared community garden.
* Develop their understanding of sustainable food production.

Children (8–13 years) should be involved in planning the fair test investigation of factors that affect plant growth:

* Deciding what to change, keep the same and measure.
* Introducing concept of a control, for comparison.
* Different groups in the class investigate different factors.
* Communication of findings from fair test investigations to community partner.

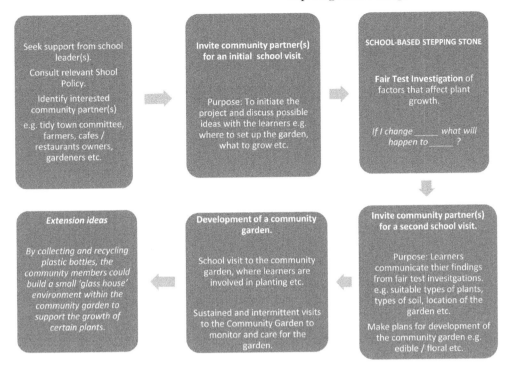

Figure 10.5 Suggested sequence to develop a school–community garden project – ready, steady grow

Involving children in planting trees is a simple and proactive way to develop carbon sinks and thus contribute to positive climate action. Tree planting provides opportunities for scientific, environmental and geographical education, as well as helping young children to think about environmental conservation. Further details for tree planting at home, in the community and in school are available on the Easy Treesie website (www.easytreesie.com).

Conclusion

This chapter has provided rationale and guidelines for supporting teachers to extend learning about climate change beyond the classroom. The suggested teaching activities outlined in this chapter develop scientific and geographical skills included in many primary curricula. The opportunities to use and develop these skills embedded in local and contextualised scenarios surpasses the often-simulated learning of these skills in classroom investigations. Pedagogies outlined support the teacher and learners in developing an on-going discussion about environmental and climate change issues.

Exemplar ideas in this chapter should be considered as longitudinal supporting a deeper and on-going discussion about environmental issues and climate change concepts. Through discussion over time, learners express, compare and analyse different ideas, thus helping them to transform their initial beliefs into reasoned views. It is envisaged that the ideas could be revisited and extended as the learners, parents and community develop greater awareness and knowledge about climate change.

Extending the learning outdoors opens possibilities to link with farmers, gardeners or horticulturists in off-site field visits to learn more about how a changing climate impacts on their everyday practices. Interacting with these professionals outside of the classroom creates opportunity for children to learn about plant growth and living things at home and in their local area. Using a scientific approach to uncover and address factors related to climate change facilitates understanding. Involving learners as leaders of school, home and community-based projects gives them ownership, pride and a sense of place as *Climate Change Champions*. Extending climate change education outside the classroom facilitates each learner's potential as an ambassador for climate action, by building on local 'funds of knowledge' (Moll et al., 1992) at home and in the community.

Useful websites

- Sustainable Energy Authority of Ireland (SEAI): https://www.seai.ie/teaching-sustainability/.
- The Global Learning and Observations to Benefit the Environment (GLOBE) Programme: https://www.globe.gov/.
- Grow It Yourself: https://giy.ie/.
- Professional Development Support for Teachers (PDST): https://pdst.ie/node/3216.
- Heritage in Schools: http://www.heritageinschools.ie/content/resources/Nature-in-the-Park_DCC.pdf.
- National Biodiversity Data Centre: https://pollinators.biodiversityireland.ie/.
- Teaching Science in Place Responsive Ways: http://geocachingforschools.co.uk/research/.
- Easy Treesie: https://www.easytreesie.com/.
- Met Éireann: www.met.ie.
- Met Office: https://www.metoffice.gov.uk.

References

Attenborough, D. (2010) *Speech to communicate conference.* Available at: https://www.bnhc.org.uk/communicate/archive/ (Accessed 25th August, 2019).

Bardsley, D.K. and Bardsley, A.M. (2007) A constructivist approach to climate change teaching and learning, *Geographical Research, 45*(4), 329–339.

Beames, S., Higgins, P. J. and Nicol, R. (2012) *Learning outside the classroom: Theory and guidelines for practice.* London: Routledge.

Bruner J. S. (1966) *Toward a theory of instruction.* Cambridge, Mass: Belknap Press of Harvard University.

Bybee, R. W., Taylor, J.A., Gardner, A., Van Scotter, P., Powell, J.C., Westbrook, A. and Landes, N. (2006) *The BSCS 5E instructional model: Origins and effectiveness.* A report prepared for the Office of Science Education, National Institutes of Health.

Department of Education (2015) *National curriculum in England: Science programmes of study.* Available at: https://www.gov.uk/government/publications/national-curriculum-in-england-science-programmes-of-study/national-curriculum-in-england-science-programmes-of-study [Accessed May 2019].

Department of Education and Science (1999) *Science-social environmental & scientific education, teacher guidelines.* Dublin: Government of Ireland.

Dillon, J. (2003) On learners and learning in environmental education: Missing theories, ignored communities, *Environmental Education Research, 9*(2), 215–226.

Dillon, J., Rickinson, M., Teamey, K., Morris, M., Young Choi, M., Sanders, D. and Benefield, P. (2006) The value of outdoor learning: Evidence from research in the UK and elsewhere, *School Science Review, 87*(320), 107–111.

Dolan, A.M. (2016) Place-based curriculum making: devising a synthesis between primary geography and outdoor learning, *Journal of Adventure Education and Outdoor Learning, 16*(1), 49–62.

Dolan, A.M. (2020) *Powerful primary geography: A toolkit for 21st century learning.* London: Routledge.

Epstein, J., Sander, M.G., Sheldon, S., Simon, B.S., Salinas, K.C., Jansorn, N.R., VanVoorhis, F.L., Martin, C.S, Thomas, B.G., Greenfield, M.D., Hutchins, D.J. and Williams, K.J. (2009) *School, family and community partnerships – Your handbook for action.* 3rd Edition. California: Sage.

Evans, G.W., Brauchle, G., Haq, A., Stecker, R., Wong, K. and Shapiro, E. (2007) Young children's environmental attitudes and behaviors, *Environment and Behavior, 39*(5), 635–659.

Flora, J., Saphir, M., Lappe, M., Roser-Renouf, C., Maibach, E. and Leiserowitz, A. (2014) Evaluation of a national high school entertainment education program: The alliance for climate education, *Climatic Change, 127*(3–4), 419–434.

Humberstone, B. and Stan, I. (2011) Outdoor learning: Primary pupils' experiences and teachers' interaction in outdoor learning, *Education 3-13 International Journal of Primary, Elementary and Early Years Education, 39*(5), 529–540.

Kerr, K. (2019) Teacher development through co-teaching outdoor science and environmental education across the elementary-middle school transition, *The Journal of Environmental Education, 51*(1), 29–43. DOI: 10.1080/00958964.2019.1604482.

Kolb, D.A. (1984) *Experiential learning: Experience as the source of learning and development.* Vol. 1. Englewood Cliffs, NJ: Prentice-Hall.

Moll, L.C., Amanti, C., Neff, D. and Gonzalez, N. (1992) Funds of knowledge for teaching: Using a qualitative approach to connect homes and classrooms, *Theory into Practice, 31*(2), 132–141.

Monroe, M.C., Plate, R.R., Oxarart, A., Bowers, A. and Chaves, W.A. (2017) Identifying effective climate change education strategies: a systematic review of the research, *Environmental Education Research, 25*(6), pp. 791–812. DOI: 10.1080/13504622.2017.1360842.

National Research Council (2012) *A framework for K-12 science education: Practices, crosscutting concepts, and core ideas.* Committee on a Conceptual Framework for New K-12 Science Education Standards. Board on Science Education, Division of Behavioral and Social Sciences and Education. Washington, DC: The National Academies Press.

Omdahl, B.L. (2014). *Cognitive appraisal, emotion and empathy.* New York: Psychology Press.

Perkins, K.M., Munguia, N., Moure-Eraso R., Delakowitz, B., Giannetti, B.F., Liu, G., Nurunnabi, M., Will, M. and Velazquez, L. (2018) International perspectives on the pedagogy of climate change, *Journal of Cleaner Production, 200*, 1043–1052.

Plutzer, E., Mccaffrey, M., Hannah, A.L., Rosenau, J., Berbeco, M. and Reid. A.H. (2016) 'Climate confusion among U.S. teachers, *Science, 351*, 664–665.

Pooley, J.A. and O'Connor, M. (2000) Environmental education and attitudes: Emotions and beliefs are what is needed, *Environment and Behavior, 32*(5), 711–723.

Somerville, M.J. (2010) A place pedagogy for 'global contemporaneity', *Educational Philosophy and Theory, 42*(3), 326–344.

Staus, N.L. and Falk, J.H. (2013) 'The role of emotion in ecotourism experiences' In R. Ballantyne and J. Packer eds., *International handbook on ecotourism* (pp. 178–191). UK: Edward Elgar Publishing Limited.

Waite, S., Davis, B. and Brown. K. (2006) *Final report: Current practice and aspirations for outdoor learning for 2–11 year olds in Devon.* Plymouth: University of Plymouth.

Wise, S.B. (2010) Climate change in the classroom: Patterns, motivations, and barriers to instruction among Colorado science teachers, *Journal of Geoscience Education, 58*(5), 297–309.

Wojcik, D.J., Monroe, M.C., Adams, D.C. and Plate, R.R. (2014) Message in a bottleneck? Attitudes and perceptions of climate change in the cooperative extension service in the Southeastern United States, *Journal of Human Sciences and Extension, 2*(1), 51–70.

Section 1 Climate change doodle designed by Lorna Gold

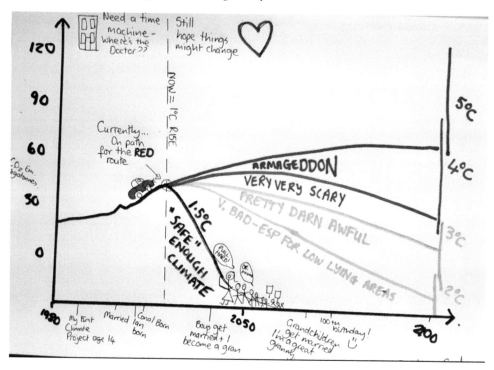

I drew this doodle in early October 2018 as I was waiting on the publication of the IPCC Special Report on Global Warming of 1.5° C. Having just published my book 'Climate Generation', I was increasingly frustrated and infuriated by the level of incomprehensible scientific jargon being used to describe the future impacts of climate change. I decided to draw what it looks like to me basing it on an existing graph of future emissions scenarios. I used that scientific graph to create a new diagram which included my own life events: when I first got interested in climate change, when I got married, the birth of my sons … and the life events into the future. I then gave colourful names to the various future scenarios.

The x-axis shows the carbon emissions (megatonnes) in the atmosphere. The y-axis plots my own lifecycle. Far from being dull and abstract, these future scenarios suddenly came to life. They were terrifying and provocative, but also strikingly clear. They cut through the jargon. Currently in line with our business-as-usual approach, we are on the red path which suggests that the average global temperature could increase by 3 degrees. The only path we want to be on is the black one and we need to change direction fast! To get onto that track, all of us need to 'pull hard' to bend the curve, so that's why I drew some stick people – a mother with some children behind her pulling on the rope by campaigning. I also drew a line between the past and the future. No matter how bad things seem, the heart in the future represents hope things can change. In some ways, it brings to mind the famous phrase of Martin Luther King about the arc of history bending towards justice. At that time, very few people had heard of Greta Thunberg or the climate strike she would spark – she had literally just sat down outside the Swedish parliament. Nobody had heard about bending the curve of a pandemic. In some ways, this little drawing captured something of the moment – of the need to urgently wake up and the power of collective action. As soon as I put it on twitter, it went viral, being shared tens of thousands of times.

Lorna Gold, author of *Climate Generation: Awakening to Our Children's Future* (2018) Dublin: Veritas

Section 2 Sample images from 'The Lost Words of Walney' a self-published book by children from South Walney Junior School in England

Section 3 Design thinking images (chapter 11)

Section 4 Examples of work from the Grow Room project (chapter 12)

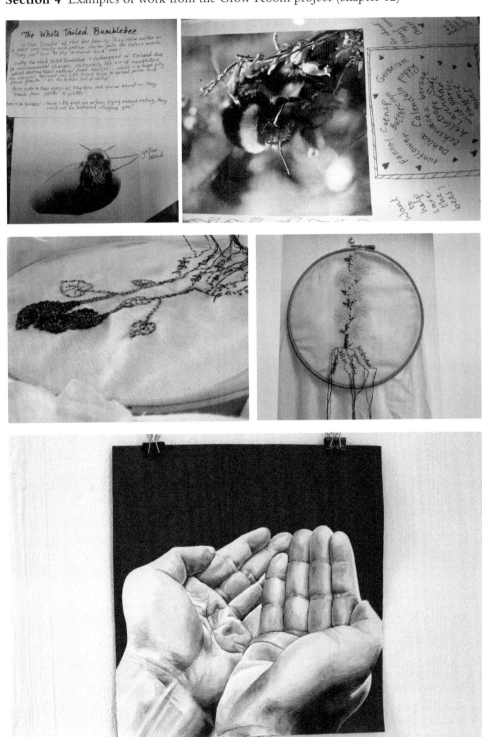

Section 5 Recycling project conducted by children from St. Augustine's Primary School, Clontuskert, Ballinasloe, Co, Galway, Ireland (chapter 13). For more information see https://soyouthinkyoucanrecycle.com/

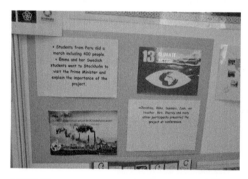

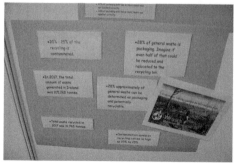

Section 6 An art piece by children (from Catherine McCauley School, Limerick) on display during a local exhibition on waste and consumption in Limerick City Hall (chapter 13)

Section 7 Selection of climate change games (chapter 18)

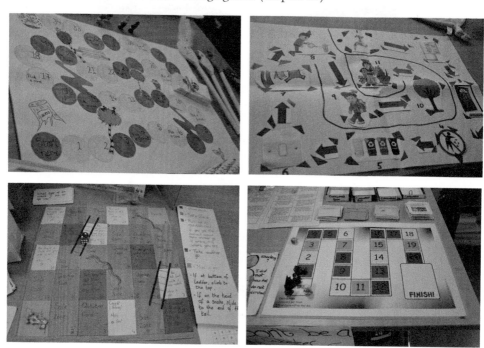

Section 8 Selection of children's climate change research

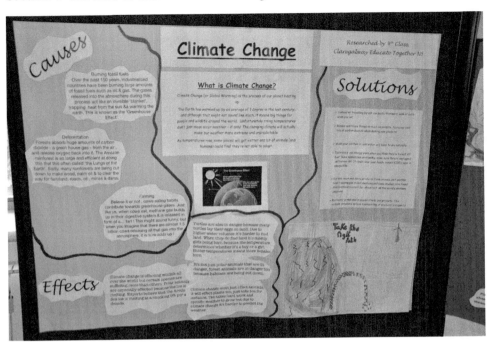

11 Do you see what I see?

A visual lens for exploring climate change

Anne Marie Morrin

Introduction

Internationally, the decline of insects, particularly bees is well-documented. More than 40% of insect species are declining and a third are endangered (Sánchez-Bayo, 2019). Insects are fundamental components of all ecosystems. They are essential for the proper functioning of ecologies as food for other creatures, pollinators, and recyclers of nutrients. While much of the conservation discussions focus on larger species including mammals, birds, and reptiles, insects are disappearing at a faster rate, eight times faster to be precise. Insects play a vital role in human and nonhuman existence. Essentially, insects provide a free service, fertilising and transporting pollen from one flower to another contributing to a thriving agricultural industry as well as the beauty and diversity of the plants in the Irish landscape.

Due to the interconnected nature of ecosystems, a decline in the insect population has far-reaching effects. For instance, insects provide an important food source for many birds, reptiles, amphibians, and fish. Without the pollinators, it will become increasingly difficult for these animals to survive. Consequently, our food sources and healthy ecosystems will be at risk.

In Ireland, the National Biodiversity Data Centre initiated the All-Ireland Pollinator Plan 2015–2020 (AIPP) highlighting the importance of bees for a functioning biosystem. The plan identifies actions and indicators to reverse pollinator decline and improve the quality of our environment and sense of well-being (AIPP, 2015–2020). Each person has a role to play in providing food and protecting the habitat of our pollinators.

At a time when insects are under threat through climate change, the approach explored in this chapter aims to raise understanding and appreciation around the biology (ecology) and the physics (behaviour) of the pollinator. The chapter presents a Science, Technology, Engineering, Art, and Mathematics (STEAM) education project entitled *Do you see what I see?* The project aims to develop appreciation and awareness about the important function of insects.

By fostering children's thoughtfulness about insects, their habitats, and their vital place in the ecosystem, this project helps children to appreciate the consequences of a declining insect population. The project *Do you see what I see?* is an arts education project for initial student teachers. Along with a group of fifth and sixth class children (11–13 years) from a local school, student teachers work alongside contemporary artists and architects, Denis Connolly and Anne Cleary.

STEAM education, creativity and climate change

Global issues such as climate change are multidisciplinary. Therefore, solutions require a transdisciplinary thinking and collaborative responses. STEAM education merges the arts with STEM subjects to improve student engagement, creativity, innovation, problem-solving skills, and conceptual understanding (Hetland and Winner, 2004; Liao, 2016; Root-Bernstein, 2015; Seifter, 2014). The 'A' in STEAM is a term that represents many art forms including liberal arts, physical arts, fine arts, design, and music. The STEAM educational model works in a cross-curricular way, creatively linking key concepts across subject areas to solve real-world problems.

The development of creativity is critical for 21st-century learners (Dolan, 2020; OECD, 2004; Saavedra and Opfer, 2012; Sawyer, 2008). Integrating STEM with the arts helps to prepare children to deal creatively, positively, and productively with global challenges. Core elements of creative thinking include: innovative, originality, applicability, appropriateness, and usefulness (Batey, 2012; Cropley, 2001; Kaufman and Baer, 2012; Mumford, 2003). STEAM education explores different perspectives, potentially generating diverse and innovative responses to big issues such as climate change. By providing new ways of seeing the world, STEAM helps to generate 'innovative thinkers to address the most pressing problems of our times' (Sheridan-Rabideau, 2010:54).

The creative spark! Artists and scientists collaborating

Historically, science and art practices are rooted in the story of humankind. The ancient Egyptian pyramids and the great Pantheon of ancient Rome are exemplars of creativity and science working together. The Renaissance (1300–1600) is the most noticeable connection of the intertwining relationship between art and science. During this time, artists integrated knowledge and sought expertise from many disciplines: art, science, engineering, and medicine. Leonardo Da Vinci (1452–1519) also known as the 'Renaissance man' was a painter, sculptor, architect, musician, engineer, inventor, and student of all things scientific.

In recent times, the STEAM model has undergone a rebirth and gained momentum, widely adapted across all sectors. One of the most noteworthy collaborations is *Project Coral*. Led by the Horniman Aquarium with international partners such as artist Sonia Levy; this project develops techniques to stimulate coral reproduction (Horniman Museum, 2013). Knowledge integration is an inherent aspect of artistic inquiry, as practice emerges from observation and perception of the world around us. The intersection of art and science provides an innovative way of seeing and a complementary mode of learning.

Design thinking: Design for climate change

Art education is widely accepted as playing a crucial role in children's development because of the affective and cognitive nature of art practice (Efland, 2002; Freedman, 2003). Art and design education is currently being rethought by art educators who are interested in big ideas (Harris et al., 2019), and design-based approaches (Vande Zande, 2016). Art practice as research (APAR) embodies a new paradigm in art education (Marshall and D'Adamo, 2011; Sullivan, 2005). Focusing on inquiry where learners are central to the process, art and design research approaches identify the research question(s) and find a solution through art practice.

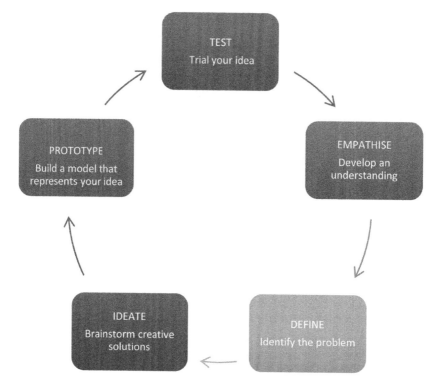

Figure 11.1 The five sequences of design thinking
Source: Adapted from the Stanford d.school design thinking process

Design thinking (DT) is a methodology for creative problem-solving and is a user-focused pedagogy in STEAM education. Do *you see what I see?* uses DT as a holistic framework for promoting creative confidence and supporting the child to understand the complexities of climate change. DT uses pedagogical approaches that are grounded within the artist/designer(s) practices. There are several iterations of DT, and the project presented in this chapter used the DT model proposed by the Hasso–Plattner Institute of Design at Stanford (Stanford d.school, 2010). The Stanford pedagogical framework has five sequences or stages; *Empathy, Define, Ideation, Prototype,* and *Test.* The phases of DT with a linear progression from one phase to another is set out in Figure 11.1. Adapted from Stanford d.school, these steps can be used interchangeably for climate education projects. As each project develops, it may be necessary to go back and forth between stages as ideas change and develop.

The little artists and the little scientists

At the centre of the creative learning experience, is inquiry including play, exploration, risk-taking, flexible-thinking, and making mistakes (Eisner, 2002; Hetland et al., 2013). Integrated STEAM project(s) nurture children's self-awareness and autonomy. In both art and science, the act of creation and investigation plays a central role. Active engagement is fundamental to the learning experience. When children engage in STEAM education, it is good practice to cast children into the dual role of artist and scientist.

Initially children's scientific discovery is facilitated through a stimulus or inquiry question. Through the creation of visual art, children have opportunities for further exploration and reflection on their scientific knowledge. The roles of the artist and scientist are interchangeable as the process develops. It is important to emphasise when planning STEAM projects, art should be valued as a complementary contribution and not just a vehicle for scientific exploration.

The project – Do you see what I see?

If a bee were a superhero, its sight would be its superpower!

About the project

The remit of this project is for children to investigate how bees function within their habitat. An endangered species, the role of hard-working bees is crucial in our planet's ecosystem. As a society, we need to act quickly to protect bees by observing and monitoring their health and welfare. By understanding the world of bees and how they function, children learn to appreciate the valuable function of bees and the importance of their conservation.

Bees are important pollinators for flowers, fruits, and vegetables. This means that they help other plants grow! Bees transfer pollen between the male and female parts of plants, allowing seeds and fruit to grow. Pollination is an essential ecological survival function. Without pollinators, the human race and all of earth's terrestrial ecosystems would not survive. Cultivating 'bee-friendly' plants and leaving some hedgerows and grass-edges free to grow and flower, enriches the environment for honeybees and other pollinators. Bees are the champions of the pollination world and they have a secret weapon: sight!

Bee vision has been a continuous source of fascination for many people in the science and the ecological community. Even though humans see colours, bees have a much broader range of colour vision. Many flowers have distinctive ultraviolet colour patterns, invisible to the human eye, but incredibly eye-catching to bees. The ability of bees to see ultraviolet light gives them an advantage when seeking nectar. Bees get energy from nectar and protein from pollen, and in the process of seeking food they transfer pollen from a flower's male anther to its female stigma. Without the super power of sight, pollination would not be possible.

Design challenge

Design a wearable device/helmet/mask to simulate bee vision. *(Note:the example given involves bees but the overall approach can be adapted to cover a whole range of insects e.g., jumping spiders, flies, and butterflies.)*

Teachers' notes

The concept for the project originated with Irish artists Anne Cleary and Denis Connolly whose art practice focuses on visual perception. Based in Paris, these two artists create innovative and participative art, focusing on perception. The *Do you see what I see project* is based on *The School of Looking* project with focuses particularly on the eye and visual perception. The project outlined was developed and implemented in a regular 5th and 6th classroom setting (for children aged 11-13 years). The lesson is based on a project carried out in Donoughmore National School in Limerick with the Visual Art Elective students at Mary Immaculate College. It follows the research, design, and construction of an exhibit to demonstrate bee vision. The lesson plan is a guide and can be adapted to meet the needs of each class. Children's active engagement using the design thinking framework is central to the learning process. Research can be conducted through further reading. A detailed list of children's literature about bees is included at the end of this chapter. Teachers and children are encouraged to research the work of artists involved in scientific conceptual understanding e.g. Connolly and Cleary, Luke Jerram and Olafur Eliasson.

Where possible teachers are encouraged to avail of current schemes/initiatives that are run by organisations such as the Arts Council in Ireland. For instance currently, the Arts in education scheme involves skilled, professional artists of all disciplines working for and with schools in the making, receiving and interpreting of a wide range of arts experiences. The Arts Council has published several reports, guidelines, and other information about arts in education http://www.artscouncil.ie/Arts-in-Ireland/ Young-people–children-and-education/Arts-in-education/.

Empathy

Empathy is central to the design thinking process. Crucially important for climate change education empathy highlights the significance of listening and discovery, learning new facts, and becoming more curious about the world around us. Phase 1 is about children finding out what they know and what they need to know.

Why are bees so important?

Firstly, let us find out about how a bee functions in the world! Bees have a secret weapon – SIGHT. Did you ever wonder what it would be like to see like a bee? What can you research and discover about bee vision?

Task 1 – Identify and research bee vision and human vision

Children are encouraged to inform themselves through research, site visits (local farms, library, science gallery), class visits from artists and scientists, and exploration of local flora and fauna.

BEE SIGHT – Did you know?

Supernatural – Bees see colours that humans cannot see for example Ultraviolet light (UV). The UV light helps bees detect nectar. How does perceiving UV light help bees find nectar?

Ingenious – Bees have two compound eyes which means they have hundreds of tiny eyes all placed around each other. This allows bees to see up to 300 pictures per second! (Humans can see approx. 65) creating a bigger picture. How might you simulate this vision?

Graphic – Bees have a mosaic-like vision.

Habitat – Bees live in hives (or colonies). The members of the hive are divided into three types. Research the three types of bees.

Target – Bees can see colour. This is what attracts bees to flowers for pollination. However, bees cannot see colours on the red spectrum e.g., red, orange, and pink. Why?

Some fun facts that need further investigation!

1 Honeybees communicate with one another by dancing. Why?
2 If bees did not exist, what would happen to the environment?
3 How many flowers will an average bee visit on a pollen collection trip?
4 How many eyes bees have?
5 Bees can see ultraviolet light. What is ultraviolet light?
6 If bees were superheroes, their power would be sight. Why?
7 Every superhero has at least one sidekick and a bee's pal is light. Why is this the case?

Possible starting points for research – **SIGHT**

Children are encouraged to look at the biology, physics, and chemistry of the eye; the processes involved in vision and the distinguishing features and differences between bee and human vision. Children are encouraged to look at the different parts of the eye, and the processes involved in vision. Children are encouraged to research science concepts, such as the electromagnetic spectrum, considering the differences between ultraviolet light and visible light.

Task 2 – Documentation of children's findings in a journal

(The research gathered and documented informs phase 3 and a drawing design project.) As part of the process and information gathering, the children are encouraged to document their research, observations, and understanding of art/science explorations in a personal A5 journal. Journaling is a valuable and fun way of documenting children's learning 'in' and 'out' of the classroom. The documentation of children's explorations and responses to the theme(s) supports each child's original responses. By documenting findings in their journals, children are encouraged to analyse and (re)interpret the challenges set out by the project.

Suggestion approach to journaling

Each child's journal will be different. The following is a guide:

1 Start at the beginning, what is your starting point? What do you know now?
2 Investigate – Document your research, the facts, science diagrams, photos, sketches, notes, your observations.
3 Development and Exploration – Develop your research and understanding by sketching and field notes.
4 Conclusion – What did you learn from the research? What are the most interesting facts?
5 Reflection – Why is it important to protect bees? From the information gathered how can you contribute to the projection of bees?

Define

The define stage is about facing the challenge and exploring the opportunities set out by the project. Each child's findings contribute to the overall findings, which defines the problem.

Presentation of research

Children are encouraged to share their observations and findings in their journals and spend time sharing ideas with their class. Each child is encouraged to listen, observe, and reflect on all the knowledge gained at the empathy phase. Examples of children's explorations can be seen in Figures 11.2–11.4.

Teacher's notes – Throughout the process, the teacher encourages children to make the connection between bees' function, habitat, and climate change. The teacher facilitates the presentation of ideas and combines all the children's insights collected in their journals.

Define the problem – Try framing the problem so that more avenues and solutions emerge. What is the best way for a human to experience bee vision? How can we make a device that allows us to see like a bee? Could we create a helmet, a set of glasses, or a space which facilitates a walk in the experience?

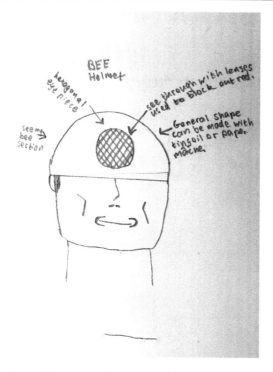

Figure 11.2 Researching bee vision – extract from a journal (12 years)

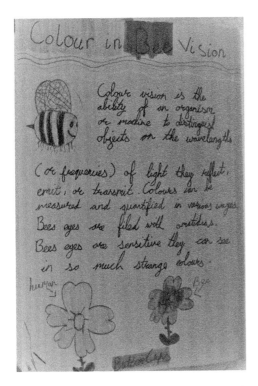

Figure 11.3 Researching bee vision – extract from a journal (12 years)

Figure 11.4 Researching bee vision – extract from a journal (12 years)

Ideation

Children's research and observations collated and presented during phases 1 and 2 provide the context for stage 3: IDEATION. After collating information and initial findings, the children choose the proposal (s) worthy of further investigation.

The ideation stage of the project should be developed in a twofold manner. Firstly, STEAM workshops should be planned and delivered in response to children's ideas and findings. Secondly, research about artists and scientists relevant to children's ideas should support this process. A framework for this stage is presented in Table 11.1.

After the workshops (or other related workshops), children can follow the following IDEATION framework.

The following stages are a guide for the IDEATION stage:

Ideas – Discussion around ideas, children are encouraged to make associations and connections by integrating their personal research and the concepts explored during the workshops (Figure 11.5).

Design – Sketch ideas for a bee vision experience/device.

Exploration – Material manipulation and exploration. Explore the form and optics of device (what might the bee vision experience look like?).

Analysis – Children are encouraged to analyse the information and pick out the main aspects of bee vision that distinguish it from human vision.

Thought – Decide which features are the most important aspect of bee vision and make connections to the function and natural environment of the bee.

Innovate – It is important to consider form and function. Refer back to the experiences of the workshop based on the pseudoscope, lenses, mirrors, and ultraviolet light (Figure 11.6).

Original –Visualise and be as imaginative as possible! Remember a bee's superpower is sight!

Negotiate – The class brainstorm and collectively decide on the best ideas to realise the bee vision experience. Children are encouraged to collaborate and co-operate throughout the entire process. Present and discuss their research, understanding, and ideas around bee vision. The class writes a design brief to set out their intentions.

(E.g., The list of design intentions established for this case study. Bee vision design brief: (1) give the viewer the feeling of hovering over a field of flowers. (2) Allow the viewer to perceive colours that cannot be viewed with the naked eye in the UV range of the spectrum. (3) Give a sense of how a bee lives in the world by creating an immersive experience. (4) Incorporate a honeycomb structure. (5) Use recycled materials where possible.)

Table 11.1 A suggested framework for STEAM workshops constructed around children's findings (using the Science Foundation Ireland [SFI] framework)

Trigger	Wonder	Exploring
Colour perception	How to change your vision of the world?	Children can make their bicoloured glasses and experience what bees see. Use a combination of coloured lenses altering the children's perception of the world.
Exploring the bee's world	Seeing in ultraviolet light.	Test out UV paint on different materials and view using a UV light. Exploring and experimenting with coloured UV paint on various surfaces will create varied effects.
Depth perception and binocular vision	How can bees survive in natural elements?	Experiments and illusions. Closing one eye, then the other, and seeing how long it takes the brain to adapt to the changing colours. How seeing the world through a blue filter makes us feel (cold?) as opposed to red (warm?).
Insect vision and natural environment	Exploring different perceptions (insect and human vision).	Children can construct a simple pseudoscope using basic materials. A pseudoscope reverses the information coming to each eye, and in so doing reverses our perception of space and distance. The pseudoscope concept begins to give children an idea of the difference between human and insect visions.
Exploring lenses, prisms, and mirrors	How light travels?	Investigating light, explore how objects may be magnified using a simple lens. Examples of children experimenting with light are included (Colour Plate, section 3).

Figure 11.5 Constructing insect-inspired pseudoscopes in the classroom (child 11 years)

Figure 11.6 Children investigating how light travels by using lenses and mirrors. Findings documented in their personal journals (child 12 years)

Prototype

Prototyping brings the ideas into vision. A variety of methods are involved in this process, which can include sketching, playing with materials to create prototypes of the final design, and ICT. Whatever method you choose for the core purpose of this stage remains the same, to create solutions, and realise your design.

The following stages are a guide the <u>PROTOTYPE</u> stage.

<u>**P**</u>**resentation** – Plan and write up a design brief with a list of the design criteria.

(<u>Re</u>)design – Provide opportunities for materials and skills exploration as the designers create and test out possibilities. Several material manipulation sessions are essential to explore the possibilities of how the design might be realised. Understanding the properties and the limitation of materials will lead to the redesign of the idea. Use of recycled materials should be used where possible.

<u>**O**</u>**riginate** – Present final design criteria.

<u>**T**</u>**echnical** – Consider all the practical elements of the design. Learning areas: design; construction; lengths, surfaces, and measurements; craft.

<u>**O**</u>**rganise** – The children organises the different elements of the design and construction.

<u>**T**</u>**rial** – Experiment with ways to all the different elements.

<u>**Y**</u>**ippy** – Remember to be *Playful* and *Experiment*.

Test

Let us have some fun and test out your bee vision.

Show, do not tell:

1   Invite other classes to interact with your bee vision experience. Images of children engaging with insect vision are illustrated in section 2 (colour section). Ask the user(s) to talk through their experience – What are they thinking? How do they feel?
2   Share your vision and explain the process.
3   Document your reflections in your journals.

Some questions to guide your thinking:

- How has this project helped you understand how bees function in our world and the value they have to a functioning biosystem?
- How can we be more responsible and provide food for bees?
- How can we protect the habitat for our pollinators?
- What are the implications of a decline in the bee population caused by climate change?

Role of the teacher

Teachers provide a learning environment in which children feel safe and in which they have permission to explore, take risks, test and fail.

Summary of learning expected learning

The teaching and learning experience will include:

- Research, critical thinking skills through experiential and practical learning in and through Geography, Visual Art, and Scientific explorations.
- The integrative nature of this project develops children's creative and imaginative potential in Visual Art, STEM, and Geography.

The main concepts explored

- Design of form (Visual Art and Engineering – design and construction).
- Vision (Science – biology of living things).
- Environmental awareness (Geography and Science, Language, and Physical Education).
- Investigation of optics using prisms and lenses (Physics, Mathematics, and Engineering).
- Properties and character of materials (Art, Science, Engineering, and Geography).
- In addition to the artworks, the children are encouraged to research, document their learning, and produce a collection of personal research journals.

Learning activities

- **Research** – Undertake specific research tasks through art-making, observation, field trips, and supervised online research.
- **Synthesise** – Synthesise their research and make notes in a designated visual journal.
- **Present and communicate** – Children will present their findings to their classmates and teachers, using sketches, drawings, and oral communication techniques.
- **Analyse** – They will be asked to analyse the results of their research and draw conclusions.
- **Design** – Based on their research, the children will brainstorm, develop problem-solving skills, and elaborate in design decisions.
- **Develop their design** – Proceeding from the design decisions, the children will do sketches and drawings of their ideas.
- **Construct** – The children will develop skills while making the final exhibit.

Conclusion

This chapter intends to provide creative and fun ways of engaging and extending children's innate curiosity to explore their immediate environment, and the impact their actions can have in the world they occupy. Nature is declining globally at rates unprecedented in human history. The loss of biodiversity is intrinsically linked to climate change. The impacts of climate change such as intense drought, flooding, and acidification of oceans are accelerating biodiversity decline. Furthermore, human activity including deforestation and intensive agriculture are major contributors to both climate change and biodiversity decline. Complex problems such as biodiversity decline and climate change require creative solutions and problem solvers. Art, design, and STEM education can be a catalyst for stimulating learning and different ways of creating knowledge. By transcending individual disciplines, STEAM approaches enhance children's understanding of the world. Seeing through the artistic and scientific lenses, the teachers and children wishing to engage with STEAM education and DT must be prepared to take a step into the unknown and explore new areas of learning.

It is essential that our school systems support novel and original thought as well as constructive outcomes when exploring big issue. DT, used effectively can generate big questions and provide opportunities for relevant research. It helps children to collaborate, reflect with a critical lens, and work as scientists and artists. DT creates innovative work that crosses artistic and scientific disciplines. Through DT, children engage with others to define and resolve problems around climate change with various lens generating different perspectives. Incorporating art and design with STEM subjects is a powerful tool in developing knowledge and understanding as well as communicating issues around biodiversity loss and climate change.

Useful websites and resources

Art and science collaboration

- https://www.nature.com/articles/nri1730.

Tools for taking action

- https://dschool.stanford.edu/resources.

All-Ireland Pollinator Plan 2015–2020. National Biodiversity Data Centre Series No. 3, Waterford.

* https://pollinators.ie/schools/.

The School of Looking

* http://www.schooloflooking.org/SoL/home.html.

de Bruin, L.R. and Harris, A., 2017. Fostering creative ecologies in Australasian secondary schools. *Australian Journal of Teacher Education (Online)*, 42(9), p. 23.

* https://creativeweb.creative-partnerships.com/guidance/090921/change-school-csdf-planning-form-guidance,descriptors-and-form.pdf.

Artists Denis Connolly and Anne Cleary

* http://www.connolly-cleary.com/Home/News.html.

Artist Luke Jerram

* https://www.lukejerram.com/.

Artist Olafur Liasson

* https://www.olafureliasson.net/.

Children's literature about bees

Picturebooks

Bee and me (2017), Alison Jay, Old Barn Books (Wordless picturebooks).
Why do we need bees? (Lift the flap, first questions and answers board book) (2017), Katie Daynes and Christine Pym, Usborne Publishing Ltd.
Bee: Nature's tiny miracle (2016), Patricia Hegarty and Britta Teckentrup, Little Tiger Kids.
Bee: A peek-through picturebook (2017), Britta Teckentrup, Doubleday Books for Young Readers.
Flight of the honey bee (nature story books) (2015), Raymond Huber, Walker Books Ltd.
The honeybee man (2011), Lela and Nargi and Kyrsten Brooker (illus), Schwartz & Wade Books.
The honeybee (2018), Kirsten Hall and Isabelle Arsenault (Illus), Atheneum Books for Young Readers.
Little honey bee (2018), Caryl Lewis and Valeriane Leblond (illus), Y Lolfa.
The boy who lost his bumble (2014), Trudi Esberger, Child's Play (International) Ltd.
Willbee the bumblebee (2019), Craig Smith, Maureen Thompson and Katz Cowley (illus), Scholastic.
The tired bumble bee (2018), Amal M Nassir, Independently published.
Five bizzy bumblebees – The fun and factual life of the bumble bee (2017), Lance Douglas, Independently published by Lance Douglas.
Bumble the bee (2016), Yvon Douran, CreateSpace Independent Publishing Platform.
You wouldn't want to live without bees (2016), Alex Woolf and David Antram (illus), Book House; Illustrated edition.
When the bees buzzed off (2019), Lula Bell and Stephen Bennett (2019), Little Tiger Press.
The honeybee man (2011), Lela Nargi and Kyrsten Brooker (illus), Schwartz and Wade Books.
The beeman (2009), Laurie Krebs and Valeria Cis (illus), Barefoot Books.
Little yellow bee (2016), Ginger Swift, Cottage Door Press.
The bee bully (2012), Anglea Muse and Ewa Podles (illus), CreateSpace Independent Publishing Platform.
The very greedy bee (2010), Steve Smalllman, Tiger Tales.
Bees in the city (2019), Andrea Cheng and Sarah Mc Menemy (illus), Tilbury House Publishers.
Thank you, bees (2017), Toni Yuly, Candlewick Press.
Zinnia and the bees (2017), Danielle Davies and Laura K. Horton (illus), Curious Fox.

Give bees a chance (2017), Bethany Barton, Viking Books for Young Readers.
Please please the bees (2017), Gerald Kelley, Albert Whitman & Company.
The magic school bus inside a beehive (1998), Joanna Cole, Turtleback Books.
Kaia and the bees (2020), Maribeth Boelts and Angela Dominguez (illus), Walker Books.
Beehive (2020), Jorey Hurley, Simon & Schuster/Paula Wiseman Books.
Are you a bee? (2004), Judy Allen and Tudor Humphries (illus), Kingfisher Books Ltd.
The hidden rainbow (2020), Christie Matheson, Greenwillow Books.
Hello honeybees: Read and play in the hive (2019), Hannah Rogge and Emily Dove (illus), Chronicle Books.
Bee and me (2017), Alison Jay, Old Barn Books.
Buzz (2010), Eileen Spinelli, Simon & Schuster Books for Young Readers.

Chapter books

The queen bee and me (2020), Gillian McDunn, Bloomsbury Children's Books.
Honeybees and frenemies (2019), Kristi Wientge, Simon & Schuster Books for Young Readers.

Non-fiction

The book of bees (2016), Piotr Socha and Wojciech Grajkowski, Thames & Hudson.
Bees: A honeyed history (2017), Piotr Socha, Harry N. Abrams.
What on earth? Bees: Explore, create and investigate (2017), Andrea Quigley and Paulina Morgan (illus), QED Publishing.
Buzz, bee! (2017), Jennifer Szymanski, National Geographic Kids.
Explore my world: Honey bees (2017), Jill Esbaum, National Geographic Kids.
The bee book (2018), Charlotte Milner, DK Children.
The bee book (2016), The wonder of bees–How to protect them–Beekeeping know how (KK Children).
What if there were no bees? (2010), Suzanne Slade, Picture Window Books.
A bee's difficult search for food (2019), Mary Ellen, Klukow Amicus Ink.
Unbeelievables: Honeybee poems and paintings (2012), Douglas Florian, Beach Lane Books.
The little book of bees (2019), Hilary Kearney and Amy Holliday, Harper Collins.

Further reading for teachers

Benjamin, A. and McCallum, B. (2019) *The good bee: A celebration of bees and how to save them.* Random House.
Benjamin, A. and McCallum, B. (2009) *A world without bees.* Random House.
Bradbury, K. (2019) *The bumblebee flies anyway: A memoir of love, loss and muddy hands.* Bloomsbury Wildlife.
Gammans, N., Comont, R., Morgan, S.C. and Perkins, G. eds. (2018). *Bumblebees: An introduction.* Bumblebee Conservation Trust.
Goulson, D. (2015) *A buzz in the meadow.* Vintage.
Hanson, T. (2019) *Buzz: The nature and necessity of bees.* Icon Books.
McCabe, P. (2010). *The Collins beekeeper's bible: Bees, honey, recipes and other home uses.* Collins.
Morrissey, J. (2020) *The bee's knees.* Dublin Currach books.
O'Brien, S. (2019) *Dancing with bees: A journey back to nature.* Chelsea Green Publishing.

References

Batey, M. (2012) The measurement of creativity: From definitional consensus to the introduction of a new heuristic framework. *Creativity Research Journal, 24*(1), 55–65.
Cheng, C.C. (2014) Creative climate, creative capabilities, and new product creativity in the internet communication space. In Shiu E. ed., *Creativity research: An inter-disciplinary and multi-disciplinary research handbook* (pp. 207–230). Abingdon: Routledge.

Creative Partnerships UK (2012) *Creative schools development framework.*

Cremin, T., Burnard, P. and Craft, A. (2006) Pedagogies of possibility thinking. *International Journal of Thinking Skills and Creativity*, *1*(2), 108–119.

Cropley, A.J. (2001) *Creativity in education and learning: A guide for teachers and educators* (1st edn.). London: Kogan Page

Dolan, A.M. (2020) *Powerful primary geography: A toolkit for 21st century learning.* London: Routledge.

Eisner, E. (2002) *The arts and the creation of mind.* New Haven: Yale University Press.

Efland, A.D. (2002) *Art and cognition: Integrating the visual arts in the curriculum.* New York: Teachers College Press.

Freedman, K. (2003) *Teaching visual culture: Curriculum, aesthetics, and the social life of art.* New York: Teachers College Press.

Harris, P., Walker, M. and Green, M. (2019) *Community-based art education across the lifespan: Finding common ground.* New York: Teachers College Press.

Hasso Plattner Institute (2019) Design Thinking, available at: https://hpi.de/school-ofdesign-thinking/design-thinking.html.

Hetland, L. and Winner, E. (2004) Cognitive transfer from arts education to non-arts outcomes: Research evidence and policy implications. In Eisner, E.W and Day, M.D. *Handbook of research and policy in art education London*: Routledge (pp. 135–162). E. Eisner and M. Day, National Art Education Association, 2004.

Hetland, L., Winner, E., Veenema, S. and Sheridan, K. (2013) *Studio thinking: The real benefits of visual arts education.* New York: Teachers College.

Horniman Museum (2013) https://www.horniman.ac.uk/about/project-coral.

Kaufman, J. and Baer, J. (2012) Beyond new and appropriate: Who decides what is creative? *Creativity Research Journal*, *24*(1), 83–91.

Liao, C. (2016) Interdisciplinary to transdisciplinary: An arts-integrated approach to STEAM education. *Art Education*, 69(6), 44–49.

Marshall, J. and D'Adamo, K. (2011) Art education as research in the classroom: A new paradigm in art education. *Art Education*, *64*(5), 12–18.

Mumford, M.D. (2003) Where have we been, where are we going? Taking stock in creativity research. *Creativity Research Journal*, *15*, 107–120.

OECD (2004) *Innovation in the knowledge economy: Implications for education and learning.* Paris: OECD.

Root-Bernstein, Robert (2015) Arts and crafts as adjuncts to STEM education to foster creativity in gifted and talented students. *Asia Pacific Education Review*, *16.* 203–212.

Saavedra, A.R. and Opfer, V.D. (2012) Learning 21st-century skills requires 21st-century teaching. *Phi Delta Kappan*, *94*(2), 8–13.

Sanchez-Bayo, F. (2019) Worldwide decline of the entomofauna: A review of its drivers. *Biological Conservation*, *232*, 8–27.

Sawyer, R.K. (2008) Optimising learning: *Implications of learning sciences research.* OECD/CERI International Conference.

Sheridan-Rabideau, M. (2010) Creativity repositioned. *Arts Education Policy Review*, *111*, 54–58.

Seifter, Harvey. (2014) *The art of science learning.* http://www.artofsciencELearning.org.

Stanford d.school (2010), "Design Thinking process guide. Hasso Plattner Institute of Design at Stanford", available at: https://dschoolold.stanford.edu/sandbox/groups/designresources/wiki/36873/attachments/74b3d/Mo deGuideBOOTCAMP2010L.pdf.

Sullivan, G. (2005) *Art practice as research: Inquiry in the visual arts.* Thousand Oaks, CA: Sage Publications.

Taylor, P.C. (2016) Why is a STEAM curriculum perspective crucial to the 21st century? In 14th Annual Conference of the Australian Council for Educational Research, 7–9 August 2016, Brisbane.

Vande Zande, R. (2016) *Design education: Creating thinkers to improve the world.* Lahham: Rowman & Littlefield.

12   The Grow Room

An artistic exploration of climate change

Tanya de Paor

Introduction

This chapter charts the ways in which creative pedagogies can foster novel forms of creating knowledge through Socially Engaged Art (SEA) practice. Socially Engaged Art SEA is a collaborative and participatory practice which involves people as the medium in the work. By opening up spaces for actualisation and potentiality (Rogoff, 2010), SEA creates a place for thinking differently and cultivating a transformative imagination (Galafassi et al., 2018). Potentially, the arts can engage individuals and communities, inspire trust and action and have a leading role to play in tackling climate change (Serota, 2018). Art can be provocative and challenging, extending the frequently asked question, what is art, to the more urgent question in these extraordinary times of what is life? (Thompson, 2012).

How can art and art education support climate change education? This chapter explores the ways in which visual art can form new constellations of collective practice to engage and empower teachers and children in the 21st century around the urgent issue of climate change. The chapter discusses key questions such as the role of art and art education in the 21st century in the context of the complex and at times paradoxical question of climate change. What are the intersectional points of encounter between art, arts education and the arts in education for climate change education? This chapter seeks to contribute to the ongoing challenge in socially engaged and relational practices, of how to share an experience that produces transformation in oneself (Holmes, 2012).

The Grow Room project is presented as a SEA project in an initial teacher education context. It opens up a space for speculative inquiry, for making and transformative thinking through visual art practice. While this project is based around a greenhouse structure within a university setting, the project can be adapted to primary, post-primary and community settings.

In the Grow Room project, undergraduate primary student teachers developed creative pedagogies to explore interactive pathways to think about climate change. Initially, students engaged in simple acts of planting seeds, gardening, researching plants, insects and artists whose work aligned with the themes of the project. Work developed through visually documenting processes, playing with ideas and testing work prior to designing individual projects which interrogated climate related issues. Students used visual methodologies to develop observational skills, to document, make work and display processes. Discussions, story-telling, story-making and creating imaginative speculative scenarios about climate, art, food, bees, butterflies, flowers or weeds emerged during the programme. Peer-to-peer learning and skill sharing was also a central component to explore climate change and the role of art in climate education. Students explored 'seeing big'

(Greene, 2000) while acting on a small scale, thereby contextualising shared human and nonhuman interconnectivity through the concept of a garden.

This chapter aims to explore climate change through the methods of SEA pedagogy and practice in an advanced visual art education module for student teachers. Through engaging in visual art pedagogy, theory and practice tutors and students develop studio habits of mind and the capacity to think through materials. Students develop ideas in a visual context and use art as a research tool to interrogate concepts, co-create work and to foster wonder and a transformative imagination in relation to the super-wicked problem of climate change. The Grow Room is a type of case study with student teachers using the garden as a site for SEA and for education in the Anthropocene. In this chapter, I give a brief outline of SEA practice. I discuss the role of the artist/educator in creating a sense of transformative wonder and outline the case study of the Grow Room project. The chapter also describes how student teachers incorporate contemporary art practice, socially engaged processes, installation work and traditional art and craft practices to develop their personal ecological projects.

Socially engaged practices and co-creating ecologies of hope

SEA, also known as social practice, has its roots in the 1960's environmental art movement. More recently art educator and cultural theorist Pablo Helguera outlines an introduction to SEA through the tools of education. The Reggio Emilia Education Model, an educational approach for early childhood education started at the end of the Second World War by Loris Malagazzi. Incorporating the pedagogical thought of John Dewey, Jean Piaget and others, the school's philosophy outlines many parallels and shared vocabularies between art and education. Here teaching and learning happens in a process of co-creation and co-construction of knowledge, where 'to participate is not to create homogeneity, to participate is to generate vitality' (Helguera, 2011:xii).

Art education can lead to a transformative imagination, facilitating agency and change (Dewey, 1916; Eisner, 2002; Galafassi, 2018; Greene, 2000; Mirzoeff, 2015). Transformative learning can be achieved through sustainable education (Sterling, 2001), by changing the educational culture towards the realisation of human potential for ecological well-being. SEA practices bring people together in novel collective and collaborative contexts. Through informal artistic collaborative projects, opportunities emerge to collectively participate in generating ideas and solutions to complex contemporary issues. Through creating a sense of togetherness, a sense that 'we' can have a shared experience, and therefore, a sense of empowerment is important in the face of a complex and paradoxical climate change debate.

Relational practices in teaching and SEA create spaces for learning, discussion and generating new ways of feeling and sensing (Hicks, 2019). They promote peer-to-peer learning and ideation. Today artists increasingly make work 'using social situations to produce dematerialised, anti-market, politically engaged projects' (Bishop, 2006:179). Models of pedagogic artistic and SEA interventions are developing to respond to the urgency of climate change. Contemporary artists are increasingly responding 'to develop a more functional relationship between art and the everyday' (Cruz, 2012:58).

Art education and risk

Art-making necessitates ambiguity, exploration and risk-taking. These are skillsets and habits of mind which are critical to cultivate in times of uncertainty and rapid change. Art, as Helguera argues, plays a role in challenging assumptions in society. Art-based approaches focus on processes, and facilitate knowledge creation as tentative and conducive towards the creation of a 'personal vision' (Eisner, 2002:44). Never before has there been such a need to cultivate the ability in the young to challenge, have a voice and develop a subjective vision for a sustainable and just future (Greene, 2000). The Fridays for Future and global school strikes for climate inspired by Greta Thunberg are evidence of an emergent civic and activist response, and indicative of a turn towards powerful ecologies of hope. There is much evidence to suggest that change will be led by the young.

Art as a research tool to foster wonder and transformative imagination in relation to climate change

In *Decolonizing Nature: Contemporary Art and the Politics of Ecology*, Demos (2016:200) cites the responsibility of artists, curators, audiences and the cultural sphere to act and react against 'neoliberal exceptionalism and its destructive ecocide'. In order to bring about a Great Transition, many scholars argue that we must 'learn to live differently' (Mirzoeff, 2015; Robinson, 2011; Stengers, 2011; Haraway, 2016). To live differently, we need to think, feel and see differently. Internationally, art and design education in the 21st century has centred on innovation, creativity and enterprise (Granville, 2012). But where in all of the innovation and enterprise is the simplicity of wonder? If, as MacFarlane (2015:25) suggests, 'in modernity, mastery usurped mystery', then we urgently need to rekindle our sense of wonder at nature, the natural world and our place in it (de Paor, 2019). Contemporary art, including design and craft are well positioned to foster wonder and a radical imagination (Biggs, 2014; Buck, 2015; Galafassi et al., 2018).

Old-fashioned wonder and the cultivation of imagination are important for thinking about sustainable visions in a time of climate change (de Paor, 2019). Encountering wonder 'is at its most basic level the function of all education, from preschool to university' (Loughran, 2015:8). Nurturing the ability to wonder is an issue of common interest to the scientist, artist, educator and cultural practitioner. Providing opportunities to wonder facilities the ability to imagine and re-imagine scenarios for environmental sustainability and climate action.

Understanding and engaging with the complexities of Anthropogenic climate change (as described in Chapter 1) demands a change in how scientific language is used in geopolitical narratives. Evidence suggests this alienates people and promotes a sense of powerlessness, crisis and fear. To achieve environmental liveability and social justice for all, human and nonhuman, we need to cultivate a togetherness and a collective will as Chantal Mouffe (2005) argues.

Imagination can be understood as a way of seeing, sensing, thinking and dreaming, which stirs students 'to wide-awakeness, to imaginative action, and to renewed consciousness of possibility' (Greene, 2000:43). Artists can present the ordinary in extraordinary ways, promoting different ways of thinking and looking at the world. Art and craft are innately human ways of shaping worlds. Arts and craft promote another way to be in and with nature, 'they allow for an enchanted, immersive state' (Buck, 2015:374).

To meet the extraordinary and unprecedented challenges of living and working in the 21st century, we need to cultivate the power of imagination to explore how to adapt to a changing world. To achieve sustainable visions for the future, we need to look forward and to see what and how children of today are learning for tomorrow. The anthropologist Tim Ingold refers to education as learning to paying attention to our experiences, stating 'education is a process of becoming wise to things, and to the world. It teaches us to attend, and to learn from what we observe' (Ergül, 2017:8). The arts provide children with the opportunity to pay attention to and look with wonder at the beauty of the natural world and to feel their place in it.

The elusive question is: what kind of tomorrow are children learning for? How will their experiences today inform their perceptions which shape tomorrow? In his 2012 TED talk on global climate change, James Hansen, the former NASA scientist and climate activist, argues that we need to act with urgency to address the escalating climate crisis. He believes that we need to act now, in togetherness to secure a future for our children and grandchildren (Hansen, 2012).

In much of contemporary society and often through mainstream education, children are actively removed from the natural world, alienated from the experience, risks and rewards of playing in nature. Reduced contact with nature reduces children's capacity to think creatively and imaginatively (Louv, 2005). Nature-Deficit Disorder describes the psychological, physical and cognitive costs of human alienation from nature, especially for children in their vulnerable developing years. When we think of species extinction, we rarely consider that 'the child in nature is an endangered species, and the health of children and the health of the Earth are inseparable' (Louv, 2005:353).

The role of art and artists

The arts can create understanding and awareness of the complexity of global climate change. Writer Linda Weintraub (2012) and renowned educator Sir Ken Robinson (2011) speak of the important role of the artist in stimulating imaginative, collaborative dialogue across different communities of knowledge. To envisage new horizons in the Anthropocene, artists have a critical role to play (Demos, 2016; Haraway, 2016; Mirzoeff, 2015; Stengers, 2012; Tsing, 2019). Contemporary artists frequently work in a transdisciplinary as well as an aesthetic context, by making artwork and through socially engaged practices. They function as public intellectuals, 'whose place it is to raise embarrassing questions, to confront orthodoxy and dogma, to be someone who cannot easily be co-opted by governments or corporations' (Said, 1994:9). Galafassi et al. (2018) identify the role of the arts and artists in environmental issues as having moved away from simply communicating climate issues to creating knowledge about the complexities and impacts of climate change. Art is a way of making social, cultural and political issues visible (O'Donoghue, 2012).

Does climate equal the weather?

Does climate change equal the weather? The weather is a focus of much talk, speculation, headshaking and annoyance, in particular in Ireland where it's not unheard of to witness all the seasons in one afternoon. We are nothing if not obsessed with the weather. It is the cultural face of climate change. It informs and shapes our everyday conversations.

Climate, as a cultural phenomenon is made visible in a daily context through the weather. By seeing the small-scale entities of our daily lives in our immediate environment, in familiar and tangible ways, we can begin to imagine how we can effect transformational change. By taking the time to notice, to touch and sense the natural world around us, we can begin to feel our inextricable interconnection with the natural world.

Contemporary visual culture presents climate and nature in a mediated way through technological digital media (Castree and Braun, 2005). It is at times presented as spectacle, as something catastrophic to be feared. But other narratives, real and imagined can be constructed. Finding relatable methods to see the crisis of climate on an everyday human scale is critical to begin to effect a positive change. In order to see Anthropogenic climate change, Mirzoeff (2015:221) suggests we 'need to unsee the past and begin to imagine a different way to be with what we call nature'.

Food production provides a useful entry point into weather and climate discussions. A universal necessity, we cannot survive without food. Food shapes our cultures locally and globally. It defines us. Food production (and its associated costs) to meet increasing consumer demands is one of the main drivers of Anthropogenic driven climate change. Interspecies and elemental interdependence is necessary for food cultivation. Weather conditions and climate have a significant impact on food production. In art, food can 'symbolize life and prosperity, consumption and commerce. It can be 'a metaphor of time and decay, and of art's power to transcend that; it also comes into its own when exploring issues of gender equality, economic inequality and social control' (Tipton, 2018).

The Grow Room: The potential of growing with initial teacher educators through a visual art elective

In 2018, Europe was struck by unusually cold weather. Nicknamed the *Beast from the East*, heavy snowfall forced schools and businesses to close. Wintry landscapes and travel delays brought a mixture of fun and frustration to many in Ireland and the UK. Shops ran out of necessities such as bread and fresh fruit and vegetables disappeared from the shelves of supermarkets. Images of empty supermarket shelves were tweeted around the world. Unusual weather patterns disrupted food production and transportation across the globe. The empty shelves in our local supermarket prompted me to consider the wider implications as I thought about where our food actually comes from, how it is produced, picked, packaged and transported? I thought about children's connection to food and nature. How do children think about food, about how it grows and about the different scales of farming that food production necessitates? What about the enormous vital role tiny insects play in crop pollination (as discussed in Chapter 11)? Or what about the insects that aerate and compost the soil?

Climate change debates generally focus attention on large scale issues. Media reports focus on fires, droughts, landscape devastation and habitat loss on a large, sometimes planetary scale. To think about climate change in a human sense necessitates a consideration of different scales.

The Grow Room operates at a small scale. The temporary makeshift structure sits outside the art studio, in a small previously disused courtyard. Soil, pots, seeds and plants are available to students. The idea initially started with a seed sharing event. Members of the college community were invited to take seedlings of vegetables, flowers and fruit to grow in their offices, gardens or at home. The practice of sharing was reciprocated through shared stories of growing plants, childhood memories of food and family recipes. Occasionally, I received photos and next generation seeds from colleagues, as illustrated in Figure 12.1.

The Grow Room operated as a Third Space (Bhabha, 1994). It was a social space where informal and formal learning and collaboration were encouraged. The space itself was central to the learning experience, facilitating students to plant seeds outside of class time, to notice emerging seedlings, to touch and feel the soil and to pay

Figure 12.1 Daniel with sunflower, Limerick.

Source: Image courtesy Sinead Dinneen

attention to the complexity and beauty of natural objects. Art and art education seeks to encourage an emergence of actualisation and potentiality (Rogoff, 2010). This garden space became 'a site through which to examine connection and care in practice' (Buck, 2015:374).

The Grow Room functioned as a physical and abstract space. Peer-to-peer conversations focused on the extinction levels of insects, on changing food tastes, art and education and existential questions about nature and our place in it. Classroom discussions ranged from the pedagogic, social and cultural to the political. These discourses fed into individual student research projects. Students' self-directed projects interrogated the potential of traditional art-based methods and contemporary practices in critical and creative pedagogies. Students also explored emerging new technologies for the production of and engagement with art. Examples of work from the Grow Room project are provided in Colour Plate, section 4.

Art, ecology and pedagogy

The theme of art and ecology informed the theoretical framework for the Grow Room programme which underpinned the advanced teacher education module in contemporary visual art theory and practice. The arrangement of the space was important for accomplishing instructional goals and promoting collaboration and sharing (Hetland and Winner, 2007). The module aimed to promote the use of new and emergent media such as digital photography, film, social media and animation with more traditional art forms. The theoretical underpinning for the module also involved visual culture theory and practices of 'looking deeply'.

Thinking ecologically

Visual Culture theory provides the framework through which we learn to see the world (Mirzoeff, 2015; Sturken and Cartwright, 2009). In the context of this module, it facilitated a way to interrogate the visual contexts surrounding climate, biodiversity, ecology, eco-art, human and nonhuman interconnectivity and ethics of climate justice in a pedagogic, political and cultural context. Students developed arts-based research methodologies such as drawing, painting and working in installation. They explored the dialogic, participatory context of socially engaged creative practices.

In Ireland, the Visual Art Curriculum (1999) focuses on interrelated strands of making art and looking and responding to art (LAR). The curricular strands include drawing, paint and colour, printmaking, clay and construction. However, greater opportunities for a curriculum to advocate for teaching and learning about contemporary practice and artists is necessary. Recent policy developments in Ireland from the *Points of Alignment Special Report* (Arts Council, 2008), *The Arts in Education Charter* (Department of Arts, Heritage and the Gaeltacht and the Department of Education and Skills, 2012) and the Arts Council (2015) initiated document, *Making Great Art Work: Arts Council Strategy (2016-2025)* now advocate for a contemporary visual arts curriculum fit for purpose to meet the challenges of the 21st century.

In the unprecedented times in which we live, students and children have a right to learn about contemporary artists in particular those who address the universal themes of our time. Artists work in a transdisciplinary context, with the ability to communicate complex ideas which connect emotionally with the public. Creative practitioners engage with socio-political, cultural and environmental issues, as they work towards a just and ecologically sustainable society (O'Donoghue, 2012). How we perceive the world today, demands more of us than looking (Gablik, 1984). I believe critical and truthful perception relies on empowerment, on what Biesta (2017) terms a grown-upness, to be a citizen in the world.

Fostering an ecological mindset can start with a seed. To observe the transformation from seed to plant, tree or flower can inspire wonder and awareness of ecological and interspecies connectedness.

Samples of student projects from the Grow Room

Turtles and Butterflies

Cornelia Hesse-Honeger is a scientist who uses art as a research and observational tool in fieldwork from nuclear fallout sites. She describes herself as a knowledge-artist. In the project Turtles and Butterflies, the student created beautiful small-scale paintings of animals and insects using watercolour paints on watercolour paper. The scale of the work and the way it was displayed, unframed directly on the wall, added to its delicate nature. The work was an exercise in careful observational looking and used analytical drawing and painting methods (as illustrated in Colour Plate, section 4).

Flowers and Weeds

The Flower and Weed exhibition initially began through the students' inquiry into the similarities and differences between weeds and flowers. One student explored the wide scale use of pesticides such as Roundup to kill weeds, a vital source of food for bees, bugs and butterflies. Part of the project involved collecting and pressing a wide range of flowers. These included pansies, daisies, roses, buttercups, thistles and various types of leaves. The pressed flowers were the stimulus for observational drawings. They developed into small scale analytical paintings and finally embroidery work (as illustrated in Colour Plate, section 4). The student also played with the idea of creating hybrid flowers under the title of Future Weeds.

The White-Tailed bee project

This project focused on the White-Tailed Bee Project. The student used visual journaling methodologies to research and visually record how the project developed (Figure 12.2). For the final exhibition, the student created an installation piece, which incorporated seed potatoes with long alien-looking roots, willow plants and a large log. At the centre of installation, she placed a dead bumblebee, which we had found and were unsuccessful in nursing back to life. This installation also encouraged participant engagement. Visitors were invited to take away bee bombs, which were little bags of seeds with bees painted on the outside, to create their own gardens. A related idea is to participate in Guerilla Gardening which creates random gardens in unusual and unused spaces (see Natalie Jerijeminko's work X Design, https://www.nyu.edu/projects/xdesign/).

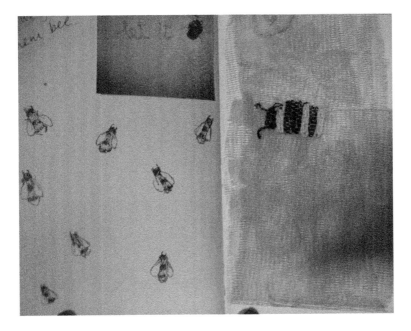

Figure 12.2 Student's design work for bee bombs

Classroom-based visual art projects

Activity for children (8–13 years)

Strand focus. Drawing and paint and colour, making work and looking and responding

OBSERVATIONAL DRAWING AND PAINTING

Pick a range of weeds, wild flowers and/or garden flowers from the school garden or from a nearby park (of course you need to make sure you have permission first). Use the flowers as your stimulus for a series of observational drawings using: (a) pencil, (b) paint and (c) oil pastels. Use good quality art materials and try different coloured and textured paper.

Fibre and fabric: Create an EcoFlag collage in fabric using scraps of brightly coloured material, yarn and thread. If possible, stitch into the flag, using small buttons, sequences (environmentally friendly ones), ribbon, lace or other objects that have interesting textures.

The flags can be displayed in school corridors or outside in the school garden in Biodiversity Areas or school gardens.

Activity for children (8–13 years)

Research one of the following projects by the artist Olafur Eliasson

In galleries and museums, it is often not permissible to touch the art. But the artist Olafur Eliasson encourages people to interact with artwork in his large-scale installations and with each other. His project **Ice Watch** encourages people to touch, smell and even lick the ice blocks he uses in the work. Eliasson has said that 'Art can change the world'. Do you agree?

Research the artist and his work through online resources and/or through art books in school or your local library. Here are links to some of his projects that focus on climate change:

The Weather Project: https://www.tate.org.uk/whats-on/tate-modern/exhibition/unilever-series/unilever-series-olafur-eliasson-weather-project-0.
The Little Sun: http://www.littlesun.com/.
Ice Watch: http://icewatchlondon.com/.

1 Write a short paragraph about the artist Olafur Eliasson, where he comes from, where his studio(s) are and what are the things that inspire him?
2 Select one of the projects listed above and write about it. Where did the artist get the idea for the work? Where was the work exhibited? Did the location of the work influence how the work was made and how audiences interacted or played with it?
3 Make a model of the work. How would you change it?
4 Did any of Eliasson's work make you think about climate change? And in what ways?

Activity for children (10–13 years)

Class debate. The topic: Does public art have the power to inspire action against climate change?

Activity: Design and then make placards and/or banners that visually communicate your ideas. Examples of placards and posters from the climate marches which can be accessed online (Some examples are included in chapter 21, p.290 in this book).

Yes, public art has the power to inspire action against climate change; or

No, public art is a waste of energy and doesn't inspire action against climate change.

Note: Take inspiration from the recent School Climate, Fridays for Future, 350.org and Extinction Rebellion.

Activity for children (8–13 years)

Dear Tomorrow www.deartomorrow.org is a digital and archive project for people to connect with the issue of climate change and to share stories with family, friends and social networks. People submit letters, videos and photographs dedicated to their children, family or future self about climate change. Write a letter, and/or submit a video or photograph dedicated to your future self about climate change. Upload to the Dear Tomorrow digital archive and/or to your school website.

Conclusion

The Grow Room Project can be tailored to suit different needs and different settings. The project provides opportunities for children, teachers and the wider school community to engage in growing, cultivating, harvesting, making and sharing together through the creation of a 'third space' of actualisation, potential and wonder. Through visual research, by honing observational skills and through documenting findings in creative arts-based methods, children have the opportunity to see and learn in an open ended exploratory, sensory and experiential capacity.

Student teachers involved in the project were initially introduced to contemporary artists working in transdisciplinary creative practices. As part of the programme, there were opportunities to consider novel, arts-based approaches to make climate change visible. The themes of the project were identified individually and collectively. These include climate change, sustainability, social justice, ecology, contemporary art and pedagogy.

This project operated as an exploratory ecological SEA project. The pedagogic intention at the heart of this project lay in fostering an ecological mindset (Bateson, 1972). The Grow Room created a space for teachers and children to have opportunities to develop creative and critical pedagogies, to explore new pathways to visualise, discuss, record and to think about complex issues such as climate change. This project is adaptable for classroom practice, as well as preschool and after school settings.

Interesting resources and websites

- The Weather Project: https://www.tate.org.uk/whats-on/tate-modern/exhibition/unilever-series/unilever-series-olafur-eliasson-weather-project-0.
- The Little Sun: http://www.littlesun.com/.

- Ice Watch: http://icewatchlondon.com/.
- James Hansen, 2012. Why I Must Talk about Climate Change, Ted Talk: https://youtu.be/fWInyaMWBY8.
- 350.0rg: https://350.org/about/.
- Bee populations: https://nuclear-news.net/2014/04/05/are-the-bees-really-dying-out-the-strange-disappearance-of-the-bees-one-japanese-farmers-experience/.
- Planting a Seed: http://www.carolanneconnolly.com/files/plantingaseedbookwebcompressed.pdf.
- Dear Climate: https://www.dearclimate.net/.
- Dear Tomorrow: https://www.deartomorrow.org/.
- Visual Art Curriculum for Primary Schools: https://www.curriculumonline.ie/Primary/Curriculum-Areas/The-Arts-Education/Visual-Arts/.
- Welcome to the Anthropocene: https://youtu.be/fvgG-pxlobk.

References

Arts Council, (2008) Points of Alignment: The Report of the Special Committee on the Arts and Education. Dublin:Arts Council http://www.artscouncil.ie/uploadedFiles/Points_of_alignment_English_2010.pdf

Arts Council (2015) Making Great Art Work: Arts Council Strategy (2016-2025) Dublin:Arts Council https://www.artshealthresources.org.uk/docs/making-great-art-work-arts-council-strategy-2016-2025/

Bateson, G. (1972) *Steps to an ecology of mind.* London and Chicago:The University of Chicago Press.

Bhabha, H.K. (1994) *The location of culture.* London: Routledge.

Biesta, G. (2017) *Letting art teach – Art education 'after' Joseph Beuys.* Arnhem: ArtEZ Press.

Biggs, I. (2014) Incorrigiblyplural? Rural lifeworlds between concept and experience. *Canadian Journal of Irish Studies*, 38(1–2), 260–279. Special issue, Text and Beyond Text: New Visual, Material, and Spatial Perspectives in Irish Studies (Accessed May 14, 2018).

Buck, H.J. (2015) On the possibility of a charming Anthropocene. *Annals of the Association of American Geographers, Futures: Imagining Socio cological Transformations*, 105(2), 369–377. (Accessed May 2019).

Bishop, C. (2006) The social turn: Collaboration and its discontents. *Artforum International*, 44(6), 178–183

Castree, N. and Braun, B. eds. (2005) *Remaking reality: Nature at the millennium.* London: Routledge.

Cruz, T. (2012) Democratizing urbanization and the search for a new civic imagination. In Thompson, N., ed., *Living as form: Socially engaged art from 1991–2011.* NY and The MIT Press Cambridge Massachusetts and London: Creative Time Books (pp. 56–63).

De Paor, T. (2019) Between three worlds: Sustainable visions in the Anthropocene (and how to achieve them). Chapter 7. In Sherman, M. ed., *International Opportunities in the Arts.* Delaware: Vernon Press, Series in Art.

Dewey, J. (1916) *Democracy in education: An introduction to the philosophy of education.* New York: MacMillan.

Demos, T.J. (2016) *Decolonizing nature: Contemporary art and the politics of ecology.* Berlin: Sternberg Press.

Ergül, H. (2017) Interview on Anthropology, education and university with Tim Ingold. *Journal of Cultural Studies*, Faculty of Communication, Hacettepe University, 4(1), 7–13.

Eisner, E.W. (2002) *The arts and the creation of mind.* New Haven & London: Yale University Press.

Loughran, G. (2015) Planting a seed and the weak power of art in education. In O Donoghue, A. and Connolly, C.A. eds., *Planting a seed* (pp. 8–12). http://www.carolanneconnolly.com/files/plantingaseedbookwebcompressed.pdf.

Gablik, S. (1984) *Has modernism failed?* New York: Thames and Hudson.

Galafassi, D., Kagan, S.J. et al. (2018). Raising the temperature: The arts in a warming planet. *Current Opinion in Environmental Sustainability, 31*, 71–79 (Accessed January 17, 2019). https://www.sciencedirect.com/science/article/abs/pii/S1877343517300714.

Government of Ireland (1999) *Primary school curriculum and teacher guidelines: Visual art.* Dublin: Stationary Office.

Granville, G. ed. (2012) *Art education and contemporary culture, Irish experiences, international perspectives.* Bristol: Intellect, The Mill.

Greene, M. (2000) *Releasing the imagination: Essays on education, the arts and social change.* San Francisco: Jossey-Bass. Education.

Hansen, J. (2012) Why I Must Talk about Climate Change, *Ted Talk.* https://youtu.be/fWInyaMWBY8.

Haraway, D.J. (2016) *Staying with the trouble: Making kin in the Chthulucene.* Durham and London: Duke University Press.

Helguera, P. (2011) *Education for socially engaged art: A materials and techniques handbook.* NY: Jorge Pinto Books (pp. x–xiv).

Hetland, L. and Winner, E. (2007) *Studio thinking: The real benefits of visual arts education.* NY: Teachers College Press.

Hicks, D. (2019) *Climate change: Bringing the pieces together teaching geography.* https://www.teaching4abetterworld.co.uk/Resources/2019%20TG.pdf (Accessed January 2020).

Holmes, B. (2012) 'Eventwork: the fourfold matrix of contemporary social movements. In Thompson, N. ed., *Living as form: Socially engaged art from 1991–2011.* NY and The MIT Press Cambridge Massachusetts and London: Creative Time Books (pp. 72–93).

Louv, R. (2005) *Last child in the woods: Saving our children from nature-deficit disorder.* London: Atlantic Books.

Macfarlane, R. (2015) *Landmarks.* UK: Penguin.

Mirzoeff, N. (2015) *How to see the world.* UK: Penguin, Random House.

Mouffe, C. (2005) *On the political: Thinking in action.* New York: Routledge.

O'Donoghue, D. (2012) Questions that never get asked about Irisheducaiton Curriculum Theory and Practice. In Granville, G. ed. *Art education and contemporary culture, Irish experiences, international perspectives.* Bristol: Intellect, The Mill.

Robinson, K. (2011) *Out of our minds.* United Kingdom: Capstone Publishing Ltd.

Rogoff, I. (2010) Turning. In O'Neill, P. and Wilson, M., eds., *Curating the Educational Turn,* Amsterdam: Open Books.

Said, E.W. (1994) *Representations of the intellectual.* New York: Vintage Books.

Serota, N. (2018) The arts have a leading role to play in climate change, *The Guardian,* https://www.theguardian.com/commentisfree/2018/nov/20/arts-climate-change (Accessed April 16, 2020).

Stengers, I. (2011) *Thinking with whitehead.* Cambridge: Harvard University Press.

Stengers, I. (2012) Reclaiming Animism, E-flux Journal # 36. https://www.e-flux.com/journal/36/61245/reclaiming-animism/ (Accessed May 2, 2019).

Sterling, S. (2001) *Sustainable education: Re-Visioning learning and change.* UK: Green Books.

Sturken, M. and Cartwright, L. (2009) *Practices of looking: An introduction to visual culture.* Second Edition. USA: Oxford University Press.

The Department of Arts, Heritage and the Gaeltacht and The Department of Education and Skills (2012) The Arts in Education Charter. *Stationary Office, Dublin.* https://www.education.ie/en/Publications/Policy-Reports/Arts-In-Education-Charter.pdf.

The Arts Council of Ireland (2015) Making great art work: Leading the developments of the arts in Ireland, Arts Council Strategy 2016–2025. http://www.artscouncil.ie/uploadedFiles/Making_Great_Art_Work.pdf.

Thompson, N. ed. (2012) *Living as form: Socially engaged art from 1991–2011.* NY and The MIT Press Cambridge Massachusetts and London: Creative Time Books.

Tipton, G. (2018) Hungry for art: Food has always been a tasty subject for art. https://www.irishtimes.com/culture/art-and-design/visual-art/hungry-for-art-food-has-always-been-a-tasty-subject-for-artists-1.3709955.

Tsing, A. (2019) KeynoteArt and the Anthropocene Conference in the Long Room Hub, Trinity College Dublin, 7–9th June 2019.

Weintraub, L. (2012) *To life! Eco art in pursuit of a sustainable planet.* Berkeley and Los Angeles, California: University of University of California Press.

13 Is plastic really fantastic or is it something more drastic?

Anne M. Dolan

Introduction

Plastic is ubiquitous. This wonder material facilitates the production of multiple products from toothbrushes to mass-produced toys, to packaging. Shops carry thousands of plastic products, all designed to make our lives easier. These include individually wrapped cakes (and sometimes vegetables), bottles of water, disposable razors, eye lenses and personal hygiene products, among others. Plastic is convenient, cheap and it provides life-saving services, including intravenous tubes, replacement hips and stents for heart operations. It has helped us access the most remote parts of the planet, from the deepest oceans to the highest mountain ranges and even beyond our atmosphere through space travel. Hundreds of millions of tons are produced each year with a significant proportion devoted to packaging. Unfortunately, plastic is also among the most pervasive and persistent pollutants on Earth.

In the 1950s, as the new plastic technology emerged and the mass production of everyday plastic products began, it was heralded as a product which would save time and energy. No more washing up. Just use plastic plates and throw them away! Since the 1950s, some 8.3 billion tons of plastic have been produced worldwide, and to date, less than 10% has been recycled (Geyer et al., 2017). Equivalent to the weight of 8 billion elephants, almost all of the plastic produced to date is still with us, along with its devastating ecological impact.

Much of this plastic ends up in the ocean. Due to the success of the BBC's Blue Planet II series, people are now more aware of the impact of plastic on the environment, ocean, ecosystems and ultimately upon our health. Moreover, there's another largely hidden dimension of the plastic crisis: plastic's contribution to global greenhouse gas emissions and climate change.

This chapter examines the nature of plastic, the extent of plastic pollution and the connections between plastic and climate change, as well as strategies for addressing the plastic issue.

What is the problem with plastic?

Plastic is a synthetic product mostly produced from oil and gas. A shortened form of 'thermoplastic', the term describes polymeric materials that can be shaped and reshaped using heat. Each step in the life of a piece of plastic, including production, transportation and disposal, uses fossil fuels and emits greenhouse gases. Notwithstanding its environmental impact, plastic is big business. Today, the plastics industry, estimated to be worth more than $4 trillion, generates more than 300 million tons of plastic a year, nearly half of which is for single use items, meaning that it will inevitably become rubbish. The extent of plastic production and its subsequent disposal is alarming. The plastic we throw away during a 12-month period could hypothetically circle the earth four times.

Single-use products are 'made to be used once only' before disposal. Indeed, the term 'single-use' has become so prolific it was named the 2018 Collins' Dictionary 'Word of the Year'. According to the dictionary, 'single-use' is defined as a 'term that describes items whose unchecked proliferation are blamed for damaging the environment and affecting the food chain'.

Microbeads are among the newer developments in the brief history of our plastic life-style. In our search for whiter teeth and smoother skin, microplastics are present in several personal-care products, such as exfoliators, body scrubs and toothpastes. Thousands of tonnes of plastic microbeads wash into the sea every year, where they harm wildlife and can ultimately be injested by people. The exact health implications of ingesting plastic have yet to be established. Potentially unnecessary personal-care products will accrue significant environmental, health and economic costs. The Stone, Bronze and Iron Ages represented historical stages in the development of humanity. So prolific is the plastic problem today that Siegle (2018) suggests we are now living though the Plastic Age.

Plastic in the ocean

Plastic pollution of our oceans is one of the greatest challenges of our time. Marine debris is litter that ends up in oceans, seas and other large bodies of water. Some plastic and marine debris comes from fishing gear, offshore oil and gas platforms and ships. But 80% of it comes from land, both from legal and illegal dumping sources. Incredibly damaging to sea life, plastic is now found everywhere from the Arctic sea ice to the world's deepest ocean trench. Seabirds, marine mammals and sea turtles can accidently eat or become entangled in plastic debris, with devastating consequences. Fishing nets lost at sea, and plastic bags trap fish and mammals, preventing them from swimming, foraging for food and mating. The problem is now so acute that there are islands of plastic in the middle of the Oceans. Referring to the collection of marine debris in the North Pacific Ocean, the Great Pacific Garbage Patch is described as the largest landfill in the world. Plastic has even been found in the Mariana Trench, the deepest oceanic trench on Earth, nearly 11 kilometres below sea level. The fear is that, as human populations grow, the amount of plastic entering the oceans will increase dramatically, if countries don't improve waste-management systems reducing the amount of plastic produced and consumed.

Plastic is not biodegradable. Once in the ocean, plastic decomposes very slowly, breaking down into tiny pieces. With exposure to ultraviolet (UV) rays and the ocean environment, plastic breaks down into smaller and smaller fragments called microplastics. These non-biodegradable tiny pieces of plastic can be found in our oceans, lakes and along our shorelines. Recognised as food by fish and animals, this plastic is ingested, and in some cases, enters the human food chain. Large plastic pieces endure, suffocate and often kill marine animals, including protected and endangered species, such as sea turtles. Some predict that by 2050, there will be more plastic (by weight) than fish in the sea.

Just as the world was beginning to comprehend the dangers of single-use plastic and several governments were in the process of initiating a ban, the global pandemic Covid-19 spread around the world. A significant increase in medical and health related plastic waste ensued. This included personal protective equipment (PPE) such as masks, gloves and gowns, disposable wipes and hand-sanitiser bottles. Demand for single-use PPE and disposable masks skyrocketed. Shops, restaurants and businesses installed perspex screens in the hope of reducing droplet transmission of Covid-19. Single-use cups and individually wrapped cutlery became popular again. Social distancing generated an increase in food deliveries wrapped in a plethora of packaging. Unfortunately, some of this waste made its way to our oceans. Beneath the waves of the Mediterranean, divers have found 'Covid waste' – gloves, masks and bottles of hand sanitiser mixed in with the usual litter of disposable cups and aluminium cans.

Plastic and climate change

Plastic is a by-product of oil, coal and gas and a key contributor to CO_2 emissions. Indeed, the plastic industry is one of the largest and fastest-growing sources of industrial greenhouse gas emissions. According to the Center for International Environmental Law's (CIEL) *Plastic and Climate: The Hidden Costs of a Plastic Planet 2019*, if the expansion of petrochemicals and plastics production continues as currently planned, by 2050 plastic will be responsible for 10-13% of our total 'carbon budget' (CIEL, 2019). Our 'carbon budget' refers to the amount of CO_2 we can emit globally and still remain below a $1.5°$ C temperature rise. Do you remember Lorna Gold's use of a balloon for explaining the concept of carbon budget? (Chapter 1). There is only a limited amount of air a balloon can take before it bursts. In climate terms, there is only a limited amount of greenhouse gases which can be released into the atmosphere before the global balloon bursts or irreversible damage occurs. The production of plastic allows the fossil fuel industry to profit from the by-products of petroleum production which would otherwise have been considered waste. Ironically, during Covid-19, restrictions on travel pushed oil prices to historic lows, in turn driving the cost of virgin plastic below that of recycled plastic.

In 2019 alone, researchers estimate that the production and incineration of plastic has contributed more than 850 million tonnes of greenhouse gases to the atmosphere (CIEL, 2019). Incineration is particularly harmful, and is the number one driver of emissions from plastic waste management. Despite a growing awareness of the environmental impact of plastic, its global production is actually increasing. The oil industry is investing more resources into plastic production, partly in response to a global move away from fossil fuel powered energy.

Of particular concern is the projected impact of plastics on the oceanic carbon sink. The world's oceans provide the largest natural carbon sink for greenhouse gases, having absorbed 30–50% of atmospheric CO_2 produced since the start of the industrial era. If microplastics were to disrupt the ability of underwater ecosystems to absorb carbon, it could seriously compromise efforts to stop global warming.

Over consumption

The production of plastic has transformed the way we consume. As Leonard (2010) argues, we have a problem with 'stuff'. We are consuming more than we need, placing unprecedented pressure on the resources of the Earth. We extract too much from nature, make it into 'stuff' we use and don't use – from chemicals to plastics to fertiliser to smart phones to meat. This stuff is then unceremoniously dumped. Siegle (2018:3) claims that the rubbish found on beaches has the same plastic brand profile as 'any homogenised high street'.

In light of an increasing population and more unequal distribution of wealth, if we continue to consume at US rates, we will need 3–5 more planets. In her book *The Story of Stuff*, Leonard (2010) tracks the life of the 'stuff' we use every day – where our cotton T-shirts, laptop computers and aluminium cans come from, how they are produced, distributed and consumed, and where they go when we throw them out. Leonard also created a YouTube sensation (*The Story of Stuff*), based on her book. Her message is very clear: we have too much 'stuff', and too much of it is toxic. Outlining the five stages of our consumption-driven economy; from extraction through production, distribution, consumption and disposal; she cleverly illuminates its frightening consequences. Leonard explores the issue of 'manufactured demand' in her YouTube clip, *The Story of Bottled Water*. This explores the marketing used to encourage us to buy billions of bottles of water every week when it already flows virtually free from the tap. While our system is in crisis, Leonard shows that we as astute consumers can stop the environmental damage, social injustice and health hazards caused by polluting production and excessive consumption. As consumers, we can avoid products containing microbeads and put pressure on companies and governments to end their use. As more than a third of all plastic is disposable packaging such as bags and bottles, we can and must limit our overall use, and reuse or recycle these items. In 2002, the Irish Government introduced an environmental levy on plastic bags at points of sale in order to reduce their consumption and adverse effects it had on Ireland's landscape. This levy with its dramatic effect on consumer behaviour led to a 90% drop in the use of plastic bags. Plastic has made life more convenient, but many of us remember a time when we got along fine without it.

The mantra *Reduce, Reuse, Recycle* has been widely adopted both in primary schools and society for some time. Given the importance of this message, the statistics are disappointing. While recycling efforts continue to grow, the recovery rates of plastic remain disappointingly low. Around 15% of the globe's plastic waste is recycled, of which 5% is turned into a recycled object or material (Siegle, 2018). Millions of tons of waste plastic still end up in landfill sites. Our relationship with plastic needs to be reconsidered (Table 13.1).

Nonetheless, consumer action alone is not enough. Plastic is a robust business model for big corporations. Ultimately, the only way to address this issue comprehensively is to stop producing fossil fuels, the primary source of plastic and to stop producing single-use disposable plastics that we don't need. Consumers can use their voting power to demand legislation which reduces the use of single-use plastic.

Learning to understand the complexity of plastic through children's literature

Children's literature and picture books in particular provide a powerful stimulus for critical thinking, creative engagement and hopeful inspiration (Dolan, 2014; Roche, 2014). There are many examples of fiction and non-fiction picture books which deal with the topic of plastic.

With beautiful illustrations by Hannah Peck, *Somebody Swallowed Stanley* (2019) tells the story of the problems a simple plastic bag can create in the oceans. Written by animal behaviourist and eco-expert Sarah Roberts, this book about plastic pollution introduces children to the character Stanley, a plastic bag who happens to look like a jellyfish.

Sip the Straw by Sam Keck Scott and Woody Heffern (2018) illustrated by Nyoman Miasa focuses on single-use plastic through the perspective of one straw. Sip starts off quite proud of his role in life ('Without straws like me, people couldn't drink'!), and is shocked to find himself dumped after one single drink. He then goes on a grand adventure through the ocean, meeting various sea creatures, such as a giant sunfish who fears the Great Pacific Garbage Patch (to which he drifts). Eventually, Sip washes ashore and achieves his dream of being recycled. The story helps children to develop a deeper understanding of how plastic waste can disrupt ecosystems.

The Tale of a Toothbrush: A Story of Plastic in Our Oceans by M.G. Leonard and illustrated by Daniel Rieley is a magical story which deals with the ecological issue of plastic

Table 13.1 Rethinking our relationship with plastics

The *reduce, reuse and recycle* mantra has now been replaced with a longer list of Rs. These options encourage us to restrict our use of plastic before we reach the recycle stage.

Reduce: Reduce the amount of material consumed and the waste produced. Practical examples include borrowing items instead of purchasing them, start a compost bin, buy products without packaging and ask retailers to source items without packaging. Ultimately the option to purchase is personal. Do not buy anything that is not needed.

Respect: Respect the true value of commodities and all of the resources used throughout the processes of production including raw materials, energy consumption, transport and labour.

Reuse: Think about reusing products instead of purchasing alternatives. This includes reusable shopping bags, plates, cups and other products often replaced by single use alternatives.

Recover: Recover the carbon from grass and prunings by composting and improving the carbon component of soil. Include a wild flower patch in gardens and school grounds to facilitate biodiversity. Plant a tree and observe its progress on a seasonal and annual basis.

Repair: A whole range of goods can be fixed or repaired. Instead of throwing out old shoes – take them to be repaired by having them resoled and reheeled. The requirement to purchase new commodities will be reduced when repairs are considered.

Return: When buying a product, keep proof of purchase and if it does not work or if it is unsatisfactory for any reason, return it to the point of purchase. Many unused items end up, either wittingly or unwittingly in the rubbish bin.

Refill: Ask local grocery shops to stock up on refill alternatives. Choose a single-use-plastics-packaging-free grocery stop over conventional retail outlets.

Refuse disposable plastics! Disposable plastics are the greatest source of plastic pollution. Plastic bags, straws, bottles, utensils, lids and cups are convenient in the short term, yet, environmentally hazardous in the long term.

Rethink: It is ultimately up to consumers to start thinking about products purchased, reasons for purchase and methods of disposal. As a consumer, think about why you are buying an item, remember your life without it, and remember how you could get by without it. Be part of the solution rather than the problem.

Replace: Instead of high carbon products look for eco-friendly alternatives.

Repurpose: If one of the previous Rs doesn't apply think creatively. – Can a home-based product be used for something else entirely? Can products be given a new life through a new purpose? This is where upcycling might come into the picture.

Recycle: This is the last item on the list, the last resort. Recycling uses a lot of energy so consider all of the options above before this final step. Many of the things consumed every day, such as paper bags, aluminum cans and milk cartons, are made out of materials that should be recycled. Materials need to be sorted, rinsed and disposed of using the correct recycling option.

pollution in an accessible way for children. The book highlights the life and journey of single use plastics through the eyes of 'Sammy' the toothbrush. Sofia is delighted with the bright yellow toothbrush she has chosen. She writes an 'S' on his tummy so everyone knows he belongs to her. However, Sammy's bristles soon wear out and Sofia's mum throws him away. In a cargo of rubbish, Sammy travels across the seas, before finding his way into a river, and from there back into the ocean to start the long journey back to

Sofia. Along the way, he meets plastic bottles, plastic straws and plastic bags, all floating in the ocean, before a kindly albatross gives him a lift for the last leg of the journey. Full of humour, the illustrations are thought provoking, bringing not only Sammy, but the shampoo bottle, the plastic bag and other characters, to life. During his journey, Sammy witnesses first-hand the considerable damage that plastic is having on the world around him. At the back of the book, there is a short informational text detailing problems associated with plastic and suggestions for how these might be overcome.

One Plastic Bag: Isatou Ceesay and the Recycling Women of Gambia (2015) by Miranda Paul is an inspirational true story illustrating the power of one person's actions. Isatou takes it upon herself to collect discarded plastic bags and recycle them. In The Gambia, discarded bags collect pools of water which attract mosquitos and disease. Animals die from eating the bags and gardens are choked by them. Isatou facilitates a change in behaviour by gathering her friends to collect and clean the bags which are then woven into beautiful purses. Selling the purses earns money to replace dead livestock and creates a healthier community.

A series of children's picture books produced by Wild Tribe Heroes deals with the topic of ocean plastics. The series introduces us to Duffy the Sea Turtle, Marli the Puffin and Nelson the Whale. Written by Ellie Jackson, these stories help children understand the relationship between the actions of humans and wildlife, and the ensuing dangers encountered in their own natural habitats. The stories focus specifically on the destructive power of plastic, while also underlining the importance of caring for our planet by suggesting simple actions which can be undertaken.

Marli's Tangled Tale: A True Story About the Problem of Balloon Releases (2017) by Ellie Jackson and illustrated by Laura Callwood is a story about a puffin who gets tangled up in balloons. It teaches children about the problems of balloon releases and suggests a number of sustainable alternatives. In the story *Duffy the Sea Turtle: A True Story About Plastic in Our Ocean* (2017), Duffy lives amongst beautiful coral reefs and colourful fish, only for Duffy to learn that not all that floats is food. As time is running out Duffy has a lucky escape when kind people step in to save the day. The third book in this series is *Nelson's Dangerous Dive: A True Story About the Problems of Ghost Fishing Nets in Our Oceans* (2018). This is the story about Nelson the Whale who discovers a hidden shipwreck and learns that what lurks below may not let you go.

Responding to the plastic crisis

While climate change is real and urgent, it is important that children do not feel scared and powerless. Children can be inspired to use their energy, creativity and sense of justice to protect our planet. Rather than focusing on doom and gloom, children can become solution-seekers. Sharing examples of children's plastic actions is a good place to begin. There are many examples of children and young people who are currently challenging the plastic conundrum:

> Fionn Ferreira, (an 18 year old student at the time of writing), won the grand prize at the 2019 Google Science Fair for creating a method to remove microplastics from the ocean.
>
> Ferreira's project used a novel, but effective methodology for removing ocean plastics. He used magnets to attract microplastics from water. Through the project, he discovered that a magnetic liquid called ferrofluid attracted tiny plastic particles and

removed them from the water. After nearly a thousand tests, his device successfully removed about 88 percent of the microplastics from water samples.

His idea came to him after finding a rock covered in oil near his remote coastal town in Ireland's southwest. He noticed tiny pieces of plastic stuck to the oil. The microscopic size of microplastics has challenged scientists looking for ways to remove them from the environment. But Ferreira was inspired.

Those microplastics, which are less than 5 mm long, come from beauty products, various textiles and larger pieces of disintegrating plastic. As they are so small, the plastic particles escape water filtration systems and end up polluting waterways. Once in rivers and oceans, marine animals, of all sizes end up ingesting them.

Since plastic and oil stick together, Ferreira wondered if the same thing would happen if he used a substance known as ferrofluid. Both microplastics and ferrofluids have similar properties, so they attract. For his experiments, Ferreira added ferrofluids to water and then stirred in a solution full of microplastics. When the microplastics found the ferrofluids, they stuck together. Ferreira then dipped a magnet to the solution, which attracted the combined ferrofluids and microplastics. It left the water clear.

Flossie Donnelly, a 12-year old student (at the time of writing) who has become synonymous with clearing South Dublin beaches of plastic waste has launched her very own charity, 'Flossie and the Beach Cleaners'. The charity was established to develop a network of south Dublin residents who wish to get involved in beach cleaning. The charity aims to: train transition year students to deliver workshops on plastic pollution in primary schools; invest in Virtual Reality (VR) headsets that give children a virtual visit to plastic-ridden rivers around the world; develop a 'Flossie and The Beach Cleaners' school network (connecting with countries most effected by plastic pollution) and hold regular beach clean-ups and other events to help educate people about plastic pollution.

The charity also strives to educate primary school children about the importance of coastal stewardship. It aims to link children in Ireland with children in countries where plastic pollution has reached crisis levels. Flossie was seven when she was kayaking in Thailand, where she observed plastic floating all around her. She immediately understood the problem of plastic. She runs a weekly blog highlighting what she finds on the shoreline.

Flossie raised over €4,000 to fund a Seabin, which currently stands in Dun Laoghaire Harbour. A Seabin is a floating rubbish bin, which is placed in the water and uses a pump to trap floating waste, such as bottles and plastic bags.

Innovative eco-activities and projects

An investigation of recycling symbols for plastic

In their study on recycling and waste management, children from St. Augustine's N.S., Clontuskert, Ballinasloe discovered that consumers are confused by the array of symbols on household packaging. Their research project aimed to address the lack of a system wide synchronisation of recycling symbols. The children conducted an extensive online survey to investigate the use of Waste Management Symbols on packaging in Ireland. By analysing the research data, the children discovered that recycling is an extremely confusing process due to vague labelling, a lack of standardisation and the absence of clear disposal instructions.

Figure 13.1 The Mobius Loop

The universally recognised recycling symbol is the Mobius Loop, a triangle composed of three arrows looping back on themselves in clockwise direction (Figure 13.1). While this symbol means an item can be recycled, it doesn't mean general acceptance by recycling centres or waste collectors. The Green Dot symbol/trade mark consists of an enclosed circle containing two interlocking arrows following a vertical axis (Figure 13.2). Images from this project are included in the Colour Plate, section 5.

The children's research focused specifically on the use of the Green Dot, as this was identified as a problematic symbol both in Ireland and the European Union. In 1994, the European Union passed the European Packaging Directive to try and

Figure 13.2 The Green Dot

reduce the amount of packaging ending up in landfill. The Directive stipulated that producers should pay towards the recycling of their packaging. Since the directive was issued, the Green Dot symbol has identified companies that financially support the collection and recycling of packaging materials. This symbol means that a financial contribution has been made towards recycling. While the packaging may or may not be suitable for recycling, the Green Dot is not a recycling symbol. It is the lack of understanding about the Green Dot trademark that has left many consumers confused about the significance of the symbol. Confusion over symbols on packaging prohibits more extensive recycling.

Many people in the children's research project confused the recycling symbols, believing that both the Green Dot and Mobius symbol indicated that packaging could be recycled. The children worked closely with a local recycling company, Barna Waste. Personnel from the company ran workshops in the school about waste management and recycling in Galway and Ireland. Their answer is simple: create a more consumer-friendly label and plastic identification system, so proper recycling techniques can be better communicated.

One of the most noteworthy elements of this research has been the degree of dissemination. The children created a website to showcase their research and findings: *so you think you can recycle.com*. They brought their project to the Galway Science and Technology Festival and the Electricity Supply Board (ESB) Science Blast in Dublin where they continued to collect data from the public. The children made presentations to two senior government ministers and subsequently received a letter of commendation from the President of Ireland Figure (Appendix 4). They also shared their findings with teachers and children in a number of countries though Skype calls. The children's work was completed as part their climate action project discussed in greater detail in Chapter 14.

Presentation of projects on waste and single-use plastic

Many local and national organisations encourage children to showcase their environmental research. Limerick City Hall hosted an art exhibition on waste and consumption. A dramatic art piece by children from Catherine McCauley School illustrates the creative response of young people to single-use items and marine litter Colour Plate, section 6.

ECO-UNESCO is Ireland's environmental education and youth organisation. The organisation works to conserve the environment and empower young people. ECO-UNESCO promotes the personal development of young people by developing and channelling the passion that young people feel about the environment into positive and creative actions to protect the natural world. Their flagship programme *The Young Environmentalist Awards* features environmental projects from people between the ages of 10 and 18 in schools, youth and community groups across the island of Ireland. There has been a dramatic increase in the number of projects dealing with the environmental impact of waste and single-use plastics (Figure 13.3).

Creating a plastic timeline: How long does it take for your rubbish to decompose?

It is useful to think about the nature of our rubbish, its final destination and the length of time it takes to decompose. Children can be given a selection of items from the list of items

Figure 13.3 Art installation inspired by the impact of plastic on ocean life (Patrician Academy, Mallow)

set out in Table 13.2. After describing the item in terms of name, properties and features they can estimate how long each item takes to decompose. Following their estimates, children can set out each item along a line creating a timeline of decomposition. After the correct answers are revealed, a class discussion to maximise learning can focus on surprise results and the implications for our consumption and dumping habits.

Table 13.2 How long does it take to break down?

How long does it take to break down?			
Paper towel	2–4 weeks	Plywood	1–3 years
Banana peel	3–4 weeks	Milk carton	5 years
Paper bag	1 month	Steel can	50 years
Newspaper	1.5 months	Foamed plastic cup	50 years
Apple core	2 months	Aluminium can	200–500 years
Cardboard	2 months	Plastic bottle	450 years
Orange peel	6 months	Plastic bag	200–1000 years

Table 13.3 What the numbers mean: numbers used on plastics

1	Polyethylene Terephthalate (PET)	Plastic drinks bottles
2	High-Density Polyethylene (HDPE)	Plastic milk cartons or shampoo bottles
3	Polyvinyl Chloride (PVC)	Cling film, plastic wrapping for bed linen and blister packs for medication
4	Low-Density Polyethylene (LDPE)	Disposable coffee cups, the plastic packaging of bread
5	Polypropylene (PP)	Yoghurt containers and takeaway containers from local deli or salad bar
6	Polystyrene (PS)	Foam-like disposable cups and containers
7	Products made from a combination of plastics	Children's toys and packaging

Exploring and categorising different types of plastics

The variety of plastics also causes confusion. Inside the three-arrow triangle, on the bottom of most plastic containers, there is a small number which ranges from one to seven. The purpose of the number is to identify the type of plastic used for the product. Not all plastics are recyclable or even reusable. If a plastic item contains the numbers '1' or '2', it can be recycled by a local waste management company. Numbers '3' through '7', are more problematic and ideally should not be purchased (Table 13.3). There are numerous plastic-based products that cannot break down and cannot be recycled.

Children can sort plastic items into different categories as indicated in Table 13.3. This kind of activity helps children to read packaging, to comprehend important information and to learn how to critically analyse mixed messages about recycling. Follow-up discussions can take place about disposal, plastic pollution and links to climate change (Dolan, 2020).

Conclusion

The fossil fuel product plastic has become an unavoidable part of modern living. Notwithstanding the problems associated with single-use plastic, other plastics provide critical functions associated with health, travel and homes. So, the battle against plastic has to target single-use, unwanted and nuisance plastic. Single-use plastic is forced upon consumers and ultimately onto the environment with devastating results. Ground breaking research is providing sustainable solutions. Researchers from the Polymer Centre, Queen's University Belfast believe they have uncovered new ways to convert single-use plastic waste, such as water bottles, into products including kayaks, canoes and storage tanks for water and fuel. Using a ground-breaking manufacturing process called rotational moulding, the researchers believe they can economically recycle large volumes of plastic waste into products including urban street furniture, marine buoys and storage tanks.

Plastic is relatively cheap to purchase, yet incredibly durable in nature. It is its durability which causes problems for disposal. Plastics illustrate the excesses of marketing and consumerism, poor resource management, excessive packaging, corporate oil interests and fragmented recycling systems. Furthermore, plastic links us to climate change and resource-based conflict through its relationship with the fossil fuel industry (Siegle, 2018). Young people are part of the solution. However, while individual actions are important, more strategic actions and political responses are required. Our political, business and corporate leaders must take steps to break our love affair with single-use plastics. Governments need to legislate to ensure that the producers of plastic waste are responsible for its ultimate recycling and disposal. Producers need to stop producing single-use plastic. Businesses need to promote plastic free policies as part of their marketing strategies. Finally, consumers should exercise their power to avoid all single-use plastic purchases. In addition, consumers can use their voices to ensure systemic changes to keep carbon in the ground. Corporate action is needed to produce sustainable alternatives and political commitment is essential for safeguarding our future.

Resources

Story of stuff: https://www.youtube.com/watch?v=9GorqroigqM
The story of bottled water: https://www.youtube.com/watch?v=Se12y9hSOM0

Picturebooks

Dorey, M. and Wesson, T. (illus) (2019) *Kids fight plastic: How to be a #2minutesuperhero*. London: Walker Books.

French. J. (2019) *What a waste: Rubbish, recycling, and protecting our planet*. London: DK Children.

Inches, A. and Whitehead, P. (illus) (2009) *The adventures of a plastic bottle: A story about recycling*. New York: Little Green Books.

Jackson, E. and Callwood, L. (2018) *Nelson's dangerous dive: A true story about the problems of ghost fishing nets in our oceans (wild tribe heroes)*. London: Ellie Jackson.

Jackson, E. and Callwood, L. (2017) *Marli's tangled tale: A true story about the problem of balloon releases (wild tribe heroes)*. London: Ellie Jackson.

Jackson, E. and Oldmeadow, L. (2017) *Duffy's lucky escape: A true story about plastic in our oceans (wild tribe heroes)*. London: Ellie Jackson.

Keck Scott, S., Heffern, W. and Miasa, N. (illus) (2018) *Sip the straw*. Herndon VA: Social Motion Publishing.

Kim, A. and Li, J. (2019) (illus) *Plastic: Past, present and future VIC*. Australia: Scribe Publications.

Lane Ferrari, S. and Valliceli, G. (2019) *Saving Tally: An adventure into the Great Pacific plastic patch*. Serena Ferrari: Save The Planet Books.

Layton, N. (2019) *A planet full of plastic and how you can help*. London: Wren and Rook.

Leonard, M.G. and Rieley, D. (2020) *The tale of a toothbrush: A story of plastic in our oceans*. London: Walker Books.

Owen, R. (2018) *Plastic pollution on land and in the oceans: Let's investigate (fundamental science key stage 1) St Austell*. United Kingdom: Ruby Tuesday Books Ltd.

Paul, M. (2015) *One plastic bag: Isatou Ceesay and the recycling women of Gambia*. Minneapolis: Lerner Publishing Group.

Roberts, S. and Peck, H. (illus) (2019) *Somebody swallowed Stanley*. London: Scholastic.

References

Dolan, A.M. (2020) *Powerful primary geography: A toolkit for 21ˢᵗ century learning*. London: Routledge.

Dolan, A.M. (2014) *You, me and diversity: Picturebooks for teaching development and intercultural education*. London: Trentham Books/IOE Press.

Leonard, A. (2010) *The story of stuff: How our obsession with stuff is trashing the planet, our communities, and our health and a vision for change*. New York: Simon and Schuster.

Roche, M., (2014) *Developing children's critical thinking through picturebooks: A guide for primary and early years students and teachers*. London:Routledge.

Siegle, L. (2018) *Turning the tide on plastic: How humanity (and you) can make our globe clean again*. Hachette UK.

Center for International Environmental Law (CIEL) (2019) Plastic and climate: The hidden costs of a plastic planet. https://www.ciel.org/wp-content/uploads/2019/05/Plastic-and-Climate-FINAL-2019.pdf.

Geyer, R., Jambeck, J.R. and Law, K.L. (2017) Production, use, and fate of all plastics ever made. *Science Advances, 3*(7), p.e1700782.

Section 4

Climate change education: Pedagogies of hope and action

14 Geography, global learning and climate justice

Geographical aspects of teaching climate change

Anne M. Dolan

Introduction

Climate change is inherently geographical. It involves physical and human processes, environmental interactions and sustainable (or the lack thereof) solutions. An understanding of environmental issues including climate change is vital for young people. Children need to understand how geographical processes interact to create unique human and physical landscapes that change over time. While climate change is a distinct geographical topic in its own right, it also informs other geographical themes including weather, coasts, rivers, ecosystems and migration. This chapter illustrates an exploration of climate change in terms of primary geography. Through creative geography, children make personal and communal connections with climate change. They explore climate change from a justice and human rights perspective through global geography in general and global learning in particular. Climate change education is examined through the lens of the Sustainable Development Goals (SDGs). Finally, the chapter presents some innovative geography from primary schools, whereby children explore the geographical dimensions of climate change.

Making a connection with climate change

The language of climate change is complex and includes terms such as *greenhouse effect, greenhouse gases, fossil fuels, carbon sink* and *the carbon cycle*. A glossary of key climate change terms is included in Appendix 1. Climate change statistics can be a little overwhelming. Many feel disconnected from the figures and narrative of climate change. It is important to help children make connections. Activities such as the game, *Climate Change Go Bingo* allow children to make simple connections with the terminology of climate change and with each other. This activity involves children by asking them to find someone in the class who matches a description or knows certain information. Additionally, this activity can be used to introduce climate change vocabulary, to activate background knowledge, and to review climate concepts. Children enjoy the mobility and sociability of this game.

Climate justice

Climate change education, climate justice and global learning are intertwined through a focus on justice and equity. Climate change is a justice issue for three reasons (Harlan et al., 2015). Firstly, its causes are generated by social inequalities, as poorer nations use less fossil fuels. Secondly, the effects of climate change have a greater impact on poorer

---

Climate Change Go Bingo

Instructions

1 **Preparation**

   Prepare 10 to 20 'Find Someone Who' statements using vocabulary or concepts that relate to climate change. For example, find someone who is able to draw the carbon cycle. Further examples are provided in Table 14.1. Create a variety of statements so that it will be easy to find a person with some characteristics, but not so easy to find others. Each set of statements can be tailor made to suit the unique climate change story of your locality/region/country. Compile these statements on a class interview sheet.

2 **Directions**

   Announce that the class is going to conduct a brief interview activity in which children will ask each other questions relating to climate change. The goal is for each child to complete his/her sheet, matching each statement with a named child. Instruct children to find someone who can answer one of their questions or say 'yes' to one of the descriptions on the interview sheet based on statements from Table 14.1. They should write that person's name on their interview sheet and move on to the next question with another person. *Important*: Each child can write a person's name only once.

3 **Complete the chart**

   Ask everyone to stand up and begin the activity for a set amount of time. The goal of the activity may be to complete the entire chart or to tick five in a row.

4 **Extension work**

   To review this exercise, the teacher can discuss each item and ask children to discuss the definitions/concepts, and to physically draw and label the carbon cycle.

---

communities locally, nationally and globally. Thirdly, policies designed to manage climate change, e.g., renewable energy sources and geoengineering schemes tend to exclude the politically marginalised.

Climate justice is a term used for framing climate change as an ethical and political issue, rather than one that is purely environmental or physical in nature. It links human rights and development to achieve a human-centred approach, safeguarding the rights of the most vulnerable people and sharing the burdens and benefits of climate change and its impacts equitably and fairly. However, according to the UN Human Rights Council (2019), the world is now increasingly at risk of 'climate apartheid', where the rich pay to escape heat and hunger caused by the escalating climate crisis while the rest of the world suffers.

By 2050, populations in low and middle-income countries will have increased. As a driver of injustice, the climate crisis will continue to widen the gap between those with and without resources. Humans and animals are competing for dwindling resources, especially in countries that contribute least to global carbon emissions. Droughts mean limited access to food and water. Rising sea levels lead to floods further exacerbating food security. Climate change will have devastating consequences for people in poverty. Even with the best-case scenario, hundreds of millions will face food insecurity, forced migration, disease and death. Climate change threatens the future of human rights and risks undoing the last

Table 14.1 *Find Someone Who* Statements for Climate Change Go Bingo (statements should be adapted in line with local social, economic and cultural factors)

Can name at least one greenhouse gas	Is able to draw the 'carbon cycle'	Can explain the term 'carbon sink'	Uses one of the following options when travelling to school
			Walks, cycles, uses public transport, carpools with another family
Name_____	Name_____	Name_____	Name_____
Can produce a reusable bottle for drinks	Is able to explain what is meant by the 'carbon cycle'	Has heard or read about climate change in the news	Has had a recent conversation with family members about climate change
Name_____	Name_____	Name_____	Name_____
Can explain the difference between weather and the climate	Has ever planted a flower or a tree	Has taken an action to address climate change (please note the kind of action taken)	Plays outside almost every day
Name_____	Name_____	Name_____	Name_____
Goes exploring in their local area	Is able to name five species of trees growing in local are	Knows the name of the government minister with the environment/climate change portfolio	Can name three causes of climate change
Name_____	Name_____	Name_____	Name_____
Can name three climate actions which can be taken by children	Has been for a walk in a woodland area in the past month	Has been on the Green School Committee at one time	Can define the term 'fossil fuels'
Name_____	Name_____	Name_____	Name_____

50 years of progress in development, global health and poverty reduction (UN Human Rights Council, 2019). Unfortunately, the injustice of climate change will be further aggravated by Covid-19. Core principles of climate justice have been identified by the Mary Robinson Foundation (n.d.) as follows:

Respect and protect human rights
    Basic rights engrained in respect for the dignity of the person should form the foundation for action on climate justice.
Support the right to development
    Current models of development perpetuate vast inequalities between rich and poor. More sustainable models of development must support low carbon resilient strategies, green technologies and a more equitable distribution of resources.

Share benefits and burdens equitably

Countries benefiting from industrialisation and fossil fuels need to contribute more towards low carbon development.

Ensure that decisions on climate change are participatory, transparent and accountable

Decisions on policies with regard to climate change taken in a range of fora from the United Nations Framework Convention on Climate Change (UNFCCC) to trade, human rights, business, investment and development, must be implemented in a way that is transparent, accountable and corruption-free. The needs of low-income countries must be understood and addressed.

Highlight gender equality and equity

Women are increasingly and disproportionately bearing the burden of the climate crisis. It often falls on women to care for growing families in worsening conditions. Women's voices must be heard as they can play a vital role as agents of change within their communities.

Harness the transformative power of education for climate stewardship

Achieving climate stabilisation requires radical change in lifestyle and behaviour. Education is required to equip us citizens to take steps to mitigate against climate change, to develop climate resilience as we learn to adapt to short-term and long-term impacts of climate change. Life-long, multidisciplinary climate change learning in justice terms is required within formal, nonformal and virtual (web-based) education settings.

Use effective partnerships to secure climate justice

Based on our interdependent world, climate justice requires partnership within and between nations involving sharing of knowledge, skills and resources. Ultimately this requires partnership with those most affected by climate change and least able to deal with it, poorly resourced nations and people.

The Sustainable Development Goals (SDGs)

In 2015, 193 United Nations (UN) member states adopted the 2030 Agenda for Sustainable Development and its 17 SDGs or global goals (Figure 14.1). Focusing on extreme poverty, climate change and world inequalities, the 17 SDGs reflect economic, social and environmental dimensions of sustainable development. Since their launch in September 2015, the UN's SDGs have been adopted by schools around the world. As global competency becomes an increasingly important requirement, the SDGs provide a unique framework for teachers for thematic teaching, global learning, sustainability and citizenship education.

The SDGs are a call for action by all countries (poor, rich and middle-income) to promote prosperity while protecting the planet. New ways of thinking and acting are required to achieve the ultimate goal of sustainable living. SDGs provide unprecedented opportunities for countries and communities to work together for a sustainable and equitable world. SDGs thinking recognises that tackling climate change must go hand-in-hand with strategies that build economic growth. They must also address a range of social needs including education, health, social protection and job opportunities, while confronting poverty and environmental protection. Although the SDGs are universal, it is recognised that each country faces its own unique development challenges. To achieve sustainable development, there are different approaches, visions, models and tools available to each country in accordance with national circumstances and priorities

Whilst urgent action to halt climate change and deal with its impacts is integral to successfully achieving all SDGs, Goal no. 13 deals specifically with climate action. The importance

THE GLOBAL GOALS
For Sustainable Development

Figure 14.1 The Sustainable Development Goals infographics

of education is also recognised within the SDGs. Education is both a goal in itself (SDG 4) and a means for attaining all the other SDGs. That is why education in general and climate change education in particular represents an essential strategy in the pursuit of the SDGs.

The SDGs provide a unique focus for work across the curriculum, supported by rich data and real-life scenarios around universal themes and current global issues. They open up debate around differing ways of tackling extreme poverty and inequality, and they provide alternative perspectives on equality and wealth.

The World's Largest Lesson introduces the SDGs to children and young people. A dedicated website (http://worldslargestlesson.globalgoals.org/) contains lesson plans created by teachers, a teachers' guide, a comic book, an animation, a global goals guide for young people and samples of innovative learning from around the global community. Also included is background information on each global goal, together with teaching tips, classroom activity ideas and links to lesson plans, film clips and teaching packs.

The World's Largest Lesson is an initiative to ensure that every child in the world grows up knowing and caring about the SDGs, and is inspired to take action to help achieve them. So far it has reached millions of children in over 100 countries, through the commitment of educators, civil society organisations, ministries and passionate individuals working across sectors.

Global learning

Geography helps to build a global perspective and to understand the connections between global and local events. It allows people to find answers to the questions about the world. Through the study of geography, learners explore and discover the processes that shape the earth, the relationships between people and environments, and the links between people and places.

In a fast-changing, globalised world, education needs to help young people understand the mechanics of the wider world, making the global connections between issues such as climate change and their own lives. While preparing young people to live and work in a global society and economy, education should ultimately help young people to make the world a better place.

Global learning is also discussed through a range of other terms, e.g., 'development education', the 'global dimension', 'citizenship education' and 'global citizenship education'. Specific themes within global learning include climate justice, global citizenship, conflict resolution, sustainability, diversity, interdependency, global poverty, aid, trade and debt, social justice and human rights. Moreover, the term *global competence* has recently featured in policy documents. The OECD/PISA (2018:4) define global competence as:

> the capacity to examine local, global and intercultural issues, to understand and appreciate different perspectives and world views of others, to engage in open appropriate and effective interactions with people from different cultures, and to act for collective wellbeing and sustainable development.

Children are 'growing up in a world of global media, in which the voices of many cultures compete for attention' (de Block and Buckingham, 2007:viii). It is therefore vital that teachers equip pupils with the ability to critically manage, assess and understand this deluge of information. Critical assessment and independent thinking have never been more important. One of the important skill-sets within global competency is the ability to formulate and articulate well-informed opinions about local, global and intercultural issues. This can be achieved through informal and formal debating as illustrated in the examples below.

Discussing and debating climate change

Debating climate change

A debate is a discussion or structured contest about an issue or a motion. A formal debate involves two sides: One supporting a motion and one opposing it. Debates may be judged in order to declare a winning side. A debate is described as a conversation between two groups that disagree, but with each trying to convince the adjudicator of the correctness of their position, and the foolishness of their opponents.

Debating is a fun, educational way of encouraging children to engage with contemporary issues and topics such as climate change. Learning to debate teaches children how to apply critical analysis, and how to prepare an argument using facts and sound research. It also teaches children valuable communication skills such as how to deliver a speech and how to effectively defend an adopted viewpoint. Debates, in one form or another, are commonly used in democratic societies to explore and resolve issues and problems. Decisions at a board meeting, public hearings or local community meetings are often reached through discussion and debate.

The purpose of debating is to succinctly express oneself using persuasive language. Effective for developing skills in oral language, public speaking, research, communication and critical thinking, debating also enhances confidence, teamwork skills and collaboration. Debating provide a unique opportunity for children to be rewarded for independent thinking. It also encourages children to explore topics from alternative perspectives. This is especially challenging for those who do not agree with the debating topic. It is particularly useful for topics such as climate change, whereby the arguments of scientists and deniers have been well publicised in the media. Information retention is another additional benefit. Debating helps children to contextualise their learning and to make links with contemporary issues.

Structuring a debate

A formal debate usually involves three groups: One supporting a resolution (affirmative team), one opposing the resolution (opposing team) and the judges. The affirmative and opposing teams usually consist of three members each, while the judging may be conducted by the teacher, a small group of children, or the class as a whole. In addition to the three specific groups, there may an audience made up of class members not involved in the formal debate. A specific resolution is developed and rules for the debate are established.

The Concern Debates

Concern is an international non-governmental organisation (NGO) implementing a range of programmes, designed to address specific causes of extreme poverty in communities across 25 countries. In Ireland, The *Concern Debates* is the organisation's flagship educational activity. While popular in secondary schools, primary schools can now participate. Schools enter a team of six children – with three children speaking and the other three acting as substitute speakers and researchers. Motions are based on contemporary development topics such as climate change, human rights and related issues. Schools can adopt the debating framework as an educational strategy. Extensive support including a primary debate handbook is available on the following link:

https://www.concern.net/schools-and-youth/debates/primary-school.

Preparing for a debate

- Develop the motions to be debated (see list below).
- Organise the teams.
- Establish the rules of the debate, including timelines.
- Research the topic and prepare logical arguments.
- Gather supporting evidence and examples for position taken.
- Anticipate counter arguments and prepare rebuttals.
- Team members plan the content and most effective order of arguments.
- Prepare room for debate.
- Establish expectations, if any, for assessment of debate.

Possible motions

- Climate change is not our problem.
- Young children should not be allowed to miss school to strike for climate action.
- To be serious about climate change is to give up using plastics.
- Public transport should be provided free of charge.
- The SDGs will not be achieved by 2030.
- Ireland should do away with cars.
- Today's children will inherit a better world.

Conducting a debate

The debate opens with one member from the affirmative team (the team that supports the resolution) presenting arguments, followed by a member of the opposing team. This pattern is repeated for the second speaker in each team. Finally, each team has an opportunity to refute the opponent's arguments. Speakers are advised to speak slowly and clearly. Judges and members of the audience are advised to take notes as the debate proceeds.

Some debating tips

1   Carefully research your debate topic.
2   Stay on topic.
3   Speak slowly, clearly, and charismatically.
4   Be confident.
5   Think about your body language and what it's telling your audience.
6   Listen carefully and take good notes.
7   Anticipate your opponent's questions.
8   Tell a story or give an example to make your point.
9   Construct a strong conclusion.
10 Respond respectfully and politely to your opponents.

Post-debate discussion and assessment

When the formal debate is finished, allow time for debriefing and discussion. Members of the audience should be given an opportunity to ask questions, and to contribute their own thoughts and opinions on the arguments presented. Members of the debate teams may also wish to reflect on their performance and seek feedback from the audience, including the teacher. Assessment can be conducted by the teacher, the judging team, or the entire class.

Walking debate

A walking debate is a useful and fun strategy to develop children's communication and critical thinking skills. Ask the children to stand. Place two signs 'Agree' and 'Disagree' on two opposing walls. Explain that children should decide whether they agree or disagree with each statement and stand close to the sign of their choice. Children should have a reason for their stance. If they are unsure, they can stand in the middle of the room. Once a child agrees with another child, he/she can move closer to the speaker. The best walking debates feature a lot of movement as children's minds are changed by powerful arguments made by their peers. Walking debates are extremely useful for giving every child a voice regardless of whether they actually speak out. They also provide an opportunity for children to explore the grey areas of difficult issues and encourage them to confront ambiguity. Sample statements for a walking debate are as follows:

1   I think the weather is very pleasant today.
2   In Ireland we do not have any extreme weather conditions.
3   Climate change is a myth. Humans are not powerful enough to change the climate.
4   We don't have to worry about climate change here in our local area. It only affects faraway places.

5 According to Greta Thunberg, no one is too small to make a difference. Do you agree?
6 Sea levels are rising at an unprecedented rate due to global warming.
7 There are actions that we can take to address climate change.
8 Human-caused global warming is changing weather systems and making heat waves and droughts more intense and more frequent.
9 Climate change is not our problem.
10 Today's children will inherit a better world.

Climate change mysteries

Mysteries are used as problem solving strategies. Particularly effective with complex issues such as climate change, they help children examine an issue in an interconnected framework. Specifically useful in teaching causes, effects and implications, mysteries promote children's geographical reasoning and relational thinking (Leat, 1998). A mystery is based on an open-ended question designed to promote children's curiosity, thinking and engagement. Teaching with mysteries incorporates three parts: First, introducing the problem/issue; second, group collaboration where children read 20–30 information strips to solve the mystery; and third, whole class debriefing and discussion (Karkdijk et al., 2019). The following two climate change mysteries (Tables 14.2 and 14.3) written by student teachers are designed to promote thinking, discussion and collaborative decision-making. There are no right or wrong answers. Children pose a solution to the problem and are required to suggest reasons for their answer. Each solution should be based on the group's deliberations, interpretation of the cards and/or reference to contemporary events. Red herrings (cards with unconnected information) may be included as a distraction.

Mystery 1. Why is Zaria worried about the animals on her family farm in Uganda (Table 14.2)?

Discussion points:

• What can we learn about climate change from this mystery?
• Horses were used for agriculture before the invention of the steam engine. What other examples of sustainable travel are available to us in our local area/region/country today?
• Richard Trevithick designed the first 'semi-portable' steam engine for agricultural use in 1804. Is this the reason that Zaria is worried about her animals? Discuss other reasons.
• What are the possible impacts of climate change addressed in this mystery?
• Can you identify any local/global connections in this mystery?

Mystery 2 Why did Jack miss the bus to Cork (Table 14.3)?

Discussion points:

• What can we learn about climate change from this mystery?
• What is causing the flooding of the River Blackwater?
• Are there other examples of extreme river flooding in Ireland, locate these examples on a map?
• What are the possible impacts of climate change addressed in this mystery?

Table 14.2 Why is Zaria worried about the animals on her family farm in Uganda?

Richard Trevithick designed the first 'semi-portable' steam engine for agricultural use in 1804, known as the 'barn engine'.	John Froelich invented the first petrol powered tractor in 1892.
In the early 1900s companies such as Ferguson and Fiat began to produce smaller and cheaper tractors.	In 1945, 'Tractor Power' overcomes 'Horse Power'.
Ciara lives on a Dairy Farm in Ireland. Ciara enjoys helping her dad on the farm.	Her favourite job is sitting in the tractor with her dad as he feeds the cows.
Ciara's younger sister thinks the farmyard and the cows are smelly.	The European Union's Agricultural Policy protects Ireland's Natural Environment.
Cows release a harmful gas called 'Methane Gas'.	The tractor and farm machinery release 'Carbon Dioxide'.
Methane gas (CH_4) and carbon dioxide (CO_2) are both greenhouse gases.	Greenhouse gases cause 'The Greenhouse Effect'. 'The Greenhouse Effect' is the rise in temperature experienced by the Earth.
Zaria is a young girl who lives on a small farm in Uganda. She helps to harvest the crops every year. Her family has one cow, one goat and three hens.	Zaria and her family harvest crops to make a living.
Crops need certain conditions to grow, mainly the right temperature and enough water.	'The Greenhouse Effect' can make it too hot to grow crops in certain countries, and drought caused by Climate Change can reduce the amount of water available for crops to thrive.
Zaria's helps on the farm by walking 3 km every day to collect water from their local water source.	Zaria goes to school every day in Uganda, so she does not always have time to collect water for the farm.
Their soil needs lots of water for the crops to grow.	Last year Zaria's family had reduced yields. Their productivity declined because of high temperatures and drought.
This year Zaria and her family are worried about their crops, because the irrigation systems cannot support the levels of drought in Uganda. There are conflicting arguments about access to fresh water in her community.	The fresh water they have is becoming scarce because new people are moving to live in her village.
Without crops to harvest, Zaria and her family will have little income, little food and little nutrition for their cow, goat and hens.	Zaria is hoping to visit Ireland later in the year and she needs money from the sale of the crops.

Written by student teacher Melissa Glynn

Table 14.3 Why did Jack miss the bus to Cork?

Jack was born in 2005 and grew up in Mallow, County Cork by the River Blackwater.	Jack is 13 years of age and he is in 6th Class in his local primary school. He and his dad are huge fans of sport. Jack supports the Cork hurlers and footballers. He also supports Cork City Football Club and Munster Rugby.
Jack and his family, especially his dad spend most weekends travelling to Cork to attend matches. They take the bus from Mallow Town Park to Cork City.	Recently, they have noticed recurring problem. Due to various storms, extreme weather and heavy rain showers, their bus stop is frequently flooded. The new flooding scheme in Mallow pushes the water from the flooded Blackwater River towards the Mallow Town Park. When flooding occurs, the bus bypasses Mallow town.
Jack has missed two vital Cork hurling games due to the flooding and the lack of a bus service in Mallow as a result. Jack and his dad are trying to figure out a solution.	Because Dad doesn't drive, the bus is the best and most affordable option in order to get to Cork. One day, they took a taxi to Cork and home. It cost €150 for the return trip. This is neither affordable nor sustainable.
Jack would like to study meteorology after his Leaving Certificate exams.	Mallow has flooded many times and the Town Park floods several times a year. Major floods have occurred in 2010, 2009, 2008, 2004, 1998, 1995, 1988, 1980, 1969, 1948, 1875 and 1853. The most severe flood occurred in 1853 when the town bridge was swept away.
Flooding in Ireland is now more common and severe than in the past and the scientific predictions are that global climate change will exacerbate the situation in years to come.	Met Éireann have a status yellow warning for heavy rain in place for Carlow, Kildare, Kilkenny, Laois, Wexford, Wicklow and Waterford until midnight.
The River Blackwater rises in County Kerry in the Mullaghereirk Mountains and initially flows south towards Rathmore before turning east, joining the Irish Sea at Youghal.	The town of Mallow benefited significantly from a flood relief scheme carried out by the OPW, Cork County Council and Mallow Town Council. This cost €36.7 M.
Jack and his Dad had a row on the day of the match.	Jack's Dad is in a bad mood. He has discovered his house is not covered by insurance due to its proximity to the river.
There are other watercourses including the Spa Glen Stream which also cause flooding problems, as it flows through the town centre, mostly beneath the streets in a series of culverts.	Due to a reduced budget, Cork Council has made many workers redundant including Jack's Dad.
Dad and Jack have had many conversations about climate change. Jack argues that human activity is changing the climate, but Dad does not agree.	At the Paris Climate Conference (COP21) in December 2015, 195 countries agreed to limit global warming to well below 2° C.
The Mallow Flood Relief Scheme cost €36.7 M.	Mallow has a long history of flooding, principally from the River Blackwater, which flows through the town.
If the rainfall continues to increase, the match may be cancelled.	Jack suffers from travel sickness on every bus journey.

Source: Student teacher Billy Madigan

Creative geographical explorations

Climate change is often perceived as a distant concept with no local repercussions. Geographical investigations based on weather, seasonal changes, impact of humans on the local environment and local planning help children make links between climate change and their local community (Dolan, 2020). Employing a geographical lens to focus on the local area can help children to appreciate the explicit and implicit impacts of climate change. Local issues provide the best starting point. These may include: Rezoning of land; controversial plans for new roads; local flooding; and the destruction of local habitats. Children have an opportunity to become immersed in, and impassioned about national and international issues such as Brexit, Migration, Covid-19 and Climate Change when considered through a local lens.

Creative geographical investigations help children to focus on what they care about and value in their own lives. Reflecting on climate change in the context of the local area makes this abstract concept more tangible for children. Recording their emotional responses can give children a voice, and can assist in the process of making personal and communal connections to climate change. Documenting these responses can occur through a variety of media, for example, narrative pieces, video recordings and haiku poetry. From the production and sharing of these documentaries, children appreciate their connections to the natural world and each other.

Writing haiku for climate change

Haiku is a form of Japanese poetry. A haiku is a three-line poem where the 1st and 3rd lines are 5 syllables and the 2nd line is 7 syllables. Traditionally, haiku poems are about nature and usually use seasonal or weather words. In Japan, these poems are valued for their simplicity, openness, depth and lightness. Haiku poets are challenged to convey a vivid message in only 17 syllables.

Haiku poems can describe anything, but are seldom complicated or difficult to understand. Almost all haiku poems have a dominant impression, or main idea, that appeals strongly to one of the five senses. Haiku is not only a way to connect to nature, but also a way to see and describe the world clearly. Since haiku is so short, the reader must be able to experience in three short lines the image in the poet's mind. Haiku poems can be written by all groups. The following haiku were written by final year B.Ed. students (Figure 14.2a–c).

Written in present tense, haiku is meant to be 'in the moment', taking something ordinary and making it extraordinary. Detailed observation and a deep love for nature can often be seen in good haiku. Haiku is usually one breath long. So, poets must listen with their ears, as well as their eyes and hearts in order to write good haiku.

After reading the 5th IPCC Report published in 2013, Seattle-based oceanographer Greg Johnson summarised the key findings in haiku poetry. He then illustrated those haiku with watercolours, resulting in a beautiful and concise visual guide to the extremely complex 2,000-page IPCC report. The images are available on-line. These images can be used to inspire children and student teachers to create their own climate change haiku poetry. Spending some time outdoors in the local area helps children to frame their haiku. The poetry can be illustrated by local area images including children's drawings and photographs.

Figure 14.2 (a) Climate change haiku

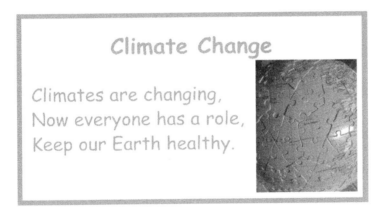

Figure 14.2 (b) Climate change haiku

Figure 14.2 (c) Climate change haiku

Case study 14.1 Climate Action Project

Climate Action Project is an annual innovative, collaborative online initiative. In 2020, 2.5 million students (6–22 years) were connected across 135 countries in six continents. This learner-centred project gives teachers an opportunity to join a global community, to share best practices and access a database of activities. With a focus on problem-based learning, students are invited to focus on real-life problems in their local area. Through researching local issues students have to explore, brainstorm, discuss, present and share their findings by uploading weekly videos on the project's webpage. Students are also required to create videos which are published on the website (www. Climate-action.info). By looking at the videos from their peers, students have access to first-hand information about climatic conditions from other parts of the world. This project showcases the nurturing of empathy, use of technology (Minecraft and Lego) and 21st-century learning skills such as collaboration, creativity, knowledge building and problem solving. The interconnected nature of global challenges such as climate change and Covid-19 require rapid adaptation and innovation from all citizens. 21st-century skills and dispositions are essential for engaged, participating citizens (Dolan, 2020). This climate action project is an outstanding example of collaboration and teaching from a perspective of hope. Delivered in partnership with the United Nations (UN), the National Aeronautics and Space Administration (NASA) and World Wildlife Fund (WWF), it has been endorsed by His Holiness the 14th Dalai Lama; Dr. Jane Goodall; The President of Ireland, Michael D. Higgins; Amnesty International; and Greenpeace. Media coverage from the BBC, CNN and National Geographic has featured the project in several countries.

The project is delivered in schools over six weeks adopting an enquiry framework (Figure 14.3, Table 14.4).

The success rates from this project have been phenomenal. In my former primary school, St. Augustine's National School, Clontuskert, Ballinasloe, I have witnessed firsthand

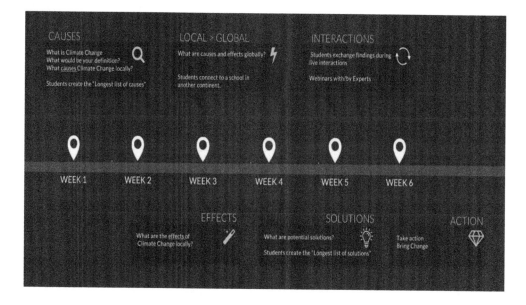

Figure 14.3 Climate Action Project: Six-week plan for schools

Source: www.climate-action.info

Table 14.4 Climate Action Project: A framework for enquiry

Week 1: Causes
What is climate change? What is your definition? What causes climate change locally?

Week 2: Effects
What are the effects of climate change locally?

Week 3: Local to global
Local to global: What are the causes and effects globally?
Connect to a school in another continent.

Week 4: Solutions
What are the potential solutions?

Week 5: Interactions and webinars
Live interactions and expert webinars.

Week 6: Action
Reflecting on work to date climate actions are designed and undertaken by students.

Source: www.climate-action.info

the impact of this project on children and teachers (Dolan, 2020). The project's work also features in Chapters 13 and 21 of this publication. Documented on the web page www.climate-action.info, the evidence of climate action adopted by young people is hopeful and future-oriented. Through the project, children have access to innovative climate change solutions from around the world (Figure 14.4). For instance, students in Malawi

Figure 14.4 Children from St. Augustine's, NS, Clontuskert discussing climate change with a class teacher in Dubai

planted millions of trees. In collaboration with a famous artist, students in Germany took to the street for a flash mob. Design thinking features strongly as students in America created a solar suitcase which was shipped to Kenya where it now supplies energy for one school. Students in Columbia made new car prototypes using cardboard. Students in India developed a solar-driven cart, while students in Indonesia created eco-bricks which were featured on national television. Most importantly, this project allows students share their stories with a global audience. Following the death of two students due to mud flows, students in Sierra Leone made an emotional video to share their story.

Information about the project is available from the following links:

Website: www.climate-action.info

Hashtag: #ClimateActionP

Conclusion

Geography, as a discipline that bridges the natural and social sciences, can provide in-depth understanding of the causes and impacts of climate change, as well as pathways for producing innovative solutions. Climate change education provides important opportunities for geographical enquiry and investigation. It also introduces concepts of sustainability and global citizenship when looking at the effects our actions have on others. Indeed, there are few areas of the geography curriculum that can be explored rigorously without at least some reference to climate change, and its human as well as physical impacts.

Children are subjected to mixed messages about climate change outside of school which can contribute to a partial or confused understanding. Climate change education helps learners to make sense of what they are hearing and experiencing. Furthermore, geography with its unique focus on futures education allows children to contemplate alternative future, including the use of green technologies and adoption of renewable energy.

Resources

Haiku by Greg Johnson (based on 5th IPCC Report) available on: http://sightline.wpengine.netdna-cdn.com/wp-content/uploads/2015/10/FULL_IPCC_HAIKU_SLIDES_OPT.pdf.

Websites

- Global dimension website: www.globaldimension.org.uk.
- Oxfam: www.oxfam.org.uk.
- Action Aid: www.actionaid.org.uk/schools.
- Amnesty International: www.amnesty.org.uk/education.
- Water Aid: www.wateraid.org/speakers.
- Christian Aid: http://learn.christianaid.org.uk/.
- Geographical Association: https://www.geography.org.uk.

References

De Block, L. and Buckingham, D. (2007) *Global children, global media: Migration, media and childhood.* New York: Springer.
Dolan, A.M. (2020) *Powerful primary geography: A toolkit for 21st century learning.* London: Routledge.

Harlan, S.L., Pellow, D.N., Roberts, J.T., Bell, S.E., Holt, W.G. and Nagel, J. (2015) Climate Justice and Inequality. In Dunlap, R.E. and Brulle, R.J., Eds., *Climate change and society; Sociological perspectives*. New York, NY: Oxford University Press, pp. 127–163.

Karkdijk, J., van der Schee, J.A. and Admiraal, W.F. (2019) Students' geographical relational thinking when solving mysteries. *International Research in Geographical and Environmental Education*, 28(1), 5–21.

Leat, D. (1998) *Thinking through geography*. Cambridge: Chris Kingston Publishing.

OECD/PISA (2018) *Preparing our youth for an inclusive and sustainable world: The OECD PISA globa; competence framework* Paris: OECD https://www.oecd.org/education/Global-competency-for-an-inclusive-world.pdf

Mary Robinson Foundation (n.d.) The Mary Robinson Foundation for Climate Justice https://www.mrfcj.org/about/mission-and-vision/

UN Human Rights Council (2019) Climate change and poverty – Report of the Special Rapporteur on extreme poverty and human rights (A/HRC/41/39).

15 Exploring climate change with an historical lens

Anne M. Dolan and Eileen O'Sullivan

Introduction

Humanity's impact on the Earth is now so profound that a new geological epoch – the Anthropocene – has been proposed. Combining the Greek words for 'humans' and 'recent time', the Anthropocene marks a turning point in the history of humanity (Ellis, 2018; Lewis and Maslin, 2018). The preceding epoch (Holocene) represented 12,000 years of stable climate since the last ice age. Since the mid-20th century, a striking acceleration of carbon dioxide emissions and sea level rise, the global mass extinction of species together with the transformation of land by deforestation and development has brought the Holocene to a close. In the 21st century, climate change (caused by human actions) has emerged as one of the pressing challenges for our collective future. However, climate change is not a new phenomenon. To understand human's relationship with weather and climate, we need to understand how people and their communities responded to and adapted to climatic challenges in the past. Furthermore, in order to appreciate events and developments in history, we need to acknowledge the roles that climate and weather have played in the past (Pfister et al., 2018). This chapter explores climate change through an historical lens. It explores significant historical climatic events and human responses. Various classroom strategies for historical exploration are presented, including story, working with time lines, developing artefacts, creating time capsules and solving historical mysteries.

Climate has always changed – An historical perspective

History education is defined as 'the study of events of the past through the development of specific historical concepts and skills' (Reynolds, 2012:152). From a climate change education perspective, an historical perspective is essential for enabling children to 'understand the origins and development of their own nation, to place that development in the context of the wider world, and to develop insights that will help them become critically aware and active citizens of the emerging world' (Hoepper, 2011:204). More specifically, the field of climate history refers to the interdisciplinary study of past weather and climate variations and their influence on human history (Pfister, 2018). Climate historians have informed the understanding of climate change in an historical context (Pfister, 2018), contributing to several reports from the Intergovernmental Panel on Climate Change Working Group.

At an elementary level, a suitable climate is indispensable for the existence and flourishing of humans. Over millions of years, climate change has influenced the evolution of the human species and the geography of the Earth. Our human ancestors evolved during a period of climate cooling. Indeed, our evolution as humans has largely been driven by climate change (Lieberman and Gordon, 2018). In Africa, where the human species originated (200,000–300,000 years ago), the opening of the Great Rift Valley led to increased aridity. Glaciation ultimately created land bridges which aided dispersal out of Africa.

Recent weather reports have made headlines with iconic statements, such as hottest day/month on record. This record refers only to the last century and a half. (Some historical weather records are available from The Met Office [metoffice.gov.uk]. These provide an invaluable source for children to explore historical records while developing their mathematical and scientific skills.) Formal weather stations provided an accurate picture of global temperatures only from 1880 onwards. However, people collected weather data themselves before the launch of weather stations. People have been measuring temperature since Galileo's time. The modern thermometer, for example, was invented in the early 1700s. Formal weather stations were gathering robust information by 1880. (More information is available from meteorological services in the United Kingdom and Ireland, listed at the end of this chapter.) Indeed, weather forecasts were of strategic importance during World War II. The Met Office, an arm of the war office was considered so important, it was moved out of London to protect it from bombing. So important was the weather to the war effort that all general forecasts were restricted for national security reasons. People were forced to use their own observations and weather folklore where appropriate.

Paleoclimatology is the study of ancient climate. The archives of nature provide much evidence as researchers develop innovative methods of collecting data, such as coring ice or drilling trees. In order to learn about climate patterns in the past, researchers have used growth rings in living trees, coral skeletons, cave deposits, fossilized wood and even timber embedded in ancient buildings to reconstruct changes in Earth's climate from antiquity to the present (Brönnimann et al., 2018). These archives provide records that extend beyond the Industrial Revolution (over 500 years ago) and provide a critical baseline for the planet's past climate. Climate warming is not a new phenomenon. Between AD 800 and 1300 (the Medieval Warm Period), the Earth enjoyed five centuries of higher temperatures in the North Atlantic. The Medieval Warm Period lasted from approximately 800–1200 AD. According to climatic data, temperatures in the North Atlantic were higher than those of today, (an argument often used by climate change deniers). As sea and land ice in the Arctic melted, this warming allowed Vikings to travel further north than had been previously possible. The Medieval Warm Period was caused by higher-than-average solar radiation and less volcanic activities (both resulting in warming). It was followed by six centuries of highly unsettled climate and cooler conditions (Fagan, 2008). Known as The Little Ice Age, this period between about 1300 and 1870 ensured that Europe and North America were subjected to much colder winters than during the 20th century. During this time temperatures dropped by as much as 2° Celsius, or 3.6° Fahrenheit. This was when London's River Thames famously froze over. This facilitated events such as 'frost fairs' – fairgrounds which were set up along the river. These events included popup shops, pubs and skating rinks everything one would expect to see of the streets of London but on ice! (Blom, 2019).

Some scholars gathered evidence of climate events and variability from European historical sources from the Middle Ages onwards, making the case for their economic and political impact (Pfister, 2018). Millions of weather reports are included in ships' logs around the world. Log books provided a general-purpose official record of the voyage (comparable to the black box of an aeroplane in today's terms). In the British Royal Navy, every officer on board was required to keep a log book which ensured a high degree of correlation. (Children can access records of these log books from the British National Archives https://www.nationalarchives.gov.uk/). The officers were highly skilled in estimating wind speed and direction from the state of sea, sails and clouds. Wind terminology used at this time ultimately evolved into today's international Beaufort Wind Force Scale. The British East India Company, which travelled extensively between 1789 and 1834, collected a significant amount of weather data. Tens of thousands of logbooks have survived in the archives of the great naval powers including the United Kingdom, France, the Netherlands and Spain. For instance, weather data from the logbooks of British whaling ships in the Arctic are noteworthy due to valuable records of sea ice cover and iceberg frequency (Pfister, 2018).

Geological time and historical consequences

Geological time is difficult to appreciate. If the story of the Earth could be compressed into one day, the first humans appear four seconds before midnight. If the 4.5 billion years of the Earth's existence could be compressed into 1 year, 1 second represents 144 years. Although geologically young, humans have imposed an overwhelming footprint on this planet. Since the dawn of the Earth, climate and life have been interconnected. Climate has never been static. Many significant changes in climate were not caused by humans. Indeed, several factors have caused the climate to change along geological timelines. The movement of Earth's tectonic plates, forcing the rerouting of ocean currents had an impact. The uplift of the Himalayas which began around 50 million years ago is associated with a cooling trend which subsequently took place. The following examples illustrate significant climatic changes which occurred during the planet's history (Park, 2018; Zalasiewicz, 2018):

1   The Precambrian is the earliest of the geologic ages (4.6 billion years ago when the Earth began to form). Laid down over millions of years, these sedimentary layers of rock contain a permanent record of the Earth's past, including the fossilized remains of plants and animals buried when the sediments were formed.

   Approximately 2.4 billion years ago, oxygen was released from the seas as a by-product of photosynthesis. Over time, the amount of oxygen in the atmosphere began to increase and the amount of carbon began to decrease. Higher up in the atmosphere, ultraviolet radiation split the molecular structure of oxygen, which in turn later recombined to form ozone. Now a billion years old, the ozone layer protects the Earth's surface from harmful ultraviolet rays.

2   Further seismic changes occurred due to the movement of the continents over hundreds of millions of years. Between 300 and 200 million years ago, the continents came together to form one super continent, called Pangaea, and then parted again. It is thought that all major continents at that time were assembled into the Pangaea supercontinent. This one-continent world existed at the start of the age of the dinosaur. Interestingly, the Pangaean world was only marginally warmer than some projections of global temperature for the next century. It was the subsequent breakup of Pangaea and formation of smaller continents that dramatically altered the planet's history and climate. Climate changes associated with the supercontinent of Pangaea and with its eventual breakup and dispersal provide an example of the effect of plate tectonics on climate. Pangaea was completely surrounded by a world ocean. The Equatorial Currents system, driven by the trade winds, resided in warm latitudes and its waters were therefore warmer.

   Indeed, scientists claim that the gradual splitting apart of the supercontinent (a process called rifting) caused substantial amounts of carbon to be released into the atmosphere (Brune et al., 2017). Furthermore, the shifting continents brought about a general rise in the diversity and abundance of life on our planet.

3　Another shift in climate patterns occurred about 100 million years ago. At that time, the climate was warmer than it is today. This may have been due to higher levels of carbon in the atmosphere and higher levels of volcanic activity. However, as continents moved, levels of carbon were reduced and as the associated greenhouse effect diminished, the earth became cooler.

4　A fourth example of climate change occurred during the ice ages. Geological data for the most recent glacial age (18,000 years ago) suggest that glacial ice covered much of North America and Europe. An ice age is a time where a significant amount of the Earth's water is locked up on land in continental glaciers. Currently, the Earth is in an interglacial period – a short warmer period between glacial (or ice age) periods. The Earth has been alternating between long ice ages and shorter interglacial periods for around 2.6 million years.

5　The Little Ice Age is a period between about 1300 and 1870 during which Europe and North America were subjected to much colder winters than during the 20th century. According to scientists, the Little Ice Age was caused by the cooling effect of massive volcanic eruptions, and sustained by changes in Arctic ice cover. Temperatures dropped by less than 1° Celsius but parts of Europe cooled more, especially in winter. For instance, in London, it was possible to walk across the River Thames, such was the level of ice coverage.

History demonstrates that our climate has always been changing for various reasons. However, in the history of human civilization, the climate has never changed so rapidly. Today, it is not the change itself which is alarming scientists, it's the speed of change. Scientists mark 1880 as the beginning of modern global weather record-keeping. This is because earlier available climate data did not cover enough of the planet to generate accurate records. However, according to recent research, our current experience of global warming and associated climate change actually dates back to the 1830s (Abram et al., 2016). This is much earlier than previously thought. The Industrial Revolution in the 18th century transformed rural, agrarian societies in Europe and America into industrialized, urban settings. Fuelled by steam power, miners were required to go deep below the Earth' surface in search of coal. The demand for coal skyrocketed throughout the Industrial Revolution and beyond, as it would be needed to run not only the factories used to produce manufactured goods, but also the railroads and steamships used for transporting them.

The 20th century witnessed an expansion of electrical power generation and distribution. Electricity is used to power the modern world of commerce, industry, shops, homes, street lighting and communications. Electricity is also used to power an increasing number of devices such as computers, phones and watches. To date generation of electricity has been heavily reliant on fossil fuels. Many countries are now investing in renewable sources (wind, wave and solar and hydro-powering of electricity). Despite the strong growth of renewables over the last few decades, fossil-based fuels remain dominant worldwide. Regardless of current commitments to renewable energy, our exponential/cumulative addiction to fossil fuels over two centuries has left us with a serious climate change problem.

Teaching activities

Waldron et al. (2021:30) propose a critical historical enquiry cycle (CHEC) framework which 'encompasses a critical, reflective and enquiry-based approach to teaching history'. This framework is specifically designed for teaching history in a manner that promotes social justice and sustainability. Similar to the geographical enquiry framework described in Chapter 14, the CHEC builds upon children's questions and research to connect the past and the present with a view to creating a more socially just and sustainable society. This cyclical framework progresses the development of conceptual understanding through five stages: (1) Generating historical questions; (2) identifying sources; (3) analysing evidence; (4) constructing evidence-based arguments and (5) reflecting and making connections.

The teaching activities described in this section are influenced by the spirit of enquiry, criticality and a belief in the importance of building capacity for democratic participation. Specifically the teaching and learning potential of activities such as building a time line, children working as historians, the use of artefacts and historical stories will be enhanced by adopting the CHEC framework.

Using a timeline to teach the history of climate change

Timelines help children understand the chronology of historical events. They provide a visual aid for identifying cause and effect relationships and they help develop an appreciation that historical events, eras and topics overlap in time. Visually less complex than pure text, a timeline is a graph showing the passage of time on a horizontal or vertical line. Timelines help children organize information in a chronological sequence. They can serve as a visual tool for studying periods of history (a day, a year, an era) and help children grasp the nuances of change and continuity and key events of historical, social and scientific significance. The history of climate change can be illustrated with a timeline. A deliberate plotting of events around climate change enhances historical understanding. Analysing a sequence of events helps children to construct meaning and examine the human experience through the historical evolution of climate change. Timelines enable children to explore the human experience behind the climate story and to appreciate that we are all part of a broader human story. Appendix 5 features cards which can contribute to a class timeline on the history of climate change. Teachers can choose the cards they wish to include and cards with visual cues can be designed for younger children. Alternatively, cards can be designed with photographs on one side and text on the alternative side. With some assistance from the teacher, children can design the cards themselves, creating illustrated timelines.

Suggested timeline activities (based on timeline cards in Appendix 5)

1 Involve the children in designing the cards for timeline tasks. Ideally, they could work in pairs or in groups of three, ensuring that each child participates as equally as possible in the task. This gives the children some ownership of the activity, while also allowing the children to construct and shape the learning experience, thereby reflecting the constructivist approach advocated in the primary curriculum. Importantly, it provides an opportunity for every child to cognitively engage with each historical point of the time line.

Give each child one card and ask him/her to select an image/draw a picture or design an emoji which best represents the information on the card.
2 Now, ask the pairs/groups of children to conduct a little class-based research on the information on the card and contribute to this information by saying what they understand it to mean.

3 On completion, these re-designed cards can be randomly displayed in the class. Then, ask each child to select one card from the display. They should select on the basis of what seems interesting to them, what might be new and strange, or what is visually appealing. In groups of five, allow the children time to discuss the information and images depicted on the cards. When ready, the children can present their cards to the teacher, who is playing the role of Museum Curator.

Each group provides an overview of their cards – what are the similarities/differences between the images? What mood or message do the images convey? What do they teach us about climate change? An important step here is to invite each group to outline the questions they might like to ask, for which they do not yet have the information.

After the group discussions, the teacher/facilitator as Curator starts inviting the children to present their chosen card(s) in chronological order and to place these on a timeline, using clothes, pegs and a string line across the classroom or in another display area of the school. Alternatively, they can be displayed on a floor space in the classroom, allowing children to interact with the images over a period of time.

4 Each child selects one unanswered question for further school/home research. He/She can explore additional information and will then be required to write a short narrative piece which will be placed on the card in the timeline, after which it will be presented to the class.

5 In constructing this timeline, a wide variety of sources should be used, as available, including internet sources, library, encyclopaedia, newspapers, interviews with parents or grandparents or other teachers. Children with an interest in digital or graphic design tools could be encouraged to create their own digital or graphic timeline. The children's creations could later be displayed on the wall/floor of the classroom, in the reception of the school or on the school website.

6 The display can be further augmented and the learning deepened by asking the children to individually design a poster based on the timeline cards. Each child selects a card, places it in the centre of an A3 blank page and considers the following questions:

How does this card/image make you feel? Why did you select it? What do you think is the relevance of this (historical event, person, symbol and concept) for our lives today? Is it in any way relevant for your life? What is the one thing that you would change in the world (inspired by this card)?

The children can be invited to use newspaper articles (images, headlines), cut them out and use them in their collage-poster creations. The completed posters can be put on display and the class can conduct a silent 'gallery walk' where children explore each other's creations. Other class groupings in the school could be encouraged to interact with the displays.

Children working as historians

History is ultimately about detective work and piecing together information and clues to help tell the story of the past. The Ps of history, designed by Buchanan (2013:25–26), provide a framework for extended historical exploration of any topic. Any of the events on a climate change timeline or indeed a cluster of events can be explored by using some aspects of Buchanan's model (Table 15.1).

Table 15.1 Activities for children based on the Ps of history framework (Buchanan, 2013:25–26)

The Ps of history framework by Buchanan (2013:25–26)	Activities for children
People – Who are key players or protagonists and what motivated them to adopt their chosen course of action?	Examine how people/communities responded to weather and climate change; how it impacted on their work/leisure; adaptation they had to make and how they attempted to control their environment?
Processes – What happened and how did people/communities respond?	Investigate what the weather/climate was like in the British Isles during the Medieval Warm Period (c.800–1300) or the cold more recent period (c.1400–1900). Children can write about and illustrate what they imagine it was like in winter and summer.
Places – Where did these events occur and what role did climate or geography play?	Select one country or region and design a timeline illustrating the impact of climate change during the Medieval Warm Period, the Little Ice Age, the Industrial Revolution and today.
Products – What happened as a result of these events? Who prevailed and prospered? Who suffered the most? Who controlled decision making and resources? Who remained or became poor and powerless?	Find out about coal mining in the 19th century and oil extraction during the 20th century and learn about how the fossil fuel industry developed. Who was responsible? Whose lives were affected as a result? What were their lives like? What differences are there between coal and oil extraction? Why was this very beneficial for certain people and societies? Why did people not anticipate the potential problems?
Proof – How do you know? What counts as evidence and why? Why are some sources more credible than others?	Conduct a 'compare and contrast' of weather using historical weather forecasts available from The Met Office. Children could learn about the difference between evidence from trustworthy sources compared with personal opinions or information which is communicated by special interest groups such as climate deniers.
Purposes – Why did people behave as they did?	Imagine what it would have been like to be able to walk across, even hold a fair on a frozen river or small lake, perhaps locally. Children can consider how long it might have lasted and such matters as how people kept warm. Artworks may be helpful for them to use. Recent local weather events, such as the big freeze in Ireland, December 2012, or the visit of the so-called 'Beast from the East' (2017) could be investigated to glean images of unusual activities, such as people skating on lakes and houses being part-submerged in snow.
	A visual display can be assembled by the children. Drawing on their personal memories, discuss the following: What can they remember? How did it impact on their lives – electricity/internet cut off for days, etc.? How did it impact on community life in general – schools/roads/motorways close/inaccessible, etc.?

Table 15.1 (Continued)

The Ps of history framework by Buchanan (2013:25–26)	Activities for children
Precursors – What were the circumstances preceding these events and what significance did they have?	Using the timeline of climate change, a (Appendix 5) select one significant historical event which took place (e.g., the Industrial Revolution). Ask children to assess its contribution to climate change.
Perspectives – What points of view were assumed by the participating people/communities or the historians reporting on their activities?	Re-write a story in history from the perspective of relevant participants, e.g., a politician, a mine worker, a factory owner dependent on an energy supply, and an environmentalist.
Progress – What technological developments might have led to, developed from or changed the outcome of events?	Children could investigate why houses were built to burn coal and who provided the coal. How did this affect the way people lived, e.g., houses with fire-places and chimneys, keeping warm, heating bath water, cooking? Why was this a 'good thing' for families? What impact did coal burning have, especially in cities, e.g., smoggy weather and the blackened walls of buildings.
Parallels or turning points – The 'what ifs?' At what points might something different been done to mitigate climate change?	Construct alternative scenarios or turning points in history whereby climate change was actually averted or reduced. What effects could these proposed historical changes have today?
Predictions – What do you think happens next?	Children could be given a scenario about the state of the weather/climate and people's lives in 2100 and asked to write a newspaper report about how things are different with the weather/climate and life in fifty, one hundred, one thousand tears time. This supports the futures aspect of teaching climate change discussed in chapter 21 (Hicks, 2014).

Historical artefacts

Artefacts are objects shaped by humans that are of archaeological, historical or cultural interest. In groups or pairs, children can create an artefact related to climate change. Based on their historical research, children can generate and collate historical evidence. Sample artefacts may include: children's recording of weather forecasts; newspaper articles selected from local/national newspaper or samples written by the children; images/photographs or drawings of climate change evidence; and postcards written and designed by the children. Each artefact should address or include historical information which focuses on the following questions: What? Who? Where? Why? When? How? Children can swap their artefacts within and between classes providing an opportunity to work as an historian.

Ask the children to create time capsules for short-term or long-term storage, including in it some of the items they have gathered above which represent ways we are currently contributing to climate change. The container may be buried in school grounds as a record, with a specific pledge to adopt climate actions at home and in school. Alternatively, digital capsules with images of the children work can be stored on the school computer. This work can be retrieved and reviewed by children on a regular basis.

Historical stories

Historical stories allow children to experience and engage with historical periods in an accessible manner. They also facilitate an understanding of the complex emotional, economic and social dilemmas facing characters who lived before them Children's literature including fiction and non-fiction can be used effectively to teach climate change from a historical perspective. There are many well-established reasons for using story in the history classroom. Children's picture books and novels stimulate curiosity, generate questions and provide contextual historical information. Picture books provide visual and contextual clues which enhance historical understanding. History textbooks often reduce important historical events and personalities to a few sentences. Children's literature can potentially situate children in a different historical era. Historical understanding can be developed as children empathise with key characters in the story. Stories can portray the complexities of issues, allowing children to understand the advantages and disadvantages of historical decisions. Multiple perspectives are presented, allowing children to engage with characters holding opposing or different viewpoints. Stories also teach children about the interpretative nature of history, demonstrating how different authors and illustrators convey their historical message. Teachers should select books which are historically correct, portray characters realistically, present authentic settings and avoid stereotypes and myths. Strategies for exploring stories are discussed in more detail in Chapters 6, 7 and 19. Books suitable for teaching climate change from a historical perspective are listed at the end of this chapter.

Conclusion

The question remains: How can we learn from the past and take action in the present which will reduce risk in the future? From a historical perspective, we need to know the story of climate change. The debate over climate change, both from natural causes and human activity, is not new (Fleming, 2005). By the turn of the 20th century, Svante Arrhenius, a Swedish chemist, was speculating that low carbon-dioxide levels might have caused the ice ages, and that the industrial use of coal might warm the planet. We are now experiencing a warming trend that is unprecedented since our ancestors hunted for and gathered food (Lieberman and Gordon, 2018). Due to historical records and scientific evidence, there is an overwhelming consensus about the impact of human activities on our current climate. For decades, we have known about the threats to humanity and the environment posed by the current episode of climate change. Warnings about global warming started making headlines back in the late 1980s.

Yet, we have tended to ignore scientific evidence. Climate change denial is alive and well. Indeed, climate change deniers often quote the Medieval Warm Period (MWP) in their attempts to disprove human influence. However, even if global temperature rise is kept to below 2° Centigrade (the current level of aspiration), many ecosystems and communities, including millions of poor and vulnerable people, face severe adverse impacts. We have the scientific evidence and knowledge to make changes. Unfortunately, certain political, economic and business interests remain to be convinced. Young people (led by activists such as Greta Thunberg) have reacted angrily. It is time to hold our political leaders to account and to demand more sustainable ways of living. It is time to reverse the trend of increased carbon emissions. History provides us with stories of people all over the world working on policies, campaigns and solutions designed to protect people and the planet. Indigenous peoples and minority communities have for centuries developed sustainable ways of living with the environments that they call home. We can learn from them and, with their consent, benefit from their know-how to inform our own efforts to find a different way of interacting with our planet. Significant short-term and long-term impacts of climate change and associated policy responses are now part of the narrative of modern history. As citizens, we have the opportunity to write history – 'to be part of, shape and change the direction of this story humankind that we're studying' (Buchanan, 2013:19).

Resources

Websites

- **Met Éireann**, the Irish National Meteorological Service, is the leading provider of weather information and related services for Ireland. https://www.met.ie.
- The **Meteorological Office**, abbreviated as the **Met Office** is the United Kingdom's national weather service. https://www.metoffice.gov.uk.
- **The National Archives** is the official archive and publisher for the UK government and for England and Wales. https://www.nationalarchives.gov.uk/help-with-your-research/research-guides/royal-navy-ships-voyages-log-books/.

Picturebooks (fiction)

Aitken, A. (2011) *Fever at the poles*. Looking Glass Library.
Bergen, L. (2008) *The polar bear's home*. Little Simon.
Bergen, L and Nguyen, V. (2008) *The polar bears' home: A story about global warming*. Little Green Books.
Bonsper, P. and Rink, D. (illus) (2015) *The problem of the hot world*. Create Space Publishing.
Cole, J. and Degen, B. (illus) (2014) *The magic school bus and the climate challenge*. Scholastic Press.
Dr. Seuss (2009) *The lorax*. Random House Books.
Dumas Roy, S. and Houssais, E. (illus) (2013) *Hot air*. Phoenix Yard Books.
Hans, D.B. (2011) *Little polar bear*. North South Books.
Herbert, M. and Mann, M.E. (2018) *The tantrum that saved the world*. World Saving Books.
Kleiner, G. and Thompson, L. (illus) (2014) *Please don't paint our planet pink: A story for children and their adults*. Cloudburst Creative.
Kyo, M. and Pak, K. (illus) (2017) *The fog*. Tundra Books.
Lisa, S. and Gott, B. (illus) (2009) *Who turned up the heat? Eco pig explains global warming*. Looking Glass Library.
O'Brien, O. and Finn-Kelcey, N. (2009) *Perry the playful polar bear*. BPR Publishers.
O'Brien, O. and Finn-Kelcey, N. (2010) *Perry the polar bear goes green: A story about global warming*. BPR Publishers.
Okimoto, J.D. and Trammell, J. (2010) *Winston of Churchill: One bear's battle against global warming*. Scholastic Canada Limited.
Tucker, Z. and Persico, Z. (2019) *Greta and the giants (inspired by Greta Thunberg's stand to save the world*. Frances Lincoln Books.
Winter, J. (2019) *Our house is on fire: Greta Thunberg's call to save the planet beach*. Lane Books.

Picturebooks (non-fiction)

Bang, M and Chisholm, P. (illus) (2014) *Buried sunlight: How fossil fuels have changed the earth.* Blue Sky Press.

Hall, J. and Lane, S. (illus) (2007) *A hot planet needs cool kids (understanding climate change and what you can do about it.* Green Goat Books.

Hepplewhite, P. (2015) *The Industrial Revolution.* Wayland.

Chapter books

Herman, G. and Hinderliter, J. (2018) *What is climate change?* Penguin.

Bradman, T. (Ed.) (2012) *Under the weather (stories about climate change).* Frances Lincoln Children's Books.

Ride, S and O'Shaughnessy, T. (2009) *Mission save the planet: Things you can do to help fight global warming.* Flash Point.

Camperini, V. and Carratello, V. (illus) Ginninderra, M. (translator) (2019). *Greta's Story. The schoolgirl who went on strike to save the planet.* Simon and Schuster.

References

Abram, N.J., McGregor, H.V., Tierney, J.E., Evans, M.N., McKay, N.P., Kaufman, D.S., Thirumalai, K., Martrat, B., Goosse, H., Phipps, S.J. and Steig, E.J. (2016) Early onset of industrial-era warming across the oceans and continents. *Nature, 536*(7617), pp. 411–418.

Blom, P. (2019) *Nature's mutiny: How the Little Ice Age of the long seventeenth century transformed the west and shaped the present.* New York: Liveright Publishing.

Brune, S., Williams, S.E. and Müller, R.D. (2017) Potential links between continental rifting, CO_2 degassing and climate change through time. *Nature Geoscience, 10*(12), pp. 941–946.

Brönnimann, S., Pfister, C. and White, S. (2018) Archives of nature and archives of societies. In *The Palgrave handbook of climate history* (pp. 27–36). London: Palgrave Macmillan.

Buchanan, J. (2013) Teaching history. In *History, geography and civics: Teaching and learning in the primary years* (pp. 19–37). Cambridge: Cambridge University Press.

Buchanan, J. (2013) *History, geography and civics: teaching and learning in the primary years.* Cambridge University Press.

Ellis, E.C. (2018) *Anthropocene: A very short introduction.* Oxford: Oxford University Press.

Fagan, B. (2008) *The great warming: Climate change and the rise and fall of civilizations.* London: Bloomsbury Publishing.

Fleming, J.R. (2005) *Historical perspectives on climate change.* Oxford: Oxford University Press.

Hicks, D. (2014) *Educating for hope in troubled times: Climate change and the transition to a post-carbon future.* London: Trentham Press/Institute of Education Press.

Hoepper, N. (2011) Teaching history: Inquiry principles. In Gilbert, R. and Hoepper, B. (Eds.), *Teaching society and environment.* Boston: Cengage Learning.

Lewis, S.L. and Maslin, M:. A. (2018) *Human planet: How we created the Anthropocene.* Yale: Yale University Press.

Lieberman, B. and Gordon, E. (2018) *Climate change in human history: Prehistory to the present.* London: Bloomsbury Publishing.

Park, G. (2018) *Introducing geology: A guide to the world of rocks* (3rd ed.). Edinburgh: Dunedin Academic Press Ltd.

Pfister, C., White, S. and Mauelshagen, F. (2018) General introduction: Weather, climate and human history. In *The Palgrave handbook of climate history* (pp. 1–17). London: Palgrave Macmillan.

Pfister, C. (2018) Evidence from the archives of societies: Documentary evidence—Overview. In *The Palgrave handbook of climate history* (pp. 37–47). London: Palgrave Macmillan.

Reynolds R. (2012) *Teaching history, geography and SOSE in the Australian primary school* (2nd ed). South Melbourne: Oxford University Press.

Waldron, Ní Cassaithe, Barry, M. and Whelan, P. (2021) Critical historical enquiry for a socially just and sustainable world. In Kavanagh, A.M., Waldron, F. and Mallon, B. eds., *Teaching for social justice and sustainable development across the primary curriculum*. London: Routledge.

Zalasiewicz, J. (2018) *Geology: A very short introduction*. Oxford: Oxford University Press.

16 Climate change education through active citizenship

Margaret Nohilly

Introduction

Citizenship education presents multiple opportunities for addressing the concerning issue of climate change. Never has our personal and collective responsibility for caring for the environment been so important with the impact of global warming and climate change that is occurring presently. The strategies and methodologies outlined are based on the principles of active learning. Through his work on education in the early part of the twentieth century, Dewey proposed active learning principles in his work on progressive education, allowing children to be more active in their learning. He saw the classroom as a microcosm of a democratic society. The teacher would model democratic ideals and the child would learn by experience (Dewey, 1933). Active learning happens when children are given the opportunity to take a more interactive relationship with the subject matter, encouraging them to generate rather than simply receive knowledge. It is a central methodology of curriculum implementation as distinct from activism for change where there are efforts or campaigns for some kind of social change. This chapter provides examples of curriculum implementation together with an overview of citizenship education. It outlines a number of active learning approaches to support climate change education through the lens of citizenship education.

Citizenship education

Citizenship education can be defined as educating children, from early childhood, to become clear-thinking and enlightened citizens who participate in decisions concerning society. The Cambridge dictionary defines a citizen as a 'member of a particular country who has rights because of being born there or because of being given rights' (dictionary. cambridge.org).

Citizenship education places the child in the context of the world in which he/she lives. It is centrally important in instilling in children a sense of hope for the future and a sense of empowerment as active agents of change. The concept of citizenship education has been strongly influenced by the participation rights afforded to children through the Convention on the Rights of the Child (1989) (Waldron et al., 2014). According to the Social, Personal and Health Education curriculum guidelines in Ireland, 'the child is encouraged to become an active and responsible citizen who understands the interdependent nature of the world in which he/she lives (Government of Ireland, 1999:12)'. Citizenship education provides opportunities for children to explore both a sense of individual and community responsibility in caring for the environment.

In the school context, an approach to citizenship education can begin by considering the school or class as a community in microcosm. By experiencing community in such a practical way, children learn what belonging and participating really mean. In a school that values caring and shared responsibility, children can learn to:

- Share and cooperate
- Set realistic goals and targets for themselves and others
- Develop leadership and administrative abilities
- Celebrate difference
- Be part of something that goes beyond personal interest and recognise that they can make a valuable contribution to society

(Government of Ireland, 1999:17)

The concept of democracy becomes real and meaningful for children as they are given the opportunity to voice their opinions, understand a variety of responsibilities, reach group decisions by consensus, listen to different points of view, work both as an individual and member of a group and be involved in decision-making. The authenticity of the participation afforded to children is considered a critical determinant. Authentic participation enables children to have meaningful opportunities to make decisions and to have those decisions implemented (Lundy, 2007).

Looking at our responsibilities for climate change in our day-to-day lives in school and the practical actions the school community can undertake to address climate change is a tangible starting point for children. As a citizen, each child will face important decisions within his/her lifetime arising from climate change. Policy decisions and commitments that are being taken to act on climate change and reduce greenhouse gas emissions will have important implications and consequences for younger generations. It is critical that young people understand their role in creating emissions, mitigating climate change and adapting to its impacts. Practical starting points and potential action projects for schools are presented later in the chapter.

Through citizenship education, children explore the diversity of the world in which they live. They are encouraged to learn about their own traditions and culture and thereafter to compare and contrast these with other ethnic or cultural groups in society. Through exploring how our day-to-day activities and lifestyle effects climate change and comparing them to cultures where more favourable approaches are adopted, this can inspire children to adapt better practices in their day-to-day lives. Furthermore, this supports children developing a rationale and a greater sense of understanding of the imperative need to adopt lifestyle changes relating to climate change. It also develops the agency and action of children from a young age, which will support them in undertaking future active citizenship roles. Through citizenship education, children are particularly encouraged to reflect on their own behaviour and to acknowledge how this could be enhanced.

Global citizenship

Children's experience of citizenship education in their local community can then be placed in the context of global citizenship. Children live in an increasingly globalised and interconnected world where the global is part of their everyday lives. We are linked to other people on every continent socially and culturally through the media, travel and migration, economically through trade, politically through international relations and environmentally through sharing one planet. Ultimately, global citizenship education promotes understanding of global issues; it encourages critical engagement with those issues, while remaining cognisant of their complexity. It involves the development of attitudes, dispositions, skills and knowledge about the unequal distribution of wealth, life changes and power and in turn the impact on climate change as addressed in the opening chapter (Oberman et al., 2012).

Oxfam sees a global citizen as someone who:

- Is aware of the wider world and has a sense of their own role as a world citizen
- Respects and values diversity
- Has an understanding of how the world works economically, politically, socially, culturally, technologically and environmentally
- Is outraged by social injustice
- Participates in and contributes to the community at a range of levels from local to global
- Is willing to act and make the world a more sustainable place
- Takes responsibility for their actions

(Oxfam, 2006:5)

For global citizenship education to achieve a level of complexity and deeper understanding, it needs to be integrated across children's learning and through a variety of curriculum subjects and methodologies, rather than an occasional and media driven learning 'stir in' (Bracken and Bryan, 2010).

Practical ideas for schools

A range of ideas to develop the concept of citizenship education and global citizenship education are presented in this chapter. These classroom initiatives and whole-school approaches simultaneously support both citizenship education and global education through a focus on climate change education. Activities presented are not specific to a particular class level and teachers can adapt activities to suit each age group.

Ideas for use within classrooms

Classroom discussion on climate change

What do I do to care for the environment?
Children are asked to reflect quietly on what they do in their own life, perhaps at home, at school or both to care for the environment. They are then asked to consider is there anything in particular that they would like to do. Children share their responses to both questions with their peers and some feedback from the class is invited from the teacher.

What can we do in our classroom to reduce our impact on Planet Earth?
There may be several initiatives underway in classrooms that reduce our impact on planet Earth and these can be emphasised with the children. Examples include recycling initiatives, tree and garden-planting projects and reducing our carbon footprint through activities such as 'Walk to School on Wednesdays'.

In groups of 3–4, children are asked to consider 3 further initiatives the classroom can undertake to generate a collective responsibility for caring for the environment. A recorder and a reporter are appointed in each group. The teachers record all of the ideas presented by the different groups. Once the ideas presented are deemed practical and doable, children have the opportunity to vote on the collective ideas. They award points to their top three ideas (three points for the idea they consider most important to implement). The ideas that are awarded the most points are then taken on board by the class. Each class, in discussion with the class teacher, will need to decide how many ideas are practical and realistic for them to implement and perhaps the ideas can be spread across the school terms.

How do you think our local and national politicians have responded to global warming?

Invite a local politician/counsellor to speak to the children. In preparation for the visit, the class prepare a list of questions that are sent to the counsellor in advance. The criteria for inclusion of questions can be based on their relevance to the theme of climate change and the government's response to the same, both at a local and a national level. It is important that children make the decision on the question schedule.

What actions do you think that local authorities, council and businesses could do in response to climate change?

Following the visits of a local politician/counsellor, in groups, children prepare a list of supporting ideas that they feel local authorities and businesses could adopt in response to climate change. These are then sent on to the relevant council or business, with the intention that the class will be kept informed of any outcomes from the process.

What could the Government do to reduce our country's impact on planet Earth?

In groups of 3–4, children are asked to prepare 3 suggestions for government action to reduce carbon emissions. Similar to reducing impact in the classroom, the ideas from all groups are collated and a voting system is implemented to choose the top five ideas. Once the final ideas are chosen, these should be communicated to the government by e-mail, direct mail or social media. It is disheartening for children if their ideas are not communicated.

This could also become a whole-school initiative with ideas presented across all class levels.

Election manifesto

Introduction

An election manifesto is essentially a list of promises (policies) that a political party says it will enact if it is voted into office at a general election. Manifestos serve a very important function, because they are the main way of telling voters why they should give their vote to a particular candidate or political party. The teacher can explain that the main focus for the next government is climate change. The children will create their own manifestos based on commitments (Table 16.1) within selected timeframes (Table 16.2).

Development

- Explain briefly how local and national elections work. Discuss the role of local politicians together with their political affiliations. Explain how each party needs to advertise itself by producing a manifesto, or a statement of its main policy intentions.

Table 16.1 Ideas for discussion

Introduce a carbon tax	More renewable energy through wind power	Plant more trees	Reduce use of fossil fuels
Introduce greener farming methods	All cars must be electric	Abolish all meat foods	Prevent the destruction of existing forests
All homes must have solar panels	All cars must be small and fuel-efficient	Introduce grants to insulate all homes	Wash all clothing in cold water
Eat a plant-rich diet	Dryers for clothes will be banned	One car per family	Change all lightbulbs to LEDs
Introduce a restriction on number of flights	All homes must grow their own food	Introduce 'Cycle Sundays'	All milk must be organic
Change all desktops to laptops	All flights must be economy class	All appliances purchased must be energy efficient	More renewable energy through solar power

- Divide the class the class into groups of three/four.
- Each group picks three/four cards from each bag (Table 16.1). They will then have a random selection of ideas to engage with. For example, a group may get two Anti cards and one Pro card, a card saying 'All cars must be electric', another saying 'Abolish all meat foods' and another saying, 'One car per family'. It is up to the group to decide which two they are against and which one they support and within which timescale (Table 16.2). For example, their timescale cards might be 'Immediately', 'Within ten years' and 'Next year'.
- Give the class a set amount of time. In this time, they must discuss and write out their proposal for the next election, with each group member contributing.
- These manifestos are then pinned up on the wall and the class take some time to travel around and read them.
- Each group then presents their manifesto to the rest of the class, favouring its own opinions while critiquing those of the other groups.

Conclusion

A 'general election' is then held and the votes counted.

Table 16.2 Timelines for implementation

In five years	Immediately	Next year	By Christmas
Ten years	This year	Now	In two years
Within a year	In six months	By the end of the decade	As soon as possible
In five years	Immediately	Next year	By Christmas
Ten years	This year	Now	In two years
Within a year	In six months	By the end of the decade	As soon as possible

Figure 16.1 Sample Beliefs Circle on climate change

Classroom circle work on climate change (Belief Circles)

The Belief Circle Game, discussed in chapter 3, is a strategy used to scaffold and structure conversations about personal beliefs among groups of participants.

- Make your own Beliefs Circles, such as the example provided in Figure 16.1, based on climate change using a pen to spin as a dial. Alternatively use a randomiser app to select topics on a circle on the interactive whiteboard
- Arrange the chairs in a circle
- Agree the rules of the game (Table 16.3)

Ideas for use at whole-school level

Challenge to change project – Scoil Bhríde, Shantalla, Galway

Scoil Bhríde is a primary school, located on the outskirts of Galway city in Ireland. The school is a 'Presentation' school. This is a Catholic school founded by the Presentation Sisters, one of many such schools both in Ireland and across the world. 'Challenge to Change' is a development education project aimed at young people attending the Presentation Sisters' primary and post-primary schools in Ireland. The initiative seeks to raise awareness and understanding of development issues and global inequality through the exploration and engagement in issues such as (in)justice, human rights, fair-trade, racism and exploitation.

The overall aims of the project include:

- To raise awareness and bring about a greater understanding of global issues
- To create and foster a critical mind set in relation to inequality, social justice and human rights

- To experience at first hand in a real and concrete way how local action can impact positively on global inequality
- To forge closer links between Irish children and those in developing countries
- To disseminate information and good practice (https://developmenteducation.ie/resource/challenge-to-change-a-development-education-project-in-presentation-schools/)

Table 16.3 Belief Circle discussion: Rules of the game

- Everybody is invited to speak but you may 'pass' should you prefer not to
- Everybody speaks from the personal in relation to their own views- 'I think', 'I feel', 'I believe'
- Everybody is invited to speak for an equal amount of time (30 seconds to 2 minutes)
- Active listening, and no interruptions, is encouraged
- One person starts by spinning the dial on the belief wheel until it lands on a topic for discussion. Everybody who wants to then has a go for speaking for the agreed amount of time
- Before the game ends the children are invited to write anonymously and briefly on a piece of card
- One thing they like about someone else's belief
- One thing they heard that made them think differently about their own belief
- What did it feel like to agree with someone else's belief?
- What did it feel like to disagree with someone else's belief?
- After 5 minutes, the cards are gathered and shuffled and placed upside-down on the floor. Children are invited to pick up a card again and going around the circle they read out the response that is written on their card

Source: The Enquiring Classroom: O'Donnell et al. (2019)

The children in fifth class (11 years) in Scoil Bhríde Shantalla participated in this project. The aims of the project, the target groups and actions undertaken are all outlined below (Table 16.4).

The children developed a menu of feasible actions for their class and for the school:

- Don't leave the TV or video on standby
- Walk, Cycle, Scoot, Skate or Bus it to school if possible
- Switch lights off when you're not in the room
- Re-cycle glass bottles, jars, newspapers and magazines and tin cans. Save then and take them to local re-cycling centres
- Re-use plastic shopping bags and envelopes, don't get new ones
- Persuade your mam or dad (or whoever does the gardening) to have a compost heap
- Put a brick in a plastic bag in your toilet cistern, then the toilet will use less water each time you flush
- Try and buy products that use less packaging
- Only fill the kettle up with the amount of water you need to boil that time
- Have showers instead of baths

The children also administered an energy audit questionnaire to the classroom teachers (Table 16.5). This encouraged the children and teachers to reflect on how they might engage in energy saving measures at school.

The children engaged in research on topics such as climate change, and renewable sources of energy such as wave, water and wind power. They presented information for the whole-school community on the project through display boards and posters across

Table 16.4 Aims, target groups and actions of the project

A green future

Scoil Bhride, Shantalla, Galway

Aims

- To educate ourselves and the school community about fossil fuels and clean energy alternatives
- To instill in ourselves and the school community a DUTY OF CARE for the future of our planet
- To see how our choices impact on everybody's future
- To make our school and home lives more energy efficient
- To organise several activities both in school and outside school that will help children learn about and subsequently promote sustainability
- To promote teamwork and develop leadership in our children's work on this project

Target group

The main group targeted in our project were the children of 5th class

The next group targeted were the children of other classes in our school and staff

Finally, we targeted the wider school community, especially parents, grandparents and visitors

Actions undertaken

One of the best thigs we did in our project was to visit a windfarm – Galway Wind Park. In working on our project, we also carried out a survey on energy use in our school interviewing teachers in their classrooms

We made posters about saving energy.

Galway wind park: We met with the manager of Galway Wind Park and learned all about it. We met the manager and learned a lot about these amazing wind turbines, from how the park was prepared and built and eventually brought to operation. It was so cool. Goudy wrote a story about our visit

Table 16.5 Energy audit questionnaire administered to classroom teachers

Survey

Energy audit questionnaire

Classroom teacher: Location:

1. Do you turn off lights at every Break time? Lunchtime? Home time?
2. Do you think you have lights on at times when they may not be necessary?
3. Do you turn OFF (not standby) your interactive whiteboard? Computer? Other devices when you leave each day?
4. Do you have mobile radiators? Are they left on unnecessarily?
5. Do you leave your classroom door/ external door open at break times?
6. Do you feel the school is sometimes too hot/ too cold/ or is the temperature appropriate?
7. Do you do anything special that helps the school save energy?
8. Have you any suggestions to make the school more energy efficient?

the school. The example of work presented in Table 16.6 below is the information the children compiled and presented in relation to global warming.

One of the highlights of the project for the school was a visit to 'Galway Wind Park' where the children learned all about the construction of the park and the purpose of the wind turbines. Table 16.7 below presents one child's account of his visit to the farm.

The outcomes of the project as detailed by the children in Table 16.8 below highlight an authentic approach to citizenship education. The children considered their school as a community in microcosm and identified goals that both individual children, teachers and the wider school community could undertake to encourage energy saving. The school community formed links with a local windfarm and furthermore believe that the messages from school will extend into the homes and wider community of the children.

Table 16.6 Sample of children's research

Climate change and global warming

What is global warming?
Global warming is the rise in temperature of the earth's atmosphere.
It's said that by the time a baby born today
In 80 years time, the world could be 6-and-a half degrees warmer than it is now!!

Is global warming bad?
The earth is naturally warmed by rays (or
radiation from the sun, which pass through
the earth's atmosphere and are reflected
back out to space again.
The atmosphere is made up of layers of
gases, some of which are called 'greenhouse
gases'. They're mostly natural and make up
a kind of thermal blanket over the earth.
This lets some of the rays back out of the
atmosphere, keeping the earth at the right
temperature for animals, plants and humans
to survive (60° F/ 16° C). So, some global
warming is **good.**
But if extra greenhouse gases are made, the
thermal blanket gets thicker and too much
heat is kept in the earth's atmosphere. That's when global warming is **bad.**

So what could happen?
If the earth gets hotter, some of these important changes could happen:

- Water expands when it's heated so sea levels would rise
- Sea levels would also rise due to the melting of the glaciers and sea ice
- Cities on coasts would flood
- Places that usually get lots of rain and snowfall might get hotter and drier
- Lakes and rivers would dry up
- There would be more droughts making it harder to grow crops
- Less water would be available for drinking, showers and swimming pools
- Some plants and animals might become extinct because of the heat
- Hurricanes, tornadoes and other storms which are caused by changes in heat and water evaporation may become more common

---

Table 16.7 A child's account of a visit to a windfarm

Our windfarm visit

By Alan (11 years of age)

On the 11th of April our class went on a trip to the windfarm in Oughterard with the teachers. We met with the manager of the windfarm and he showed us some pictures and videos about how long it took them to build the wind turbines and what they thought they would do in case a fire started. Then they asked us some questions about how we thought they got all the pieces of wind turbines delivered and how long it took them to build the wind Turbines in different weather.

The blades had to be brought in by ship to Galway port and then transported overnight on huge trucks. A road under a bridge had to be lowered so that the trucks could fit under it! And the corner on the road where it had to turn up had to be widened so that the trucks could turn safely. The 14-mile journey from Galway, which would normally take 25 minutes, took 6 hours!!!

The Oughterard windfarm is the biggest windfarm in Ireland, it has about approximately 58 wind turbines in whole entire farms. When we were finished answering the questions and talking about the wind turbine, they gave us pencil cases at the end. And then we were on our way to go see one of the wind turbines up close.

It was a very long walk that some people stopped at half way and wanted to go back. Finally, we got to our destination in front of the wind turbine, it looked huge. It was like when you get closer to the wind turbine, it feels like it's going to fall on top of you but it doesn't. Mr. White took some pictures and videos of us in from of the wind turbine. Then we were on our way back to school on the bus.

Honestly this was a very fun and educational experience for all the class. I think I'd like to go there again sometime.

Table 16.8 Outcomes of the project

Project outcomes

- The children of 5th class (11–12 years) learned about fossil fuels and clean energy.
- They understand the future depends on the world moving away from fossil fuels and using sustainable clean energy alternatives instead.
- We learned about the effects of climate change on people in other parts of the world like Honduras. It is very unfair that countries that cause very little pollution are the one who suffer the most from its effects.
- We learned that we should try and reduce the amount of energy we use as it uses up so much of our natural resources and can cause pollution.
- If we all make small changes, we can make a difference.
- The staff and children in our whole school are more aware of their energy use and are making bigger efforts to reduce how much energy we use.
- We hope that the children of Scoil Bhride are bringing this message home and saving energy at home too.

'Our daily lives at school' project

'Our daily lives at school' project is an idea aimed at starting with the realistic and everyday changes individuals, families and communities such as a school community can undertake that will make positive changes towards addressing climate change. This inspires the concept of both individual responsibility for addressing climate change as well as collective responsibility through the communities we engage with on a daily basis.

One class in the school is tasked with looking at the day-to-day activities that take place in each classroom.

- What measures are underway in each classroom that support climate change?
- What more could be done in the classroom to help to address climate change?

Other activities that take place outside of classrooms, such as the staff room, the Art room, the Computer room or other spaces in the school are also included so a comprehensive picture of the school initiatives that support climate change are outlined and also the areas where the school could improve are detailed. It is important to discuss the impact of personal and collective actions on climate change. However, feelings of guilt should be avoided. Instead, there should be a focus on positive climate actions. The school could then link with another similar sized school in their own country or more favourably in another country and both compare and learn from approaches adopted.

'Our Diamond 9' for climate change

Each class in the school prepares a ranking exercise or 'Diamond 9' outlining their agreed actions to address climate change in the school. The arrangement takes the form of a diamond where nine pictures or statements are used, with the most important placed at the top of the diamond, the least important at the base, and the others placed in between (Figure 16.2).

Following on from this, the results of all classes can by displayed and discussed and an overall 'Diamond 9' agreed and displayed in the school, which will outline the actions the school will undertake to address climate change.

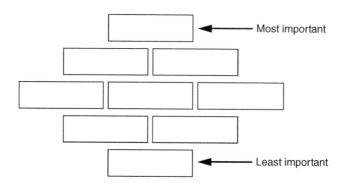

Figure 16.2 Sample 'Diamond 9'

Examples of statements might include:

- Introduce recycling bins into each classroom
- Introduce a Walk to and from School day once a week
- Have a meat free lunch day once a fortnight
- Ensure all electrical equipment in the school is plugged out by the end of each school day
- Grow a school garden
- Plant some trees in the school grounds
- No plastic bottles allowed in school- reusable drink containers only
- Turn off all lights at break times
- No plastic wrapping on any lunch items

Conclusion

Encouraging children to reflect and realise their potential as active citizens to impact positively on climate change will enable them to realise not only their independent and collective responsibility to make a difference but the absolute necessity that they do so. It is the children in our classrooms today that will become the real advocates and leaders in matters relating to climate change into the future. As has been highlighted in this chapter and in Chapters 7 and 21, it is so important to give children a sense of hope for the future and a sense of empowerment as active agents of change. This is what citizenship education is all about!

Useful websites and resources

- Amnesty: https://www.amnesty.ie/.
- Development Education: http://www.developmenteducation.ie/.
- Oxfam: http://www.oxfam.org.uk/.
- The enquiring classroom: Values, identity, exploration. Available at: http://nebula.wsimg.com/b34a2e21e05d30983c68342cf6de3918? AccessKeyId=C0264DFDC5E0FBB4FF37&disposition=0&alloworigin=1.
- UNICEF: http://www.unicef.org/siteguide/resources.html.

References

Bracken M. and Bryan A. (2010) The reflective practitioner model as a means of evaluating development education practice: Post-primary teacher's self-reflections on 'doing' development education. *Policy and Practice: A Development Education Review*, *11*(2), 22–41.

Dewey, J. (1933) *How we think*. Boston: D.C. Heath.

Government of Ireland (1999) *Social, personal and health education teacher guidelines*. Dublin: Stationery Office.

Lundy, L. (2007) 'Voice' is not enough: The implications of Article 12 of the United Nations Convention on the Rights of the Child for Education. *British Educational Research Journal*, *33*(6), 927–942.

Oberman R., Waldron F. and Dillon S. (2012) Developing a global citizenship education programme for three-to-six-year-olds. *International Journal of Development Education and Global Learning*, *4*(1), 37–60.

O'Donnell A., Kieran P., Cherouvis S. and Bergdahl L. (2019) The enquiring classroom: Values, identity, exploration. Available at: http://nebula.wsimg.com/b34a2e21e05d30983c68342cf6de3918?AccessKeyId=C0264DFDC5E0FBB4FF37&disposition=0&alloworigin=1 (Accessed 6 June, 2019).

Oxfam (2006) *Education for global citizenship: A guide for schools*. London: Oxfam.

Waldron F., Ruane B. and Oberman R. (2014) Practice as prize: Citizenship education in two primary classrooms in Ireland. *Journal of Social Science Education*, *13*(1), 34–45.

17 Ecological awareness

A cornerstone to developing a healthy Christian spirituality

Maurice Harmon

Introduction

The greatest gift you have, and which you can develop and nourish in yourself and the people you meet, is imagination. Imagination is nourished by the world you inhabit. If you live in a sterile, arid environment, your imagination will be the same, whereas if you live in a world of colour, beauty and bountiful life, then your imagination will be alive, and you will flourish as a human being. When you view the world as a place in which your imagination is enriched, then you have a responsibility to care for it. The world is a gift that allows the imagination to grow. If that gift is neglected, then you neglect the nourishment of your imagination and, as a result, you are personally challenged. This chapter explores the importance of the spiritual development of the person through the gift of the world in which he/she lives. The world that nourishes the mind is also the gift that nourishes the spiritual self. Many would claim that humanity has lost touch with its connectedness to the earth, resulting in the current ecological crisis and loss of spiritual awareness. This chapter proposes ecological awareness as a core to developing a healthy spirituality, which will help to stem the tide on climate change, through reawakening each person's moral duty as a steward of creation. It also offers practical ideas to teachers and teacher educators for use in their educational settings with children (9–13 years).

Spirituality

The concept of spirituality is widely contested in literature; so, too, is its connection or relationship to religion. Spirituality is a word that is readily used in society to describe 'something' that is beyond the self; or an 'ultimate concern' in life (Lipscomb and Gersch, 2012; Rolheiser, 1998; Rossiter, 2010, 2012; Ryan, 2007; Tracey, 2005; Wright, 2000). The literature argues that spirituality is innate in all and that it slumbers in the unconscious, awaiting expression (Harmon, 2018; Hay and Nye, 1998; Tracey, 2000). An analysis of the literature illustrates some common ground. Nevertheless, this does not allow for a clear, shared definition of spirituality (Eaude, 2009; Hart, 2003; Hay and Nye, 1998, 2006). Much of this commonality lies in the idea of wonder and awe in the beauty of creation; belonging to a community; intellectual stimulation; search for meaning; and, for some, a connection with the Transcendent.

Many scholars link spirituality to religion, while others have a broader understanding which does not include a religious component. Meehan describes secular spirituality as 'seeking to find meaning and purpose in universal human experience rather than religious experience *per se*' (Meehan, 2002:292). Hay and Nye (2006) regard this form of spirituality as also being concerned with one's relationship with the other, nature and the world, but not with God. A religious spirituality allows people of a religious belief system to engage with the world through a particular lens (Ryan, 2006; Trousdale, 2005). Others claim that spirituality can only be developed within a faith tradition and that this allows for it to be focused on developing a relationship with a God (Eaude, 2009; Fisher, 2007).

The concept of spirituality linked to religious tradition is widely supported. However, a secular spirituality is equally valuable for those who do not profess a faith background. Both are valid within an educational system. When writing of spiritual education, Alexander and McLaughlin (2003) refer to education 'from the inside', meaning working from within a religious tradition and 'from outside', meaning from outside any faith tradition. While appreciating the complexity of spirituality, this chapter explores it from a religious perspective and more particularly a Christian one, that is, a spirituality based on the life and teaching of Jesus. Ronald Rolheiser (1998) claims that there are certain elements that are non-negotiable and consequently unique to those upholding a Christian spirituality. These include: (1) private prayer and private morality; (2) social justice; (3) mellowness of heart and spirit and (4) community as a constitutive element of true worship. The world has changed dramatically since Rolheiser documented these elements. In his encyclical letter *Laudato Si'*, Pope Francis (2015) invites people to reflect on consumerism, irresponsible development and their subsequent impact on the world. Personally, I believe that ecological awareness should be highlighted in its own right when exploring the non-negotiables of a Christian Spirituality. Pope Francis (2015) says that climate change is a result of human activity and calls for a swift and unified global action. Drawing from the rich tradition of Catholic teaching on the care of creation, the encyclical calls for an ecological spirituality, that will counteract against climate change and encourage people to once again become active stewards of creation, for it is the natural world that nourishes the imagination, and this in turn nourishes the spiritual self.

Ecological awareness

As teachers and parents, one of the central questions we ask ourselves is what kind of world we want our children to live in. Answering such a question is multi-layered, but it is predominately about relationships: those with others, the environment, and for some, the Transcendent (God). Pope Francis's (2015) *Laudato Si'* highlights the challenge of developing beneficial and fruitful relationships with the earth in the context of an extensive 'throwaway culture'. Ecological awareness is about caring and respecting our common home for the flourishing of all. St. Francis of Assisi is widely known as the patron saint of ecology in the Christian world today. He is well-known for his sense of caring for 'our common home', for the world which we share with all its inhabitants, whether fellow-humans, plants, animals, or nature in general. Pope Francis' environmental awareness in his encyclical is clearly influenced by the ecological sensitivity of St. Francis. As Pope Francis (2015:110) says, 'the earth is our environment to protect and the garden to tend'. Embracing this understanding of our relationship with the environment, and a renewed appreciation of the natural world, a dialogue needs to take place on how best the environment can be protected and, in some cases, rejuvenated. Pope Francis calls for nothing less than 'a bold cultural revolution' (2015:114) and a profound ecological conversation. The starting point for much of this is a reconciliation between humanity and the environment. To be a person of Christian faith, is to be a person fully alive in the presence of Jesus, which includes a just relationship with the earth and all its inhabitants, thus seeing the wonder and awe of God in all things. That is, a respectful relationship with every drop of water, plant, insect, tree, animal, fish of the sea and all living people: 'all creatures are moving forward with us and through us towards a common point of arrival, which is God' (Pope Francis, 2015:83). Ecological awareness is about stewarding creation. Each person is a steward, ensuring that this diverse planet is cultivated and sustained. From the Christian tradition, the person who embodies this most is St Francis of Assisi, who in his *Canticle of the creatures* blesses and thanks God for all creation. He also described all parts of creation as his family, his brother sun and sister moon. For St. Francis, it was a love relationship with the world that he inhabited; and when one experiences that deep sense of love, one shares a deep respect.

Laudato Si' (2015) calls on people to begin a dialogue on how we can reshape the future of the planet, especially issues pertaining to the environment, as they concern all who share it. A key element of the letter, according to Fr. Sean McDonagh, is that all parts of creation, from the smallest plant or animal, is of key importance to the world and the relational importance of humanity with God, as well as humanity and the earth. Ecological awareness is more than just an environmental issue: it is one of justice and, more specifically, climate justice (described in more detail in Chapter 1). Climate change impacts are felt globally but people in poorer communities are facing the brunt of the crisis. In exploring one's spirituality, a key question is how our relationship with the environment affects our brothers and sisters in our common home, the world. Collectively, there is a need for us to examine our relationship with the environment and the impact of this on other people locally and globally. Pope Francis (2015:114) claims that caring for the environment includes the capacity to live together and 'that we have a shared responsibility for others and the world and that being good and decent is worth it'.

As a person of faith, you should be encouraged through spirituality to get to know the natural world more thoroughly, appreciate what is threatening it and do all you can to create a friendly world for every human, creature and plant to flourish.

In your classroom

This section outlines four different activities that you can use to develop the spirituality of the child through the environment. Designed to develop a sense of wonder and awe for children (9–13 years), these activities provide children with opportunities to experience the presence of God and to generate a connection with nature. While promoting connectedness and stewardship (Fisher, 2011; Haugen, 2018; Hyde, 2008), this can occur during peak moments that foster a sense of magic in the environment, while promoting connectedness and stewardship. Such moments have been called 'spiritual relational moments' (Scott, 2003:124). All suggested activities promote active learning and allow for children to reflect both as individuals and collectively, as a group. This is core: children must have time to develop and nourish their personal understanding, before engaging with others, who then will help them to shape, develop, reassess and confirm their viewpoint.

Becoming aware of your environment

The following activity takes place over four days. It aims to help children to appreciate places of beauty in their life and of others by focusing on their responsibility to care for their place. Children are also invited to reflect on the impact of actions on places of beauty across the world. The world as a whole is a gift from God. Each person is a steward of creation and has an important part to play in protecting this gift.

Day 1: Invite the children to think of a place in nature that is special for them: a place with memories; a place they like to visit; a place where they feel happy and close to nature. The children can write or draw about this special place in nature and what it means to them. *(The next day, the children may bring a photograph or drawing of this place.)*

Pair and share: When they have completed their work, invite the children to share it with their neighbour. Each child must listen respectfully to the other and pick one positive thing they like about what their partner has shared.

Whole-class activity: Invite the class to return to the full group and, if possible, sit in a circle. Invite the children to share something about their conversations and place their images or words on a display board. Explore how they would feel if this place became damaged or was no longer beautiful. How could humans affect this place?

Homework: Invite each child to bring in a photograph of their favourite place if possible.

Day 2: Review the work of day 1. Add the children's images and photographs to the display board. Highlight key words from the previous day's conversations. Ask the children to consider their special place being harmed or damaged, building on the conversation from the previous day. Once again explore how that might happen, focusing the conversation on the effects caused by others or themselves. If the children do not bring up climate change, you may offer it to the conversation. These conversations can be held in groups and reported back to the class. After the feedback sessions, introduce the children to the concept of a carbon footprint, that is, the amount of carbon dioxide released to the atmosphere by the activities of a person, group or nation. Invite the children to brainstorm on how carbon dioxide is entering the atmosphere, once again moving from the global to the local. Record answers and place then by the display board with pictures created earlier. End the lesson by asking the children to reflect on how carbon dioxide emissions will affect their special places and the impact of their actions.

Homework: Invite each child to calculate their carbon footprint. http://meethegreens.pbskids.org/features/carbon-calculator.html

Day 3: Begin reflecting on day 2 with the children. Highlight main words from the previous day's conversations. Invite the children to draw and cut out their footprint on light cardboard. Following this, invite them to draw their carbon footprint, based on their findings from their homework the previous night. When they have finished, invite them to share their work with another child. Finally, invite them to place their carbon footprints on the cardboard, over all the images and words that were put up the previous day. Ask them the following questions: now that we have layered the images with our carbon footprints, what do our beautiful places look like? How do you feel? How has our carbon footprint effected the collection of images of our beautiful places? What can we do to see the images again?

Homework: Ask the children to reflect on ways in which they can change their lifestyle to decrease their carbon footprint.

Day 4: Reflect on discussion from the previous class. Ask the children the following questions: how did you feel when your carbon footprints covered your favourite places? Last night you were asked to reflect on how you could reduce your carbon footprint. Can you share some of your ideas?

Invite the children to take their cardboard carbon footprints off the display board. When each carbon footprint has been retrieved, ask the children to physically cut out parts which they potentially can change. Encourage them to be realistic about what they plan to change. When they have cut out what they feel is appropriate, ask the children to hold up their cardboard carbon footprints. It should now be possible to look through each cardboard carbon footprint. Invite the children to replace their carbon footprints back on the display board and ask them the following questions: what can we see? How is it different from earlier? What can we see of our special places? Through our actions in reducing our carbon footprint, we can protect these beautiful places. If we can do this for these places, can you imagine what it will do for places in the Global South?

You can then share the following reflection with the children:

> Your imagination and your memory are nourished through these special places and every person has a special place. We saw this at the start of the week. Just as you all have a special place, so does everybody in the world. That special place makes everyone feel happy and brings them closer to nature or, for some, to God. But, if we allow our carbon footprints to increase at this rate, we will be damaging these beautiful places and taking them away from people. We all have to work to protect the environment; we all have a responsibility to care for our common home, in becoming ecologically aware in our lives. We need to respect the environment, not just for the good of ourselves, but for all our brothers, sisters, plants and animals across the whole world.
>
> Thought for the week: the earth was here before us and was given to us by God. The world is a gift to be cherished and protected, not to be thrown away. What can I do in the future to protect my special place?

Meditation

'Today, with gratitude to God, we remember that our body contains the elements of the planet: its air is that which gives us breath, and its water revives and restores us' (Pope Francis, 2019).

Each member of the class interacts daily with the world around them in a variety of ways, so these meditations are given to allow for some personal reflection time. Some have a Christian spirituality focus, while others do not. It is suggested that each meditation should take two to three minutes, with some reflective music playing in the background. Alternatively, a reflective walk through nature can be organised and each meditation can be used as a stop for reflection along the journey. Each meditation begins with a one-minute focus: where do I see the wonder and awe of God in this place and moment in time?

How present am I to the world around me? How do I show my love for God through my respect for creation and my neighbour? Take time to look at or imagine a tree; think of all that goes on inside the bark, to allow it to grow. Now move your attention to a leaf of the tree; notice the complexity of the leaf. Look at the veins in the leaf; they allow the nourishment it needs to flow throughout – air, water, light. Hold the leaf (or imagine you are holding it); feel the gift of life in it. This is a gift from the earth – the earth that is gifted to you by God.

How can I move away from a throwaway culture? How can I show care for creation and solidarity with my brothers and sisters and the most vulnerable people in the world?

Where are the most polluted areas of your community and in the world? Who lives in them? How do my daily actions contribute to the pollution of the world? What can I do to change, and to become more aware of the harm I am causing others?

How do I use water throughout the day? Do I use the gift of water responsibly? How does my use of water affect the supply of clean water for my community and that of people in other parts of the world? Do I appreciate the gift of clear water and use it respectfully?

Do I appreciate that eating has an effect on climate justice? Do I respect food? Do I eat quickly or slowly? Do I take time to reflect on where my food comes from? Do I take more than I need? Do I waste a lot of food, when many are hungry in the world? What do I do with waste food? Is it recycled? Am I aware of where my food comes from; how it is grown; how far it has had to travel; if those who grew it were given a just price for it; and its effect on the climate? What are the environmental impacts of my eating habits?

As a Christian, do I take God's Word seriously in my duty to care for the environment? God spoke: 'Let us make human beings in our image, make them reflecting our nature so they can be responsible for the fish in the sea, the birds in the air, the cattle, and, yes, Earth itself, and every animal that moves on the face of Earth' (*Genesis 1:26*). Do we take seriously God's request to care for the world? Do we protect the wildflowers for the pollinating bees? Do we ensure that all animals have clean water?

Ecological awareness tree

Trees are beautiful and come in a variety of shapes and sizes, depending on where you are in the world. Take time with your class to reflect on the trees that grow in your county. I am from Ireland and we have a beautiful tree called the Irish oak. It is a large, broadleaf tree and is native to my country. It has deep roots and takes many years to grow to maturity. However, we do not grow as many of these as we did in the past. The majority of the trees now grown in my country are coniferous and are not the best for nourishing the earth. As a society, we make choices about what we grow, what we eat, or the cars we drive. Each day, we make choices and these choices effect the environment – some positively and others negatively.

In you class, you can create an ecological awareness tree (Figure 17.1). You will need the following: a branch of a tree; cut-outs of tree leaves (some on brown paper and some on brightly coloured paper) and cords to attach the leaves to the tree branch.

Invite the children to take a brown leaf and to write or draw something that they or their community are doing that is harmful to the environment. Hang all the leaves on the tree branch. Take time with the children to reflect on how it looks. Here are some prompt questions:

- How does the tree look?
- How does the tree make you feel?
- Are you a good steward of God's creation?
- How can we change some for our actions?

Over the coming weeks, invite the children to change their actions or promote change in their community. When their actions become part of their normal routine, they can then go and take a coloured leaf and write or draw what they have done to effect this change. Going to the tree, they can remove the brown leaf and replace it with a coloured one,

Figure 17.1 Ecological Awareness Tree

which is the positive action they have taken. Over time, the tree should change colour and the children will see how, through their actions, the world can become a better place; and, in doing so, they become more ecologically aware. In becoming more ecologically aware, they are more grounded in the life presence of all in the world and for some, this will deepen their connection with the Transcendent (God).

The season of creation

The Season of Creation is marked throughout the Christian world from 1 September to 4 October (Feast of St Francis of Assisi). Its focus is to celebrate the created world and to encourage awareness of environmental issues from within a Christian faith perspective. This is a lovely way to start a new school year and it can signal Climate Change as a school priority. You could look up your local Christian community website to review available resources. Here is a link to an Irish website: https://www.catholicbishops.ie/2019/07/17/season-of-creation-2019/.

Conclusion

Spirituality and religion are complex areas, particularly for children. The literature suggests that children are innately spiritual (Harmon, 2018; Hay and Nye, 2006, 1998; Tracey, 2000;). The environment is real and tangible for all and thus allows an avenue for people to explore their spirituality either from a secular or religious position. This chapter places ecological awareness as a non-negotiable element within a professed Christian spirituality. We should take heed of Pope Francis's call, in *Laudato Si'* (2015:23), for an ecological spirituality, based on an appreciation of our 'common home', reminding us that 'the earth is our environment to protect and the garden to tend'. Education needs to reflect on the dignity of the natural world and the relationship between that natural world and human beings and so counteract against the negative effects of climate change. Pope Francis when speaking on education says education takes place, through the head, hands and heart.

To truly counteract against climate change, our education system is called: to educate children's minds about it; to invite children to become active citizens in effecting change, through action; and to help children discover a renewed love and awareness for the gift of the natural world, our common home. The activities in this chapter are designed to inspire children to care for the world that has been gifted to them, and to appreciate that they are the stewards for future generations.

'*We remember that our body contains the elements of the planet: its air is that which gives us breath, and its water revives and restores us*'. (Pope Francis, 2019).

References

Alexander, H. and McLaughlin, T. (2003) Education in religion and spirituality. In Blake, N., Smeyers, P., Smith, R. and Standish, P. eds., *The Blackwell guide to philosophy of education*. Oxford: Blackwell, pp. 365–376.

Eaude, T. (2009) Happiness, emotional well-being and mental health: What has children's spirituality to offer? *International Journal of Children's Spirituality*, *14*(3), pp. 185–196.

Fisher, J.W. (2007) It's time to wake up and stem the decline in spiritual well-being in Victorian schools. *International Journal of Children's Spirituality*, *12*(2), pp. 165–177.

Fisher, J. (2011) The four domains model: Connecting spirituality, health and well-being. *Religions*, 2, pp. 17–28, https://doi.org/10.3390/rel20 10017 (Accessed 17 June 2019).

Harmon, M. (2018) 'I am a Catholic Buddhist': The voice of children on religion and religious education in an Irish Catholic primary school classroom. http://doras.dcu.ie/22639/ (Accessed 10 July 2019).

Hart, T. (2003) *The secret spiritual world of children*. Maui: Inner Ocean.

Haugen, H.M. (2018) It is time for a general comment on children's spiritual development. *International Journal of Children's Spirituality*, *23*(3), pp. 306–322. https://doi.org/10.1080/13644 36X.2018.1487833 (Accessed, 10 May 2019).

Hay, D. and Nye, R. (1998) *The spirit of the child*. London: Harper Collins.

Hay, D. and Nye, R. (2006) *The spirit of the child* (Rev. ed.). London: Jessica Kingsley Publishers.

Hyde, B. (2008) Weaving the threads of meaning: A characteristic of children's spirituality and its implications for religious education. *British Journal of Religious Education*, *30*(3), pp. 235–245. https://doi.org/10.1080/01416200802170169. (Accessed 9 July 2019).

Lipscomb, A. and Gersch, I. (2012) Using a 'spiritual listening tool' to investigate how children describe spiritual and philosophical meaning in their lives. *International Journal of Children's Spirituality*, *17*(1), pp. 5–23.

Meehan, C. (2002) Resolving the confusion in the spiritual development debate. *International Journal of Children's Spirituality*, *7*(3), pp. 291–308.

Pope Francis. (2015) *Laudato Si'*. Dublin: Veritas.

Pope Francis. (@Pontifex) (2019) Today, with gratitude to God, we remember that our body contains the elements of the planet: Its air is that which gives us breath, and its water revives and restores us. #BeatAirPollution #LaudatoSì (Twitter), 5 June. Available: https://twitter.com/pontifex/status/1136256359819644929?lang=en (Accessed 25 March 2020).

Rolheiser, R. (1998) *Seeking spirituality: Guidelines for a Christian spirituality for the twenty-first century.* London: Hodder & Stoughton.

Rossiter, G. (2010) Religious education and the changing landscape of spirituality: Through the lens of change in cultural meanings. *Journal of Religious Education, 58*(2), pp. 25–36.

Rossiter, G. (2012) Perspective on children's spirituality and Catholic primary school religious education: A key starting point for reviewing issues in content and pedagogy. *Journal of Religious Education, 60*(1), pp. 31–40.

Ryan, M. (2006) *Religious education in Catholic schools: An introduction for Australian students.* Melbourne: David Lovell Publishing.

Ryan, M. (2007) Theorists informing early years religious education. In Grajczonek, J. and Ryan, M. eds., *Religious education in early childhood: A reader.* Brisbane: Lumino Press, pp. 32–43.

Scott, D.G. (2003) Spirituality in child and youth care: Considering spiritual development and 'relational consciousness'. *Child and youth care forum, 32*(2), 117–131, https://doi.org/10.1023/a:1022593103824 *(Accessed 20 April 2019).*

Tracey, D. (2000) *Re-enchantment: The new Australian spirituality.* Aldershot: Ashgate Publishing Limited.

Tracey, D. (2005) *The spirituality revolution: The emergence of contemporary spirituality.* New York: Routledge.

Trousdale, A. (2005) Intersections of spirituality, religion and gender in children's literature. *International Journal of Children's Spirituality, 10*, pp. 61–79.

Wright, A. (2000) *Spirituality and education.* New York: Routledge Falmer.

18 Creating teaching resources in response to the rapidly changing nature of climate change

Brighid Golden

Introduction

Teaching controversial issues is challenging. Teachers may feel hesitant about engaging with issues such as climate change due to lack of knowledge about content and methodologies. While there are numerous resources available for teaching about climate change, these often pose a challenge for teachers in that they require adaptation to suit the needs of a particular class group or purpose. Additionally, the knowledge in relation to climate change is constantly evolving so data becomes redundant. Keeping up-to-date with statistics can be demanding. Carefully created teaching resources enhance climate change education for all age groups. I have worked with organisations to create resources applicable to wide audiences, and also supported student teachers to design and develop resources to use with specific class groups. This chapter will draw on these experiences to guide you through your own resource design for your particular setting.

What is a teaching resource?

A teaching resource is anything that you create to support your teaching about a topic in the classroom. Very often we purchase resources or use free resources to support our teaching, but from time to time it becomes necessary to create something to meet the specific needs of a learner group or because what we need does not exist. A teaching resource is generally thought to be something physical (such as a game, a poster or a book) or a strategy for approaching a topic (such as structured questions or a drama activity).

What is a climate change teaching resource?

A climate change teaching resource supports teaching and learning about climate change, and facilitates the engagement of children with climate change through the development of knowledge, skills, values and attitudes in relation to climate change.

A climate change teaching resource may focus specifically on knowledge and understanding. This includes the causes of climate changes, the effects of climate change or climate actions. Alternatively, climate change resources may focus specifically on skill development. Some of the skills which are integral to climate change education include critical thinking, discussion and debate strategies. These skills support children to engage

Table 18.1 Beginning the process

Where to start when designing a resource?

Phase one: Assess children's prior knowledge and interest levels. This will help to pitch teaching resource at the appropriate content level and will give an indication of the children's interest in the topic.

Phase two: Decide on key learning objectives in terms of what knowledge, skills and attitudes to be fostered through the use of this resource. Having clear objectives will help guide teacher research. Consult current information in relation to climate change and choose the appropriate content. A teaching resource may focus on one particular area of climate change (such as causes, effects or mitigation strategies) or a more general overview may be more appropriate for children at this time.

Phase three: Consider the different mediums for resources. This chapter offers suggestions for a number of different options, but it is not an exhaustive list and teachers may have other ideas.

Phase four: Planning and piloting initial ideas. It is a good idea to chat to a friend or a fellow teacher about your idea before implementing the final version of your resource with your group. Having another set of eyes and ears considering your resource can be crucial to its success and improvement.

Phase five: Create it and use it!

Source: Developmenteducation.ie, Dóchas and IDEA (2014) guidelines for producing development education resources

with others around climate change outside of the classroom, and help to spread awareness and understanding of the issues.

Climate change is a very topical and sometimes controversial topic. Teaching resources should also support children to examine and develop their own values, attitudes and beliefs around climate change. An effective climate change resource can help children to connect this global issue to their own lives, by supporting them to identify appropriate actions they can take to tackle climate change. Ideas for beginning the process of creating a resource are set out in Tables 18.1 and 18.2. This chapter provides tips and ideas for the creation of teaching resources; however, teachers are advised not to be disappointed if they don't work first time. The examples in this chapter are the culmination of multiple piloting attempts.

Examples of resource types

Board games

Board games provide interactive and memorable methods for learning about climate change. There can be a significant amount of hidden learning taking place in games without the children realising. Games also give children an opportunity to apply their learning in a safe environment, as they are often required to use their knowledge to progress through the game. Examples of board games designed by teachers and children are demonstrated in Figures 18.1 and 18.2, and in the Colour Plate, section 7.

Table 18.2 Choosing resource type

Choosing a type of resource

When deciding about the type of resource to create, there are a few questions to consider:

How much time is available for research and creation?

Some resources require minimal preparation (such as discussion prompts or using videos and photographs) while others rely on more significant input (at the creation stage) to create a complete resource before use (such as board games or quizzes).

Will the resource be created by the teacher or in consultation with children?

Depending on learning objectives, one of these approaches may be more appropriate than the other. If time is limited, consider including the creation of the resource in consultation with children as part of the learning process.

What materials do you have available to you easily?

Every teaching resource will require some materials; however, some are more material heavy than others. For example, access to a computer and projector, facilitates use of photographs and videos. Alternatively, resources such as a board game will require physical materials with associated costs.

How will the resource be used?

It is important to consider if the resource is required for a large group, or if multiple copies are required for smaller groups. For example, board games generally do not work with more than six or eight children at a time, whereas simulation games can be used with 60 children simultaneously by just adapting the numbers.

Benefits

- Board games are natural tools for climate change education and engagement;
- They allow players to build empathy by taking on various roles and perspectives;
- Through navigating carefully selected climate scenarios, children learn from playing the game rather than listening to the teacher.

Figure 18.1 Climate change around the world

Source: Designed by children in St. John the Apostle, National School, Knocknacarra, Galway

Figure 18.2 Twisted game of climate change

Source: https://www.trocaire.org/education/resources/twisted-game-climate-change

Considerations

- Sometimes games are designed to trick players;
- Elimination games are usually fast paced and require good coordination;
- Often the same children are left out repeatedly;
- Games can be discouraging and damage self-esteem;
- Competition can distract from the aim of the game.

Therefore …

Good educational games must be inclusive, cleverly designed and should not be focused on competition (unless that is the learning).

Examples

Adapting well-known existing board games with an established rule set. For example:

Snakes and Ladders: You could change the snakes to lines of smoke and the ladders could be made from arms holding hands to show that we need to work together to move forward. You could also introduce an additional element to the game where questions about climate change are included on different squares on the board and must be answered in order to progress.

Table 18.3 Sample cards for taboo game

Carbon dioxide	Climate change	Emissions	Greenhouse gas
Gas	Weather	Gas	Carbon dioxide
Greenhouse	Human activity	Greenhouse	Emission
Pollution	Extreme	Atmosphere	Global warming
Emissions	Warming	Cause	Methane

Taboo: In this game, participants must describe a given term or phrase for their team mates to guess without using a list of words provided. These words can be changed and adapted depending on what children are learning about. For example, on the cards (Table 18.3) the participant must describe carbon dioxide, climate change and emissions of greenhouse gas without using any of the words in the boxes below them. This can be easily adapted for younger children; they could be permitted to use one or two or three of the words while describing. This is a card game that children could create themselves after learning about climate change and use to test each other on their knowledge.

Twister: It is a classic party game played on a large mat spread on the ground. The mat has six rows of large coloured circles on it with a different colour in each row: Red, yellow, green and blue. A spinner is used to determine where the player has to put their hand or foot. The spinner is divided into four labelled sections: Left foot, right foot, left hand and right hand. Each of those four sections are divided into the four colours (red, yellow, green and blue). After spinning, the combination is called (for example: 'right hand yellow'), and players must move their matching hand or foot to a circle of the correct colour. An adaptation: The *Twisted Game of Climate Change* was created by two student teachers and published by the non-governmental organisation (NGO) Trócaire (Figure 18.2).

Simulation games

A simulation game is a recreation of a real-world event whereby children have an opportunity to experiment with new ideas and strategies in a safe environment. Children are provided with a simple framework of rules and roles through which they can learn interactively. Simulation exercises look at complex issues taking place in reality and simplify them so they can be mimicked in the classroom in a more accessible way. They are a useful methodology for engaging with a complex topic such as climate change.

Benefits

They allow children to discover key learning for themselves during memorable, active games and activities.

Simulation exercises usually require children to explore multiple perspectives related to the topic they are exploring, and encourages them to develop their communication skills to progress the game.

Considerations

Significant time is required to conduct the full simulation. Additional time is also required for discussion or reflection following the game itself to draw out and consolidate the learning involved.

Simulation games can only capture the basic principles of the topic being explored and the reality of the situation is always more complex. This is an important point to highlight during discussions following the games.

Examples

One example of a simulation game to aid in understanding the impact humans have had on climate change is the use of a web. This can be used to explore the carbon cycle or the water cycle, both cycles are critical to understanding the ways in which human beings have altered natural ecological cycles, causing climate change.

Carbon cycle web simulation game

Step 1: Exploring the basics of the carbon cycle to help children develop their understanding of where carbon is stored, how it is used and how it moves between different stages of the cycle. Simple diagrams can be easily found online.

Step 2: Children should be given the opportunity to draw their own examples/interpretations of the carbon cycle.

Step 3: Once children have an understanding of the different elements of the cycle and the ways in which they relate to each other, the simulation exercise can begin.

  a Assign role cards to each child, which can be tied on a string around their neck or stuck on their jumper. Role cards include different elements of the carbon cycle – plants (name specific plants), animals (name specific animals), sun, atmosphere and ocean (name different oceans or other bodies of water).

  b A ball is handed to the child assigned the role of the sun, he/she then must throw it to an element of the carbon cycle that links to the sun, explaining the link as they do so – for example, they may throw it to a tree explaining that sunlight is used by trees during photosynthesis to take in carbon dioxide, release oxygen and store the carbon.

  c Once the ball has been thrown to all children at least once and everyone can explain the connections, the simulation can be advanced. At this stage, you can add in human activity to the carbon cycle, this will include the ways in which fossil fuels are used such as factories or transport systems. This can continue with the use of the ball, or you may introduce string to begin building a web.

  d To build the web, the ball of string will begin with the child assigned the role of the sun, who will pass it to another child while continuing to hold the end of it, this will continue in the same way as the ball was used, but now a physical web will be created using the string. The use of the string will allow children to see a visual representation of the carbon cycle and the ways in which human activity has impacted on it.

  e The web can now be tested to progress, challenge and deepen learning about the carbon cycle. Whilst still holding the web together, children can begin discussing what element of human activity is having a negative effect on the carbon cycle (i.e., releasing too much carbon into the air and removing it from its stores in the ground or oceans). At this stage, different elements can release their hold on the web to examine what impact that would have on the overall web.

Questions to explore while looking at the web:

- In what way is the carbon cycle affected by deforestation?
- How would the carbon cycle be affected by reduced fossil fuel use?
- What do you think will happen to the carbon stored in fossil fuels as the world population increases?
- What can we do to make the carbon cycle more balanced so that less carbon dioxide is added to our atmosphere?

Sample role cards can be found in Table 18.4. Depending on the number of participants in the group, the same role card can be assigned to multiple participants. The only role card which cannot be used more than once is the Sun as it is the starting point for the activity (Table 18.4).

Posters

Posters can be used in a variety of ways. They are educational tools designed and created by the teacher, to be used to support learning in the classroom. Alternatively, they can be created with children and used as a means to feature learning and share it with others. When teaching about climate change, it is crucial that the learning extends beyond the classroom. Posters are an excellent way to spread awareness and include others in the learning process.

Benefits

- Allow for creative expression and provide visual aids in teaching;
- Can be used to assess learning;
- If created by children (in full or in part) posters provide an opportunity for them to apply their learning;
- Authentic – spreading awareness and understanding to others makes the learning real and connects the classroom to the wider global or local community.

Table 18.4 Role cards for carbon cycle simulation

Basic	Human activity	Specific examples
Plants	Deforestation	Oak Tree
Animals	Factories	Vegetable garden
Sun	Cars	Fox
Atmosphere	Trains	Horse
Oceans	Rubbish dumps	Atlantic Ocean

Considerations

If posters are to be shared with the wider school, local or online community, it is crucial that the information on the poster is correct. This will require you, as the teacher, to keep a close eye on what is being included on the posters.

As statistics and information in relation to climate change are constantly changing, it is important to update posters regularly. Some sustainable options for updating posters are as follows:

- Clear pockets where information can be regularly checked and revised;
- Include laminated sheets where statistics are written with a whiteboard marker so they can be wiped off and updated;
- Create removable parts of the poster by using Blu Tack or Velcro strips to allow you or children to change the information when necessary.

These tips will help you to ensure you create a sustainable poster that does not need to be destroyed in order to be kept up-to-date.

Quizzes

Quizzes can be used at all different stages of the learning process to assess learning, be it at the beginning to establish levels of prior learning, in the middle for formative assessment or at the conclusion for summative assessment. Quizzes are extremely adaptable resources which can be engaging and interactive for children. Children can also formulate their own quiz questions based on the glossary in Appendix 1. There is a large body of information in relation to climate change. While different levels of information are appropriate for different age groups or learning stages, there will always be some dense knowledge acquisition required. Quizzes can be used to make this learning more engaging for children.

Benefits

For a teacher, quizzes are a useful way to assess children's knowledge and ability levels as well as obtaining an indication of their values and attitudes in relation to climate change. Quizzes are very adaptable and customisable. Similar formats can be used, but it is advisable to change questions depending on focus, class group or an individual child's needs.

Considerations

The following issues should be considered when designing a quiz:

- *Different types of quiz questions* include multiple choice, scales or short answers.
- *Different purposes:* Are children required to answer the questions individually or collectively? Should children answer questions from recall or to investigate the answers as they complete the quiz?
- *Different styles:* Quizzes can come in many formats. They can be a list of questions in written or online format. They can also be constructed as a treasure hunt where the

answer to one question leads them to another question and helps them to build a picture of their learning all together. *Climate Change Go Bingo* (in Chapter 14) is an example of a quiz. It is a good idea to use a mixture of different question styles and different stimuli during the quiz. Photographs and quotations may be included. It is also important to engage children both cognitively and emotionally through your questions.

- If using categories of questions, a spinner or dice could be used to determine which category of questions is to be answered next. Similarly, formats adapted from television quiz programmes (e.g., *Who wants to be a Millionaire*) could be used.
- *Categories for designing questions include:* Causes of climate change; effects of climate change; and actions against climate change (as discussed in Chapter 1.).

Discussion stimulus

Discussion allows children the opportunity to reflect on their learning through engaging with other perspectives. Discussion also supports children to build their confidence around engaging with climate change in a dynamic manner. There are numerous approaches to discussion; however, the examples below will offer some structured approaches which will link skill development with knowledge acquisition and application for children.

Benefits

Discussions in the classroom can be a great way to engage children and give them the opportunity to share their own opinions and experiences in a safe manner. Very often engagement in discussions is the stimulus which sparks interest and longer-term engagement with an issue for children as it allows them to authentically consider their own opinions and responsibilities.

Considerations

Facilitation of diverse perspectives – it is crucial that ground rules are established prior to discussions in relation to controversial issues such as climate change. There can be divergent opinions and experiences in the group, all of which should be given the opportunity to be shared.

A good example of ground rules used to create a safe space for discussions around controversial or sensitive issues are those used in the methodology Open Space for Dialogue and Enquiry (OSDE) developed by the Centre for the Study of Social and Global Justice. There are multiple versions of these ground rules offered but the most accessible version for groups of all ages includes the following rules:

- No one should feel left out;
- There should be a good atmosphere;
- No one should tell you what you should think;
- No one – not even the teacher – has all the answers;
- Everyone should attempt to do their best in relation to the three key challenges: Staying focused, thinking hard and working as a team.

Examples

Dice discussion: For this methodology, children roll a dice to decide what question they are going to talk about. The questions can be stuck to the sides of a large dice, or the questions can be provided on the board or a handout and numbered 1–6 to indicate which one to discuss when the dice is rolled. Keeping the questions separate from the dice makes it easy to change the questions each time you use the methodology depending on your lessons and learning objectives. It is a good idea to have a mix of recall, evaluative, analysis and values-based questions.

Ranking activities: As discussed in Chapter 16, this methodology requires children, individually or in groups, to prioritise competing alternatives and explain their choices. Statements can be ranked along a line beginning with the most important statement and ending with the least important statement (in the opinion of the children). Alternatively, statements can be ranked in the shape of a diamond. Children can place their first priority card on top, followed by two in second place, three in third place, a further two and then the card which represents the lowest priority at the bottom. This forms a diamond as shown on page (236). Children should strive for consensus amongst themselves. This may involve various discussions on the order of cards involving justifications. Afterwards the class discussion can focus on lessons learnt and children's observations about the exercise. Ranking cards may include the causes of climate change, effects of climate change and/or best solutions to address climate change.

Walking debates: As discussed in Chapter 14, walking debates a commonly used methodology, gives children an opportunity to express their opinions or questions that don't have simple right or wrong answers. It is important to remember that we can change our opinions and thoughts based on things we hear and experience so listening to each other can help us to grow and change our opinions.

Final tips to consider when creating your own resources

Ensure they are <u>adaptable</u>: This means when facts and figures change, resources can be easily updated. This could involve: (1) keep your word file safe so it is easy to change and reprint if necessary, and (2) thinking carefully about the format of your resource. For example, if you are creating a game or quiz, make sure that fact-based questions or answers are on separate, easily changeable pieces. This will help to keep your resource fresh and minimise work involved when you need to update your resource.

Make your resource <u>applicable</u> across more than one curricular area or curricular element so that it can meet numerous objectives at once.

Make it <u>sustainable</u>: Although it is crucial to environmental protection to limit your use of plastics generally, laminating or using contact paper to preserve parts of your resource can be a good idea to ensure its longevity.

Make sure you have had a look at what is <u>already available</u>: You want to make sure you don't waste time creating something that already exists. At the end of this chapter is a list of useful websites to keep up-to-date with resources on climate change.

Make it <u>interactive</u>: The information surrounding climate change can be challenging to understand. It is easy to fall into patterns of 'chalk and talk' to ensure core knowledge is covered. However, we know that all of us internalise and understand information at a deeper level when we have the opportunity to engage with it, discuss it and put it to use.

Ensure your resource is helping to develop *critical thinking* and not just internalising information. We know that tackling climate change involves creative thinking and making connections with our own lives and between issues. These skills are as important to develop as the transfer of knowledge about the causes and effects of climate change.

Where possible, ensure that the resource allows children to engage in *self-directed learning*. This means having open-ended elements that allow children to explore their own interests.

Fact based – if you are using stories, photographs or case studies as part of your resource, ensure that they are based on real people and real events. Many NGOs such as Trócaire or Christian Aid often have case studies available to the public that can be used to inform your own teaching. If you would like to create fictional characters, ensure that they reflect real life situations.

Include a focus on *justice and human rights* principles by ensuring that you challenge stereotypical views, include a commitment to equality in the language you use and provide space for children to develop their skills as critical thinkers and ultimately engage in action to mitigate the impacts of climate change.

Conclusion

Teachers should feel free to pilot a resource as it is being developed and make changes in response to comments from children and other colleagues. When creating a climate change teaching resource, striking a balance between over-simplification of data and inclusion of excess data is challenging. It is important to avoid situations where children may feel upset or hopeless. While it is crucial that climate change education highlights the reality of the situation, the aim should be to inspire a feeling of responsibility and hope leading to engagement in action. Therefore, it is a good idea to think about appropriate actions children could engage in and provide time for them to plan and carry these out. Resources may deal exclusively with climate actions. Using teaching resources described in this chapter can transform climate change teaching. Being able to use adaptable resources that are tailored to individual setting, will support interactive lessons and encourage meaningful engagement from children.

Weblinks for more information about climate change

Stop Climate Chaos: https://www.stopclimatechaos.ie/.
The World Bank (Climate Change): https://www.worldbank.org/en/topic/climatechange.
The Intergovernmental Panel on Climate Change: https://www.ipcc.ch/.
Environmental Protection Agency, Ireland: http://www.epa.ie/climate/.
United Nations Climate Change: https://www.un.org/en/climatechange/.
NASA Global Climate Change: https://climate.nasa.gov/.

References

Centre for the Study of Social and Global Justice (n.d.) Open space for dialogue and enquiry methodology. *OSDE Ground Rules*. Available: http://www.osdemethodology.org.uk/groundrules.html (Accessed 30 August 2019).

Developmenteducation.ie, Dóchas and IDEA (2014) *Guidelines for producing development education resources*. Dublin: developmenteducation,ie, Dóchas and IDEA.

19 Negotiating environmental protection through drama

Margaret O'Keeffe and Joanna Parkes

Introduction

Given that education plays a critical role in supporting the development of environmental awareness, it is critical that learners are empowered with an understanding of their role as change agents in the context of environmental justice. In this regard, the importance of working towards climate justice so that future generations can live in harmony with nature needs consideration.

This chapter is concerned with the role of drama in facilitating children to engage meaningfully with climate change. It will contribute to understanding the specific way drama can support enquiry into issues around climate change. The content, knowledge and pedagogical strategies required to implement drama lessons will be outlined along with the theoretical underpinnings. An overarching theme embedded in each lesson relates to citizenship and the capacity of an individual to be a 'good citizen'. A 'good citizen' has a justice orientation with a desire to act in a responsible manner.

Drama and learning

In the context of climate change, drama is a powerful medium to examine questions related to the impact of human actions on the environment. Drama is a unique curricular subject or lens, as it enables participants to connect deeply with content through engaging cognitively and affectively with knowledge and underlying themes (Murphy and O' Keeffe, 2006). It enables creative, critical and reflective thinking as learners engage in the co-construction of a story and negotiate meaning through the process of embodied experience. Drama supports learning through the employment of a multiplicity of pedagogical approaches including mime, still image, improvisation and teacher in role. As attention is drawn to differences and similarities between 'other' and 'self', drama can help in an ever-changing world as learners are supported to understand different perspectives. Developing an understanding of other people's perspectives happens as participants enter into 'the shoes' of another, and make meaning through the creation and development of a story. The story provides a fictional lens for participants to explore complex themes such as climate change. Depending on the story, each fictional lens is different providing children with a safe environment, while ensuring they do not feel threatened or exposed. The following section provides a detailed outline of two sample schemes – one for the junior end of the primary classroom (children 5–8 years) and the second for the senior classes (children 9–13 years). The aims of the schemes are as follows:

The lessons seek to give children opportunities through an engaged and embodied experience to:

- Appreciate nature and to care about the richness and beauty of the natural world.
- Become aware of the impact of an individual's actions on the immediate environment and the wider world.
- Develop a growing awareness of the lives of people in other places and how interdependent we are on each other.
- Become more aware of the role we can play in addressing environmental concerns in our daily lives, in terms of buying less and using less, re-using items, passing things on, recycling, saving energy and water conservation.
- Become aware of some alternative ideas and strategies that need to be considered with regard to environmental protection – such as green energy options.
- Develop a sense of agency so children and young people feel they can be part of the solution.

Can the two little pigs build better sustainable homes? (children 5-8 years)

Background

This drama scheme developed for children (5–8 years) demonstrates how a well-known story can be adapted. By giving a new focus and emphasis to a story such as *The Three Little Pigs,* children can engage with the topic of climate change in an accessible fashion. In this example, two of the three little pigs, Peter and Paul, are re-imagined as environmentally aware pigs who are trying to build sustainable houses. The first time they try to build their houses from local materials, wood and straw, they fail to do enough research so their houses fall down when the wolf comes to visit. The Wolf is also depicted as a friendly wolf.

These two little pigs write a letter to the children asking for their help to build strong and cosy houses in a sustainable way that will not damage the earth. The children conduct some research and use this information to help build stronger wooden and straw houses for the pigs.

However, the third little pig, Percy, does not care about the environment. He just wants to show-off and have a bigger house than his brothers. He orders very expensive bricks and he uses up the local water supply when making the concrete. In the end, his brothers don't want to visit him as they are so annoyed with all the damage he has caused. Percy finds himself all alone in his house made of bricks.

In this drama, the children participate as part of the whole class drama, miming and demonstrating the actions. The teacher also participates in and leads the drama.

Lesson One: Introducing the three little pigs – Peter, Paul and Percy

Introduction

Invite children to sit in a circle formation and discuss what materials could be used to build a house – enable children to consider materials which could damage the environment and materials which would be good for the environment, e.g., wood and straw are environmentally friendly.

Engage in a discussion about building materials which hurt the environment, discuss the use of materials that are not produced locally and the issue of transportation. Use talk and discussion to elicit that materials that are not produced locally are often transported from across the country or even from overseas. The transportation required for shipping these materials has an impact on air quality and contributes to global warming. This introduction can be adapted based on the age, interests and ability of the children

Organise children in a semi-circle

Invite children to listen to the following story which will involve introducing the children to the first two little pigs, Peter and Paul. The children are informed that the two pigs were trying to build a house from materials they could find locally, as they wanted to protect the environment by using natural materials.

Peter's story: Peter Pig tried to build his house from wood and sticks, but he didn't get help or advice and the house fell down when the wolf came to visit. It was a very windy day and the wolf had a very bad cold. The wolf's sneezing could have knocked the house over! The wolf was very upset as he was looking forward to visiting Peter.

Paul's story: Paul tried to build a house from straw, but he didn't wait for the mud to dry so it fell apart on the first day of heavy rain – which was also the day the wolf came to visit. The wolf was allergic to the straw and was sneezing a lot so that might also have been the reason the house fell down. The wolf was very upset as he was looking forward to visiting Paul.

Elicit how the wolf felt when the house fell down and explore if the children think that the wolf did it on purpose?

Percy's story: The children are then introduced to the third little pig, Percy. Percy doesn't care about the environment or looking after the world, he just wants the best house in the neighbourhood. He is a bit of a show-off and he wants a bigger and better house than his brothers. He says to his builders, 'I want the biggest and best house around, I want everyone to look at my house and say wow who lives there, he must be very important'. Percy orders very expensive bricks that come from the other side of the world. The builders have to use so much water when making the concrete that all the water in the river is used up and the ducks have nowhere to swim. But Percy Pig said, 'as long as my house is the biggest and the best I don't care'. When the wolf came to visit his new house, Percy felt he wasn't important enough to let in, so he locked his door and sent him away. The Wolf was very upset.

1 **Peter and Paul send the children a letter as they need help: Letter and discussion**

  The children are told a letter has arrived for them from Peter and Paul; Peter and Paul have a problem and need the children's support.

Dear friends,
Please can you help us. Our brother Percy Pig is being such a show-off. He keeps laughing at us because our houses fell down in the storm, on the day when the wolf came to visit. He says his house is the best and that our houses will never be as good as his house. But we want to build houses that are strong, good for the environment

and are made from things that are found nearby. Can you help us? We need help to make a warm, cosy, safe and strong house that does not hurt the world.

Thank you from two of the little pigs.

Peter and Paul.

Exploring the letter

- The children are asked if they think they can help the two little pigs. Think/Pair Share: Elicit what materials Peter and Paul need to use. These materials must be strong enough to use for building a house and must be found in the local environment.
- Record ideas on the white board. It is expected that children will suggest that Peter and Paul can use trees from their environment. Remind children of the importance of planting new trees to replace the ones they will be chopping down.

2 **Researching and creating a wooden house: Drawing and mime**

- Direct the class to look at some pictures of wooden houses online and make a list of all the things they might need to build a strong wooden house, e.g., saw, ladder, nails, hammer, etc.
- Drawing Activity: Individually the children are encouraged to design/draw a wooden house.

3 **Exploring the pedagogy of mime: Helping Peter build his house: Drawing and mime**

- The children will be invited to start helping Peter build his house. (Make it clear that when we are building the house, we are going to use our imagination and we will not use any props or real objects). Remind children to consider what steps will be required to build a wooden house. What are the considerations? What will they need to do first, second, etc.?

Teacher model miming actions

- The teacher demonstrates miming using an axe to chop down a tree.
- Invite children to discuss what is happening.

Individual or small group mime

- Children are invited to start building their wooden house. If working in a small group, they are encouraged to work together and help each other out, e.g., this wood is very heavy so two people are needed to carry it. As the children work to build the (imaginary) wooden house, the teacher can move around the room, joining in the building, side coaching as they proceed, e.g., 'you're doing a great job, and can I help you? Will I hold the wood while you bang in the nail? Do you need help sawing that wood?'

Reflection: Class discussion

- The children are asked to sit down and reflect on progress so far. How is the house progressing? What are they pleased with? What was challenging?

Creating the interior of the house

- The children are invited to think about the next stage of the house build – what needs to happen inside the house and how can we ensure that it is environmentally friendly? Make a list of jobs that need to be completed? What materials can be used? What about paint? The use of plastic? Make a list of materials and decide which items are environmentally friendly and which ones are not.

Decorating the inside of Peter's wooden house: Mime

- The children are encouraged to go back to work; making doors, windows, furniture, painting walls, sewing curtains. (Move around as before offering help and advice).
- After some time, the children are invited to sit down and imagine what the house looks like now it has been finished. They are asked to finish the following sentence adding their own ideas at the end; 'I look at Peter Pig's lovely wooden house and I see .... a red door, blue curtains and comfy bed.'
- Discuss to what extent is the house environmentally friendly? How many trees do you think are required to build a house? A discussion on using natural heating options will enable children to reflect on renewable and nonrenewable resources of heat and energy.

Replanting the trees

The children are reminded that they need to plant new trees to replace the ones they chopped down.

Researching trees

- Spend some time researching the types of trees that can be planted, discuss the benefits of trees for the environment, e.g., removal of carbon dioxide. Discuss the growth timeframe of new trees.
- Invite children to think about why they might need to plant new trees and then to imagine the room is the forest so they decide where they might dig a hole to plant the tree (move around as before helping and side-coaching as they plant the trees).

Reflection through drawing

- The class are told that Peter Pig is delighted with his new wooden house and knows it will stay strong regardless of the weather, and that it was built using resources which will not harm the environment.
- He decides to invite the wolf for tea the following week to show him around and prove that his house is made from sturdy materials which are environmentally friendly.

4   Meeting the Wolf: Teacher in role

- The children are told that when the wolf is invited to tea, he mentioned his concern about Peter's house that it might fall down again if he sneezes near it. He tells the children that before he visits the house, he wants to hear how strong the house is. He also informs the children that he has heard about the importance of protecting the environment and is interested to see what Peter has done in this regard.

Preparing children for teacher in role

- The teacher will adopt the role as Wilma or Wilfred Wolf. To prepare the children, explain that when teacher uses a specified prop (e.g., a scarf or tie), he/she will become Wilma or Wilfred Wolf.
- At this point, the children will take on the role of Peter Pig. In this role, the children will have to explain how Peter's house was constructed. They will be required to outline how the house was built and decorated to ensure that it is both sturdy and environmentally friendly.
- The children, in role as Peter, will explain how their house can withstand harsh weather conditions. They will also demonstrate how materials that have been used do not damage the environment. Eventually, the children will persuade the wolf that Paul's new house is safe to visit and a new invitation to tea is issued.

Lesson Two: Helping Paul Pig make a sustainable, cosy, warm house using straw bales

Inform the children that they are going to investigate houses for Paul, which can be made out of straw bales.

1 **Researching straw houses: Drawing**

Children can explore how to construct straw houses including their aesthetic and environmental benefits. Using images and YouTube clips, the children can look at the process of building a straw house. Compare the benefits of using straw-bale houses versus wooden houses. It is important they do some detailed research into the potential of straw-bale houses.

The class make a list of all the things they might need to build a strong straw-bale house, and explore the different design options available such as round and curvy houses. Cross-curricular links with shape can be made here.

2 **Helping Paul build his house of straw: Mime**

The children are invited to start helping Paul build his house. The children are encouraged to think about what they need to do first, e.g., cutting the straw and packing it into even-shaped bales and tying them up with string, placing the bales beside each other to make the walls of the house, leaving gaps for the door and windows, then putting a second layer of bales on top of the first layer, and together lifting a third row of bales on top. The teacher can offer suggestions such as: 'let's use the straw bales to make the shape of the house, remember we can make round or curvy shapes', 'let's put the bales on top of each other', and 'don't forget to leave a gap for the door and windows'.

Covering the house

- The children are told that the straw bales now need to be covered with a mixture of mud, straw and little stones. They are asked to imagine they have a big bucket of mud and they can use their hands to spread the mud over the straw bales.
- After some time, the children are told that the first coat of mud has to dry. This is what Paul forgot to do last time. They are encouraged to pretend to go to sleep and see if it is dry tomorrow.
- They are 'woken' up and all encouraged to check if the mud is dry. 'Oh dear it's not dry yet – back to sleep we'll check it again tomorrow'. The children can be

encouraged to check if the mud is dry and go back to sleep a couple of times. When the first layer of mud is eventually dry, they are invited to add another layer of mud and then they can paint and decorate the house.

- The children are asked what they need to do to finish the house.

Drawing

- Individually, the children are encouraged to draw a picture of a straw-bale house for Paul, focusing on the question: What design should he use?

Reflection

- When Paul's house is finished, the children are invited to complete the sentence 'I look at Paul's round and curvy house and I see ....'
- Elicit from the children the environmental benefits of using straw bales.
- Paul is delighted with his new straw house and cannot wait to invite everyone around to view his lovely round, warm, cosy straw house.

3 Exploring the Wolf: Thought-tracking

- The children are told that Wilma/Wilfred Wolf has concerns and is very worried that the straw house might fall on his/her head again. He/she doesn't want to visit.

Sculpting the Wolf

- What words would you use to describe the Wolf? How might we show the Wolf? How might he/she stand? The children are asked if a volunteer will come to the front of the class and take on a position to show how Wilma/Wilfred Wolf might look as he/she looked at Paul's house. Ask the child to freeze as if he/she is the Wolf at the top of the class.
- Invite children to speak the wolf's thoughts (thought-tracking) as they look at the straw house. What thoughts are going on in his/her head?

Meeting the wolf: Teacher in role

- The children are told they have a second opportunity to meet Wilma/Wilfred Wolf. Once again, the teacher moves into role as the Wolf (using the same prop as before to indicate when in role) and this time the class, in role as Paul, have to reassure the wolf that his straw house is safe to enter and is environmentally friendly.
- The teacher in role will challenge the children to describe what research they did in order to ensure their new straw house is strong enough to withstand all weather conditions. They can also demonstrate how they used natural materials to design a warm and cosy house that not only looks attractive but also does not harm the environment. Eventually, the wolf may be persuaded that it is safe to visit Paul's house for tea.

4 Percy Pig and his house of bricks?

Remind the children of Percy's story. Percy doesn't care about the environment; his only concern is that he has a more impressive house than his brothers. He wants people to think he is important because his house is so big and imposing. He doesn't care where his building materials come from so he chooses bricks from the other side of the world and uses so much water making concrete that the river dries up.

Exploring Percy using an empty chair technique: Thought-tracking and teacher in role

- The children are asked to imagine that Percy is sitting on his own in his house of brick. His brothers are annoyed with him, as he has caused so much damage when building his house. No one has visited him and he is feeling rather lonely.
  Do they think he might feel sorry about wanting to have the biggest house?

Do they think Percy might change his mind?

- Invite children to suggest thoughts which might be going through his head as he looks out the window and sees his brothers with lots of visitors while no one visits poor Percy (thought-tracking).

Teacher in role

- The children are asked if they think they might be able to offer some advice to Percy, if so, teacher can move into role as Percy and children can talk directly to him/her. The children could suggest things Percy can do to reduce his impact on the environment (environmental and climate actions). They might also be able to suggest things Percy could do in order to improve his relations with Peter and Paul (community resilience actions).

Letter-writing

- Guided writing could be used to compose a letter to Percy explaining that his house is not environmentally friendly and that a big house will not make him happy. The children can also engage in this activity individually or collectively.

5 Conclusion

- If you were to build a house what kind of house would you build?
- What house is the most environmentally friendly?

Why do we need to protect the environment?
What can you do to help protect the environment?

Second drama: An embodied exploration of local and global effects of deforestation in the Amazon rainforest through the lens of Amazon tribal communities (children 9–13 years)

Background

Supporting children to be equipped with knowledge and understanding of the importance of protecting the environment is fundamental, given the global challenges which face our humanity. This lesson demonstrates how drama can be employed to enable children to engage emotionally with the issue of deforestation through the lens of the tribal people. Children are enabled to engage cognitively and emotionally with the topic through the integration of the mind/body in the learning process.

The body becomes a vehicle to support the production of knowledge and new insights. Reflection is stimulated through an embodied experience, as children engage in meaningful enquiry into their beliefs and practices with regard to their role as change agents for the environment.

In the culture of tribal people, an intimate connection exists with the land and the universe. The land serves both a spiritual and practical function for indigenous people.

The traditions and beliefs of tribal people guide their practices in the sustainable use of natural recourses. A tribal community was discovered in the Amazon rainforest in May 2008 along the border between Brazil and Peru. Until that date, the people had lived in harmony isolated from the developments of modern society. The following drama examines the life of this tribe and the implications of the discovery on the tribe and the broader impact on the environment.

Lesson 1: What is the cultural, social and environmental impact of deforestation on a tribal community?

1 **Introduction**

- Use a map of the world to locate Brazil and provide some background on the Amazon forest. A lesson on the Amazon could be conducted in advance.
- Distribute a picture of a Brazilian tribal community to small groups or place an image on PowerPoint. There are many images available on the internet. The New York Times published this article on the discovery of a hidden tribe: https://www.nytimes.com/2018/08/23/world/americas/brazil-amazon-tribe.html
- Consider the following questions to facilitate reflection on the image:
  - What else do you notice/see?
  - What is the dwelling made of?
  - How does the picture make you feel?
- Narrate the following information/background

The children are informed that this picture shows a tribe discovered for the first time by outsiders along the border between Brazil and Peru. The tribe had lived isolated from the developments of modern society. When the helicopters circulated overhead, the people began firing arrows at the helicopter. Why might the tribe be doing this? Why do you think that the tribe was never discovered by outsiders?

Explore the newspaper caption, which may have been used to accompany this picture in the New York Times.

2 **Moving the children into role: Guided imagery**

Guided imagery

- Children are asked to close their eyes and imagine that they are one of the tribal people – Imagine what can be seen, heard, smelt – what does the environment look like – consider the location of rivers, rainforest, waterfalls, open grassland. How do you think the people survive? Why is the environment important for their survival?

Reflection through diary entry, discussion or drawing

- A diary entry is a useful way of enabling children to meaningfully engage with the context of the drama and, consequently, help children connect in a deeper way with the learning outcome of the lesson. Children could be invited to write a short diary entry from the perspective of one specific character.

Think/pair share

- Enable children to engage in paired discussion on what has been imagined.

Whole class feedback or invite children to sketch an outline of the world they created.

3 **Embodying knowledge using mime and still image: Exploring the tribal people lifestyle and the moment of discovery**

Preparing children for mime

- Ideally, lessons about indigenous tribes in the Amazon rainforest should be covered during geography and history lessons.
- Source a YouTube clip, which provides children with an insight into life of an indigenous tribe. If you do not have a clip, you can stimulate discussion using think/pair share.
- In pairs discuss how the local environment provides for the tribe. Consider materials, tools, shelter, food, leisure, animals and plants.
- Discuss the possible make up of a tribal family unit? Discuss how each family member contributes to the tribe? Fathers and sons engage in hunting and gathering while women and girls are involved in cooking and child rearing.
- Record on the whiteboard the specific jobs that members of the tribe do each day.

Enabling children to move into role as a tribal member

- Narrate the following – in a few minutes I want you to imagine that you are a member of the tribe – will you be a child, a parent – mother, father, or an elder. How do you support your family and community? What job do you have in your community? Alternatively, teacher designed role cards can be distributed to the children.
- Model an example, e.g., mime fishing action.
- Note: Provide clear instructions with regard to the setup of the mime – explain that children have to work independently and focus on their character.

Individual miming action

- Invite children to practice their mime individually as a whole class. Encourage children to work silently. Move around the space and praise all efforts.

Whole class sharing

- Once children have had an opportunity to practice their mime, they can be invited to share their mime with the class.

4 **Deepening children's engagement with the problem/tension: Still image**

Preparing children for still image

- Children will be broken up into small groups and asked to discuss the following for approximately 5 minutes.

  - An ordinary day in the life of the tribal people in the rainforest.
  - What it was like for the people when they realise that their way of life is going to be under threat?

- While children are seated, ask them to consider who/what character they would like to represent. Inform them that they will be creating a frozen picture of an ordinary moment in the lives of the tribal people, a moment which gives us an indication of their way of life.

- *Building tension:* Once children have created the first moment, they can be invited to create a frozen picture which captures their concern about their future.
- *Adding dialogue:* Request children to add two lines of dialogue to depict the emotion that was felt by the people at this time. 'I feel …'.
- *Reflection and analysis:* Invite each group to share with the class and engage in critical refection on the consequence of the discovery for the tribe. Thought-tracking can also be employed to capture the thoughts of the native people.

  - How did the tribal people feel?
  - What are they most concerned about?

5 Exploring the tribal peoples' perspective: Role on the wall, empty chair and thought-tracking

Role on the wall

- Role on the wall is a strategy used to enable learners to infer meaning about a character onto an outline representing the character. The relationship between characteristics (emotions) can be captured. Draw an outline of an individual on the whiteboard, and invite children to decide what words could be used to describe how the tribal people might feel when they realised that their way of life could change due to the disruption caused by the arrival of outsiders.

Empty chair: Thought track

- Place an empty chair at the top of the class.
- This seat is for the elder of the tribe. Inform the children that the elder takes this seat and considers the position of the tribe. Invite children to consider what the elder may be thinking about at this time – what are his concerns? Think/pair share can be employed in advance to support higher order thinking. Encourage children to share thoughts in the first person – 'I feel, I am concerned …', etc. Elicit responses such as tree logging, loss of home, food, shelter, fear of violence against them, loss of medicines due to tree logging and damage to flora and fauna.

Additional option: Sculpting

- Explain the idea that a character can be depicted using gesture and body position. Invite a child to the top of the class to demonstrate a tribal person's reaction to the arrival of the helicopter – discuss with the class how this image may be presented, e.g., How we might use gesture, space to depict the character? How might a subtle change of body position influence the meaning being portrayed?
- Thought track. Ask the class to consider what the person might be thinking at this time?

Conclusion

- Explore the broader implications of the discovery for the tribal people and the environment.
- Explore who has an interest in the rainforest and why?

- Do the people of the forest have any power against these that have an interest in the rainforest?
- What can the people do to protect themselves?
- How does deforestation impact specifically on the global environment and what can you do to help?

Lesson Two: What power do tribal people have to deal with deforestation?

This lesson seeks to make connections between deforestation and other broader environmental concerns.

1 **Exploring the dilemma: Teacher in role**
   The children are told that the elder of the tribe decides to consult with the other elders as he has serious concerns about what will happen in the future. He decides to hold a meeting.
   Set up teacher in role using the following guidelines:

   Before teacher in role: Contract

   - Teacher narration: 'I want you to imagine in a few moments that I will no longer be the teacher, but instead I will become the elder of the tribe – do you think you can IMAGINE and BELIEVE that I am no longer the teacher'?
   - Invite children in pairs to consider how they are going to advise the elder.
   - Once children have been given an opportunity to come up with ideas for the elder, inform them that when teacher sits on the chair, he/she will no longer be the teacher but will become the elder.

   Conducting the meeting: Considerations

   - One volunteer can be assigned to chair the discussion.
   - Ensure each child puts up his/her hand and redirects answers to the whole class to enable children to engage in peer exploration of the issues.

   Out of role reflection

   - What did you learn?
   - What advise did the elder receive?
   - What should happen next?

2 **Place an object in the centre of the circle, which represents the rainforest**

   - What would you say to those in power about the importance of protecting the rainforest and the people that live there?

3 **Challenging rainforest exploitation using improvisation**

   - *Step one:* Examine who from the outside world might have an interest in this tribe? Elicit the following groups: Scientists, anthropologists, loggers, media people, mining companies, medical research teams, tourism and multinational companies.
     Break children into small groups and assign areas of research to each group. Each group has to create the benefits of the rainforest for those with a vested interest in the rainforest. Explore the impact of deforestation on the environment.

- *Step two:* Discuss who might have an interest in protecting this tribe and why? Explain that a conservationist is trying to challenge those that are exploiting the rainforest. The children are told the conservationist has asked to meet with those that engage in logging. Remind the children that timber companies cut down huge trees such as mahogany and teak and sell them to other countries to make furniture. The roads that are created to remove the timber lead to further damage.
- This can be followed with paired improvisation between a conservationist and a group with a vested interest in exploiting the land for commercial purposes. Divide children into pairs and request partner A to imagine that he/she has a vested interest in the land and feels that the tribe would be better placed in a city with more modern resources. Partner B challenges the logging company, he/she wants to protect the environment and the people.

Building belief

- Enable children to engage in dialogue. Explain that it is important that children really work at speaking from the perspective of the character, even if the character does not hold the same opinion as themselves.
- *Reflection/conclusion:* Once children have been given sufficient time to discuss in role, enable children to reflect on the impact of the modern world and its technology on the tribe and the environment – the benefits and potential harm to the tribe and the environment – consider deforestation, ecosystem, etc.

4 *Poetic action*

In groups, children create a presentation in slow motion which depicts the sound of machines roaring and trees falling and the reaction of the people as they are forced to leave their homes.

5 **Advocacy**

Letter writing or presentation

- In an effort to enable children to reflect on broader issues relating to the environment, the children are asked to write a letter to someone in power outlining the concerns they have for the environment. Arguments can be made about the potential actions individuals and society/government can undertake to protect the environment.
- A letter can be written to the Brazilian government about the impact of deforestation on the tribal people and the future of the environment.

Small group presentation/making a film

The children are told that the film company is looking for people to take part in a film, which highlights environmental issues and, in particular, issues associated with deforestation. Children can be given the option of adding sound or movement to their presentation – body percussion can be employed.

The form can be presented using story, a documentary style or a rap.

Groups can be invited to perform for the class who can be placed in role as the government. Question children on the issues which need to be addressed in the film. What themes could be explored? Elicit the following: Rainforest – forest fires, deforestation, biodiversity; pollution – water, air, ozone depletion; rising sea levels; increased temperature; and extreme weather.

6 **Final reflection/conclusion**
Why is environmental degradation considered one of the most pressing issues of our time?

What can we do as a society or individually to protect the environment? What can be done by politicians?

Conclusion

Supporting children to be equipped with knowledge and understanding of the importance of protecting the environment is fundamental, given the global challenges which exist. This chapter demonstrated how drama can be employed to enable children to engage emotionally and cognitively with the topics presented. Actions can be designed and discussed in relation to climate justice and community resilience. As has been highlighted, drama has a unique capacity to enable children to engage in content through a multiplicity of pedagogical approaches. It enables learners to integrate the mind/body in the learning process. The body becomes a vehicle in the creation of knowledge. As was demonstrated in the samples provided, children can become engaged in meaningful enquiry into their beliefs and practices with regard to environmental protection using 'The three Little Pigs' and 'The Hidden Tribe' drama frameworks.

References

Murphy P. and O' Keeffe M. (2006) *Discovering drama, theory and practice for the primary school.* Dublin: Gill and Macmillan.

Additional resources

Environmental Education Research Journal.
Curtis, D., Howden, M., Curtis, F., McColm, I., Scrine, J., Blomfield, T., Ryan, T. (2013). Drama and environment: Joining forces to engage children and young people in environmental education. *Australian Journal of Environmental Education, 29*(2), 182–201. doi:10.1017/aee.2014.5.
ADEI (Association of Drama in Education Ireland): https://www.adei.ie.
National Drama UK: https://www.nationaldrama.org.uk.
Trocaire: https://www.trocaire.org/sites/default/files/resources/edu/creating-futures-lesson.

20 Moving towards change

The contribution of physically educated communities

Richard Bowles

Introduction

Peter is a teacher in Sunnyvale, a primary school in the centre of a small rural village. Mona, on the other hand, teaches in Hollypark Primary School, which is located in a busy suburban setting. While their teaching situations are very different, they are both very interested in heightening an awareness of climate change issues among the children they teach. This chapter aims to show how they, and teachers like them, can adopt strategies to do this through curricular physical education (PE) and extracurricular physical activity (PA).

Whitehead (2010:12) describes physical literacy 'as the motivation, confidence, physical competence, knowledge and understanding to maintain physical activity throughout the lifecourse.' The potential impacts of climate change, including altered weather patterns and the increasing frequency of hazardous weather events, may adversely affect our ability to maintain regular PA participation. Higher levels of physical inactivity and the development of more sedentary lifestyles may, in turn, contribute to the conditions that impact negatively on our climate, including an increased dependency on modes of transport powered by fossil fuels. In addition, Sanderud et al. (2019:1) suggest, 'children in contemporary Western societies spend less time in nature than previous generations and are less physically active than their parents were.' Consequently, this chapter explores ways to enhance children's physical literacy development while, at the same time, embedding practices that can help to address climate change issues, develop responsible citizenship and foster an appreciation for nature and outdoor activities. In doing so, teachers like Peter and Mona can make a positive contribution to the lives of the children they teach and, consequently, facilitate positive environmental impacts in the wider community. Specifically, they can foster the development of 'an appreciation of and concern for the natural environment, while also heightening their sensitivity to the impact of their actions on others' (Stiehl et al., 2015:257).

Teaching about climate change through PE: Using curriculum models

The adoption of models-based practice (MBP) has been proposed as an alternative, and potentially more effective, means of teaching PE compared to traditional approaches that are teacher-centred and focused on the acquisition of a narrow range of sport skills (Kirk, 2013). Metzler (2011) has suggested that instructional models are beneficial when used to plan, implement and assess an entire unit of learning coherently. These models can provide teachers with clear pedagogical structures that support the planning and realisation of well-defined learning outcomes. They are 'focused and theme-based and represent a particular philosophy' (Lund and Tannehill, 2015:166), enabling teachers to select specific models with a clear purpose in mind. While there is a growing range of distinct models within PE, some authors have argued that adopting a multi-model approach may help teachers to address a wide range of learning outcomes in different aspects of PE (Casey, 2014; Haerens et al., 2011). In that context, this chapter aligns with the approach taken by Fernandez-Rio (2014) where he suggested combining aspects of two such models, *Cooperative Learning* and *Teaching Personal and Social Responsibility* (TPSR), in a hybridised format. The following sections outline why, and how, combining aspects of these models can be a useful approach for the teaching of climate change awareness through curricular PE and co-curricular PA. By adopting some of these pedagogical strategies, teachers can help children to develop patterns of personally and socially responsible PA as they grow older, impacting positively on their lives and on their communities.

Using Cooperative Learning in PE and PA contexts

Grounded in social constructivist theories of learning, the Cooperative Learning model can help 'to create an authentic, relevant and meaningful learning environment' (Goodyear et al., 2014:717). Examples of Cooperative Learning are also discussed in several chapters of this book. This section outlines how the model can support teachers to explore climate change themes though integrated teaching with PE and related activities. Significantly, the teacher's role within a cooperative approach is to facilitate learning (Goodyear and Dudley, 2015). As a result, this provides opportunities to support discussion and reflection that, perhaps, may be absent from more traditional, teacher-directed, approaches to teaching PE. The approach allows for the attainment of learning outcomes through 'exploring the interrelation between teaching, learning, content, and context' (Casey and Goodyear, 2015:58). For Mona and Peter, adopting a Cooperative Learning pedagogical approach to explore climate change issues involves a very inclusive approach to learning, where teachers and children are positioned as co-learners (Dyson and Casey, 2014). The learning that occurs is inherently linked to social skill development, with a clear process, rather than product orientation (Metzler, 2011). Cooperative Learning can enhance learning in PE by fostering social and emotional skills through collaboration and problem-solving.

What are the features of this approach?

By its nature, Cooperative Learning involves a considerable amount of group work where individuals not only learn for themselves, but also help others to learn. The five elements of Cooperative Learning, as outlined by Dyson and Casey (2016) are summarised in Figure 20.1.

   This means that Peter and Mona can design learning situations where children must work together to solve specific challenges; where encouragement and positive comments underpin their group work; where each child has a defined role in order to help complete the assigned task; where decision-making and problem-solving skills are fostered in small groups; and where regular reflection is undertaken to consolidate learning. Practical examples to illustrate these points will be outlined later in this chapter.

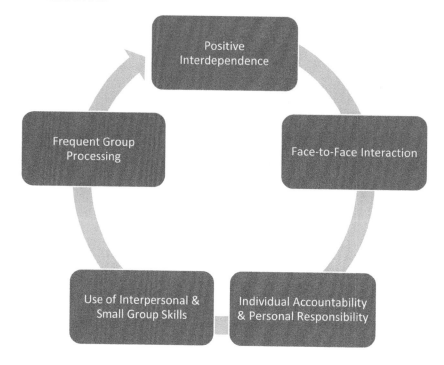

Figure 20.1 The elements of Cooperative Learning

Source: Dyson and Casey (2016)

Teaching Personal and Social Responsibility (TPSR) in PE and PA contexts

This chapter also draws on the Teaching Personal and Social Responsibility (TPSR) curriculum model (Hellison, 2003). The originator of TPSR, Don Hellison, sought to teach in a way that went beyond the basic delivery of curricular content. Instead, he wanted to help his students become more aware of their personal and social responsibilities within, and outside, the classroom. He was influenced by the work of Nel Noddings (1992:48) who argued that:

> The physical self is only part of the self. We must be concerned also with the emotional, spiritual, and intellectual self…We separate and label them for convenience in discussion but it may be a mistake to separate them sharply in curriculum.

Consequently, his model focuses on character development in the context of social awareness, democratic values and mutual respect, within the overall context of PE and PA. In particular, with a focus on the explicit teaching of personal and social responsibility, children can learn 'about their role in society as responsible citizens' (Severinsen, 2014:84). This approach also aligned with Mona and Peter's objectives – to develop citizenship skills that would enable the children in their classes to participate effectively in society as children, and also set sound foundations to becoming responsible, engaged citizens throughout their lives. Given the immediacy of climate change issues, Peter and Mona both saw the potential for engaging with these issues through PA.

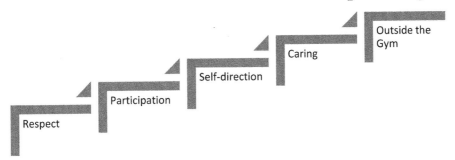

Figure 20.2 Five progressive levels for Teaching Personal and Social Responsibility (TPSR)

Source: Hellison (2003)

What are the features of this approach?

When describing his TPSR approach, Hellison (2003) proposed five progressive levels for teachers and learners to focus on (Figure 20.2).

Beginning with a focus on *Respecting the rights and feelings of others,* learners display self-control, resolve conflicts appropriately and include others respectfully at Level 1, leading to greater awareness of others, and of the world around them. Making a positive contribution to the class through *Participation and Effort* is integral to Level 2. *Self-direction* is central to Level 3, as learners begin to take more responsibility for their own learning and general well-being. Level 4 (*Caring*) involves helping others and displaying leadership skills. At each of these levels, the development of these aptitudes and attitudes can help the children become aware of the positive role they can play within their school community. Finally, Level 5 requires learners to transfer skills learned to situations *Outside the Gym*. In the context of raising climate change awareness, learning undertaken at this level can have a positive impact at home and in the wider community.

> More information on the TPSR model can be found at: www.tpsr-alliance.org

Adopting a hybrid approach to enhance teaching and learning about climate change

Having outlined the core characteristics of the Cooperative Learning and TPSR models, this section identifies their common features and presents an argument for combining these features to teach about climate change in a holistic way. The TPSR model can develop social consciousness by creating a bridge between school-based PE programmes and community-based activity initiatives (Beale, 2016). Because of this focus on personal and social responsibility in schools and in the wider community, the TPSR model offers the potential to connect work done within curricular PE with initiatives designed to address climate change in society as a whole. Similarly, a Cooperative Learning approach can support the development of social and interpersonal skills in individual classes and at a whole-school level (Dyson and Casey, 2016).

Because the approaches are underpinned by similar philosophies, combining them to teach about climate change appealed to Mona and Peter. In particular, the centrality of personal responsibility in both models provides an important starting point for climate change education, as does the focus on individual and group reflection (Fernandez-Rio, 2014).

Exploring climate change within curricular PE using the hybrid model approach

Exploring climate change through outdoor education

PE, by its very nature, provides a range of learning opportunities in outdoor contexts, and this is recognised in PE curricula internationally. The Outdoor and Adventure Activities strand of the Irish primary PE curriculum, for example, is focused on the provision of 'alternative avenues for pupil achievement and encouragement to adopt a healthy lifestyle based on an enjoyment and appreciation of the outdoors' (Government of Ireland, 1999:5). Dolan (2016, 2020) has argued for an integrative approach to link primary geography and outdoor learning. Learning about, and in, outdoor contexts is also an approach that aligns well with the objectives of this chapter. As Stiehl et al. (2015:256) highlight, this outdoor learning in PE 'demands a responsible and tolerant attitude; that is, individuals must be concerned about their own welfare as well as the welfare of others and their surroundings.' Outdoor education in a PE context, therefore, involves the development of 'technical, intellectual and social skills and sharing decisions' (Stidder and Haasner, 2011:79), and a wide range of activities can be explored in the immediate school surroundings. This can lead to deep, authentic cross-curricular learning experiences where the learners take more responsibility for their learning in, and about, their own local place (Beames et al., 2009; Beames and Ross, 2010). Furthermore, outdoor learning outcomes in PE are 'nearly always real and uncertain' (Lemmey, 2008:108). While this may be demanding for teachers in terms of planning and organisation, these authentic experiences can have deep meaning for the participants, with opportunities for social and affective learning (O'Connor, 2018). Other examples of outdoor learning to support climate change awareness can be found in Chapter 10 of this book.

The next part of this chapter outlines strategies that are situated in PE and PA contexts, grounded in the Cooperative Learning and TPSR models. Filiz (2017) has proposed a template for a lesson based on the TPSR approach that involves the following steps: (1) Relational Time: *Where the teacher has informal conversations with individual participants to foster personal relationships*, (2) Awareness Talk: *Outlining clear objectives and responsibilities*, (3) Physical Activity Time: *Including a focus on learner responsibility and awareness*, (4) Group Meeting: *Giving participants a chance to share opinions and give feedback* and (5) Reflection Time: *Prompting to think about their own learning, and their contribution to the day's lesson*. In conjunction with this, the elements of Cooperative Learning (Figure 20.1) guided the pedagogical approaches adopted by Peter and Mona. These include: The allocation of clear roles and responsibilities to each group member so that their efforts are crucial to the completion of assigned tasks; use of strategies such as *Think, Pair, Share, Perform* to prompt reflection on learning; and the provision of task cards to support groupwork. More examples are available from Dyson and Casey (2016). Peter and Mona incorporated these suggestions into their regular teaching, and they used the following exemplars to explore climate change using specific examples of outdoor education content.

Exemplars exploring climate change through outdoor education

1: Walking activity

Peter designed an outdoor walking activity through which to explore climate change. The first activity, *Walk to the Well,* focused on developing empathy with people affected by climate change in other countries. Using the World Water Day resource pack to teach thematically about water across the whole curriculum, he focused specifically on water consumption through the *Where is Water?* video clip (www.youtube.com/watch?v=b1f-G6v3voA). While exploring a range of related resources, the children were amazed to hear that Angela, a 10-year-old girl in Malawi, must walk over 2 km each morning to collect clean drinking water for her family (see Trócaire: Climate Change Climate Justice). Peter and the children measured and marked a looped route of 100 m around the school yard. Teams consisting of 3 children were constructed and, working in a relay formation, they were given a target to cover a distance of 2 km during lunchtime each day. Their experiences formed the basis of group discussions later, where they contrasted their own lifestyles with the situations faced by children elsewhere, especially where the effects of climate change may be more pronounced.

The resources mentioned are available at: www.worldwaterday.org and https://www.trocaire.org/education/climate-change/primary.

2: Bicycle education

Because active travel has been identified as a way to encourage choices that have the potential to combat climate change, Mona decided to develop the cycling skills of the children in her class during PE. Through the Sprocket Rocket programme, the children were enabled to learn basic bike-handling skills such as *balancing, braking, cornering* and *pedalling* in the school grounds. As their skills developed, Mona and the children designed simple trails using cones and other suitable obstacles. She also facilitated them to provide peer feedback as they learned to manoeuvre around the trails. These activities were supported by group discussions focused on safety awareness and the need to act responsibly to protect themselves and others. A central aspect of these discussions was a focus on how travel choices affect climate change. Specifically, issues such as carbon emissions, air pollution and fossil fuel use were discussed, and children were encouraged to continue these conversations about viable alternatives in their own home contexts.

More details about the Sprocket Rocket initiative can be found at: http://www.cyclingireland.ie/page/programmes/sprocket-rocket.

3: Appreciating the outdoors

The next activity has been selected for Peter and Mona's contexts so that they help children to appreciate their surroundings in meaningful ways. It can be adapted to suit the specifics of their contrasting school environments.

Geocaching might be described as a treasure hunt using GPS technology, and can be an engaging activity to foster a sense of place. It is now a worldwide activity where participants use smartphones or GPS devices to search for hidden objects (caches). Using the acronym CITO (Cachers Improve the Outdoors), participants adhere to the environmental protection ethos of 'leave no trace,' building a sense of care and appreciation of their surroundings. In a school context, a temporary geocache trail could be designed by the teacher using the following steps:

1   Place clues to solving a puzzle or age-appropriate environmental quiz questions in a set of clean empty plastic containers with waterproof lids (items from the recycling bin would be perfect!).
2   Hide each container in a safe location around the school grounds. Using a GPS device, write down the exact coordinates of each location (a mapping app such as Google Maps would work too!).
3   Back in the classroom, give pairs of children a worksheet containing a list of the different co-ordinates (pairs might search for the objects in a particular order to avoid groups from following each other).
4   Once each pair finds a cache, they record what they find and replace the cache exactly as they found it.
5   When they have found all the caches, they return to the classroom and solve the problem posed. To encourage Cooperative Learning, two pairs might work together, each collecting different information at separate locations, before working together to complete their challenge.

Geocaching can enhance children's mapping skills, enable them to work with a partner or team and can incorporate a *jigsaw learning* approach. Most importantly in the context of climate change awareness, it can encourage children to understand more about their environment. In addition, geocaching activities can be promoted as a family pastime, connecting the learning done in school to the home context.
   Find out more:
   www.geocaching.com.
   https://www.geocaching.com/blog/category/environment/.
   www.geocachingforschools.co.uk.

Exploring climate change through extracurricular PA initiatives

Active School Travel (AST)

Typically, AST interventions have been designed to address concerns about children's physical inactivity (Buttazzoni et al., 2018), and there is evidence to suggest that active travel to school can have positive impacts on health and cardiovascular fitness (Lubans et al., 2011). Significantly, Khreis et al. (2019) have identified how improved transport infrastructure in urban areas (including safe cycling and walking routes, and regular public transport) can produce benefits relating to climate change, PA, air quality, noise reduction and safety. From that perspective then, it is imperative that policy makers plan for the provision of 'supportive environments, or pro-AST cultures' (Buttazzoni et al., 2019:213) or, as Berry et al. (2010:2) describe them, 'walkable neighbourhoods.'

Developing an awareness of the impact of transportation methods on climate can be a central part of our strategy to foster responsibility within, and beyond, the school environment. Exploring ways to reduce our use of fossil fuels as we travel to and from school can be an important starting point. International studies identify a number of factors that can support positive choices regarding AST. Initiatives promoting AST work best for children living within 3 km of their school, for those living in urban and suburban settings, and for those who are in upper primary school classes and beyond (Mammen et al., 2014).

Levels of active travel to school in Ireland are low when compared to other European countries (Murtagh et al., 2016). In that context, the work of O'Keeffe and O'Beirne (2015) acknowledges parental concerns about children's safety when they are outside generally, and specifically when they are involved in independent travel. Their research suggests that over 50% of journeys to primary schools are made in cars, while approximately 25% of children walk and with fewer than 3% travelling by bicycle. Consequently, embedding a culture of active travel to school could be a starting point from which teacher, parents and children would choose to travel actively in other contexts too. Changing these travel patterns could then be a positive climate action locally, nationally and internationally.

AST exemplars

Exemplar 1: A Cycle to School initiative

While parents frequently recall very positive memories from their own youth about cycling in their own locality, personal safety concerns are regularly identified as reasons for not allowing their children to engage in active travel in contemporary settings (Jordi-Sánchez, 2018). In order to counteract this perception among the parents in her school, Mona decided to organise a cooperative Cycle to School project. This built on the bike awareness work she had completed during her curricular PE lessons. Influenced by the stages of development used by the Galway Cycle Bus initiative (https://galwaycyclebus.weebly.com/), she has now planned a similar programme using the following structure, and incorporating a range of cross-curricular links:

Step 1: Viability
> As part of an English writing activity, Mona helped her class to design a questionnaire for distribution to all families. This questionnaire elicited information about current school travel methods, commuting distances and attitudes towards active travel. The results, analysed during Maths class, showed that parents viewed the idea favourably.

Step 2: Engaging stakeholders
> Having established that the initiative had broad parental support, a series of meetings were held with a variety of groups within the school community (parents, children, school management, teachers, local police and community groups, etc.) and a *leadership team* was established. This team recruited a group of volunteers that undertook to marshal the cycling bus on a rotational basis.

Step 3: Route mapping

As part of a series of PE orienteering lessons, integrated with Geography, the children in Mona's class carried out a mapping activity to explore possible routes for the cycling bus. Their results were shared with the leadership team, leading to agreement about the most viable routes. Pick-up and drop-off points and times were identified along the routes.

Step 4: Developing safety protocols

Part of the route mapping process involved identifying any safety hazards on the agreed routes. In addition, rules were established about safe-cycling practice (well-maintained bikes, appropriate clothing and helmets and cycling etiquette) and these were discussed and practiced during PE class time. Separately, marshals agreed their duties and teams of five were assigned to each daily bus commute (lead position, rear position, junction marshal and two support marshals cycling parallel to the group, available to assist the others when the need arose).

Step 5: Reviewing progress

The Hollypark leadership team undertook regular reviews of the programme. Two key issues arose:

1 Speed of the bus: Because there was a large age-range among the children using the bus, the cycling experience and ability of the cyclists varied greatly. This became an issue for some of the older children as they wished to cycle more quickly. This issue was addressed through in-class conversations framed within the TPSR/Cooperative Learning structure (group processing), and it was agreed that the younger, less experienced cyclists should dictate the pace.

2 Informing the wider community: As the cooperation of the wider community was essential for the safe operation of the cycling bus, it was decided to increase local publicity about it. The children designed posters to be placed in local shops, and the leadership team used social media and other local communication channels to inform other road users about how the bus operated, with a view to raising awareness and empathy for the young cyclists.

For additional information about designing safe travel environments near schools, check out this example from Scotland: https://www.sustrans.org.uk/scotland/schools/ active-travel-funding-schools.

Exemplar 2: A Walk to School initiative

Due to its location in the centre of a small rural village, the majority of children are driven to Sunnyvale school by car. Safe walking or cycling paths are not available outside the village boundary. Despite this, Peter has implemented a modified Walk to School initiative. His main aim was to help parents and children to reflect on the impact of their travel choices. The process they designed is summarised in the following steps:

1 Building on aspects of the PE and Geography curricula, Peter and his class conducted a 'walkability audit' of the immediate vicinity of the school. During this audit, they identified three parking locations in different parts of the village that each allowed for a safe 'park and walk' journey to school of about 500 m.

2   The children designed posters and notes for parents, encouraging them to think about using the 'park and walk' option at least once a week. Peter engaged in discussions with his class in order to raise awareness of potential to incorporate some aspects of active travel into daily commutes. These discussions then formed the basis of homework assignments where families reviewed their current travel practices and agreed on some modifications. In that way, active travel came to be viewed as a responsible choice within the school environment, with the potential for this awareness to be transferred to other contexts too.

3   This was formalised into a Walk on Wednesdays (WoW) initiative, where cars were left at the designated parking areas and parents walked with their children to school. In addition, families were encouraged to continue to do this informally on other days. This was framed within the context of a decrease in the proportion of their distance travelled by car, and an increase in their daily PA.

For additional information about other walk to school initiatives, check out these examples from Ireland: https://greenschoolsireland.org/themes/travel/.

Drawing everything together

There is scope for a range of PA initiatives that can lead to a variety of positive health and environmental outcomes. An important factor in any such increase would be a willingness on behalf of policymakers to make the environment close to schools more suitable for walking and cycling. Writing in the Australian context, (Carver et al., 2019) argue for the provision of infrastructure that facilitates children's independent travel to school. For this to happen, policymakers will need to be aware of the health and environmental benefits that can be derived from appropriate infrastructural adjustments. Very often, this awareness stems from the success of school and community-based initiatives, where small-scale activities can be provided to suit the constraints of local contexts. Within educational settings, the use of curriculum models such as TPSR and Cooperative Learning can provide suitable evidence-based frameworks with which to support behaviour change in schools and in the wider community embedding, potentially patterns of active living that enhance health and wellbeing and actions that combat the negative impacts of climate change. *Taking responsibility* within the classroom and outside it, can lead to 'a positive outcome of a positive choice' (Parker and Stiehl, 2015:175), while *Learning cooperatively* fosters positive interdependence and teamwork skills that can have lifelong benefits (Dyson and Casey, 2016). Taken together, these can be integral components of a climate change education approach through PE. Mary Robinson (2018:106) argues: 'when faced with the enormity of the climate change problem, it is easy to throw our hands up and admit defeat. But individual empowerment leads to confidence.' In the context of this chapter, individual teachers like Peter and Mona, through their approaches to teaching PE, can become important catalysts to facilitate and empower change in their schools and, subsequently, in their wider communities.

282   *Richard Bowles*

References

Beale, A. (2016) Making a difference: TPSR, a new wave of youth development changing lives one stroke at a time. *Journal of Physical Education, Recreation & Dance, 87*(5), 31–34. Available: http://dx.doi.org/10.1080/07303084.2016.1157392.

Beames, S., Atencio, M. and Ross, H. (2009) Taking excellence outdoors. *Scottish Educational Review, 41*(2), 32–45.

Beames, S. and Ross, H. (2010) Journeys outside the classroom. *Journal of Adventure Education and Outdoor Learning, 10*(2), 95–109. Available: http://dx.doi.org/10.1080/14729679.2010.505708.

Berry, T.R., Spence, J.C., Blanchard, C.M., Cutumisu, N., Edwards, J. and Selfridge, G. (2010) A longitudinal and cross-sectional examination of the relationship between reasons for choosing a neighbourhood, physical activity and body mass index. *International Journal of Behavioral Nutrition & Physical Activity, 7*, 57–67. Available: http://dx.doi.org/10.1186/1479-5868-7-57.

Buttazzoni, A.N., Clark, A.F., Seabrook, J.A. and Gilliland, J.A. (2019) Promoting active school travel in elementary schools: A regional case study of the school travel planning intervention. *Journal of Transport & Health, 12*, 206–219. Available: https://doi.org/10.1016/j.jth.2019.01.007.

Buttazzoni, A.N., Coen, S.E. and Gilliland, J.A. (2018) Supporting active school travel: A qualitative analysis of implementing a regional safe routes to school program. *Social Science & Medicine, 212*, 181–190. Available: https://doi.org/10.1016/j.socscimed.2018.07.032.

Carver, A., Barr, A., Singh, A., Badland, H., Mavoa, S. and Bentley, R. (2019) How are the built environment and household travel characteristics associated with children's active transport in Melbourne, Australia? *Journal of Transport & Health, 12*, 115–129. Available: https://doi.org/10.1016/j.jth.2019.01.003.

Casey, A. (2014) Models Based Practice: great white hope or white elephant. *Physical Education & Sport Pedagogy, 19*(1), 18–34.

Casey, A. and Goodyear, V.A. (2015) Can Cooperative Learning achieve the four learning outcomes of physical education? A review of literature. *Quest, 67*(1), 56–72. Available: http://dx.doi.org/10.1080/00336297.2014.984733.

Dolan, A.M. (2020) *Powerful primary geography: A toolkit for 21st century learning.* London: Routledge.

Dolan, A.M. (2016) Place-based curriculum making: devising a synthesis between primary geography and outdoor learning. *Journal of Adventure Education and Outdoor Learning, 16*(1), 49–62. Available: http://dx.doi.org/10.1080/14729679.2015.1051563.

Dyson, B. and Casey, A. (2014) Introduction: Cooperative Learning as a pedagogical model in physical education. In Dyson, B. and Casey, A. eds., *Cooperative learning in physical education: A research-based approach.* Abingdon: Routledge.

Dyson, B. and Casey, A. (2016) *Cooperative Learning in physical education and physical activity: A practical introduction.* Abingdon: Routledge.

Fernandez-Rio, J. (2014) Another step in models-based practice: Hybridising Cooperative Learning and teaching for personal and social responsibility. *Journal of Physical Education, Recreation & Dance, 85*(7), 3–5. Available: http://dx.doi.org/10.1080/07303084.2014.937158.

Filiz, B. (2017) Applying the TPSR Model in middle school physical education. *Journal of Physical Education, Recreation & Dance, 88*(4), 50–52. Available: http://dx.doi.org/10.1080/07303084.2017.1281672.

Goodyear, V. and Dudley, D. (2015) "I'm a facilitator of learning!" Understanding what teachers and students do within student-centered physical education models. *Quest, 67*(3), 274–289. Available: http://dx.doi.org/10.1080/00336297.2015.1051236.

Goodyear, V.A., Casey, A. and Kirk, D. (2014) Hiding behind the camera: Social learning within the Cooperative Learning Model to engage girls in physical education. *Sport, Education and Society, 19*(6), 712–734. Available: http://dx.doi.org/10.1080/13573322.2012.707124.

Government of Ireland (1999) *Physical education curriculum*. Dublin: The Stationery Office.

Haerens, L., Kirk, D., Cardon, G. and De Bourdeaudhuij, I. (2011) Toward the development of a pedagogical model for health-based physical education. *Quest*, *63*(3), 321–338. Available: http://dx.doi.org/10.1080/00336297.2011.10483684.

Hellison, D. (2003) *Teaching responsibility through physical activity*. Champaign: Human Kinetics.

Jordi-Sánchez, M. (2018) Social perceptions of the promotion of cycling as a mode of transport for children in Andalusia (Spain). *Journal of Transport Geography*, *72*, 86–93. Available: https://doi.org/10.1016/j.jtrangeo.2018.08.014.

Khreis, H., Sudmant, A., Gouldson, A. and Nieuwenhuijsen, M. (2019) Transport policy measures for climate change as drivers for health in cities. In Nieuwenhuijsen, M. and Khreis, H. eds., *Integrating human health into urban and transport planning*. Cham: Springer International Publishing.

Kirk, D. (2013) Educational value and models-based practice in physical education. *Educational Philosophy and Theory*, *45*(9), 973–986. Available: http://dx.doi.org/10.1080/00131857.2013.785352.

Lemmey, R. (2008) Creativity and outdoor education. In Lavin, J. ed., *Creative approaches to physical education*. Abingdon: Routledge, 108–117.

Lubans, D.R., Boreham, C.A., Kelly, P. and Foster, C.E. (2011) The relationship between active travel to school and health-related fitness in children and adolescents: A systematic review. *International Journal of Behavioral Nutrition and Physical Activity*, *8*(5), 1–12.

Lund, J. and Tannehill, D. (2015) *Standards-based physical education curriculum development*, 3rd ed. Burlington: Jones & Bartlett Learning.

Mammen, G., Stone, M.R., Buliung, R. and Faulkner, G. (2014) School travel planning in Canada: Identifying child, family, and school-level characteristics associated with travel mode shift from driving to active school travel. *Journal of Transport & Health*, *1*(4), 288–294. Available: https://doi.org/10.1016/j.jth.2014.09.004.

Metzler, M. (2011) *Instructional models for physical educational*, 3rd ed. Scottsdale: Holcomb Hathaway.

Murtagh, E.M., Dempster, M. and Murphy, M.H. (2016) Determinants of uptake and maintenance of active commuting to school. *Health & Place*, *40*, 9–14. Available: https://doi.org/10.1016/j.healthplace.2016.04.009.

Noddings, N. (1992) *The challenge to care in schools*. New York: Teachers College Press.

O'Keeffe, B. and O'Beirne, A. (2015) *Children's independent mobility on the Island of Ireland*. Limerick: Mary Immaculate College.

O'Connor, J. (2018) Exploring a pedagogy for meaning-making in physical education. *European Physical Education Review*, *25*(4), 1093–1109. Available: http://dx.doi.org/10.1177/1356336x18802286.

Parker, M. and Stiehl, J. (2015) Personal and social responsibility. In Lund, J. and Tannehill, D. eds., *Standards-based physical education curriculum development*, 3rd ed. Burlington: Jones & Bartlett Learning, 173–205.

Robinson, M. (2018) *Climate justice*. London: Bloomsbury Publishing.

Sanderud, J.R., Gurholt, K.P. and Moe, V.F. (2019) 'Winter children': An ethnographically inspired study of children being-and-becoming well-versed in snow and ice. *Sport, Education and Society*, 1–12. Available: http://dx.doi.org/10.1080/13573322.2019.1678124.

Severinsen, G. (2014) Teaching personal and social responsibility to juniors through physical education. *Asia-Pacific Journal of Health, Sport and Physical Education*, *5*(1), 83–100. Available: http://dx.doi.org/10.1080/18377122.2014.867793.

Stidder, G. and Haasner, A. (2011) Learning and teaching through on-site outdoor and adventurous activities. In Stidder, G. and Hayes, S. eds., *The really useful physical education book*. Abingdon: Routledge.

Stiehl, J., Parker, M. and Coulter, M. (2015) Outdoor education. In Lund, J. and Tannehill, D. eds., *Standards-based physical education curriculum development*, 3rd ed. Burlington: Jones & Bartlett Learning, 255–276.

Whitehead, M. ed. (2010) *Physical literacy: Throughout the lifecourse*. Abingdon: Routledge.

21 Pedagogy of hope

Futures teaching for climate change

Anne M. Dolan

Introduction

Humankind is not a stranger to traumatic events including war, natural disasters and pandemics. Such systemic and pervasive crises can cause a deep level of hopelessness and alienation. Climate change is the most challenging environmental, social and political issue we face today. Together with the coronavirus pandemic and the massive civil rights protests ignited by the unjust death of George Floyd, a sense of hopelessness is widespread.

Psychologists have identified hope as an important element for engaging people in solving problems (Snyder, 2000a). Research indicates that climate change education programmes need to focus on promoting hopefulness, as well as an understanding of the issue (Ojala, 2015). Hope is not just a pleasant feeling, it also serves as an important motivational force. Hopeful people are more likely to become active agents in mitigating and adapting to climate change. One of the most hopeful signals to date is the voice of children and young people. Through widespread protests, these voices clearly articulate an urgent need for climate action. People will only become engaged in climate action if they remain hopeful. This book is written in a spirit of hope by calling educators to take action in their classrooms. It is written by teacher educators who are committed to equipping teachers, student teachers and young people with the knowledge, skills and attitudes, for dealing with the transition to a zero-carbon society.

This chapter:

- Underlines the importance of hopeful pedagogies
- Discusses the connections between hope and action
- Highlights lessons which can be learnt from Covid-19
- Illustrates the value of rediscovering the wonders of nature and outlines strategies for reconnecting with the Earth
- Considers the possibility of evoking hope by re-imaging the future through story and art
- Highlights the need for conducting transformative climate change education
- Outlines six school-based actions which can be adopted by children supported by their teachers

A pedagogy of hope

Climate change affects every region of our planet. Scientific evidence is clear that our climate is changing. Extreme drought, heat, rainfall and coastal deluges are projected to get worse in many parts of the world. There's little reason to be optimistic about climate change. For those facing imminent danger, communities in the Arctic, indigenous people in the Amazon and fishermen in the Tropics, hope is a luxury. Yet, the alternative, despair is disempowering and fails to recognise human ingenuity.

To date, many attempts to educate the public and our children about climate change have relied on scare tactics focusing on superstorms, massive floods and ominous weather patterns to generate fear. But fear can actually inhibit the desire to learn more and take action – particularly in young people. Norwegian psychologist and climate researcher Per Espen Stoknes (2017) popularised the language of apocalypse fatigue. He argues that rhetorical strategies which attempt to motivate climate action by pointing out the facts of environmental losses or potentially bleak futures actually overwhelm us into feelings of powerlessness.

Patrisse Cullors one of the founders of Black Lives Matter described the movement's mission as to 'provide hope and inspiration for collective action to build collective power to achieve collective transformation, rooted in grief and rage but pointed towards vision and dreams' (Solnit, 2020). This poignant statement is powerful because of its hope and the recognition that hope can coexist with suffering and human cruelty.

Marlon et al. (2019) describe two types of hope – false and constructive. False hope is employed when people believe that climate change will be solved by God, nature or some undiscovered technological innovation. People who are constructively hopeful believe that it is in our power as humans to design and deliver the solutions. Several commentators suggest that hope is not enough (Scoffham, 2020). This is certainly the case in relation to false or unrealistic hope. However, Ojala (2012) identifies three sources of hope. The first source is positive re-appraisal, whereby children re-assess an issue focusing on solutions. The second, concerns a trust in sources outside oneself. This refers to trust in environmental organisations, experts and technological innovations. The third theme refers to trust in one's own ability to influence environmental problems. This includes action projects such as awareness campaigns and energy conservation. The plastics project conducted by children in St. Augustine's NS, Clontuskert, Ballinasloe described in Chapter 13, underscores these three sources of hope (Table 21.1).

Bonnett (2013) is concerned that classroom actions may support an illusion that we can continue as normal in spite of the catastrophe that is unfolding around us. Hence, the concept of hope is problematic. While focusing on hope may be pedagogically desirable, the potential of individual behaviour to solve the climate crises is unrealistic. Classrooms actions are important for personal and social development, but their impact could be considered limited in light of the magnitude of the climate crises. On the other hand, focusing on 'doom and gloom' scenarios engender feelings of helplessness which inhibit a sense of agency. While global climate protests have generated increased awareness about climate change, there has also been a corresponding increase in psychological distress or 'eco-anxiety' otherwise known as fears for the future of the earth.

Psychologists (Snyder, 2000a) believe hope is generated when people make connections between their current situation and a desired future state. It emerges from three elements: Personally determined goals; the identification of pathways to reach these goals; and agency thinking, the motivation to use these pathways. Hope is profoundly linked with action. According to Rebecca Solnit (2016:xii), 'hope locates itself in the premises that we don't know what will happen and that in the spaciousness of uncertainty is room to act.' She is very clear that hope 'is not the belief that everything was, is or will be fine' (2016:xi), arguing that it is an alternative to the persistent narratives of both optimists and pessimists. Research also indicates that people with a high degree of hope are more likely to take action to achieve their goals (Snyder, 2000b).

Table 21.1 Three sources of hope from children's investigative project work on plastic packaging and recycling symbols

Positive re-appraisal (focus on solutions)	Trust in other sources	Trust in one's ability
Children studied plastic as a topic including its production, use and disposal.

Children conducted research about the public's knowledge of recycling symbols.

A website was created: So youthinkyoucanrecycle.com.

The children revised their project several times following feedback from other schools and local experts. | Children invited a speaker from Barna Waste to address their class. Subsequently, a class visit to the site was planned. Barna Waste is a waste transfer company based in Galway. It offers a wide range of domestic and commercial waste collection, recycling, compost and environmental services.

The author of this chapter was invited to run some workshops with the children on connections between plastics and climate change.

Through their local, national and international collaborations, children have had discussions with schools and experts about plastic. | Children are now recognised for their expert knowledge on plastics.

Their research has been shared widely with members of the public locally, nationally and internationally.

This research has informed government policy in Ireland.

The project now features as part of the Climate Action project (https://www.climate-action.info/).

Throughout the project the children have acquired important skills in critical thinking, collaboration, group work, communication and presentation skills. |

Source: This work was conducted by children in St. Augustine's NS, Clontuskert, Ballinasloe (more information is detailed in Chapter 13)

Indeed, as Freire (1994:3) argues, 'one of the tasks of the progressive educator ... is to unveil opportunities for hope, no matter what the obstacles might be.' Hence, climate change education should focus attention on futures and possible pathways to a sustainable future to promote hope in children (Ojala, 2015). Part of climate change education involves imagining a carbon-free future and outlining actions which need to be taken to achieve this. Therefore, climate change education needs to provide a forum for hope informed by narratives of resiliency, well-being, health and sustainability.

Hicks (2014) has an ongoing interest in how teachers and learners can stay optimistic and hopeful in such difficult times. He makes a distinction between aspirational hope (e.g., hoping that we will have a day off school tomorrow) and more radical or active hope, essential for survival in challenging circumstances. The latter is ontological in nature; it is what keeps us going in the most difficult of times. Hicks provides us with sources of hope which we may need to draw upon, as we transition to a carbon-free lifestyle (Table 21.2).

Action 1: Weaving a thread of hope through the curriculum

There are many reasons for despair. But equally, there are many reasons for hope which ultimately inspires individual and collective action. Research indicates that those who feel hopeful and are supported by hopeful beliefs, are more likely to engage in pro-environmental behaviours and to support environmental policies (Ojala, 2015). There are many examples of curricular and cross-curricular hopeful pedagogies in this book. Whole school approaches such as climate action days and a youth assembly (described in Action 2) maximises the learning potential from children's discussions and research. They also provide a platform for sharing and celebrating children's work. Furthermore, this work can be shared with parents and the wider community through school websites, social media and information evenings.

Planting trees is a well-documented climate action (discussed in greater detail in Chapter 10). As part of the process of decarbonising our way of living, trees are the most powerful weapons in our fight against climate change. Trees take the greenhouse gas, carbon dioxide out of the air and turn it into trunk, branches and roots, locking it away for years. Invaluable in urban settings, trees generate cooler, moister microclimates, and create more aesthetic surroundings while enhancing our collective mental health and well-being.

Picturebooks such as *The Promise* by Nicola Davies (illustrated by Laura Carlin) provide a gateway to discussing the importance of trees. In response to extreme poverty, a young girl resorts to shoplifting to find money and food to eat. When she snatches the bag of an older woman, she is caught; the woman demands that in exchange for the bag the girl must promise to plant the contents. The girl concedes and when she discovers the bag is full of acorns,

Table 21.2 Key sources of hope

The natural world	*Other people's lives*
A source of beauty, wonder and inspiration which ever renews itself and ever refreshes the heart and mind.	The way in which both ordinary and extraordinary people manage difficult life situations with dignity.
Faith and belief	*Humour*
May be spiritual or political. Offers a framework of meaning in both good times and bad.	Seeing the funny side of things, being able to laugh in adversity, having fun, celebrating together.
Mentors and colleagues	*Collective struggles*
At work and at home who offer inspiration by their deeds and encouragement with their words.	Groups in the past and the present which have fought to achieve the equality and justice that is rightfully theirs.
A sense of self	*Relationships*
Being aware of one's self-worth and secure in one's own identity which leads to a sense of connectedness and belonging.	The experience of being loved by partners, friends and family that nourishes and sustains us in our lives.
Roots	*Human creativity*
Links with the past, childhood, history, previous generations, ancestors, the need to honour continuity.	The constant awe-inspiring upwelling of music, poetry and other arts – an essential element of the human condition.
Human creativity	*Visionaries*
Both individual and community, music, song and dance, painting and sculpture, books, stories, poetry and utopia.	Those who offer visions of an Earth transformed and who work to bring this about in different ways.

Source: Hicks (2006)

she embarks on a journey that changes her own life and the lives of others for generations to come. Inspired by the belief that a relationship with nature is essential to every human being, and that now, more than ever, we need to renew that relationship, *The Promise* is the story of a magical discovery about the power of nature. *The Promise* can also be read in the context of climate change and climate justice. The story reflects the world's reality that climate change places a larger burden on those least responsible. A cross-curricular plan for exploring the theme of tree planting in the context of climate change is provided in Figure 21.1.

Cross-curricular plans with a focus on any topic can be reframed through a climate action lens.

Theme: The Importance of tree planting
Enquiry question: Why is tree planting an important climate action?

Literacy: Reading: Initial response to the story What did you enjoy most about the story? What can we learn from the story? Think of 5 words which describe how the story made you feel **Literacy: Oral language:** Discussing the importance of trees Why are trees important in our lives? What would the world be like without trees? **Literacy: Writing** Tell the story in your own words using a comic strip Write a note of advice to the girl. State the reasons for the advice and suggested course of action. Write two diary entries for the girl one before she received the acorns when she was sad and living in a dreary community and the second after planting the acorns and subsequently changing the life of her community. Write a proposal to the town council proposing ideas for the care and enhancement of the local environment.	**Whole school activity** Tree Planting ceremony **Cross-Curricular Plan based on *The Promise* by Nicola Davies and Illustrated by Laura Carlin** **Drama** Role on the wall: Display an image of girl on whiteboard. At different stages of the story ask the children to discuss what we know about the girl and reasons for their answers. Hot seating: Adopting the role of the main character, the teacher can answer questions from the children addressing different stages in her life. Role play: Children make 3 frozen images depicting three scenes from the story and use thought tracking to depict the thoughts of each character. Conscience Alley: a child in role as the girl walks between wo rows of classmates who offer opposing opinions on what she should do with the seeds.	**Citizenship Education: What can we do to help?** **Snowballing activity** On a piece of paper, each child writes a note to the girl telling her what she should do e.g.. should she keep the promise or not? Reasons for this advice should be included. When all children have finished they should scrunch up the paper into a 'snowball' and on 1,2,3... throw across the room. Every child picks up a snowball and reads the note. Each child writes a reply in role as the girl – are you going to follow the advice? Will you keep the promise or not? Repeat the snowball throwing when all children have written their reply. Discussion about our needs and wants Why did the girl in the story have to steal? Discuss the value of helping and being kind to each other and to the environment. Devise a list of actions for reducing greenhouse gas emissions
Literacy: Poetry Using haiku or acrostic formats, write a poem based on the story. **Art** Explore the illustrations in the book, before and after the acorns were planted. Discuss use of colour and artistic technique used to convey emotion Symmetrical painting. Divide a page into two with a sketch of a symmetrical house and field on each side of the page. On the left-hand side, depict a scene before the trees are planted, with a scene with the trees on the other side. Using samples created in science, children can create an artist's impression of a tree focusing on texture, line and space.	**Whole class activity** Design a picturebook which explores the theme of the importance of Trees. This can be in an A-Z or traditional illustrated format. The finished product should be available for local audiences and it can be sold to raise funds to support the children's choice of climate actions. **Geography: Climate Change** Explore the role of trees as part of the carbon cycle. Learn about solutions to address climate change. Take a walk in the local area. Assess evidence of biodiversity and local habitats. Indicate areas where improvements can be made. Write a letter to local council with maps, suggestions and a request for improvements.	**Science: Why do trees matter?** In the story, what did the trees mean for the girl and her community? Explore our connections with trees How does planting trees improve urban living? Discuss the conditions required for successfully planting seeds Conduct a tree study in school grounds or local area. Using an identification key, children can learn how to identify trees in their locality. Collect samples of bark, seeds and leaves (for art).

Figure 21.1 Sample cross-curricular plan for climate change education based on the book *The Promise* by Nicola Davies and illustrated by Laura Carlin

Acquiring hope through action

Agency involves empowerment, shared decision-making and action-taking. Constructivist and enquiry-based approaches to education prioritise child agency. Greta Thunberg, a Swedish teenage activist, was alarmed by her country's lack of radical action on climate change, so she decided to protest. Every Friday (at the time of writing this chapter) instead of going to school, she sat quietly on the cobblestones outside parliament in central Stockholm. Her protest captured the imagination of a country that has been struck by heat waves and wildfires during its hottest summer since records began. Thunberg herself has risen rapidly in prominence and influence. During her 2018 speech to the United Nations Climate Conference in Katowice, Poland (COP24), she urged young people to raise their voices by coming out together on Fridays. In her one-minute speech she managed to capture the urgency of what the world is facing. Subsequently, she addressed the World Economic Forum at Davos, the European Union's (EU) European Economic and Social Committee and the United Kingdom Parliament. Greta called on citizens to take action as if their houses were on fire. She spoke eloquently and clearly about the challenges facing our civilisation:

> Solving the climate crisis is the greatest and most complex challenge that Homo sapiens have ever faced. The main solution, however is so simple that even a small child can understand it. We have to stop our emissions of greenhouse gases.
>
> (Thunberg, 2019a:21)

Through her *Ted Talk,* she has chastised world leaders for behaving like irresponsible children (Thunberg, 2019b). Greta was subsequently nominated for a Nobel Peace Prize. In 2019, she undertook a two-week sailing journey to the United States of America where she was invited to speak at a United Nations climate summit. She refused to fly because of aviation's inordinate carbon footprint. While she has commanded international support, her actions have also been met with contempt and abusive comments.

Thunberg's actions have instigated an international climate revolution. Demonstrations by tens of thousands of school and university students have taken place in Australia, Belgium, Germany, the United States, Japan, Ireland and the United Kingdom among others. This rebellion is an inspiration for all and is supported by many including parents, teachers, third-level students, non-governmental organisations (NGOs) and members of the public. Greta Thunberg (2019a:56–57) reminds us that hope has to be earned: 'you can't just sit around waiting for hope to come – you're are acting like spoiled irresponsible children. You don't seem to understand that hope is something that you have to earn.'

On 15 March 2019, youth climate strikes were held in 105 countries. Over 2,000 events were attended by tens of thousands of young people. In Ireland, hundreds of school children staged a protest. More than 11,000 young people marched to *Dáil Éireann* (the Irish Parliament) at lunchtime seeking urgent action to address the growing threat of climate breakdown. A total of 37 rallies were staged around the country in solidarity with the global movement. In addition, numerous schools, especially primary schools, staged other climate events on their own premises.

These weekly protests are part of a global coalition of young people acknowledging their frustration with the lack of climate action adopted by politicians and civil society. Social media has been used extensively to communicate the message. Twitter handles and hashtags such as #FridaysForFuture and @climatestrike spread the message throughout the world of social media. Eye-catching banners have been designed by the students (Figure 21.2). A further case of youth action is illustrated in the Youth Assembly on Climate (case study 21.1)

Through innovative chants, a striking call for climate action has been brought to city centres (Table 21.3).

Figure 21.2 Examples of protest banners

Table 21.3 Selection of slogans from protest banners

Banners on protest cards	Sample protest chants
1 Are you fracking kidding me?	Save Planet Earth, There is no Planet B.
2 I speak for the trees, for the trees have no tongues.	We're going to go to our TD (Note: Teachta Dála a member of Dáil Éireann or the Irish Parliament)
3 Can we fix it? Yes we can.	We're going to go to Dáil Éireann.
4 No planet B.	1,2,3,4 Climate is what we are fighting for!
5 Sea levels are rising, so are we.	WE DON'T NEED NO EDUCATION!
6 We are the first generation to feel the effects of climate change and we are the last that can do anything about it!	We need you to take control! No more excuses, We need action!
7 We can't drink oil, we can't breathe money.	Hey TAOISEACH! LEAVE FOSSIL FUELS ALONE!
8 Sorry I can't tidy my bedroom, I have to save the planet.	*(Note Taoiseach is the Irish word for leader or Prime Minister.)*
9 Global warming. Oh no!	**Chant:**
10 Learn to change or learn to swim.	Save Mother Earth, She's been with us since birth!
11 You say you love your children but you are destroying their future.	Save Mother Earth, She's been with us since birth!
12 Respect existence or expect resistance.	Where is your emotion, There's plastic in ocean! Where is your emotion, There's plastic in ocean!

Case study 21.1 Youth assembly on climate

The global student mobilisation on climate change is a source of great hope for democracy, a type of democracy which incorporates equality, social justice, protection for the environment and genuine climate action. The Youth Assembly featured in this case study recognises the importance of providing a platform for young people to articulate their views and an opportunity for them to design and shape climate actions and solutions.

The national Irish broadcasting service Radio Teilifís Éireann (RTÉ) and the National Parliament (Houses of the Oireachtas) facilitated the country's first ever Youth Assembly on Climate in Leinster House, Dublin, (home of the national parliament). This was a chance for young people to discuss what Ireland needs to do to tackle issues around the climate crisis. Children/young people between the ages of 10 and 17 could apply, with a parent or guardian's permission. As part of the application, children included information about climate or environmental projects they have been involved in, as well as a one-minute video pitch. Some 157 applicants were selected. These children/young people from all over Ireland gathered in the Dáil to discuss the climate crisis and look at solutions. On Friday, 15 November 2019, the Youth Assembly on Climate, called on adults and elected representatives to take action on their recommendations on climate change.

Sitting in the seats of their TDs (Teachta Dála or Members of Parliament) the children focused on and debated climate disruption's growing impact on environment, economics, food and farming, energy and education. The event was chaired by Ceann Comhairle (Speaker), Seán Ó Fearghaíl and broadcast live on national television in two sessions: The first setting the agenda, the second to ratify a climate proclamation – coinciding with the centenary of the first Dáil (first meeting of Irish Parliament). An 11-year-old girl from St. Augustine's NS, Clontuskert, Ballinasloe highlighted the global impacts of climate change, especially on the poorest people, and the need to end fossil fuel use, deforestation and biodiversity loss.

The delegates issued this statement:

'We, the youth of Ireland, call on our elected representatives and on adults to listen. We put forward our recommendations for action to stop climate breakdown. We are NOT experts. In our recommendations we offer ideas but we do NOT have answers. It is a starting point for adults and particularly for those elected to protect and progress our society. We call on you to listen to the science, to take on board our Recommendations and to work on our behalf to ensure that we – and you – have a future.'

The 157 delegates of the RTÉ Youth Assembly issued these 10 recommendations:

1   From your corner store to your supermarket, we call on the house to incentivise and obligate the installation of glass doors on open refrigerators.
2   For Ireland to ban the importation of fracked gas and invest solely in renewables.
3   Implementing measures that will allow that Irish goods be both eco-sustainable and affordable in todays' Irish Market.
4   Implement a tiered tax on emissions from large companies including those under capital Emissions Trading Scheme (ETS). This tax must be increased every year while threshold decreases, shifting the burden from individuals to corporations.

5 Investment in industrial hemp facilities to provide a viable, sustainable and alternative land use for farmers as well as employment in rural Ireland.
6 A labelling and pricing system showing the climate impact of food products based on criteria such as impact of packaging and distance travelled.
7 Ireland to outlaw acts of ecocide – the widespread and systematic loss of ecosystems, including climate and cultural damage.
8 Protect existing forests and make compulsory that at least 10% of all land owned for agricultural uses is dedicated to forestry.
9 A targeted nationwide information campaign to educate the population about the climate crisis regarding the causes, the effects and the solutions.
10 Mandatory 'sustainability' education from primary level to the workplace including a new compulsory Junior Cycle and optional Leaving Certificate subject.

Action 2: Organise a school assembly on climate

Teaching about climate change requires dedicated allocated time. This book demonstrates that many curricular objectives can be achieved through climate change education. Following a climate change month of activities in school, or participation in any climate change project described in this book, an assembly can be organised whereby each class is invited to devise one climate recommendation or action. These recommendations can be shared with the school community during an assembly. Additional excitement is generated by inviting guests to listen to the children, by recording the presentations and by generating a framed portrait of the school's climate charter.

Remaining hopeful during challenging times: Covid-19 and climate change

From a climate change point of view, there is much to learn from the global response to Covid-19. Indeed, the pandemic itself may have been a manifestation of the dysfunctional relationship between humans and the natural world. While Covid-19 crept upon us like a silent fog, we have had years of warning about climate change. Scientists have long recognised that carbon dioxide emissions and their resulting effects have been increasing exponentially. Nevertheless, political and societal responses are slow. Even in the face of a looming crisis such as Covid-19, societies reacted too slowly despite undisputable evidence and exponential growth (Klenert et al., 2020). Yet action when it was taken was decisive and effective. Delays in containment measures are costly. From a climate perspective, decisive action now will ultimately reduce future costs and damages dramatically.

In some jurisdictions, scientists were hailed as heroes during the pandemic. In a minority of cases, they were demonised for allegedly spreading misinformation. In any event, epidemiologists, virologists and immunologists became household names. Advances in clinical care, prevention, treatment and the speed of vaccine development were unprecedented, driven by global collaboration and data sharing. In effect, science became fashionable. Surely, we have now surpassed the time to act on the scientific evidence of climate change. During Covid-19, the importance of international organisations, such as the World Health Organisation, was illustrated. It is even more pertinent for us to heed the advice of international bodies such as the UN, the Intergovernmental Panel on Climate Change (IPCC) and international treaties such as the Paris Climate Agreement. Vaccinations for Covid-19 became a metaphor of hope. Unlike Covid-19, there is no vaccination which can be taken to avert the impact of climate change. In medical terms, we need to treat the disease of climate change, manage its symptoms and roll out the cure (decarbonisation) in a manner which is equitable, fair and just. If left untreated, this disease will kill humanity.

States were able to mobilise an extraordinary amount of physical, economic, political and social resources to deal with Covid-19. A similar impetus in the long-term resource mobilisation towards combatting climate change is required. The many benefits from such investment include a greener, safer, more sustainable and humane society. A multi-billion global investment in green energy will not only save lives, it will ultimately be economically cost efficient in the long term.

The European Commission has launched a European Green Deal which will mobilise €100 billion over the period 2021–2027 (European Commission, 2019). By moving to a clean, circular economy and by taking actions to restore biodiversity, this Green Deal provides an action plan to boost the efficient use of resources. Described by the EU Commission President Ursula Van der Leyen as a 'European man on the moon moment,' the Green Deal is a sign of hope, solidarity and consensus.

During Covid-19 we were given a glimpse of a different world. Difference is possible, a prospect which may be hopeful for some while worrying for others. There will be no time when society is back to 'normal' as Covid-19 has changed our concepts of 'normal.' We now have a space between old concepts of normal and new, re-imagined, better ideas about 'normal.' In any event 'normal life' was not good for everyone. New stories might now be recalled, crafted and remade for this time and place. This is the time for a pedagogy of hope.

Action 3: Climate legacy digital time capsule project.

In some schools in Ireland, children were invited to compile a time capsule to record their experiences of the Covid-19 pandemic and subsequent lockdowns. Time capsules are a well-recognised but underutilised resource for documenting a school's story. The year 1995 was designated as *European Nature Conservation Year.* To mark the year, a project entitled *20–20 vision* was launched in the United Kingdom and Ireland. Commencing in 1995, the project ran throughout the year, concluding with the burial of time capsules in February 1996. Children in schools across England, Wales, Scotland, Northern Ireland and the Republic of Ireland were encouraged to think about their environment, to consider what had happened to it over the previous 25 years, and to predict how it might change over the following 25 years by 2020. Various environmental themes were discussed at the time.

The time capsules give a fascinating insight into how children in 1995 imagined the year 2020, as shown by the contents of the capsule retrieved by different schools. In some capsules, the material was damaged and information could not be retrieved.

Contents included the following; children's vision for 2020; an audio tape of interviews with various people comparing the 1970s with 1995, and looking ahead to 2020; newspaper cuttings from the 1970s and 1995; school projects on recycling, global warming, greenhouse effect, and pollution; photographs of the school and of the participants; video footage of the school and its environs; information on endangered animals; messages to the children of 2020; and letters from people in the local and national community.

It is now possible to compile a digital climate change capsule. Such capsules unlike physical versions do not require physical storage. They can be archived on a computer and retrieved regularly. Such an archive could include the following:

- Children's letter to their future selves
- Newspaper clippings documenting climate change events
- Samples of climate change projects and research
- Interviews with parents and local people

Compiling a climate time capsule provides an opportunity to document personal, school-based, local and national climate change actions. The act of documenting children's work provides a focus for several curricular areas including literacy, numeracy, geography and art. More importantly, such resources will provide invaluable historical data for children in a relatively short-time scale.

Inspiration for hope from nature: Rediscovering the wonders of Earth

Nature is constantly a source of hope, inspiration and beauty. As a species, humans are intimately tied to nature. We need clean air to breathe, water to drink and healthy soil for the production of nutritious food. However, nature is now flashing red warning signs of system failure. We must urgently fix our broken relationship with nature. Without urgent action, significant damage to human and ecological well-being is inevitable. A revival or rewilding of the natural world has to be part of our transition to a sustainable way of living. According to David Attenborough (2020), rewilding the world is the most efficient means of recapturing carbon and restoring biodiversity. Nature is our greatest ally; therefore, it is in our interest to work with rather than against nature. The renowned conservationist urges us to look to nature for solutions. Such solutions recognise that our economies and societies are underpinned by nature. They include actions that protect, sustainably manage, restore and enhance ecosystems. Such actions include planting more forests, changing the way we farm, changing our diet and methods of soil carbon sequestration.

In schools, children need to learn about the wonders of nature and how nature works. Many curriculum theories for primary education advocate outdoor learning, play and direct contact with nature. Pestalozzi influenced by the work of Rousseau promoted a holistic approach to education which involved a balance between the hand, heart and head. Froebel pioneered play as learning and outdoor play was a central element in his philosophy of learning. Frobel's notion of the 'kindergarten' (literally translated as children's garden) includes a key focus on the natural environment. Montessori developed ideas about outdoor sensory play and the importance of using natural materials for teaching children. Steiner education incorporates outdoor time both for informal play and for the formal learning curriculum. These philosophical theories highlight the importance of outdoor learning for all children (Dolan, 2016). Nonetheless, concerns about children's current and future relationships with the environment are well documented. Louv's (2010) discussions about 'nature-deficit disorder' describe the human cost of alienation from nature, including physical and emotional illness, reduced use of the senses and attention difficulties.

Action 4: Rediscover the power of nature through biomimicry

Biomimicry is innovation inspired by nature. Other than humans, living organisms know what works and what is appropriate for living on this planet. For instance, leaves represent the world's best water distribution network. In biomimicry, biologists are brought to the design table to share nature-based solutions. How is a leaf designed to maximise its potential as a solar cell for photosynthesis? How does nature hold and store liquids? How does nature repel liquid? (Benyus, 2009).

Biomimicry is popular in the design disciplines including engineering and architecture because people are searching for sustainable solutions. Scientists and engineers use observations from nature to develop some of the most innovative technologies. For example, the design of a bullet train was informed by a kingfisher's bill. A mechanical arm was created based on the design of a seahorse tail. One of the oldest examples of innovation inspired by nature is Velcro created by George de Mestral, a Swiss Engineer. One day, on returning home from hunting in the Alps, he noticed many burr seeds stuck to his clothes and his dog's fur. He then examined the seeds under a microscope and noticed many tiny hook-like structures throughout the seed's surface. These small hooks connected with multiple loops on surfaces of fabric, hair or fur. This was the same principle used by de Mestral to create what was later to become known as Velcro, an easy durable and safe material used to bind objects together. Velcro is found everywhere from home to outer space. Indeed, it proved invaluable in the Aerospace industry when it was used to allow astronauts to manoeuvre in and out of their bulky space suits. The name Velcro, is derived from the French word velour ('velvet') and crochet ('hook').

By mimicking the shapes, materials and structures found in nature, we can develop new products, materials and architecture to solve human design challenges. Design thinking described in Chapter 11 is heavily influenced by biomimicry. Nature offers many lessons in waste reduction and elimination, re-use of resources and regeneration of natural systems. Moving our systems from a make-use-dispose approach to a more circular model not only saves resources, but it is also much more cost efficient. Children and teachers become involved in such design activities when they take time to learn from the natural world. The following tasks allow children to focus on sustainable solutions by adopting a problem-solving approach.

Design task (using natural materials)

1   Design a seat for Teddy in the garden using natural materials ensuring the structure is robust and comfortable.
2   Build a bird's nest with twigs, fabric and moss.
3   In a woodland area design a village.

During the discussion, focus on observations and key learning moments. Ask the children to notice the position of the sun as a source of heat. By looking around their creations, children can identify opportunities and threats in the locality such as a river, a tree or evidence of a badger's den. Children can discuss reasons for their choice of materials, division of labour and choice of location. They can consider advantages and disadvantages of their creation. The experience can be recorded though pictures, maps, video and narrative writing in the classroom.

Design task (using LEGO)

Robotics is an evolving industry along with a new generation of learning using LEGO robotics. Also known as Lego Mindstorms, LEGO robotics involves the use of robots for teaching coding and logical reasoning in schools. Through LEGO Robotics, children of all ages are introduced to engineering, mathematics and robotics principles. They are also given the opportunity to develop their critical thinking and problem-solving skills.

The FIRST LEGO League (FLL) is an international competition involving children (11 to 16 years) from over 90 countries. FIRST is an acronym for 'For Inspiration and Recognition of Science and Technology,' and the FLL encourages children to think like scientists and engineers, developing practical solutions to real-world issues. Every year, FLL releases a new Challenge based on a real-world, scientific theme. Sustainability themes feature regularly. For *Climate Connections,* children were invited to focus on the Earth's past, present and future climates. Children researched a local climate problem, devised solutions and shared their results. For the challenge, *Food Factor,* children were invited to improve the quality of food by finding ways to prevent food contamination. Children have had the opportunity to explore awe-inspiring storms, quakes, waves and natural disasters to address the theme *Nature's Fury.* Solutions for the waste problem were devised by children as part of the *Trash Trek* challenge. The transportation, use and disposal of water featured in the *Hydro Dynamics Challenge* (Figure 21.3). Through the City Shaper project, children worked as architects. Addressing the concept of sustainable cities, children were invited to address the challenges facing cities including transportation, accessibility and even natural disasters.

Specific challenges from the City Shaper project included the following (Ruiz et al., 2020:9696):

1   Expert in biodiversity and energy
    Challenge 1. Build a sustainable garden or orchard in a city (Sustainable roof).
    Challenge 2. Create an energy source that takes advantage of wind gusts (Wind Turbine).

Figure 21.3 Problem solving with LEGO

2 Expert in mobility and energy
  Challenge 3. Build a marquee that reacts to traffic and emits light (Marquee).
  Challenge 4. Create an energy source that takes advantage of sunlight. (Photovoltaic field).
3 Expert in efficiency and recycling
  Challenge 5. Create a lighting system that optimises and saves light (Urban lighting).
  Challenge 6. Make a building for recycling (waste separation).

Even if children are not participating in FLL, all of these challenges are applicable for design thinking using LEGO. Once again in teams, the children can research their ideas, create a model and present their work to a wider audience. Solutions inspired by nature will extend the children's experience of biomimicry.

Evoking hope: Re-imagining the future through story and art

There is an urgent need to introduce new ways of thinking, new ways of seeing ourselves as part of a larger whole, where we all take responsibility for our actions and expressions (Cagle, 2014). Ultimately, we need to revise or re-visualise our view about what a normal society looks like (Boyle, 2012) – one based on renewable energy sources. The age of fossil fuel no longer serves our best interests. We, and future generations, need to understand, share and help enact, a new low or zero-carbon story (Hicks, 2018).

Telling stories is a familiar aspect of primary education. The decision to tell stories about the environment in general and climate change in particular is political in nature. Those who are afraid to discuss controversial issues with children, tend to avoid these stories, while other teachers welcome the accessibility of stories for engaging children's thoughts and opinions. Children need a narrative of hope. Stories of progress over time demonstrate that humanity has achieved so much in terms of quality of life, mortality rates and technological developments. Learning about the successful resolution of past adversities also highlights human agency. Indeed, the number of new children's books looking at the climate crisis, global warming and the natural world have dramatically increased. Some publishers are referring to this renewed interest in environmental publications as the 'Greta effect.' Illustrations and stories from children's environmental picturebooks provide a powerful resource for developing critical visual literacy (Dolan, 2014; Roche, 2014). Authors such as Nicola Davies, author of *The Promise* (Figure 21.1) presents a lifelong love of nature in her books. Her writing focuses on the natural world and human relationships with it. Picturebooks provide multiple opportunities for exploring environmental themes in general and climate change, in particular, critically and creatively (Dolan, 2014).

Stories can be told using text-based and visual formats. The visual arts provide a powerful medium through which children can reflect on people, the environment and the interconnections between the two. In many cases, the visual message of art can be more accessible and easier to grasp than the message in a written text (Vasudevan, 2008). For younger children in particular, the visual message of art is more accessible. Art has always been a powerful tool when pointing out injustice, human rights violations or damage to the environment (Desai, 2002). Artists today explore ideas, concepts, questions and practices that examine the past, describe the present and imagine the future (Hicks and King, 2007). Through art, children can create new understandings about climate change which are informed by other curricular areas, e.g., literacy and science. Artists, in whatever medium they work, can create works that explore the causes, impacts and solutions of climate change. Art allows children to make sense of complex issues such as climate change.

Action 5: Create a picturebook about climate actions and solutions

Creating a class picturebook allows children and teachers to think critically, creatively and hopefully about climate change. Children can create an A-to-Z book of climate change and its impacts on their locality, country and world. Alternatively, a story based on a dilemma caused by climate change, followed by a solution provides an opportunity for children to consider potential solutions.

One teacher, Rachel Collins worked with her class exploring the issue of climate-related migration through the lens of the Syrian civil war. Links between the Syrian conflict and climate change have been well documented (Selby et al., 2017). Climate change was a contributory factor to the extreme drought experienced in Syria, prior to civil war. This exacerbated socio-economic distress, which eventually contributed to Syria's descent into war. Large-scale migration ensued. Eleven-year-old children in Rachel's class researched the war in Syria and the associated journey of Syrians fleeing for safety. The children were invited to create a class story, illustrating the journey of a child from Syria to Greece. Younger children in the school (8-year-old children) were invited to illustrate the story (Figure 21.4).

Transformative climate change education

Climate change education, handled in an age-appropriate and sensitive way (Sobel, 2008), equips and empowers children for their future. Well-designed action projects which facilitate children's climate actions are both hopeful and future-oriented. Such initiatives offer hope in uncertain times (Hicks, 2014). They encourage children to reconsider their own agency and think positively about their futures. Some argue that individual actions are insufficient, as climate change is a systemic problem requiring a complete overhaul of national and international values. However, Waldron et al. (2019) present a dynamic picture of climate change education which 'conceptualises children as present citizens capable of collective action.'

Calls for more action from education have increased in the light of mounting anxiety over environmental problems. While there are numerous policy instruments and technical solutions for mitigating and responding to climate change, changing the behaviour of individuals and organisations is one critical element of the process. Some education programmes have enhanced our understanding of the causes of climate change. However, there is little evidence to suggest that this knowledge is sufficient to change the behaviours responsible for climate change (Eilam and Trop, 2012). Ironically, it is often those who are well educated, who live the most intensive carbon lifestyles. It is now time to close the gap between knowledge and action. Notwithstanding the importance of individual actions, there is a greater need for industries, governments and multi-corporations to address the challenges posed by climate change. A politically astute electorate has the power to elect politicians committed to prioritising climate change action.

There is widespread consensus in the literature that education has a key role to play in our attempts to realise ecologically sustainable development (Bamber, 2019). To facilitate transformative climate change education, children need to have opportunities to

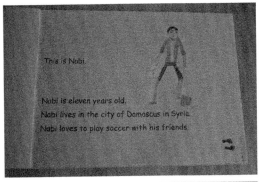

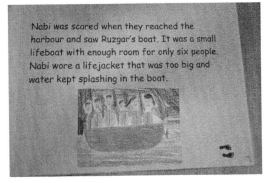

Figure 21.4 A selection of pages from *Nabi's Story*: The picturebook created by second class (8 years) and fifth class (11 years) children

Source: Collins and Dolan (2020:27)

Table 21.4 Key elements of climate change education

Knowledge and understanding	Skills	Values and attitudes
Sustainable development	Creative and critical thinking	Concern for the environment and commitment to sustainable development
Human rights	Co-operation and conflict resolution	Belief that people can bring about change
Globalisation and interdependence	Ability to manage complexity and uncertainty	Respect for people and human rights
Power and governance	Informed and reflective action	Commitment to social justice and equity

Source: Trócaire (2018:2)

design and participate in actions which address the causes and solutions of climate change. This involves connecting children with nature, assisting them to co-construct knowledge about environmental and sustainability issues, and enabling them to participate in positive change for sustainability.

Transformative climate change education values, encourages and supports children to be problem-solvers, problem-seekers and action-takers in their own environments (Davis, 2014). Teachers who operate within a transformative framework provide children with opportunities to follow open-ended and self-directed paths of learning. This makes links with children's experiences and issues, explores alternative ways of thinking about issues such as climate change, and gives children power (MacNaughton, 2003).

Many schools are involved in innovative and transformative climate change education. Table 21.4 illustrates key elements of climate change education.

Action 6: Taking action for climate change

Hope, personal agency and action are interrelated. As the title of Greta Thunberg's (2019a) book suggests 'no one is too small to make a difference.' Greta's collection of speeches is sobering but tentatively hopeful. Encouraging and inspiring individuals to take personal actions to mitigate climate change is promoted by many (Lorenzoni et al., 2007; O'Neill and Nicholson-Cole, 2009; Wolf and Moser, 2011). Such actions include those outlined in Table 21.5.

Conclusion

We can be absolutely certain that climate change will have a significant impact on all aspects of our lives. Nevertheless, the world appears to be unprepared for the anticipated political, cultural and economic events which will unfold over the next 30–50 years. As educators we have a moral duty to tell the story of climate change. Rebecca Solnit (2016:ix) reminds us that 'progressive, populist and grassroots constituencies have had many victories' and that 'popular power has continued to be a powerful force for change.'

Table 21.5 Actions for climate change

Actions to address climate change

Food: Buy local organic food. Reduce consumption of meat and encourage vegetarian options. Animals emit methane and other greenhouse gases. A meat-free diet contributes to a reduction in global warming.

Spread the message about climate change: Spend time discussing climate change. Conduct research about its causes and impacts. Write an article about climate change reflecting your research for your local newspaper

Everyone in the school community should know and understand the impact climate change has on children. Based on your research create a quiz for each class level.

Curriculum: Explore links to climate change across all subject areas.

Create a climate change game and market your game as a birthday and/or Christmas present

Interview a person who is conducting positive action to combat climate change, e.g., a person who eats less meat, or lives in a highly efficient energy home.

Energy and Transport: Conserve energy. Switch off lights. Turn down the heating. Wear extra clothes. Insulate and ventilate. Investigate the possibility of using renewable energy

Encourage children to walk or cycle to school. For those who travel in cars highlight the importance of car-pooling.

Materials: Recycle everything. Ban the use of single-use plastics. Use biodegradable cleaning materials. Set up a swap day or sharing library for items that children do not use every day.

Carbon footprint: Calculate the school's carbon footprint and set annual targets for its reduction. Devise a list of actions for reducing our carbon footprint. Illustrate, publish and disseminate this list as widely as possible.

Support the work of organisations addressing the issue of climate change:

Invite a guest speaker to address your class about climate change actions.

Conduct a fund-raising activity for a non-governmental organisation which supports communities affected by climate change.

Political action: Many schools have a green-schools or eco-committee. Such a committee can address the issue of climate crisis in a democratic forum.

Make a climate change presentation to a local councillor and/or politician. This is particularly important at election time. Record this presentation and place it on the school website.

Write a letter to the President/ Prime Minister about your climate change work.

Hope does not mean denying the realities of climate change, it means facing and addressing them while adopting actions for change.

Archbishop Desmond Tutu (2011) describes himself as a 'prisoner of hope,' whereby he argues that within every challenging scenario there are rays of light which can support action. For Tutu, hope brings energy. Indeed, it is imperative for educators to remain hopeful and to use hope as an educational strategy. Covid-19 inspired a fundamental rethinking about the role of science and knowledge, the importance of competent leadership including global cooperation, and how the fate of the most vulnerable anywhere affects the fortunes of all citizens everywhere. The pandemic has shown us that we are capable of timely, creative and urgent responses.

The student movement to save the planet from climate change seems to have appeared suddenly and spontaneously. Social networking enabled its rapid spread. History shows us that such organisations can disappear quickly. There is a need to link this call for action with political mobilisation. At a time when so many people are alienated from politics, it is easy to despair. Issues such as climate change may potentially generate feelings of hopelessness and fear. In the interest of empowering citizens to take action, climate change education is imperative for political and business leaders, as well as in all levels of education. Indeed, many young people are protesting because they have experienced climate change education in primary and secondary schools.

This book is written from a perspective of hope. I would like to invite all primary teachers to try out some of the activities documented in this book, to share them with colleagues and to create a curriculum for hope in their school. The activities in this book will only achieve their potential if adopted by schools. Feel free to share some of your success stories, images and testimonials with the authors of this book.

Children have a right to be hopeful and ultimately, they deserve a sustainable future. Should current levels of unsustainable living continue, it is our children who have the most to lose as they will have to deal with the inevitable impacts of unsustainability in the future. Children are entitled to a pedagogy of hope. In the worlds of Michelle Obama (2011:np) 'don't ever underestimate the impact you can have, because history has shown us that courage can be contagious, and hope can take on a life of its own.'

References

Attenborough, D. (2020) *A life on our planet: My witness statement and a vision for the future.* London: Random House.

Benyus, J. (2009) *Biomimicry in action.* TED Talk 2009. https://www.ted.com/talks/janine_benyus_biomimicry_in_action?language=en.

Bonnett, M. (2013) Normalising catastrophe: Sustainability and scientism. *Environmental Education Research, 19*(2), 187–197, DOI: 10.1080/13504622.2012.753414.

Boyle (2012) *Renewable energy: Power for a sustainable future.* Oxford: Oxford University Press.

Cagle, L. (2014) *Transformative learning and systems thinking: NWEI's pedagogy for sustainability.* Retrieved from: http://www.nwei.org/assets/Transformative- Learning-and-NWEI-Overview.pdf.

Chawla, L. (1999) Life paths into effective environmental action. *Journal of Environmental Education, 31*(1), 15–26.

Collins, R. and Dolan, A.M. (2020) Understanding migration through children's literature. *Primary Geography, 101,* 28–29. Sheffield: Geographical Association.

Davies, N. and Carlin, L. (illus) (2014) *The Promise.* Somerville, MA: Candlewick.

Davis, J.M. (ed.) (2014) *Young children and the environment.* Cambridge: Cambridge University Press.

DES, DOH & HSE, (2015) *Well-being in primary schools guidelines for mental health promotion.* https://www.education.ie/en/Publications/Education-Reports/Well-Being-in-Primary-Schools-Guidelines-for-Mental-Health-Promotion.pdf.

Desai, D. (2002) The ethnographic move in contemporary art: What does it mean for art education? *Studies in Art Education, 43,* 307–323.

Diamond, J. (2019) *Upheaval: Turning points for nations in crises.* New York: Little Brown.

Dolan, A.M. (2012) Futures talk over story time. *Primary Geography*, 78(2), 26–17. Sheffield: Geographical Association.

Dolan, A.M. (2014) *You, me and diversity: Picturebooks for teaching development and intercultural education.* London: Routledge.

Dolan, A.M. (2016) Place-based curriculum making: Devising a synthesis between primary geography and outdoor learning. *Journal of Adventure Education and Outdoor Learning*, 16(1), 49–62.

Dolan, A.M. (2020) *Powerful primary geography: A toolkit for 21st century learning.* London: Routledge.

Eilam, E. and Trop, T. (2012) Environmental attitudes and environmental behavior – Which is the horse and which is the cart? *Sustainability*, 4(9), 2210–2246.

European Commission. (2019) *Communication from the commission: The European green deal.* Brussels: European Commission.

Freire, P. (1994) *A pedagogy of hope.* London: Continuum.

Gough, I. (2017) *Heat, greed and human need: Climate change, capitalism and sustainable wellbeing.* Cheltenham, SA: Edward Elgar Publishing.

Hayes, K. and Poland, B. (2018) Addressing mental health in a changing climate: Incorporating mental health indicators into climate change and health vulnerability and adaptation assessments. *International Journal of Environmental Research and Public Health*, 15(9), 1806.

Hicks, D. (2006) Stories of hope: A response to the psychology of despair. In *Lessons for the future: The missing dimension in education.* Victoria, BC: Trafford, pp. 68–77. Available online at www.teaching4abetterworld.co.uk (last accessed 10 June 2013).

Hicks, D. (2014) A geography of hope. *Geography*, 99(1), 5–12.

Hicks, D. (2018) Why we still need a geography of hope. *Geography*, 103(2), 78–85.

Hicks, D. The Geographer as Scout: Engaging with climate change.

Hicks, L. and King, R. (2007) Confronting environmental collapse: Visual culture, art education, and environmental responsibility. *Studies in Art Education*, 48(4), 332–335.

Kelsey, E. and Armstrong, C. (2012) Finding hope in a world of environmental catastrophe. In Wals, A. and Corcoran, P. eds., *Learning for sustainability in times of accelerating change.* Netherlands: Wageningen, pp. 187–200.

Klenert, D., Funke, F., Mattauch, L. and O'Callaghan, B. (2020) Five lessons from COVID-19 for advancing climate change mitigation. *Environmental and Resource Economics*, 7, 751–778.

Lorenzoni, I., Nicholson-Cole, S. and Whitmarsh, L. (2007) Barriers perceived to engaging with climate change among the UK public and their policy implications. *Global Environmental Change*, 17(3–4), pp. 445–459.

Louv, R. (2006) *Last child in the woods. Saving our children from nature-deficit disorder.* Chapel Hill: Algonquin books.

Louv, R. (2010) *Last child in the woods: Saving our children from nature-deficit disorder.* Atlantic Books.

Louv, R. (2016) *Vitamin N: The essential guide to a nature-rich life.* Chapel Hill: Algonquin Books.

Lowe, I. (2007) Climate change and our children's future. *Every Child*, 13(1), 4.

MacNaughton, G. (2003) *Shaping early childhood learners, curriculum and contexts.* Berkshire, England: Open University Press.

Marlon, J.R., Bloodhart, B., Ballew, M.T., Rolfe-Redding, J., Roser-Renouf, C., Leiserowitz, A. and Maibach, E. (2019) How hope and doubt affect climate change mobilisation. *Frontiers in Communication*, 4, 20.

O'Neill, S. and Nicholson-Cole, S. (2009) 'Fear won't do it' promoting positive engagement with climate change through visual and iconic representations. *Science Communication*, 30(3), 355–379.

Obama, M. (2011) *Address to the young African Women Leaders Forum.* Soweto, South Africa: Regina Mundi Church. https://obamawhitehouse.archives.gov/the-press-office/2011/06/22/remarks-first-lady-during-keynote-address-young-african-women-leaders-forum.

Ojala, M. (2012) Hope and climate change: The importance of hope for environmental engagement among young people. *Environmental Education Research*, 18(5), 625–642.

Ojala, M. (2015) Hope in the face of climate change: Associations with environmental engagement and student perceptions of teachers' emotion communication style and future orientation. *The Journal of Environmental Education*, 46(3), 133–148.

Paterson, M. and Newell, P. (2010) *Climate capitalism: Global warming and the transformation of the global economy*. Cambridge: Cambridge University Press, pp. 129–140.

Roche, M. (2014) *Developing children's critical thinking through picturebooks: A guide for primary and early years students and teachers*. London: Routledge.

Ruiz Vicente, F., Zapatera Llinares, A. and Montés Sánchez, N. (2020) 'Sustainable city': A steam project using robotics to bring the city of the future to primary education students. *Sustainability*, 12(22), 9696.

Scoffham, S. (2020) 'Hope is not enough' paper delivered at the TEESNET online conference *Education as a Pedagogy of Hope and Possibility: The Role of Teacher Education in Leading Narratives of Change*. Thursday September 17th.

Selby, J., Dahi, O.S., Fröhlich, C. and Hulme, M. (2017) Climate change and the Syrian civil war revisited. *Political Geography*, 60, 232–244.

Snyder, C.R. (2000a) *The psychology of hope*. New York: Free Press.

Snyder, C.R. (2000b) The past and possible futures of hope. *Journal of Social and Clinical Psychology*, 19, 11–28.

Sobel, D. (2008) *Childhood and nature: Design principles for educators*. Portland, ME: Stenhouse Publishers.

Solnit, R. (2016) *Hope in the dark: Untold histories, wild possibilities*. Chicago: Haymarket Books.

Solnit, R. (2020) *The impossible has already happened: What Coronavirus can teach us about hope*. The Guardian. https://www.theguardian.com/world/2020/apr/07/what-coronavirus-can-teach-us-about-hope-rebecca-solnit.

Sterling, S. (2001) *Sustainable education: Re-visioning learning and change. Schumacher briefings*. Schumacher UK: CREATE.

Stoknes, P.E (2017) *How to transform apocalypse fatigue into action on global warming*. Ted Talk. https://www.ted.com/talks/per_espen_stoknes_how_to_transform_apocalypse_fatigue_into_action_on_global_warming?language=en.

Thunberg, G. (2019a) *No one is too small to make a difference*. London: Penguin.

Thunberg, G. (2019b) The disarming case to act right now on climate change Ted Talk https://www.ted.com/talks/greta_thunberg_the_disarming_case_to_act_right_now_on_climate.

Tutu, D. (2011) *God has a dream: A vision of hope for our times*. New York: Random House.

Vasudevan, L. (2008) A picture can do things words can't: Transforming representations in literacy research. In Flood, J., Lapp, D. and Heath, S.B. eds., *Handbook of research on teaching literacy through the visual and communicative arts*, Vol. 2. Mahwah, NJ: Lawrence Erlbaum Associates, pp. 187–194.

Waldron, F., Ruane, B., Oberman, R. and Morris, S. (2019) Geographical process or global injustice? Contrasting educational perspectives on climate change. *Environmental Education Research*, 25(6), 895–911.

Wolf, J. and Moser, S.C. (2011) Individual understandings, perceptions, and engagement with climate change: Insights from in-depth studies across the world. *Wiley Interdisciplinary Reviews: Climate Change*, 2(4), pp. 547–569.

Appendix 1

Climate Change Glossary

Anthropocene A proposed geological age, viewed as the period during which human activity has been the dominant influence on climate and the environment.

Anthropogenic This describes a process or result generated by human beings.

Atmosphere The mass of air surrounding the Earth.

Building Energy Rating (BER) A BER certificate indicates a home's energy performance. It is similar to the energy label for household appliances. The certificate rates the energy performance of a home on a scale of A–G. A-rated homes are the most energy efficient and will tend to have the lowest energy bills. In Ireland, BER ratings are carried out by BER Assessors registered with the Sustainable Energy Authority of Ireland.

Biodegradable waste Organic waste, typically from plant or animal sources (for example, food scraps and paper), which other living organisms can break down.

Biodiversity or 'biological diversity' This means the variety of life on this planet and related interactions within habitats and ecosystems. Biodiversity covers all plants, animals and micro-organisms on land and in water.

Bioenergy All types of energy derived from biomass, including biofuels.

Biomass A source of fuel made from living and recently-dead plant materials such as wood, leaves and the biodegradable part of industrial and municipal waste.

Biofuels Renewable fuels derived from biological materials including crops such as maize and sugar cane, and some forms of waste.

Business as usual A 'business as usual' scenario represents a worst case where countries continue to burn oil, gas and coal unabated – in contrast with a world where emissions have been dramatically reduced, and global warming is more moderate.

Carbon Carbon is a chemical element, like hydrogen, oxygen, lead or any of the others in the periodic table. In the context of climate change, 'carbon' is commonly used as a shorthand for carbon dioxide, the most important greenhouse gas released by humans. Technically, however, this isn't accurate. Carbon only becomes carbon dioxide when each atom of carbon joins with two atoms of oxygen (hence the chemical formula of carbon dioxide, CO_2). Carbon molecules move around the Earth system in the carbon cycle.

Carbon cycle The carbon cycle is nature's way of reusing carbon atoms, which travel from the atmosphere into organisms in the Earth and then back into the atmosphere over and over again. Most carbon is stored in rocks and sediments, while the rest is stored in the ocean, atmosphere and living organisms. These are the reservoirs, or sinks for carbon. Marine organisms from marsh plants to fish, from seaweed to birds, also produce carbon through living and dying. Sometimes dead organisms become fossil fuels that go through combustion, giving off CO_2, and the cycle continues. Flowers, plants and trees need CO_2 to stay alive. They take it out of the atmosphere when they breathe in as part of the carbon cycle.

Carbon credit   A carbon credit is a tradable permit or certificate that provides the holder of the credit the right to emit one ton of CO_2 or an equivalent of another greenhouse gas. The main goal for the creation of carbon credits is the reduction of emissions of CO_2 and other greenhouse gases from industrial activities to reduce the effects of global warming. (See carbon offset)

Carbon dioxide (CO_2)   Carbon dioxide is a colourless gas in the Earth's atmosphere. It is produced naturally from animals and people in exhaled air and the decay of plants. It is also a by-product of human activities such as burning fossil fuels. It is removed from the atmosphere by photosynthesis in plants and by dissolving in water, especially on the surface of oceans. CO_2 is the principal anthropogenic (caused by humans) greenhouse gas. The use of fossil fuels for energy is increasing the concentration of CO_2 in the atmosphere, which is believed to contribute to global warming.

Carbon emissions   In the context of climate change, CO_2 is released when substances, especially oil, gas and coal, are burned by vehicles and planes, by factories and by homes.

Carbon footprint   A measure of the impact our activities have on the environment. This is reported in the amount of carbon emitted by an individual or organization, in a given period of time, or the amount of carbon emitted during the manufacture of a product.

Carbon leakage   Carbon leakage refers to the situation that may occur if, for reasons of costs related to climate policies, businesses were to transfer production to other countries with laxer emission constraints. This could lead to an increase in their total emissions.

Carbon neutral   Carbon neutral is a term used to describe the state of an entity (such as a company, service, product or event), where the carbon emissions caused by them have been balanced out by funding an equivalent amount of carbon savings elsewhere in the world.

Carbon offset   A unit, equal to one ton of CO_2, that individuals, companies or governments buy to reduce short-term and long-term emissions of greenhouse gases. The payment usually funds projects that generate energy from renewable sources such as wind or flowing water. Individuals can choose whether to buy an offset (for example to compensate for air travel), but governments and large industries are sometimes required to buy them to meet international targets aimed at reducing greenhouse gases.

Carbon sink   Any process, activity or mechanism that removes carbon from the atmosphere. The biggest carbon sinks are the world's oceans and forests, which absorb large amounts of CO_2 from the Earth's atmosphere.

Carbon sequestration (carbon capture and storage)   The process involved in carbon capture and the long-term storage of atmospheric CO_2 or other forms to mitigate or defer global warming. It has been proposed as a way to slow the atmospheric and marine accumulation of greenhouse gases which are released by burning fossil fuels.

Carbon source An organism or landscape which emits carbon.

Carbon tax A tax on fuels according to their carbon content. Carbon taxes are designed to encourage people and businesses to use fuels with less carbon and reduce the amount of energy they use.

Carpooling Sharing a car to a destination to reduce fuel use, pollution and travel costs.

Chlorofluorocarbons (CFCs) Short for 'chlorofluorocarbons', which are chemicals used in manufacturing (and, in the past, in aerosol cans and refrigerators), which can damage the ozone layer.

Circular economy (cyclical economy) An economic system that aims to eliminate waste and the continual use of resources. Circular economies employ sharing, reuse, repair, refurbishment, remanufacturing and recycling to create a closed-loop system. All waste becomes food for the next process. This is in contrast to the traditional linear economy, which adopts a take-make-use-discard model of production.

Climate The pattern of weather in a particular region over a set period of time, usually 30 years. The pattern is affected by the amount of rain or snowfall, average temperatures throughout the year, humidity, wind speeds and so on. Ireland has a temperate climate in that it doesn't get too hot or too cold.

Climate change A change in the climate of a region over time due to natural forces or human activity. In the context of the UN Framework Convention on Climate Change, it is the change in climate caused by higher levels of greenhouse gases in the atmosphere due to human activities as well as natural climate changes. See also global warming, and UN Framework Convention on Climate Change.

Climate change scenario A plausible description of how the future may develop, based on a coherent and internally consistent set of assumptions about key relationships and driving forces (i.e., rate of technology change, prices). Note that scenarios are neither predictions nor forecasts, but are useful to provide a view of the implications of the social, economic and political drivers of change

Compost A rich soil-like material produced from decayed plants and other organic matter, such as food and animal waste, that decomposes (breaks down) naturally. Most food waste is compostable.

Composting The process of deliberately allowing food, garden and other suitable organic wastes to break down naturally over time to produce compost. This may take a long time to break down and may attract unwanted pests.

Deforestation The permanent removal of standing forests that can lead to significant levels of CO_2 emissions.

Ecology A branch of science that studies the interactions and relationships among organisms and between organisms and their environment.

Electric vehicle A vehicle that is powered by an electric motor or battery and is generally less noisy and less polluting than common combustion engine vehicles.

Emissions Emissions is the term used to describe the gases and particles which are put into the air or emitted by various sources.

Energy efficiency Energy efficiency means using less energy to perform the same task, While renewable energy technologies also help accomplish these objectives, improving energy efficiency is the cheapest and often the most immediate way to reduce the use of fossil fuels.

Energy rating   A rating given to electrical appliances such as ovens, washing machines, dishwashers and refrigerators according to how much energy they use. Ratings are on a scale from A to G, with A-rated appliances using the least energy and G-rated needing the most. An energy efficient appliance is more cost effective and eco-friendly.

Environmental impact statement   A statement about the expected effects on the environment of a proposed project or development such as a new road or waste water treatment plant, including how any severe effects on the environment will be addressed.

Feedback loop   In a feedback loop, rising temperatures on the Earth change the environment in ways that affect the rate of warming. Feedback loops can be positive (adding to the rate of warming) or negative (reducing it). The melting of Arctic ice provides an example of a negative feedback process. As the ice on the surface of the Arctic Ocean melts away, there is a smaller area of white ice to reflect the Sun's heat back into space and more open, dark water to absorb it. The less ice there is, the more the water heats up, and the faster the remaining ice melts. Essentially, feedback loops make the impacts of key climate factors stronger or weaker, starting a cyclical chain reaction that repeats again and again.

Fossil fuels   Natural resources, such as coal, oil and natural gas, containing hydrocarbons. These fuels were formed in the Earth over millions of years producing CO_2 when burnt.

Fracking   A pressurized process in which underground rock formations (shale) are cracked, or fracked, to release trapped oil and gas.

Fuel poverty   A household is said to be in fuel poverty when its members cannot afford to keep adequately warm at a reasonable cost, in the context of total income.

Global average temperature   The mean surface temperature of the Earth measured from three main sources: (1) satellites, monthly readings from a network of over 3,000 surface temperature (2) observation stations and (3) sea surface temperature measurements taken mainly from the fleet of merchant ships, naval ships and data buoys.

Glaciers   Glaciers and ice caps form on land. Glaciers accumulate snow, which over time becomes compressed into ice. On average, glaciers worldwide have been losing mass since at least the 1970s.

Global warming   Global warming is the long-term heating of the Earth's climate system observed since the pre-industrial period (between 1850 and 1900) due to human activities, primarily fossil fuel burning, which increases heat-trapping greenhouse gas levels in Earth's atmosphere. In the natural cycle, the world can warm, and cool, without any human interference. Global warming occurs when CO_2 and other air pollutants and greenhouse gases collect in the atmosphere and absorb sunlight and solar radiation that have bounced off the earth's surface. Normally, this radiation would escape into space – but these pollutants, (which can last for years to centuries in the atmosphere), trap the heat and cause the planet to get hotter.

Greenhouse effect   The greenhouse effect is the natural warming of the earth that results when gases in the atmosphere trap heat from the sun that would otherwise escape into space. When fossil fuels are burnt to produce electricity, heat and more, they emit greenhouse gases such as CO_2 and methane. These gases trap the sun's energy in the Earth's atmosphere as heat. As more and more greenhouses gases are released, more heat gets trapped and the planet warms up, disrupting the long-standing, delicate climate systems that have made life on Earth possible. (See also greenhouse gases and global warming.)

Greenhouse gases   Gases such as CO_2 and methane, which tend to trap heat radiating from the Earth's surface, cause warming in the lower atmosphere. The major greenhouse gases that cause climate change are carbon dioxide (CO_2), methane (CH4) and nitrous oxide (NO2). (See also greenhouse effect and global warming.)

Greenwashing   This is a form of deceptive marketing in which a company, product or business practice is falsely or excessively promoted as being environmentally friendly.

Gulf Stream   A warm current that originates in the Gulf of Mexico and (together with the North Atlantic Drift) crosses the Atlantic Ocean. It transports heat from low to high latitudes and keeps northwest European winter temperatures higher than they would otherwise be.

Hockey stick   The name given to a graph published in 1998 plotting the average temperature in the Northern hemisphere over the last 1,000 years. The line remains roughly flat until the last 100 years, when it bends sharply upwards. The graph has been cited as evidence to support the idea that global warming is a human-made phenomenon, but some scientists have challenged the data and methodology used to estimate historical temperatures. (It is also known as MBH98 after its creators, Michael E. Mann, Raymond S. Bradley and Malcolm K. Hughes.)

Incinerator   A furnace that is designed to burn waste at very high temperatures under controlled conditions and is licensed by national regulatory authorities. Most modern and efficient incinerators generate heat and energy from burning waste.

Insulation   Insulation refers to the use of any material to fill the spaces (including little gaps, crevices and hard-to-reach places behind walls and above ceilings) of a home to reduce heat flow by reflection and/or absorption.

Keeling Curve   The Keeling Curve is a graph that represents the concentration of CO_2 in the Earth's atmosphere since 1958. The Keeling Curve is named after its creator, Dr. Charles David Keeling.

Kyoto Protocol   The Kyoto Protocol is an international agreement that aimed to manage and reduce CO_2 emissions and greenhouse gases. The Protocol was adopted at a conference in Kyoto, Japan, in 1997 and became international law on February 16, 2005.

Jet stream   These ribbons of very strong winds, (9–16 km), found above the Earth's surface, can reach speeds of 322 kmph (200 mph) and move weather systems around the globe.

La Niña   This large-scale weather phenomenon is characterised by colder-than-usual surface ocean temperatures circulating in the tropical East Pacific.

Mass extinction   A widespread and rapid decline in the biodiversity of Earth. A mass extinction event has occurred at least five times in life's history including that which brought an end to the dinosaurs.

Methane   Methane is the second most important greenhouse gas. Sources include both the natural world (wetlands, termites, wildfires) and human activity (agriculture, waste dumps, leaks from coal mining, etc.).

Meteorology   Meteorology is the part of science that looks at the physical processes in the atmosphere in order to understand the weather.

Meteorologist   A meteorologist studies the weather and atmosphere using scientific research and mathematical models to predict patterns and forecast changes in weather conditions. This involves investigating and researching the physical nature of the laws governing air movement, pressure and temperature changes to determine the causes which bring about the various atmospheric conditions. Today, meteorologists play a vital role by studying the causes and effects of climate change, raising awareness and advising others on global environmental issues.

Mitigation   Climate change mitigation refers to efforts to reduce or prevent emission of greenhouse gases. Mitigation can mean using new technologies and renewable energies, making older equipment more energy efficient, or changing management practices or consumer behaviour. It can be as complex as a plan for a new city, or as simple as design improvements to a cook stove. Efforts underway around the world range from high-tech subway systems to bicycling paths and walkways.

Nature-based solutions   The use of nature to jointly tackle social and environmental issues including climate change, food security, access to water and pollution. Relatively cost effective, nature-based solutions have the significant benefit of increasing biodiversity.

Natural greenhouse effect   The natural level of greenhouse gases in our atmosphere, which keeps the planet about 30° C warmer than it would otherwise be – essential for life as we know it. Water vapour is the most important component of the natural greenhouse effect.

Ocean acidification   The ocean absorbs approximately one quarter of human-made CO_2 from the atmosphere, which helps to reduce adverse climate change effects. However, when the CO_2 dissolves in seawater, carbonic acid is formed. Carbon emissions in the industrial era have already lowered the pH of seawater by 0.1. Ocean acidification can decrease the ability of marine organisms to build their shells and skeletal structures and kill off coral reefs, with serious effects for people who depend on fishing as a source of food and income.

Ozone layer   The thin protective layer of gas 10 to 50 km above the Earth that acts as a filter for ultraviolet (UV) radiation from the sun. High UV levels can lead to skin cancer and cataracts and affect the growth of plants.

Permafrost   Ground often below the surface that remains continually frozen. As the globe warms, the permafrost is predicted to thaw, releasing methane, a greenhouse gas into the atmosphere.

Pre-industrial levels of CO_2   The levels of CO_2 in the atmosphere prior to the start of the Industrial Revolution. These levels are estimated to be about 280 ppm (by volume). Today, CO_2 levels are 40% higher than they were before the Industrial Revolution began; they have risen from 280 ppm in the 18th century to over 400 ppm in 2015. At the time of writing this book, levels have reached 411 ppm.

Plastic bag levy   An environmental tax that customers must pay when they accept a plastic or laminated bag from a retailer. There is no tax on small bags, such as those for fresh meat or loose fruit and vegetables. Money raised from the tax is put into a special fund that is used to protect the environment.

Renewable energy   Renewable energy is the energy created from sources that can be replenished in a short period of time. The five renewable sources most often deployed are: biomass (such as wood and biogas), the movement of water, geothermal (heat from within the earth), wind and solar.

Recycle   To break waste items down into their raw materials, which are then used to re-make the original item or make new items.

Reforestation   The process of planting trees in forest lands to replace those that have been cut down.

Refuse   Another name for waste.

Renewable energy   Energy from renewable resources such as wind power, solar energy or biomass.

Rewild   The process of restoring and expanding biodiverse systems, communities and spaces reversing biodiversity loss and ensuring that humankind becomes more sustainable.

Reuse   To use an item more than once for the same purpose, which helps save money, time, energy and resources.

Solar panel   A panel fixed to the roof of a building that uses special cells to collect energy from the sun and convert it to electricity. This source of energy is used to heat the building and/or power lights, appliances or equipment.

Sustainable development   Development using land or energy sources in a way that meets the needs of people today without reducing the ability of future generations to meet their own needs.

The Intergovernmental Panel on Climate Change (IPCC)   This is a scientific body established by the United Nations Environment Programme and the World Meteorological Organization. It reviews and assesses the most recent scientific, technical and socio-economic work relevant to climate change, but does not carry out its own research. The IPCC was honoured with the 2007 Nobel Peace Prize.

Tipping point   A tipping point is a threshold for change, which, when reached, results in a process that is difficult to reverse. Scientists say it is urgent that policymakers halve global CO_2 emissions over the next 50 years or risk triggering changes that could be irreversible.

UN Framework Convention on Climate Change   An international treaty signed by 192 countries that has the goal of preventing 'dangerous' human interference with the climate system and sets general rules for tackling climate change.

Weather   Weather is the mix of events that occurs each day in our atmosphere. Weather varies in different parts of the world and changes over minutes, hours, days and weeks. The term 'weather' refers to the temporary conditions of the atmosphere, the layer of air that surrounds the Earth. This involves atmospheric phenomena such as temperature, humidity, precipitation (type and amount), air pressure, wind and cloud cover. The average weather pattern in a place over several decades is called climate.

WEEE (Waste Electrical and Electronic Equipment)   These appliances include any unwanted devices with a plug or battery – from a remote control or digital camera to a vacuum cleaner or fridge freezer. These devices must be disposed of carefully to avoid damage to the environment. Unwanted devices can be brought to a civic amenity site or left with a retailer when buying a new device. All WEEE left in retail outlets and civic amenity sites are collected for recycling.

Wind energy   Energy harnessed from the wind at wind farms and converted to power. See also wind turbine.

Wind turbine   An engine or machine, usually mounted on a tower, that captures the force of the wind and converts it to electricity.

Zero emissions   Zero emissions refers to an engine, motor, process or other energy source that does not release any harmful gases directly into the environment.

Zero waste   The conservation of all resources by means of responsible production, consumption, reuse and recovery of materials without incineration or landfilling.

Appendix 2

Sample lesson plans (as Gaeilge)

Athrú Aeráide trí mheán na Gaeilge Seachtain 1. / Ceacht 1 – 30nd Rang 3 / 4

Snáitheanna: Feasacht agus Cúram Imshaoil & Teanga Ó Bhéal, Léitheoireacht, Scríbhneoireacht

An Córas Análaithe

Aidhmeanna Ábhair: Athrú Aeráide

a tuiscint ar an gcóras ánálaithe sa chorp
b scileanna, eolas agus dearcadh a fhorbairt

Scileanna:

ag ceistiú / ag breathnú / ag tuar / ag imscrúdú agus ag tástáil / ag meas agus ag tomhas / ag anailísiú / ag clárú agus ag cur in iúl

Aidhmeanna Teanga: Gaeilge / teanga na foghlama

a an t-ábhar a theagasc trí mheán na Gaeilge le modhanna teagaisc suimiúla agus oiriúnacha chun tuiscint agus foghlaim a chinntiú
b deiseanna cumarsáide a eagrú chun deiseanna a thabhairt don rang cleachtadh a dhéanamh ar an teanga agus chun dul i ngleic le heolas nua nuair a thagann an deis chun cinn

Scileanna: Éisteacht, Labhairt, Léitheoireacht, Scríbhneoireacht

Modhanna Múinte:

An modh díreach (fearas)

Modh na sraithe (sraith pictiúr)

Modh na lánfhreagartha gníomhaí (geáitsí)

An modh closlabhartha (athrá)

An modh closamhairc (pictiúir)

Modh na ráite (ráiteas)

Áiseanna:

íomhánna ón idirlíon de dhaoine ag caitheamh mascanna ag siúl na sráideanna i gcathair Shanghai san Ind / cathair mhór san Áis agus léarscáil don domhain,

pictiúir le lipéid,

clár bán / marcóir

púicín

Straitéisí:

múnlóireacht ar straitéisí, ar theanga, ar ghníomhaíochtaí

obair bheirte (oscailte agus dúnta)

ceisteanna chun tuiscint a chinntiú agus ag lorg eolais

obair phraiticiúil

leabhar nótaí speisialta ag na páistí (treisiú)

tascanna scríbhneoireachta iata m.sh. líon na bearnaí / fíor nó bréagach / abairtí a chur in ord / abairtí a iomlánú (rogha)

léaráidí: an corp / na scámhóga agus an córas análaithe / an cúrsa fola,

luaschártaí réamhullmhaithe (téarmaíocht / an téarmaíocht i gcomhthéacs)

balúin chun na scámhóga a mhíniú

fiseán den chóras análaithe ón idirlíon

ábhar ar Chlár na Gaeilge chun tacú leis an teanga (m.sh. briathra san Aimsir Láithreach; an t-ainm briathartha) / téarmaíocht / tearmaíocht i gcomhthéacs / léaráidí

leabhar nótaí ag na páistí

tascanna scríbhneoireachta réamhullmhaithe

Cuspóirí Foghlama: *Ábhar & Teanga* Ba cheart do pháistí a bheith in ann

a tuiscint a bheith acu ar an gcóras análaithe agus conas a oibríonn sé
b an nasc idir análú agus an cúrsa fola a thuiscint
c eolas a bhailiú ar O2 & CO2 agus a dtréithe
d O2 & CO2 i saol an pháiste féinig a aithint
e an téarmaíocht agus an teanga a bhaineann leis an gcóras análaithe a fhoghlaim, a thuiscint agus iarrachtaí a dhéanamh chun an teanga a úsáid go cumarsáideach
f na feidhmeanna teanga seo a leanas a bhaint amach: ceisteanna a fhreagairt; eolas a thabhairt agus a lorg; iarracht a dhéanamh dearcadh a léiriú
g díriú ar ghné d'fhoirm na teanga – an t-ainm briathartha (ag _____)

Comhtháthú leis an rang Gaeilge (an tseachtain roimh ré):

Briathra san Aimsir Láithreach (Gach lá) – Tógann sé, Súnn sé, Cuireann sé, Déanann sé, Faigheann sé

Gníomhaíochtaí & Caitheamh Aimsire: ag rith, ag snámh, ag _____ srl.

Teanga: éadaí, dathanna, aimsir (Cad atá á chaitheamh acu? Cén saghas éadaí atá ar na daoine sa phictiúr? Cén fáth? srl)

Teanga an Cheachta

Teanga na Foghlama (foclóir +
eiseamláirí teangat)

ocsaigín nó O2,

gás, dofheicthe,

boladh, blas, an corp,

ag análú, scámhóga,

fuil, an cúrsa fola

ag sú isteach, ag sní / ag taisteal
/ ag rith timpeall an choirp,

aer úr, aer salach, **truailliú**
san aer nó sa timpeallacht,

dé-ocsaíd charbóin san
aer nó sa timpeallacht

Na **tréithe** atá ag O2:

Is gás é. Ní féidir linn é a
fheiceáil.

Tá sé dofheicthe.

Níl boladh uaidh Níl blas
uaidh.

ag análú / na scámhóga /
aer glan úr ón atmaisféar

an cúrsa fola / fuil ag taisteal
nó ag sní nó ag rith timpeall
an choirp

an croí – cosúil le hinneall
an chairr – brúnn sé an fhuil
timpeall agus ní stopann sé ag
obair. (bás / marbh)

CO2 – na tréithe

Is gás atá anseo freisin.

Ní féidir linn é a fheiceáil.
Tá sé dofheicthe.

Níl boladh uaidh. Níl blas
uaidh.

Teanga don Fhoghlaim (f + et)

San aer timpeall orainn tá
. . . . (sa timpeallacht)

aer glan / aer úr

aer salach / truailliú san aer

Ní féidir linn é a fheiceáil. Tá sé
do-fheicthe.

Níl boladh uaidh. Níl blas
uaidh.

Baill an choirp (an corp):
lámha, cosa, ceann, ...

Bíonn fuil ag rith / ag sní /
ag taisteal ó na barraicíní go
barr an chinn (suas go dtí do
inchinn).

Bígí ag análú. Tóg isteach aer
sna scámhóga. Coimeád istigh
é. Scaoil amach é go mall.
Tógaimid isteach ocsaigín
nó aer glan úr ón atmaisféar.
(cosúil le balún)

Tógann an cúrsa fola, le
cabhair ón gcroí, ocsaigín
timpeall an choirp ar
fad – ó na barraicíní go dtí
an inchinn.

Ní féidir linn maireachtáil gan
ocsaigín. Gheobhaimid bás
gan é.

Tá ocsaigín i ngach áit timpe
all orainn – san atmaisféar,
san aer, san uisce.

Nuair a dhéanamimid análú
amach cuirimid dé-ocsaíd
charbóin (CO2) nó aer
salach amach san aer nó san
atmaisféar.

Tá CO2 san atmaisféar
timpeall orainn agus tá
leibhéal sláintiúil
riachtanach ACH tá an
leibhéal seo ag ardú in
aghaidh na bliana.

Teanga de thoradh na Foghlama
(f + et)

An féidir leat? Is féidir liom /
ní féidir liom . . . . . .

Cad a tharlaíonn nuair
a bhíonn aer salach san
atmaisféar?

Cén fath go bhfuil an t-aer
glan anseo agus an t-aer salach
i . . . . . . ?

Sa phictiúr, tá . . . . Feicim _____
sa phictiúr/ sa scannán.

An bhfuil cead agam triail a
bhaint as anois?

Ní féidir liom an balún seo a
shéideadh? Cén fáth nach
féidir . . . . Cén fáth
gur . . . . Phléasc
sé. Cén fáth?

Tá sé deacair / éasca an pictiúr
_____ a tharraingt.

Sraith abairtí chun cur síos
a dhéanamh ar an obair
a dhéanann an croí / na
scámhóga a úsáid san ord ceart.

Cur síos a dhéanamh ar na
tréithe atá ag O2 / CO2.
(an teanga seo a úsaid le
boladh gáis sa teach / boladh
ó phairceanna an fheirmeora
agus é/í ag cur amach aoiligh.

Cad is féidir linn a dhéanamh
chun an t-aer sa timpeallacht a
fheabhsú? (sa bhaile / ar scoil /
sa tsráidbhaile / sa bhaile mór /
sa chathair / sa domhan mór)

Cathain a bíonn an t-aer
truaillithe / a lán CO2 san
aer? Nuair a . . . .

Cathain a bhíonn an t-aer glan
nó sláintiúil / a lán O2 san aer?

Nuair a . . . .

Cad eile a bhíonn riachtanach
chun go mbeadh daoine
sláintiúil ar an saol?

Tús

1   Pictiúr / plé: Pictiúr de chathair mhór san Áis a phlé ag leibhéal teanga bunúsach. Beidh ceisteanna dúnta & íseal-oird ar dtús ón múinteoir chun iarrachtaí teanga agus muinín a spreagadh. *Cad atá sa phictiúr? Cad eile a fheiceann sibh? (éadaí / foirgnimh / rudaí suimiúla eile dóibh) Cad atá á dhéanamh acu? Cá bhfuil siad? → Cén fáth?* Cuirfidh an múinteoir eochair fhocail / an teanga i gcomhthéacs abairte (go háirithe má athraíonn préamh an fhocail) / luaschártaí ar an gclár bán mar a thagann siad chun cinn agus déanfar aithris agus athrá orthu chun iad a threisiú. Lig dóibh an téarmaíocht nua nó cuid de a chur sa leabhar nótaí ag an bpointe seo. (É, L, L, S – na scileanna ar fad in úsáid go minic)

Forbairt

2   Ansin le cabhair léaráidí múinfidh an múinteoir ábhar an cheachta bunaithe ar O2 / CO2 / an corp ag análú / an córas análaithe. Déanfar forbairt ar an réamheolas atá acu ag deimhnniú go bhfuil an teanga atá roghnaithe roimhré á teagasc (Teanga an Cheachta) agus go bhfuil na cuspóirí ábhair agus teanga á bhaint amach chomh maith.

3   Ansin déanfar **cleachtadh fisiciúil** leis na balúin chun obair na scámhóga a thuiscint - ag análú isteach & amach chun an fhoghlaim a dhaingniú – isteach leis an ocsaigín (aer glan, úr) – amach le dé-ocsaíd charbóin (aer salach le truailliú / truaillithe). Le híomhánna, lipéid, fearas is gá a chinntiú go bhfuil tuiscint agus foghlaim ag tarlú ar an gcóras análaithe agus ar an gcúrsa fola agus is gá dul siar go rialta chun treisiú ar an teanga nua agus ar an ábhar.

4   Arís beidh deis anseo an teanga nua a chur sa leabhar nótaí agus cúpla léaráid le lipéid a tharraingt chomh maith m.sh. an corp / na scamhóga / an croí.

Críoch

5   Ar ais linn go dtí an pictiúr de Shanghai – Cad atá ar eolas againn anois faoin aer sa phictiúr seo? Ceisteanna ard-oird – cén fáth?

6   Obair Bheirte: ceisteann ar an gclár bán le freagairt

   a   An bhfuil an t-aer sa scoil seo mar Shanghai? Cén fáth? 2 chúis ó gach beirt
   b   Tá gach duine ag tógaint isteach O2 agus ag cur CO2 amach sa seomra ranga seo. Conas is féidir linn an t-aer a choinneáil glan?
   c   Ainmnigh 2 áit sa tír seo nó sa cheantar seo ina bhfuil a lán O2 agus a lán CO2 san aer.
   d   Conas is féidir linn leibhéil O2 a ardú timpeall na scoile?

7   Tasc Scríbhneoireachta dúnta:((Rogha) Líon na bearnaí / Fíor no bréagach / abairtí a chur in ord / abairtí a iomlánú agus beidh orthu an tasc a dhéanann siad a ghreamú sa leabhar notaí.

8   Teagasc foirm-dhírithe: an t-ainm briathartha tríd an cur chuige a) ag tabhairt faoi deara b) feasacht c) cleachtadh

Éagsúlacht Chumais

Is fiú tascanna difriúla scríbhneoireachta a ullmhú don Críoch m.sh. Líon na Bearnaí A (O2); Líon na bearnaí B (CO2); Fíor nó Bréagach A – 3 abairt ar an gcroí. Fíor nó Bréagach B – 3 abairt ar na scámhóga.

a   Is féidir leis na páistí a tasc féin a roghnú
b   Beidh tascanna éagsúla le déanamh ag grúpaí éagsúla
c   Beidh deis ag páistí áirithe na habairtí a léamh seachas a scríobh
d   Spreagfar páistí áirithe chun tascanna breise a dhéanamah.

Measúnú

Breathnóireacht an oide le linn tascanna / obair bheirte. Ceisteanna dúnta & oscailte.

Na tascanna scríbhneoireachta a cheartú: Líon na bearnaí / Fíor nó Bréagach

Athmhachnamh an mhúinteora

Appendix 3

Sample lesson plans

Please note: additional lesson plans are available on the padlet which accompanies this book – https://padlet.com/annedolan/uir0u3bwz3octwz0

Climate change through the medium of English: Week 1 / Lesson 1 – 30 min Grade 3 / 4

Strands: Environmental awareness and care & oral language, reading, writing

The respiratory system

Content-based learning outcomes: Climate change

a An understanding of the respiratory system
b The development of skills, knowledge and attitudes

Skills: Questioning / observing / predicting / investigating and experimenting / estimating and measuring / analysing / recording and communicating

Language learning outcomes: English / requisite language

a Teaching the content through the medium of English using interesting and appropriate methodologies to ensure understanding and learning
b Organising communicative tasks and opportunities to ensure children get to use and practice the language and the new learning with the teacher and with one another

Skills: Listening, speaking, reading, writing

Language teaching methods

The Direct method

The Series method

Total physical response (TPR)

The Audio-Lingual Method

The Audio-Visual method

The Phrase Method

Resources

Images from the internet of people wearing masks while walking the streets of Shanghai in India or in another large Asian city and a world map

Pictures with labels

White board and marker

Blindfold

Strategies

Modelling strategies / language / activities

Pair work (open / closed)

Questions to seek knowledge & to ensure understanding

Practical work

Notebook per student to document & consolidate the learning

Closed writing tasks, e.g., fill the blanks, true or false, putting sentences in the correct order, completing sentences (choice)

Large diagrams of the body / the lungs & the respiratory system / the blood stream

Pre-prepared flashcards of the relevant terminology / the terminology in context

Balloons to help explain the lungs and their function

A video from the internet of the respiratory system

A large pin board / notice board made available at the back of the room with relevant terminology / terminology in context / support materials, e.g., verbs in the Simple Present tense, verbal nouns / diagrams with labels etc.

A notebook per student

Pre-prepared writing tasks

Learning objectives: Content and language

Children should be enabled to:

a Understand the respiratory system and its function
b Understand the link between breathing and the blood stream
c Build on their knowledge of O_2 & CO_2 and to identify their characteristics
d Identify O_2 & CO_2 in their own environment
e Learn and understand the terminology and the language of the respiratory system and to make efforts to use this language communicatively
f Achieve success in using the following language functions: answer questions, impart and seek knowledge; sharing an opinion
g Focus on an aspect of language form, e.g., verbal nouns (ending in –ing)

Integration with the language lessons (the previous week)

Verbs in the Simple Present Tense (every day) – He takes / They take, It soak / They soaks, She puts / They put, It makes / They make, He gets / They get

Activities & Pastimes – ending in – ing

Other relevant vocabulary: clothes, colours, weather. (What are they wearing? Why? etc.)

Language

Language of Learning

(Vocabulary & sentence structures)

Oxygen or O_2

An invisible gas, smell, taste, the human body, breathing, lungs, blood, the blood stream

To take in or to soak in, flowing, travelling, travelling through or around the body

Fresh air or clean air, polluted air / unclean air / pollution in the air or in the environment

Carbon dioxide in the air or in the environment

The characteristics of O_2: it is a gas. It is invisible. We cannot see the gas. It has no smell. It has no taste

Breathing / lungs / clean air from the atmosphere

The blood stream / travelling or flowing through or around the body

The heart – like an engine in a car – it forces / pushes the blood around the body and it never takes a break (death / dead)

CO_2 – characteristics

This is also an invisible gas. It has no smell. It has no taste

Language for Learning (V + SS)

In the air or in the atmosphere or in the environment around us ....

Clean air / fresh air

Dirty air / unclean air / polluted air

_____ is an invisible gas. We cannot see it. It has no smell. It has no taste

Body parts – arms / hands / legs / feet / head ....

Blood runs / flows / travels from your toes to the top of your head up to the brain

Giving instructions and modelling: Breathe in and out. Inhale fresh air into your lungs. Hold it in. Exhale slowly. We inhale oxygen or fresh clean air from the atmosphere and we fill our lungs like we fill a balloon

The blood stream with the help of the heart takes oxygen around the whole body from the lungs to the brain to the toes

We cannot exist / survive without oxygen. We will die without it

Oxygen is in the air, in the atmosphere everywhere around us

When we exhale or breathe out, we exhale CO_2 into the atmosphere or into the environment

CO_2 is also in the atmosphere around us and a healthy level is vital. However, these levels are rising every year

Language through Learning (V + SS)

Can you ....? I can ..... ; I cannot ......; I can't ....

What are the effects of air pollution in the atmosphere?

How come the air conditions are clean in _____ but polluted in _____?

In the picture / clip / video, I see _____

Can I try it now / take a turn?

I cannot blow up this balloon? Why not? It burst? How come ....?

It is very difficult / easy to draw this picture

A series of sentences to describe the work of the heart and the lungs being utilised in the correct order

Describing the characteristics of O_2 / CO_2 and being able to apply this language to household gas / slurry etc.

How can we improve air conditions in our own environment (home / school / village / town / city / in the wider world)?

When / Why is the air polluted?

When are there high levels of CO_2 in the air?

When is our atmosphere clean and healthy?

When are there high levels of O_2 in the air?

What other factors are important to ensure we live healthy lives?

Introduction

1   Visual image / discussion: A visual image of a normal day in a large Asian city can be used to stimulate language already known to the learner. Closed questions and lower order questions will support scaffolding and support to recall language and to build their confidence. *What can you see in this picture? Tell me about their clothes, the buildings, any other interesting things you note. What are these people doing? How many people can you see?* Key words & important sentence structures should be recorded on the white board with pre-prepared visual prompts used to ensure the lesson holds a climate change focus while placing a conscious effort on the language required and pre-planned above. This language needs clarity of pronunciation and plenty of repetition to ensure consolidation of learning.

Allow the learners to document the language / discipline-specific language in their notebooks ensuring the regular use of all language skills – L / S / R / W.

Development

2   The teacher then teaches the relevant content noted in the above learning objectives while using diagrams and visual prompts based on O_2 / CO_2 / breathing / the respiratory system. Their prior knowledge will be developed while also ensuring the pre-planned vocabulary and language structures above are included and the learning objectives are being achieved.

3   Using the balloons, the teacher will employ interactive methodologies and cooperative learning strategies which will ensure learner involvement and comprehension of the following: the function of the lungs / physically inhaling or taking in O_2) and exhaling (polluted air with CO_2).

While using images, labels, concrete materials all avenues must be explored to ensure that the children are understanding & learning and every opportunity must be taken to revise the new language and the new content in question.

4   Again allow the learners to document more new language and discipline-specific language in their notebooks.

Conclusion

5   We return to our Asian city scene – What do we now know about this picture? Can anybody describe the environment in the picture? This picture will allow an opportunity for pair/group work. Can somebody explain why people are wearing masks? What do you think? Why?

6   Pair work (applying the learning to the children's environment). Providing focus questions on the whiteboard will also help the learners.

   a   Is the air in our school similar to the air in Shanghai / Asia? Why / Why not? 2 reasons
   b   Everybody inhales O_2 & exhales CO_2 in this school. How can we ensure we are inhaling clean / non-polluted air?
   c   Name 2 places in this country / in this area where there is normally a lot of O_2 / CO_2?
   d   How can we increase levels of O_2 in our locality / area / school yard?

7   A Closed Writing Task: A choice of writing tasks can be administered to different groups – Fill the blanks / True or False / Putting sentences in the correct order / Completing sentences and the completed task can be included in their notebooks.

8   Form-focused instruction: the verbal noun using the following approach a) noticing b) awareness c) practicing activities.

Differentiation

To cater for different learners a variety of closed writing tasks can be prepared, e.g., Fill the blanks (O_2 based); Fill the blanks (CO_2 based); True or false A – three sentences based on the heart. True or false B – three sentences based on the lungs.

a Children can choose their own task
b Different groups can be asked to try particular tasks
c Children can read & complete the task orally or in written form
d Some children can be encouraged to complete more than one task

Assessment

Teacher observation during tasks. Closed and open questions

Correction of writing tasks

Teacher reflections

Appendix 4

Letter from the President of Ireland to the children in St. Augustine's NS, Clontuskert, Ballinasloe

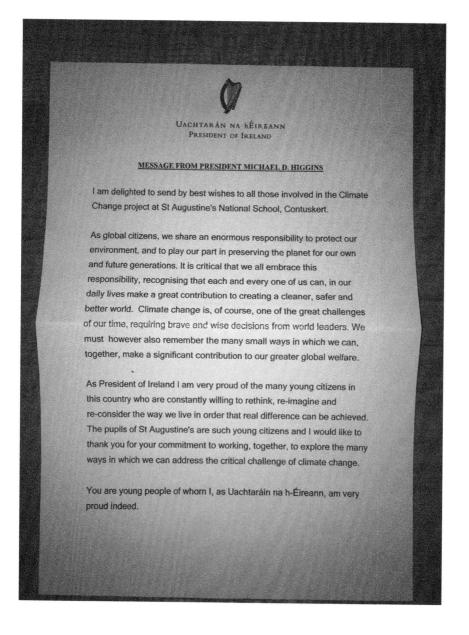

UACHTARÁN NA hÉIREANN
PRESIDENT OF IRELAND

MESSAGE FROM PRESIDENT MICHAEL D. HIGGINS

I am delighted to send by best wishes to all those involved in the Climate Change project at St Augustine's National School, Contuskert.

As global citizens, we share an enormous responsibility to protect our environment, and to play our part in preserving the planet for our own and future generations. It is critical that we all embrace this responsibility, recognising that each and every one of us can, in our daily lives make a great contribution to creating a cleaner, safer and better world. Climate change is, of course, one of the great challenges of our time, requiring brave and wise decisions from world leaders. We must however also remember the many small ways in which we can, together, make a significant contribution to our greater global welfare.

As President of Ireland I am very proud of the many young citizens in this country who are constantly willing to rethink, re-imagine and re-consider the way we live in order that real difference can be achieved. The pupils of St Augustine's are such young citizens and I would like to thank you for your commitment to working, together, to explore the many ways in which we can address the critical challenge of climate change.

You are young people of whom I, as Uachtaráin na h-Éireann, am very proud indeed.

Appendix 5

Timeline cards: History of climate change

Note: These cards can be used with children or as a resource for teachers. It is important to edit the cards in line with specified learning objectives, age level of children and teacher requirements.

Timeline 1: 900–1970

900–1300	1350–1850	1709
The Medieval Warm Period. Europe enjoys warmer weather.	The Little Ice Age cools part of the northern hemisphere.	At end of the Little Ice Age, Europe experiences an unusually cold winter.
1800–1870	**1863**	**1890s**
First stage of the Industrial Revolution. Coal, railroads and land clearing speed up greenhouse gas emission, while better agriculture and sanitation speed up population growth.	Irish scientist John Tyndall identifies carbon dioxide and water vapour as key components of the atmosphere which trap radiant heat energy in the Earth's climate system.	Scientists discover that the burning of fossil fuels could lead to global warming, but they do not realise that the process might already have begun.
1815	**1827**	**1873**
The Tambora volcanic eruption causes a drop in temperature globally.	Jean-Baptiste Joseph Fourier, a French mathematician is the first to use a greenhouse analogy.	The International Meteorological Committee is founded in Vienna.
1890s–1940	**1940–1970**	**1957**
Average surface air temperatures increases by 25° C. A period of severe dust storms known as the American Dust Bowl (in the Southern Plains from Texas to Nebraska) is recognised as evidence of the greenhouse effect by some scientists. The opening of the Texas and Persian Gulf oil fields heralds an era of cheap and plentiful fossil fuel energy.	Globally, temperatures decrease and scientists lose interest in the greenhouse effect. **1950** The world population is 2.5 billion. The International Meteorological Committee became the World Meteorological Organisation under the direction of the UN.	David Keeling sets up the first continuous monitoring of CO_2 levels in the atmosphere. In the mid-'60s, this curve (known as the Keeling Curve) is shown to a small undergraduate class which includes one Al Gore, sparking his lifelong interest in the issue.

Timeline 1: 1970–recent events

1970s	1979	1985
A series of studies by the US Department of Energy increases concerns about future global warming.	The first World Climate Conference brings together a range of scientists. This strengthens the coordination of their research efforts as they call upon Governments to foresee and prevent potential human-made changes in climate.	First international conference on the Greenhouse effect at Villach, Austria.
1973		
The Arab oil embargo produces the first big energy crisis in the industrialised world. A series of reports by the US Department of Energy in the 1970s increase concern about future global warming.		

1987	1988	1990
Warmest year since records began. The Brundtland Commission report defines sustainable development as "meeting the needs of the present generation without compromising the ability of future generations to meet their needs".	In 1988, a group of scientists from many nations began working together to examine the evidence for climate change. This group is called the Intergovernmental Panel on Climate Change (IPCC).	First report of the Intergovernmental Panel on Climate Change (IPCC) shows evidence of global warming.

1991	1992	1995
The eruption of Mount Pinatubo in the Philippines helps to interrupt the warming trend.	In 1992, representatives from most of the world's countries gathered at a United Nations (UN) conference in Rio de Janeiro, Brazil. During this Earth Summit, it is agreed to begin a series of conferences to establish worldwide agreement to slow climate change. Subsequently, most countries joined the United Nations Framework Convention on Climate Change.	The hottest year on record. The IPCC predicts that, under a "business as usual" scenario, by the year 2100 global temperatures will have risen by between 1° C and 3.5° C.
Future rises in sea levels is a concern for small island states. In 1991, The Alliance of Small Island States is established. This is a group of 44 small island and low-lying coastal states including Fiji, Kiribati and the Marshall Islands.		Berlin, Germany. The first Conference of the Parties to the UNFCCC agrees to negotiate carbon emission cuts for industrialised countries.

1997	1998	2000
Representatives from 192 countries gathered in Kyoto, Japan. Here they begin to try and agree what to do about climate change. In the Kyoto Protocol, while many promises were made, commitments remained unfulfilled. Many people consider the Kyoto Protocol a failure. Pollution by greenhouse gases continued to climb.	This is the hottest year in the hottest decade of the hottest century of the millennium.	A series of major floods around the world reinforce public concerns that global warming is increasing the risk of extreme weather events. Ireland publishes its first National Climate Change Strategy.
2001	**2002**	**2003**
Washington DC, United States of America, March. Newly elected U.S. President, George W. Bush, renounces the Kyoto Protocol because he questions the science and he believes it will damage the US economy.	Antarctica's Larsen B ice sheets breaks up.	Europe experiences the hottest summer in 500 years with an estimated 30,000 fatalities as a result. Extreme weather costs an estimated record of US$60 billion around the world this year.
2004	**2005**	**2006**
Hollywood blockbuster *The Day After Tomorrow's* plot is based on an exaggerated climate change scenario.	Scientists link global warming to more severe US hurricanes and accelerated melting of Arctic sea ice and Siberian permafrost. In August, Hurricane Katrina makes landfall in New Orleans, United States of America. The 2005 Atlantic hurricane season is the most active in recorded history, shattering all previous records	Al Gore's climate change film An Inconvenient Truth becomes a box-office hit. Carbon dioxide emissions are found to be rising faster than in the 1990s. This informs the creation of the "hockey stick" graph.

2007	2008	2009
The 4th IPCC report firmly blames human activity for accelerated levels of global warming. Al Gore and the IPCC are awarded the Nobel Peace Prize.	The polar bear is listed in the United States' Endangered Species Act. Barack Obama becomes president of the United States and promises increases in science funding.	China overtakes the United States as the world's largest greenhouse gas emitter – although the United States remains well ahead on a per-capita basis. 192 governments convene for the UN climate summit in Copenhagen with expectations of a new global agreement high; but they leave only with a controversial political declaration, the Copenhagen Accord.

2011	2013	2015
Human population reaches seven billion. This population growth has generated a demand for even more food, clothing and general goods. This has resulted in more fossil fuel extraction, forest fires and related issues such as pollution and climate change.	The first part of the IPCC's fifth assessment report says scientists are 95% certain that humans are the "dominant cause" of global warming since the 1950s.	The Paris Agreement is the first truly global commitment to fight the climate crisis. In 2015, 195 countries signed an agreement that aims to keep global warming to well below 2°C (3.6°F). The 17 Sustainable Development Goals (SDGs) are the world's best plan to build a better world for people and our planet by 2030. Adopted by all United Nations Member States in 2015, the SDGs are a call for action by all countries – poor, rich and middle-income – to promote prosperity while protecting the environment. Goal 13 deals specifically with climate change.

2016	2017	2018
Donald Trump is elected President of United States of America. Year 2016 marks the third year in a row that record global temperatures were set.	Exxon, Chevron and BP each donate $500,000 for the inauguration of Donald Trump as President of United States of America.	Fifteen-year-old Greta Thunberg begins protesting outside the parliament building in Stockholm, Sweden. According to scientists we have 12 years to take action for global warming to be kept to a maximum of 1.5° C. Even an additional half a degree will significantly worsen the risks of drought, floods, extreme heat and poverty for hundreds of millions of people.

2019

Young people organise massive protests across the globe reflecting a growing sense of urgency to take action on climate change.

About 1.6 million students walk out of classrooms during a coordinated day of strikes across more than 120 countries in March.

"Climate strike" is named 2019 word of the year by Collins Dictionary.

2020

The greatest disaster since World War II, Covid-19 leaves thousands dead, millions vulnerable, while all citizens are required to stay at home.

However, Covid-19 has taught us new lessons about well-being, resilience, interconnections and the importance of nature.

2021

Joe Biden is elected as the 47th President of the United States of America. He moved to reinstate the US to the Paris climate agreement just hours after being sworn in as president.

THE Irish Government publishes a revised edition of the Climate Action Bill, which commits to Ireland becoming carbon neutral by no later than 2050.

The future

Please write your anticipated climate predictions for the next 1/ 5/10 years.

Index

acting, children 99–109
active learning 107, 226, 240
Alexander, H. 239
alpine flora 101–102
The Amazon Synod 55
ancient sea turtle 100–101
Anders, William 1
Anthropocene 3, 15, 46, 169, 171, 214
Arabacioğlu, S. 77
art education 110, 153, 168, 169, 173
Attenborough, D. 138, 294

Bailey, J. 132
Bardsley, A.M. 142
Bardsley, D.K. 142
belief circles game 48–50
beliefs 47, 48, 50, 51, 58, 61–63, 265, 266, 271, 285, 288
Berry, T.R. 278
bicycle education 277
Biesta, G. 174
biodiversity 14–15, 82, 99, 148, 152, 164, 174, 176, 185, 270, 291, 293, 294, 296
Black Lives Matter 285
Boggs, G.L. 90
Bonnett, M. 285
Bonsper, P. 91
The Boy Who Harnessed the Wind 132
Bronfenbrenner, U. 75
Buchanan, J. 219
business as usual 10, 17, 25
busy bee 102–103

Callwood, L. 186
Cammarata, L. 115
carbon cycle 197, 198, 252, 253
carbon dioxide (CO_2) 1, 10, 21, 214, 241, 251–253, 262, 287, 292
carbon emissions 12, 17, 198, 222, 229, 277
carbon footprint 2–3, 54, 228, 241–242, 289
carbon sequestration 294
carbon sink 183, 197
Casey, A. 273, 276

The Centre on the Developing Child, Harvard University 74
children 65, 76, 77, 93, 140, 218, 219, 221, 227, 229, 241, 260, 262–265, 267, 270, 296, 298; activity for 68; being part of the solution 96–97; learning 31, 65, 72, 73, 76, 139, 140, 228; reflective activity for 65
children literature, choosing 90–91; books for raising awareness 91; global warming and climate change, information 91; interdependency, world inhabitants 91
circular economy 293
citizenship 226–237
citizenship education 5, 132, 200, 202, 226–228, 234, 237; practical ideas, schools 228
classroom-based visual art projects 176–177
classroom methodologies 48–52; belief circles game 48–50; enquiring 48–52, 54; interbelief environmental dialogue café 50–52; Origami moment 54
Cleary, Anne 152
Climate Action Project 210–212
climate change: adaptation 22; art, ecology and pedagogy 173–174; art and artists, role 171; art education and risk 169–170; artistic exploration of 168–177; and biodiversity 14–17; causes 21; challenge to change project 231–235; children as historians 219; classroom circle work on 231; classroom discussion on 228–229; co-creating ecologies, hope 169; Content and Language Integrated Learning (CLIL) approach 110–116; creative geographical explorations 208; debating 202–205; denial 22; election manifesto 229–230; exploring with historical lens 214–223; geological time and historical consequences 216–217; historical artefacts 221; historical perspective 214–216; historical stories 222; impacts 20–21; making connection with 197; mitigation 22–23; moral dimension of 18–19; mysteries 205–207; 'our daily lives at school' project 236;

'Our Diamond 9' for 236–237; questions about 2–3; research tool, art 170–171; responding to 19–23; science of 10–13; socially engaged practices 169; STEM challenges 121–134; suggested timeline activities 218–219; teacher educators, visual art elective 172–173; teaching activities 217–222; teaching resource 247, 257; thinking ecologically 174; timeline to teach history of 218; transformative imagination 170–171; visual lens for exploring 152–164; and weather 171–172; whole-school level, ideas 231–237; writing haiku for 208; *see also individual entries*

climate change education 3, 4, 23, 60, 61, 63, 64, 66, 138, 140, 142, 148, 197, 212, 247, 286, 298, 302; beliefs, values & assumptions 62–64; citizenship and 226–237; critical reflection and 61–70; early childhood education (ECE) 72–76; early childhood pedagogy 76–83; fostering positive dispositions 72–84; hope and action, pedagogies 5; learning, dimensions 23–25; learning science and geography, rationale 139; literacy-based approaches 4; longitudinal approach at school 142–145; outdoor learning, practical considerations 139–140; outside the classroom 138–150; personal beliefs about 64; personal biography 62–64; recalling experiences in nature 64; reflective approach to 60–71; school, home and community links 140–141; scientific & geographical skills, pedagogical approaches 141–142; STEAM (STEM + art) 4–5; stepping stones to learning 148–149; supporting learning at home 147–148; theories and practices of 4

Climate Change Go Bingo 198

Climate Generation: Awakening to Our Children's Future 328

climate justice 197–200; discuss and problematise issues 95–96; response 17–18

colourful coral 104–105

Comber, B. 90

compost 172, 185

Connolly, Denis 152

Content and Language Integrated Learning (CLIL) approach 4, 110–116; curriculum content 114; language proficiency, target language 112–113; language teaching methodologies 113–114; lesson in classroom 111–115; proactive pre-planning for 114–115; teachers 111, 112, 114, 115; teaching and learning, second or foreign language 110–111; understanding 111–112

Cooperative Learning 273, 276, 278, 281

Cooper. J.M. 61

Covid-19 16, 17, 183, 199, 210, 284, 292, 293, 301

Coyle, D 110, 112

critical literacy 89–90, 92, 94

critical reflection 61–70; beliefs, values & assumptions 62–64; examination stage 64–65; personal biography 62–64; struggle stage 66–68; teacher reflection activity 63–64; transformation stage 68–70

critical thinking 94–95

Critical Thinking and Book Talk (CT&BT) 92

Cullors, Patrisse 285

Decolonizing Nature: Contemporary Art and the Politics of Ecology 170

define stage 158

deforestation 14, 17, 95, 164, 214, 253, 265, 266, 269, 270, 291

de Graaff, R. 111

design thinking (DT) 153–154, 164, 295, 297

Dillon, P. 139

Dolan, A.M. 148, 276

Donnelly, J. 91

Dorling, D. 18

Dream, Invent, Create 132

Dream Big: Engineering Our World 132

Duffy the Sea Turtle: A True Story About Plastic in Our Ocean 186

Dyson, B. 273, 276

early childhood 72, 73, 76, 77, 84, 226; classroom 72, 73, 76, 77, 82, 83

early childhood education (ECE) 72–76; children and lives, early childhood 73–74; children connections with others 74–76; children's learning and development 76

early childhood pedagogy 76–83; our changing environment 79–83

Earth's atmosphere 10, 234

Echterling, C. 96

ecological awareness 174, 238–241, 243, 245; becoming aware of environment 240–242; meditation 242; season of creation 244; tree 243–244

ecology 15, 47, 152, 170, 173, 174, 177, 239

ECO-UNESCO 189

education 22, 23, 29, 73, 111, 121, 122, 138, 169, 170, 200–202, 245, 298

emotions 29, 95, 268, 290

empathy 156

engineering design process (EDP) 128, 132–134

Engineering Habits of Mind (EHoM) 134

environmental education 73, 139, 141, 189

environmental problems 138, 285, 298

environmental protection 25, 42, 256, 258, 259, 261, 263, 265, 267, 269, 271; drama and learning 258–259; global effects of deforestation, Amazon tribal

communities 265–271; little pigs build better sustainable homes 259–265; negotiating 258–271
Esprívalo Harrell, P. 30
European Nature Conservation Year 293
A European Union that strives for more 1
experiential learning 140, 141

false hope 285
Fernandez-Rio, J. 273
Filiz, B. 276
first language 111, 116
FIRST LEGO League (FLL) 296, 297
food 14, 103–105, 152, 155, 172, 175, 182, 243, 267, 268, 288, 291
footprints 69, 216, 241, 242
foreign language 4, 110, 116
Foreman, M. 91
fossil fuels 9–11, 21, 22, 24, 181, 184, 197, 198, 200, 217, 252, 253
Francis, P. 19, 55, 239–240, 242, 245
'The future of critical literacy' 94

Galafassi, D. 171
geocaching 277, 278
Gibbons, P. 115
glaciers 217, 234
global average temperature 10
global citizenship 227–228; education 202, 228
global climate disruption 46–58
global learning 132, 197, 200–202
global warming 9, 12, 20–23, 25, 46, 48, 50, 51, 126, 205, 226, 234
Gold, L. 11
The Great Irish Weather Book 91
Green Dot symbol 188, 189
greenhouse effect 10, 12, 197, 217, 293
greenhouse gases 10–12, 14, 18, 21, 22, 181, 183, 251, 287, 289
Grow Room programme 168–177

habitats 14, 15, 107, 139, 152, 155, 157, 158, 163
Haley, C. 115
Hansen, James 9
Harris, J. 111
Hay, D. 238
healthy Christian spirituality 238–245; in classroom 240–244
Heffern, W. 184
Hellison, D. 275
Hello Mr World 91
Herman, G. 91
Hicks, D. 286
Hinderliter, J. 91
hooks, bell 71
hope, pedagogy 284–302; challenging times, Covid-19 292–293; climate legacy digital

time capsule project 293–294; earning through action 288–294; inspiration from nature 294–297; organise school assembly 292; picturebook about climate actions and solutions 298; power of nature, biomimicry 295–297; story and art, evoking hope 297–298; thread of hope through curriculum 286–288; transformative climate change education 298–300; wonders of Earth, rediscovering 294–297
human rights 18, 198–200, 202, 203, 231

ideation 160, 161
inquiry-based learning (IBL) 72, 76–84
insects 14, 52, 54–57, 82, 152, 155, 168, 172–174
Intergovernmental Panel on Climate Change (IPCC) 12
Irish language 110, 111
Irish teaching 111

Jackson, E. 186
Janks, H. 94

Kamkwamba, W. 132
Keck Scott, S. 184
Keeling, Charles David 10
Keeling Curve 10, 11
Khazem, D. 18
Khreis, H. 278
Kindergarten Teachers 74
Klein, N. 22
Kurlansky, M. 91

language 20, 25, 90, 93, 110–116; learning 112–113, 115, 116
Larrivee, B. 61, 66
Laudato Si' 240, 245
learning activities 164
learning outcomes 29, 266, 273
learning process 77, 156, 249, 253, 254, 265, 271
Leonard, M.G. 183
lesson plans, sample 317–321
listening, children 99–109
Lorna Gold 328
Loughman, S.B. 32
Louv, R. 295

MacAree, F. 91
Macfarlane, R. 170
Marli's Tangled Tale: A True Story About the Problem of Balloon Releases 186
Marlon, J.R. 285
mass extinction 214
McLaughlin, T. 239
Mercer, N. 67
Met, M. 115
Metzler, M. 272

Miasa, N. 184
microplastics 182, 183, 186, 187
Mirzoeff, N. 172
Mobius symbol 189
monotheistic religions: Christianity 55; Islam
    55–56; Judaism 55; teachings, snapshot from
    55–56
Mouffe, C. 170

National Council Curriculum Assessment Ireland
    (NCCA) 121
nature-based solutions 295
*Nelson's Dangerous Dive: A True Story About the
    Problems of Ghost Fishing Nets in Our
    Oceans* 186
New Zealand 77
Nohilly, Margaret 5
Nye, R. 238

Obama, M. 302
O'Beirne, A. 279
Ó Ceallaigh, T.J. 112
Oğuz-Ünver, A. 76–77
Ojala, M. 285
O'Keeffe, B. 279
*One Plastic Bag: Isatou Ceesay and the Recycling
    Women of Gambia* 186
Organisation for Economic Co-operation and
    Development (OECD) 202
outdoor learning 138–142, 150, 276, 294

Paris Agreement 19
Paris Climate Conference 9
Paul, M. 186
Peck, H. 184
physical education (PE) 3, 111, 272–274, 276,
    277, 281
physically educated communities 272–281;
    active school travel (AST) 278–281; climate
    change through outdoor education 276–278;
    cooperative learning 273; curriculum models
    272–273; positive health and environmental
    outcomes 281; teaching and learning, hybrid
    approach 275–276; teaching personal and
    social responsibility (TPSR) 274–275
picturebooks 89, 91–92, 96, 97, 288, 297, 298
PISA 202
planting trees 15, 149, 287, 288
plastic pollution 181, 182, 184, 185, 187, 191
plastic production 182, 183
plastics 5, 100, 181–192, 256, 262, 290;
    and climate change 183; exploring and
    categorising 191; fossil fuel product 191; in
    ocean 182–183; over consumption 183–184;
    problem with 181–182; recycling symbols,
    investigation 187–189; responding to
    crisis 186–187; timeline, creating 189–190;

understand the complexity, children's literature
    184–186; waste and single-use plastic, projects
    presentation 189
pollination 103, 107, 155, 157
positive dispositions 72, 74, 76, 77, 83, 84
powerful polar bear 105–106
Prensky, M. 121, 122
President of Ireland, letter 322
primary classroom 3, 99, 100, 110, 111, 115, 116,
    124, 142, 258
primary school children 12, 89, 91, 93, 95, 97,
    141, 187
The Problem of the Hot World 91
professional learning 4
prototypes 128, 131, 132, 134, 154, 162, 212

re-acting, children 99–109
reflective approach 60, 61, 63, 69, 71
reflective practice 4, 60, 62, 68
reflective teaching 60–71
religions 18, 46–48, 51, 58, 238, 244; and beliefs
    47, 48; Buddhism 53; Hinduism 52; Jainism
    52–53; teachings, snapshot from 52–53
religious traditions 4, 46, 47, 50, 51, 58, 239
renewable energy 22, 125, 198, 212, 217, 297
research projects 125, 126, 187
research tool, art 170–171
Rink, D. 91
Robinson, K. 171
Robinson, M. 281
Roche, M. 91
role cards 252, 253
Rolfe, G. 68
Royal Academy of Engineering 123, 134

Saint Francis of Assisi 55
Sanderud, J.R. 272
school day 83, 111, 237
Schultz, M. 66
Science Blast 12–13
Science Capital 123, 124, 134
second language 110, 111
Shepardson, D.P. 23
Siegle, L. 182, 183
single-use plastics 182, 184, 189, 191, 192
Sip the Straw 184
skills 29–32, 60, 74, 107, 111, 113, 123, 128, 139,
    149, 247, 257
Solnit, R. 285, 300
Somebody Swallowed Stanley 184
species 4, 14, 15, 54–56, 58, 99, 100, 103, 104
spirituality 3, 47, 238–240, 244
Start Engineering 132
STEAM (STEM + art) 3–5, 152–154; artists and
    scientists collaborating 153; design challenge
    155; design thinking 153–154; education,
    creativity and climate change 153; little artists

and scientists 154–155; project 155; teachers' notes 155–156
STEM (science, technology, engineering and math) 4–5, 121–134; climate change, primary classroom 124; clubs 125; consultation and mentoring 125; coping with extreme weather conditions 131; cross-curricular STEM challenges and projects 129; debates/ridiculous arguments 125; education 5, 122–124, 128, 132, 133, 164; engagement strategies 125–128; engineering design process (EDP) 128–129; impacts of climate change, solutions 129–130; importance of 122; literacies 122–125, 128; media 125; open-ended STEM projects 132; research 132–133; research projects 125–126; *Science Capital* 123–124; science communication activities 125–128; Science Talk Ball 126; social responsibility and active citizenship 122–123; sustainable development, engineering 133; sustainable world 132; thinking cap activities 126; 'What If, ' Plus Minus Interesting Activities 126–128
Stiehl, J. 276
Stockton, F. 91
Stoknes, P.E 285
straw houses 259, 263, 264
student projects, Grow Room programme: Flowers and Weeds 175; Turtles and Butterflies 174; White-Tailed bee project 175
student teachers 2, 24–26, 169, 177, 205, 208, 251, 284
suggested activities 106–108; art and creativity 107–108; hope, generating 108; learning moments, stories 107; living thing, hot seat 107; problem-solving 108; pupils, researchers 107
Sunflower investigation 79
sustainable development 9, 55, 125, 126, 132–134, 197, 200, 202, 298
Sustainable Development Goals (SDGs) 9, 126, 197, 200–201, 203

target language 111–114, 116
teacher educators 2, 99, 238, 284
teacher reflection activity 63, 64
teachers 3, 24, 30, 31, 60, 64, 66, 73, 76, 77, 90, 92, 93, 99, 107, 139, 140, 263, 269, 272; of climate change education 60, 61, 64; and learners 149, 275, 286

teaching ideas 142
teaching personal and social responsibility (TPSR) 274–276
teaching resources 247–257; board games 248–251; carbon cycle web simulation game 252–253; climate change 247–248; discussion stimulus 255–256; posters 253–254; quizzes 254–255; simulation games 251–252; tips, creating resources 256–257
test 163
The Enquiring Classroom (TEC) 48
thematic teaching 4, 29–31, 43, 44, 200; considerations in using 31–32; disadvantages 31; step by step 32–43; value of 31
theme, of climate change 32, 36, 38, 229
'*Think of an Eel*' 91
Thunberg, G. 288–289, 300
time capsules 221, 293
timeline 63, 203, 218–221; cards 323–328
transformative climate change education 284, 298, 300
tribal people 265–270
Tutu, D. 301

UN Human Rights Council 198
United Nations Framework Convention on Climate Change 9, 23, 200

visual culture theory 174
von der Leyen, U. 1

Waldron, F. 217, 298
walking activity 277
Wall, S. 76
Weintraub, L. 171
What is Climate Change? 91
What's the Point of Being Green? 132
Whitehead, P. 272
wind turbines 233–235, 296
wind turbines 235, 296
Woodworth, P. 19
world's religious traditions 46–58; classroom methodologies 48–52; extension activities 56; powerful resources, human responses 46–47
World Wildlife Fund's Living Planet Report 11
A World Without Fish 91